THE NEW EMILY DICKINSON STUDIES

This collection presents new approaches to Emily Dickinson's oeuvre. Informed by twenty-first-century critical developments, the Dickinson that emerges here is embedded in and susceptible to a very physical world, and caught in unceasing interactions and circulation that she does not control. The volume's essays offer fresh readings of Dickinson's poetry through such new critical lenses as historical poetics, ecocriticism, animal studies, sound studies, new materialism, posthumanism, object-oriented feminism, disability studies, queer theory, race studies, race and contemporary poetics, digital humanities, and globalism. These essays address what it means to read Dickinson in braille, online, graffitied, and internationally, alongside the work of poets of color. Taken together, this book widens our understanding of Dickinson's readerships, of what the poems can mean, and for whom.

Michelle Kohler is Associate Professor of English at Tulane University and author of *Miles of Stare: Transcendentalism and the Problem of Literary Vision in Nineteenth-Century America* (2014).

TWENTY-FIRST-CENTURY CRITICAL REVISIONS

This series will address two main themes across a range of key authors, genres, and literary traditions. The first is the changing critical interpretations that have emerged since c. 2000. Radically new interpretations of writers, genres, and literary periods have emerged from the application of new critical approaches. Substantial scholarly shifts have occurred too, through the emergence of new editions, editions of letters, and competing biographical accounts. Books in this series will collate and reflect this rich plurality of twenty-first-century literary critical energies, and wide varieties of revisionary scholarship, to summarize, analyze, and assess the impact of contemporary critical strategies. Designed to offer critical pathways and evaluations, and to establish new critical routes for research, this series will collate and explain a dizzying array of criticism and scholarship in key areas of twenty-first-century literary studies.

Forthcoming Books in This Series:
VICTORIA AARONS *The New Jewish American Literary Studies*
JEAN-MICHEL RABATÉ *The New Samuel Beckett Studies*
JOANNA FREER *The New Pynchon Studies*
MARK BYRON *The New Ezra Pound Studies*
MATT COHEN *The New Walt Whitman Studies*
JENNIFER HAYTOCK & LAURA RATTRAY *The New Edith Wharton Studies*
KIRK CURNUTT & SUZANNE DEL GIZZO *The New Hemingway Studies*
DOUGLAS MAO *The New Modernist Studies*

THE NEW EMILY DICKINSON STUDIES

EDITED BY
MICHELLE KOHLER
Tulane University

CAMBRIDGE
UNIVERSITY PRESS

University Printing House, Cambridge CB2 8BS, United Kingdom

One Liberty Plaza, 20th Floor, New York, NY 10006, USA

477 Williamstown Road, Port Melbourne, VIC 3207, Australia

314–321, 3rd Floor, Plot 3, Splendor Forum, Jasola District Centre,
New Delhi – 110025, India

79 Anson Road, #06–04/06, Singapore 079906

Cambridge University Press is part of the University of Cambridge.

It furthers the University's mission by disseminating knowledge in the pursuit of education, learning, and research at the highest international levels of excellence.

www.cambridge.org
Information on this title: www.cambridge.org/9781108480307
DOI: 10.1017/9781108648349

© Michelle Kohler 2019

This publication is in copyright. Subject to statutory exception and to the provisions of relevant collective licensing agreements, no reproduction of any part may take place without the written permission of Cambridge University Press.

First published 2019

Printed and bound in Great Britain by Clays Ltd, Elcograf S.p.A.

A catalogue record for this publication is available from the British Library.

Library of Congress Cataloging-in-Publication Data
NAMES: Kohler, Michelle, 1974– editor.
TITLE: The new Emily Dickinson studies / edited by Michelle Kohler.
DESCRIPTION: Cambridge, United Kingdom ; New York, NY : Cambridge University Press, 2019. | Series: Twenty-first century critical revisions ; volume 1 | Includes bibliographical references and index.
IDENTIFIERS: LCCN 2019003487 | ISBN 9781108480307 (hardback : alk. paper)
SUBJECTS: LCSH: Dickinson, Emily, 1830–1886 – Criticism and interpretation. | Dickinson, Emily, 1830–1886 – Influence.
CLASSIFICATION: LCC PS1541.Z5 N49 2019 | DDC 811/.4–dc23
LC record available at https://lccn.loc.gov/2019003487

ISBN 978-1-108-48030-7 Hardback

Cambridge University Press has no responsibility for the persistence or accuracy of URLs for external or third-party internet websites referred to in this publication and does not guarantee that any content on such websites is, or will remain, accurate or appropriate.

Contents

List of Illustrations *page* vii
List of Contributors viii
Acknowledgments xii
Abbreviations and Textual Note xiii

    Introduction: Dickinson Dispersed 1
    Michelle Kohler

    PART I POETICS AND THE IMAGINATION 15

1 Collaborative Dickinson 17
   Alexandra Socarides

2 Generic Dickinson 33
   Michael C. Cohen

3 "Success in Circuit lies": Dickinson, Media, and Imagination 49
   Eliza Richards

4 "Criterion for Tune": Dickinson and Sound 66
   Christina Pugh

    PART II THEORETICAL FRAMEWORKS 83

5 Dickinson's Object-Oriented Feminism 85
   Michelle Kohler

6 "The Vision – pondered long": Dickinson, Chronic Pain, and the Materiality of Figuration 100
   Michael D. Snediker

7	Emily Dickinson's Posthuman Worlds: Biopoetics and Environmental Subjectivity *Colleen Glenney Boggs*	118
8	Dickinson and Historical Ecopoetics *Gillian Kidd Osborne*	136

PART III NINETEENTH-CENTURY HISTORIES   153

9	Dickinson's Physics *Cody Marrs*	155
10	Dickinson's Geographic Poetics *Grant Rosson*	168
11	Global Dickinson *Páraic Finnerty*	187
12	Dickinson and George Moses Horton *Faith Barrett*	204
13	Dickinson and the Diary *Desirée Henderson*	220

PART IV RECEPTIONS, ARCHIVES, READERSHIPS   237

14	Textures Newly Visible: Seeing and Feeling the Online Dickinson Archives *Seth Perlow*	239
15	Coloring Dickinson: Race, Influence, and Lyric Dis-reading *Evie Shockley*	258
16	Dickinson, Disability, and a Crip Editorial Practice *Clare Mullaney*	280
17	Emily Dickinson in Baghdad *Naseer Hassan*	299

Suggested Further Reading   308
Index   312

Illustrations

1 (13.1) Lavinia Dickinson, Diary, 1851. Dickinson family *page* 226
    papers, 1757–1934. MS Am 1118.95 (226). Houghton Library,
    Harvard University, October 30, 1851.
2 (16.1) "In this short life" (F1292). 286
    About 1873. Six lines written in pencil on the inside
    of an upside-down envelope flap. The seal is partially present.
    MS252. Courtesy of Amherst College Archives and Special
    Collections, Amherst, MA.
3 (16.2) "Dont put up my Thread + Needle" (F681A). Copied 290
    and included in Fascicle 32 in 1863. MS Am 1118.3 214b,
    Houghton Library, Harvard University.

Contributors

FAITH BARRETT is Associate Professor of English at Duquesne University. With Cristanne Miller, she coedited *Words for the Hour: A New Anthology of American Civil War Poetry* (University of Massachusetts Press, 2005). She is the author of *To Fight Aloud Is Very Brave: American Poetry and the Civil War* (University of Massachusetts Press, 2012), and she has also published articles on the poetry of Abraham Lincoln, George Moses Horton, and Dave the Potter.

COLLEEN GLENNEY BOGGS is Professor of English at Dartmouth College. She is the author of *Animalia Americana: Animal Representations and Biopolitical Subjectivity* (Columbia University Press, 2013) and *Transnationalism and American Literature: Literary Translation 1773–1892* (Routledge, 2007), as well as articles in such journals as *American Literature*, *PMLA*, *Cultural Critique*, and *J19*. Her work has been supported by the National Endowment for the Humanities, the American Philosophical Society, and the Mellon Foundation.

MICHAEL C. COHEN is Associate Professor of English at UCLA. He is the author of *The Social Lives of Poems in Nineteenth-Century America* (University of Pennsylvania Press, 2015) and coeditor of *The Poetry of Charles Brockden Brown* (Bucknell University Press, forthcoming), as well as many essays on nineteenth-century American and Victorian poetry.

PÁRAIC FINNERTY is Reader in English and American Literature at the University of Portsmouth. He is the author of *Emily Dickinson's Shakespeare* (University of Massachusetts Press, 2006) and coauthor of *Victorian Celebrity Culture and Tennyson's Circle* (Palgrave Macmillan, 2013). His next book, *Dickinson and Her British Contemporaries*, is forthcoming from Edinburgh University Press.

List of Contributors

NASEER HASSAN is an Iraqi poet and translator of poetry and philosophy. He has published four poetry books, and translated into Arabic the work of Emily Dickinson, Luis Borges, Robert Frost, Langston Hughes, Wallace Stevens, Schopenhauer, Kierkegaard, and Derrida. His most recent poetry collection *Dayplaces* was translated into English by Jon Davis and Christopher Merrill and published in the United States by Tebot Bach in 2017. He was awarded the 2008 David Burke Distinguished Journalism Award for working in a highly dangerous situation as a member of the Baghdad Bureau of Radio Free Iraq.

DESIRÉE HENDERSON is Associate Professor of English at the University of Texas Arlington, where she specializes in American literature and women's writing. She is the author of *Grief and Genre in American Literature, 1790–1870* (Ashgate, 2011), as well as essays published in *a/b: Autobiography Studies, Early American Literature, Legacy: A Journal of American Women Writers, Studies in American Fiction,* and *Walt Whitman Quarterly Review,* among other scholarly journals. She is currently completing a book titled *How to Read a Diary: Critical Contexts and Interpretive Strategies for 21st Century Readers* (Routledge, forthcoming).

MICHELLE KOHLER is Associate Professor of English at Tulane University and author of *Miles of Stare: Transcendentalism and the Problem of Literary Vision in Nineteenth-Century America* (University of Alabama Press, 2014). She has published in such journals as *ESQ, Nineteenth-Century Literature, The Emily Dickinson Journal, Arizona Quarterly,* and *American Literary Realism.*

CODY MARRS is Associate Professor of English at the University of Georgia. He is the author of *Nineteenth-Century American Literature and the Long Civil War* (Cambridge University Press, 2015), the editor of *The New Melville Studies* (Cambridge University Press, 2019), and the coeditor of *Timelines of American Literature* (Johns Hopkins, 2019).

CLARE MULLANEY received her PhD in English from the University of Pennsylvania in August 2018 and is currently a Visiting Assistant Professor of Literature and Creative Writing at Hamilton College. Her research and teaching focus on nineteenth- and early twentieth-century American literature, disability studies, and material text studies.

List of Contributors

GILLIAN KIDD OSBORNE is a co-instructor (with Elisa New) for all Poetry in America courses at the Harvard Extension School and the co-editor (with Angela Hume) of *Ecopoetics: Essays in the Field*. She holds a PhD in English from the University of California Berkeley and was a postdoctoral fellow at the Harvard University Center for the Environment from 2015 to 2017. Her work on Dickinson has been supported by several awards from the Emily Dickinson International Society and the Dickinson Critical Institute.

SETH PERLOW is an assistant teaching professor in the Department of English at Georgetown University. He is the author of *The Poem Electric: Technology and the American Lyric* (University of Minnesota Press, 2018) and editor of *Gertrude Stein's Tender Buttons: The Corrected Centennial Edition* (City Lights, 2014). His essays on poetry, new media, and gender and sexuality have appeared or are forthcoming in *Criticism*, *Paideuma*, *Letteratura e Letterature*, *Convergence*, *The Wallace Stevens Journal*, and elsewhere.

CHRISTINA PUGH is Professor of English at the University of Illinois at Chicago and consulting editor for *Poetry* magazine. She is the author of four books of poems, including *Perception* (Four Way Books, 2017) and *Grains of the Voice* (Northwestern University Press, 2013). She was the recipient of a 2015–2016 Guggenheim fellowship in poetry, as well as fellowships and awards from the Poetry Society of America, the Illinois Arts Council, and the Bogliasco Foundation. Her critical articles have appeared in *The Emily Dickinson Journal*, *Twentieth Century Literature*, *Poetry*, *The Cambridge Companion to Poetry since 1945*, and other publications.

ELIZA RICHARDS is an associate professor in the Department of English and Comparative Literature at UNC-Chapel Hill. She teaches and writes about American literature and culture before 1900, with a particular emphasis on poetry. She is the author of *Gender and the Poetics of Reception in Poe's Circle* (Cambridge University Press, 2004) and *Battle Lines: Poetry and Mass Media in the US Civil War* (University of Pennsylvania Press, 2019) and the editor of *Emily Dickinson in Context* (Cambridge University Press, 2013). She was awarded a National Humanities Center Fellowship to work on this project.

GRANT ROSSON is a doctoral student in English at the University of California, Los Angeles, where he is writing a dissertation on nineteenth-century American literature and geography. He earned a BA, with High Distinction, from the University of Virginia for his thesis on the publication history of Emily Dickinson's letters and poems.

EVIE SHOCKLEY, Professor of English at Rutgers University-New Brunswick, is the author of *Renegade Poetics: Black Aesthetics and Formal Innovation in African American Poetry* (University of Iowa Press, 2011) and several collections of poetry, most recently *semiautomatic* (Wesleyan University Press, 2017) – finalist for the Pulitzer Prize and the *LA Times* Book Prize, and winner of the 2018 Hurston/Wright Legacy Award – and *the new black* (Wesleyan University Press, 2011), which received the 2012 Hurston/Wright Legacy Award. Shockley's work has been supported and recognized with the 2015 Stephen Henderson Award for Outstanding Achievement in Poetry, the 2012 Holmes National Poetry Prize, and fellowships from the Radcliffe Institute for Advanced Study, the Schomburg Center for Research in Black Culture, and the American Council of Learned Societies.

MICHAEL D. SNEDIKER is Associate Professor of English at the University of Houston. He is the author of *Queer Optimism: Lyric Personhood and Other Felicitous Persuasions* (University of Minnesota Press, 2009) and two books of poems, *The Apartment of Tragic Appliances* (Punctum Books, 2013) and *The New York Editions* (Fordham University Press, 2018), as well as many articles on American literature, poetics, queer theory, and disability. He is currently working on a second critical book, titled *Contingent Figure: Aesthetic Duress from Ralph Waldo Emerson to Eve Kosofsky Sedgwick*, a reading of disability theory and aesthetics across the very long American nineteenth century (under contract, University of Minnesota Press).

ALEXANDRA SOCARIDES is Associate Professor of English at the University of Missouri. Her first book, *Dickinson Unbound: Paper, Process, Poetics*, was published by Oxford University Press in 2012. She is the coeditor (with Jennifer Putzi) of *A History of Nineteenth-Century American Women's Poetry* (Cambridge University Press, 2016) and coeditor (with Michael Cohen) of the forthcoming *The Charles Brockden Brown Electronic Archive and Scholarly Edition, Volume 7: Poetry*. Her articles and essays have appeared in, among other places, *Nineteenth-Century Literature*, *Legacy: A Journal of American Women Writers*, and *Los Angeles Review of Books*.

Acknowledgments

I'm very grateful to Ray Ryan for commissioning this volume and to the staff at Cambridge University Press for ushering the manuscript through the publication process. It has been an enormous pleasure to work with the sixteen scholars whose essays appear here, and I thank each of them for their hard work and inspiring intellectual contributions. I am also immensely thankful for the work of the many other Dickinson scholars cited throughout these pages and feel lucky to be part of such a robust intellectual community. For their generous advice during the editing process, I'm particularly grateful to Eliza Richards, Alexandra Socarides, Faith Barrett, Cody Marrs, and Scott Oldenburg. I'm also grateful to Hannah Newsom for her indispensable help in the project's final stages. The Department of English at Tulane University also provided essential support, and for that I owe thanks to Rebecca Mark and Barb Ryan. For other kinds of crucial intellectual support and cheerleading, I thank my Tulane colleagues Katherine Adams, Rebecca Mark, Travis Tanner, and Karen Zumhagen-Yekplé. My deepest thanks go to Karen Jackson Ford, Scott Oldenburg, and, for their genuine enthusiasm about this project, my children, Maja, Wesley, and Sam.

Abbreviations and Textual Note

EDJ   *The Emily Dickinson Journal* (Johns Hopkins University Press).
F   Franklin, R. W., ed., *The Poems of Emily Dickinson: Variorum Edition* (Cambridge, MA: The Belknap Press of Harvard University Press, 1998).
L   Johnson, Thomas H., and Theodora Ward, eds., *The Letters of Emily Dickinson* (Cambridge, MA: The Belknap Press of Harvard University Press, 1958).

Unless otherwise indicated, quotations from Dickinson's poems follow the text of Franklin's variorum edition, and Franklin numbers are cited parenthetically within the text. Dickinson's letters are cited by the numbers in Johnson and Ward's edition.

Introduction: Dickinson Dispersed
Michelle Kohler

The most startling encounter I've had with Emily Dickinson's poetry was in New Orleans in December 2014 at the breathtaking ExhibitBE, a massive, collaborative graffiti exhibit initiated by artist Brandan "Bmike" Odums. Graffiti artists painted the exhibit on the vast exterior and interior walls of DeGaulle Manor, an abandoned five-story, block-long public housing complex with a long history of racial and economic struggle. Over 100 families, largely African American, were evicted from the DeGaulle apartments just days before Thanksgiving in 2006. When I approached the entryway to the exhibit, I faced a brilliant orange brick wall and was surprised to see, in bright green letters shadowed in white, a line I know well: FOREVER IS COMPOSED OF NOWS. The line was painted without attribution to Dickinson, and the graffiti artist did not identify him- or herself. (Moreover, the wall stood just outside the gated area that enclosed the official exhibit, so when I recently queried Odums regarding who the artist might be, he said s/he was likely not among the thirty-five named collaborators.) Once a person walked past this wall, he or she entered the stunning scene of ExhibitBE: towering paintings on exterior walls that were awaiting demolition[1]; chilling installations inside apartments, memorializing evicted families; enormous portraits of and quotations from Martin Luther King, Jr., Malcolm X, James Baldwin, and other civil rights leaders.

There are many components of ExhibitBE that warrant attention, and the line from Dickinson is pretty far down the list. And, in part, I begin *The New Emily Dickinson Studies* with this example precisely because of this demotion – its placing of Dickinson in the margins, unattributed, subordinate to the urgency of the twentieth- and twenty-first-century politics that shaped both the history and the artistry of the space. Paul Crumbley has recently described Dickinson as one who sought to be a writer of memes, of phrases that anonymously enter the "linguistic stream," offering up detachable fragments of her poems to be placed in entirely new contexts without attribution.[2] Herein lies the capacity for language to do its most revolutionary work, argues Crumbley: not in its transcendence of norms or in the uniqueness or personhood of its author but in its absorbability, its becoming generic, its collaborative reach toward future readers and writers, its propensity to circulate and recirculate, to fall into an ongoing stream of Nows that belong to everyone and no one. Dickinsonian details did not matter at ExhibitBE (indeed, how many of its 30,000 visitors even knew the words were hers?). The line was missing the dashes and capitalizations of the original ("Forever – is composed of Nows –"); it was pulled from its context in Fascicle 32; it was not in Dickinson's handwriting but someone else's; it created new line breaks ("FOREVER IS / COMPOSED / OF NOWS"); it was drawn into a new visual field, with "Q ^{N} A / =" painted in black above it among other non-Dickinsonian marks in sky blue, hot pink, purple, and yellow, all against that bright orange backdrop. But I have never thought more about what this line might mean than I did at ExhibitBE. The line's original context – a three-stanza poem that thinks about the phenomenology of eternity – was supplanted by a graffiti exhibit that insisted on the phenomenology of racial and socioeconomic *history* and the need to attend to the real, felt, often violent Nows that compose it. The anonymous graffiti artist pulled the line into new political meaning alongside quotidian domestic spaces from which people were unexpectedly evicted (thousands of household possessions remain uncannily in the apartments, as if arrested in time); the line was made adjacent to depictions of crucial moments in civil rights history and to the entire structure's own temporariness in the face of its impending demolition. Regardless of what Dickinson herself intended by this line, or whether she would have embraced the exhibit's politics, or whether Crumbley is right that Dickinson wanted her poetry swept into the linguistic stream, here the line powerfully expressed the political refusal of a temporality in which Nows don't matter in the eternal scheme of things and in which the later of Forever is a way to dismiss the socioeconomic suffering of Now. It is a call to activism that Dickinson almost certainly did not intend.

There is no question that Dickinson and her poems are the focus of the chapters that follow. But the volume blurs Dickinson in ways exemplified by this opening example. Many of these chapters find her in unfamiliar contexts – off-center, embedded in collaborative spaces, and caught in circulations she does not control. And while much of the volume situates her in the nineteenth century, the chapters also often look toward the ways she might (or might not) further our thinking about contemporary issues. Such decentering is not easy to do with a writer like Dickinson, for

Dickinson scholarship has invested a great deal of intellectual energy insisting on her strength and exceptionality. This insistence has been a crucial project, pushing against stubborn mythologies that had rendered Dickinson isolated and deviant, an accidental writer of symptomatic poems. Over the past fifty years, scholars have productively recast her isolation and deviance, first characterizing her as a skillful proto-modernist (even if, in David Porter's terms, one "without a project") and then as a strategic, sovereign feminist.[3] These moves toward emphasizing Dickinson's control over her own poetics laid the groundwork for the late twentieth-century/early twenty-first-century Dickinson with whom we are familiar: a poet who is decidedly not withdrawn from the world but is attentive to many nineteenth-century American cultural, literary, and political contexts.

The transformation of Dickinson from alone and idiosyncratic (for better or for worse) to avidly engaged and often exemplary in her critical and poetic acumen has crucially deepened our understanding of Dickinson's canny attention to her nineteenth-century world. Given the mythical versions of her biography and the feminist politics at stake, it has been important to outline not only Dickinson's cultural engagement but also her agency, to see this woman poet *choosing*, even when her choice is, as Sharon Cameron argues, not to choose.[4] We have turned symptom to skill; recluse to citizen; a confined feminine body to a capacious human mind. As we often know her now, Dickinson thinks and writes firmly *in* the world; she is firmly in control of her engagement with the world; and she is engaged with everything: nineteenth-century religion, war, politics, literary culture, philosophy, music, art, science, Darwinism, trains, and telegraphy. She is war critic, legal analyst, political theorist, wry lampooner of transcendentalism, William Jamesian philosopher, and avid reader of popular and journalistic discourses.[5]

This emphasis on agency and engagement remains important – anyone who has taught Dickinson's poetry knows well that cultural myths about her still shape initial tendencies to read her poetics as unwitting and symptomatic. At the same time, while the attention to her intellectual sovereignty has given us a more sophisticated, saner Dickinson, it also to some extent perpetuates a notion of bounded, controlled selfhood and authorship that we resist (indeed, deconstruct) in many other critical contexts in the wake of post-structuralism. If we have celebrated Dickinson's own penchant for yielding to the unpredictable play of meaning and for destabilizing centers of meaning, we have often proceeded to insist on a stable Dickinson, one who may think through a variety of competing thoughts about faith, war, womanhood, and so on but who nonetheless thinks those competing thoughts with a coherent, conscious mind. When we insist, however, that she is sane, not mad; able, not disabled; mind, not body; agent, not victim, we uphold a kind of old-fashioned humanism. In other contexts, we have come to understand that such humanist notions of autonomous subjectivity rely on binary structures of exclusion that reinforce the very problematic cultural categories from which we have sought to rescue her.

Both building on and pivoting from this deliberate, engaged Dickinson, the new Dickinson that has begun to emerge in scholarship, and that this volume explores, does not just engage the world actively from her lookout but is inextricably embedded in a very physical world, deeply susceptible to and permeated by it, caught up in unceasing circulations of organic and inorganic material, sounds, printed texts, technologies, identities, and physical sensations. She is decentered, embodied, and not necessarily exceptional. She is enmeshed in changing environments and co-evolving with others (human and nonhuman) within intellectual, political, and material networks and ecological systems.[6] More, the *poems* themselves are caught up in material circulations and contexts, in nineteenth-century and twenty-first-century reading formats and locales that draw the poems away from Dickinson-as-center and away from even our own reading conventions: we find the poems not just graffitied but also online, in braille, described aurally, in contemporary verse, photocopied in Baghdad, and translated into Arabic. Such material processes exert many kinds of pressures on Dickinson's thought and experience, on what her poems can mean and for whom. To recognize the contingencies of reading is to undermine the sovereignty we have so often attributed to her.

I opened with an example that explores this decentering in relation to US racial politics, and without leaving that behind, I would like to add a second way of articulating this blurred Dickinson. Many of the chapters in this volume engage, explicitly or implicitly, the various lenses of twenty-first-century posthumanism, defined by Pramod K. Nayar as the "radical decentering of the traditional sovereign, coherent and autonomous human in order to demonstrate how the human is always already evolving with, constituted by and constitutive of multiple forms of life and machines."[7] The human of posthumanism cannot be separated from material environments, nor can consciousness be separated from either the body or the environment with which the body interacts. Consciousness, rather, emerges through these material interactions and is even distributed among multiple entities. Posthumanist discourses derive in part from

Introduction: Dickinson Dispersed

new developments in computer technologies, biology, science studies, and environmental studies that variously undermine the notion that the human is unique and bounded. Moreover, posthumanism focuses on demonstrating the erroneous ways we have relied on discourses of animality, monstrosity, and disability to define the human against a marginalized nonhuman Other (whether animal, machine, or non-normative human).[8] These discourses are coextensive with new materialism, a set of emergent theories across the sciences, social sciences, and humanities that variously emphasize matter's primacy and the ongoing processes of materialization: the self-organizing power, material force, and dispersed processes of nonhuman agents and systems both within and without humans.[9]

While posthumanist discourses do not explicitly inform more than a handful of the book's chapters, these discourses have triggered much interest in environments, blurred identities, complex interactions, and new kinds of embodiment that provide a range of ways to consider Dickinson's poetry anew. They invite us to resist hyperbolizing Dickinson's agency and exceptionality and thus to resist inadvertently reinforcing the dualistic construction of an unexceptional Other against which our notion of a sovereign Dickinson depends. (Such an unwanted effect has been evident in the way we have marginalized so many of the not-Dickinson women poets of the nineteenth century as we underscore Dickinson's genius; as Jennifer Putzi and Alexandra Socarides argue, with "the rise of Emily Dickinson to a position of exceptional prominence ... you quite quickly have a deeply entrenched perception of nineteenth-century American women's poetry as unsusceptible to study.")[10] To take a more positive tack, posthumanist discourses suggest rich ways of approaching a Dickinson whose body, consciousness, politics, and poems are inevitably enmeshed in environments and interactions. In terms of the state of Dickinson scholarship, we are perhaps especially ready to make this particular pair of decentering moves now for a couple of reasons. Once marginalized (decentered in the decidedly negative sense), Dickinson's centrality to literary studies is no longer in question. Because we have successfully emphasized her poetic power, we can now think of destabilizing her without losing her to the margins of literary study and without impugning her literary genius. But, to put it another way, we have perhaps overemphasized her power and agency and thus would *do well* to destabilize them now, to reconsider her authorship in light of theoretical developments (both long-standing post-structuralist theories and still-emergent posthumanist ones) that we readily apply to other authors and subjects. We would also do well to be more willing to critique the racial and class politics that emerge in her writing, which an investment in Dickinson's exceptionality has made hard to do.[11] The fact that we have accrued a wide understanding of Dickinson's interest in many historical and intellectual contexts means that we are poised, indeed have begun, to think in new ways about how context functions and how it forms subjectivity, embodied experience, poetics, and the political scope of her poems.

The book is divided into four sections: Poetics and the Imagination; New Theoretical Frameworks; Nineteenth-Century Histories; and Receptions, Archives, Readerships. The first section gathers essays that consider new ways of thinking about the literary imagination in terms of environments and systems, arguing for the need to move away from models of authorship that focus on isolation, genius, and agency in favor of such concepts as collaboration, media networks, generic conventions, non-public circulations, and historical readerships. As Socarides argues in Chapter 1, "Collaborative Dickinson," many of these frameworks have been hard for us to apply to Dickinson but are in fact very much aligned with the ways nineteenth-century poets and readers encountered poems. These models of literary creativity allow us to consider interactions that fall beyond the writer's control and that either deliberately or unwittingly include other agencies and influences. In part, this is Dickinson's creative process seen through the lenses of historical poetics, which aims to understand genre, prosody, and other elements of form in terms of historical-political readerships and conventions. It might also be seen as a poetics Wai Chee Dimock has described as a "cumulative reuse ... [that is] profoundly unoriginal" and that prides experimental reception over originality or exceptionalism.[12] In Chapter 2, "Generic Dickinson," Michael C. Cohen argues that Dickinson's notion of what poetry is and does, which we have repeatedly cast as unique, is profoundly conventional. Both Socarides and Cohen build on Virginia Jackson's *Dickinson's Misery*, which radically rethinks Dickinson's relationship to genre by asking us to historicize reading practices and consider audience and address in terms of actual historical circulations rather than contemporary notions of lyric.

In Chapter 3, "Dickinson, Media, and Imagination," Eliza Richards looks at Dickinson's own ways of figuring the imagination as a faculty that works less like an inspired solitaire and more like part of an external network or circuitry: her poems experiment with tracking the mind's movement through complex layers of human media networks and "elemental media" (the weather, for example), obliterating the boundaries of individual thought and perception. Chapter 4, Christina Pugh's

"Dickinson and Sound," joins emerging scholarship that supplements long-standing critical attention to the visual features of Dickinson's manuscripts by attending both to the sonic features of Dickinson's poems (meter, rhyme, and so forth) and to the extra-poetic sounds that filled her nineteenth-century physical surroundings (technology and music, for example); Pugh argues that Dickinson's poems embrace sound as a crucial component of prosody and daily life, even as the poems issue sharp critiques of sounds that risk captivating the ear at the expense of reason and complexity.

Section 2 brings Dickinson into conversation with theoretical developments in feminist theory, disability studies, queer theory, posthumanism, animal studies, and ecocriticism. In all cases, it is not only that these frameworks help us say something about Dickinson's poems but also that the poems help us, to echo Jed Deppman, "try to think" about these twenty-first-century discourses in all their urgency. My own essay in Chapter 5 enlists object-oriented feminism (a wry off-shoot of/retort to object-oriented ontology) to elicit new readings of Dickinson's poems that resonate with twenty-first-century feminisms and feminist politics, shifting attention from individual subjectivity to camaraderies with objects, human and nonhuman. In Chapter 6, Michael D. Snediker reads chronic pain and its relationship to figuration within the context of queer phenomenology and disability studies. Resisting Sharon Cameron's long-standing account of Dickinson's lyric pain as "atemporal," he attends to the *chronicity* of pain in "chronic pain," arguing that time is in fact the medium of pain. Figuration, he argues, is the mode of language most akin to how chronic pain works because the two share a similar temporality; Dickinson's work exemplifies this relationship. Snediker's chapter is one of several in the volume that help us consider the way making poetry is an embodied activity: how, these chapters ask, do Dickinson's poems register the unavoidable, ongoing force of the body's being-in-the-world?

Whereas Snediker focuses on the *body*'s being-in-the-world (as does Clare Mullaney in a later chapter on disability and editing), Colleen Glenney Boggs's Chapter 7, "Emily Dickinson's Posthuman Worlds," stresses the way meaning-making is fundamentally tied to being-in-the-*world*. She situates Dickinson's poetry within conversations about biosemiotics, arguing that Dickinson was preoccupied by how relationships to the nonhuman world fundamentally shape subjectivity and produce meaning. In her Chapter 8, on "Dickinson and Historical Ecopoetics," Gillian Kidd Osborne similarly argues that locale matters for the production of texts, though she ultimately lands on a historical ecopoetics attentive to the environmental context of *reading*. Poetry, she argues, is "comprised of relation ... [I]ts own nullifications, absences, holes, can guide us to read both through and with a text, towards both the time and place in which it appeared and into the time and place where it is received."

Chapters in Section 3 turn to various nineteenth-century contexts in ways that are new both for the histories they address and for the ways these histories come into view differently via twenty-first-century perspectives on science, new materialism, globalization, and race. In Chapter 9, "Dickinson's Physics," Cody Marrs explores Dickinson's treatment of force and matter in light of nineteenth-century physics and twenty-first-century posthumanism; Dickinson, he argues, might help us theorize the latter anew. Grant Rosson, in Chapter 10, examines Dickinson in relation to geography, a nineteenth-century school subject and popular discourse that has received scant attention from Dickinson scholars; he demonstrates her surprising pattern of using specific geographic methods and lexicons not to refer to foreign places but to map out for readers the space of her own home and of heaven.

By contrast, Páraic Finnerty's Chapter 11, on "Global Dickinson," comprehensively explores Dickinson's references to foreign places and their entanglements with the United States. Drawing on Dimock, Finnerty argues that Dickinson folds this global expansiveness into the compressed space of her poems, intensifying her depiction of global interdependence and its shaping of nineteenth-century subjectivity. Finnerty also considers Dickinson's use of racial and ethnic stereotypes and notes how much more work remains to be done to understand her racial logic and politics. In Chapter 12, Faith Barrett's essay "Dickinson and George Moses Horton" brings Dickinson's poems into surprising conversation with Horton, an enslaved poet; Barrett argues that reading Dickinson's references to confinement alongside Horton's underscore the whiteness of her feminism. Desirée Henderson's Chapter 13, on "Dickinson and the Diary," considers Dickinson in relation to a nineteenth-century archive that seems to be on Dickinson's periphery at best and has thus not been seen as an important context for interpreting her poems. Henderson's chapter offers not only a reading of Dickinson's poetic treatment of diary-keeping but also a meditation on how such peripheral archives might enrich Dickinson scholarship and, conversely, how bringing Dickinson into the conversation might inform our understanding of such archives.

Section 4 includes essays that newly address a range of receptions and the bibliographic contexts for those receptions. But reception and context become (or require) intervention in each case. Taking up the reading context that has perhaps seemed the least subjected to editing, Seth

Introduction: Dickinson Dispersed 9

Perlow's Chapter 14 examines the online Dickinson archives from Amherst College and Harvard University, arguing that our long-standing desire for experiential contact with Dickinson's manuscripts, paired especially with the entrenchment of Harvard's print editions, shapes these archives in ways that limit access to productive scholarly research, including the most promising forms of digital research. In Perlow's estimation, the new archives are more old than new and warrant significant rethinking. Evie Shockley's Chapter 15, "Coloring Dickinson: Race, Influence, and Lyric Dis-reading," examines why and how women-of-color poets choose to engage Dickinson's work despite the racism (or elision of race) they may find there: Gwendolyn Brooks and Marilyn Chin engage in what Shockley calls *lyric dis-reading*, a process by which poets neither embrace nor oppose their white canonical forebears (who did not write for readers of color) but rather perform creative labor that racializes their forebears' work. Such dis-reading makes Dickinson's poetics of use to poets of color while also leaving open the possibility of exposing, or at least not excusing, Dickinson's exclusion of non-white readers.

Clare Mullaney, in Chapter 16, "Dickinson, Disability, and a Crip Editorial Practice," takes up another problem of exclusion, asking how we might edit the poems with disability in mind. Mullaney argues on one hand that we should use editorial restraint to avoid erasing textual manifestations of fragility and eyestrain (she questions, for example, the way Marta Werner and Jen Bervin "liberate" the brittle envelopes into the thick, glossy *Gorgeous Nothings*). On the other hand, Mullaney considers the kinds of editorial interventions needed to make the poems accessible to readers with disabilities. Her chapter grapples with the tensions between these two sets of concerns and seeks to establish the ethics and principles of what she calls a crip editorial practice.

The volume concludes with "Emily Dickinson in Baghdad," a striking narrative from Iraqi poet and translator Naseer Hassan, who in Chapter 17 tells the story of finding and translating Dickinson's poems in Baghdad during the 1990s under the threat of political violence from Saddam Hussein's regime. Hassan's narrative, which includes an interpretation and Arabic translation of "Because I could not stop for Death," in many ways resists Western ways of reading Dickinson, circumventing familiar academic pathways and theoretical frameworks – even as Hassan finds that Dickinson's poetry registers as utterly, even uncannily, familiar to Iraqi readers: "it expresses exactly the feeling of a whole people which she almost didn't hear of."[13] Hassan's framing of the way violence might shape writing, reading, and accessibility – and of the way texts resonate across time and space – is an apt conclusion to a volume that aims in part to think in new ways about our contexts for reading Dickinson. If, as Virginia Jackson has argued, contemporary approaches to lyric reading are so much the critical air we breathe that we cannot see our reading practices as the product of our own constructions, then perhaps Western readers would do well to startle themselves by finding Dickinson's poetry elsewhere and thus to be thrown off-center themselves.[14]

I began this introduction with a focus on US racial politics and then pivoted to posthumanism, enlisting these two frameworks to cast Dickinson into environments that exceed her control and our expectations. Hassan's closing essay invokes a third frame that might help us further reconfigure Dickinson along these lines, in this case to think more cross-culturally and trans-temporally about the relations Dickinson's poems can enter and how they do so. Hassan describes Dickinson as "reaching out to other worlds [she] doesn't know about"; upon reading her, he felt "a friendship of two worlds distant in space and time." As Hassan and I corresponded about his essay during the drafting process, I asked him to do more to emphasize cultural or linguistic differences that come to the fore during the translation process. No, he responded after some thought; Dickinson's poems, particularly those about death, pain, and loss, matter to him and to the Iraqi readers he's talked with because the poems' disposition is similar to theirs – astonishingly and comfortingly so. (As he told me in an exchange, one of his Iraqi readers reports that she carries his translations of Dickinson in her purse, a permanent companion wherever she goes.)

This friendship across space and time is akin to what Dimock posits in *Through Other Continents: American Literature Across Deep Time*, where she aims to upend the national and temporal borders of literary scholarship. She urges us to think not primarily of American literature but of the literature of a "global civil society."[15] "[T]hink of the planet as a plausible whole," she argues: a "crisscrossing set of pathways, open-ended and ever multiplying, weaving in and out of other geographies, other languages and cultures ... input channels, kinship networks, routes of transit, and forms of attachment ..."[16] Such pathways "thread America[n] texts into the topical events of other cultures, while also threading the long durations of those cultures into the short chronology of the United States."[17] Just as Pramod K. Nayar radically decenters the "traditional sovereign, coherent and autonomous human," Dimock's crisscrossing of cultural networks and entanglements radically dissolves the boundaries of "sovereign, coherent and autonomous" national literatures that continue to shape our discipline

Introduction: Dickinson Dispersed

even amid the moves toward transatlanticism and globalism. Reading transgresses boundaries: the act of reading, writes Dimock, "generates relational ties that can ... extend for thousands of miles and thousands of years," and this is the tie that might create a whole, a readership comprising a global civil society.[18] Socarides argues in this volume that in poems about death Dickinson is collaborating with *future readers*, seeking to join a "larger conversation about how to represent the crisis" of the Civil War. In light of Hassan's essay, we might see an even larger conversation, an unwitting collaboration with a network of future readers in "other worlds [she] doesn't know about," as he puts it, readers who are likewise in crisis, likewise struggling to understand violence and death.

Hassan's essay insists on a cross-cultural, trans-temporal relatedness, satisfying Dimock's call to "think of the planet as a plausible whole" – in this case, to think of an increasingly global Dickinson readership. But his description of struggling to find Dickinson in 1996 Baghdad, where she is "almost no[where]" to be found, also underscores the fact that planetary wholeness requires *open* channels. The Ba'athist regime and international sanctions had closed pathways, impeding the accessibility of Dickinson's poems in ways we should consider when we talk about making the poems accessible. As we discuss digitizing the manuscripts, putting the poems in the public domain, making them readable for those with visual impairments, and translating them, we should also note that accessibility can be a geopolitical issue of borders, sanctions, censorship, and violence.

The threads that render the planet whole are thus tenuous. The whole may be a vast system that decenters and outlasts any singular subject, but such a system also relies precariously on the filaments of many single individuals, on the will of a reader, a writer, a translator, a librarian. As we see in Hassan's essay, a pathway that creates a text's route of transit depends on the embodied making of that pathway, of real feet forming a path on a street, of hands operating a photocopy machine, of a technician maintaining that machine, of a translator wrestling with shades of meaning. And sometimes these actions rely on a body doing them despite the violence that might be done to that body. Hassan's narrative reminds us that to think of a global readership one must think of bodies doing, bodies being done to: fragile bodies doing despite being done to.

One aim of this volume, then, is to think of the planet as a plausible whole, in all of the connectivity, fragility, embodiment, activity, activism, imagination, tenacity, and precarity implicit in that formulation, and to let that thinking redirect our approach to Dickinson's poems in myriad ways. If posthumanism invites us to recognize the inevitably open networks in which we are enmeshed, Hassan at once offers another a model of interconnectivity and reminds us that not all pathways are in fact inevitably open, that some must *be opened* in what might sometimes be an act of sheer will and risk. And as Evie Shockley notes, this act of will often comes from readers who do not comprise any kind of audience Dickinson may have imagined for herself and who choose therefore to open up the poems themselves and "dis-read" them, tell them slant. In turning to a radically decentered understanding of the networks, environments, and temporalities that shape writing and reading – and to a decentering of Dickinson herself – we might continue to find new contexts, new readerships, new histories, new ways of articulating what is at stake in her poems, and new ways of using her poems to attend to what is most urgent in contemporary politics and discourses.

Notes

1. As this book goes into press, DeGaulle Manor has not undergone demolition and remains abandoned; it was recently purchased, though plans for it are unclear. See Chelsea Brasted, "The 'failure' of ExhibitBe: Crowds, not change, for an Algiers neighborhood," *The Times-Picayune* (New Orleans), July 11, 2018.
2. Paul Crumbley, "Back Talk in New England: Dickinson and Revolution," *EDJ* 24.1 (2015): 17.
3. See, for example, David Porter, *Dickinson: The Modern Idiom* (Cambridge: Harvard University Press, 1981), and Sharon Cameron, *Lyric Time: Dickinson and the Limits of Genre* (Baltimore: Johns Hopkins University Press, 1979). For an overview of the rich trove of twentieth-century feminist scholarship on Dickinson, see my own essay in Chapter 5 of this volume, especially n. 1 and n. 2.
4. See Sharon Cameron, *Choosing Not Choosing: Dickinson's Fascicles* (Chicago: University of Chicago Press, 1992).
5. Recent edited collections, companions, introductions, and encyclopedias have collated discussions of these engagements, most notably *Emily Dickinson in Context*, Eliza Richards (ed.) (Cambridge: Cambridge University Press, 2013), but also *The Cambridge Introduction to Emily Dickinson*, Wendy Martin (ed.) (Cambridge: Cambridge University Press, 2007), and *A Companion to Emily Dickinson*, Martha Nell Smith and Mary Loeffelholz (eds.) (Hoboken: Wiley-Blackwell, 2008).
6. Recent work in this vein includes the essays collated in the special issue of *ESQ* 63.2 (2017) on "Dickinson's Environments," edited by Paul Crumbley and Karen Kilcup; Christine Gerhardt, *A Place for Humility: Whitman, Dickinson, and the Natural World* (Iowa City: University of Iowa Press, 2014); Juliana Chow, "'Because I See – New Englandly': Seeing and Species in the

Nineteenth Century and Emily Dickinson's Regional Specificity," *ESQ* 60.3 (2014): 413–449; and Theo Davis, *Ornamental Aesthetics: The Poetry of Attending in Thoreau, Dickinson, and Whitman* (Oxford: Oxford University Press, 2016). See also Midori Asahina, "'Fascination is absolute of Clime': Reading Dickinson's Correspondence with Higginson as Naturalist," *EDJ* 14.2 (2005): 103–119; Gillian Osborne, "Dickinson's Lyric Materialism," *EDJ* 21.1 (2012): 57–78; and Colleen Glenney Boggs, *Animalia Americana: Animal Representations and Biopolitical Subjectivity* (New York: Columbia University Press, 2013).
7. Pramod K. Nayar, *Posthumanism* (Cambridge: Polity, 2013), 2. See also Cary Wolfe, *What Is Posthumanism?* (Minneapolis and London: University of Minnesota Press, 2010). Posthumanism has its roots in Donna Haraway's work, especially her "A Cyborg Manifesto," in *Simians, Cyborgs, and Women: The Reinvention of Nature* (New York: Routledge, 1991), 149–182.
8. Nayar, 29.
9. On new materialism and related discourses, see Karen Barad, *Meeting the Universe Halfway: Quantum Mechanics and the Entanglement of Matter and Meaning* (Durham: Duke University Press, 2007); Jane Bennett, *Vibrant Matter: A Political Ecology of Things* (Durham: Duke University Press, 2010); Diana Coole and Samantha Frost, "Introducing the New Materialisms," in *New Materialisms: Ontology, Agency, and Politics*, Diana Coole and Samantha Frost (eds.) (Durham: Duke University Press, 2010), 1–43. See also Gilles Deleuze and Félix Guattari, *A Thousand Plateaus: Capitalism and Schizophrenia*, trans. Brian Massumi (Minneapolis: University of Minnesota Press, 1987); Manuel De Landa, *A Thousand Years of Nonlinear History* (New York: Zone, 1997); Bruno Latour, *Reassembling the Social: An Introduction to Actor-Network-Theory* (Oxford: Oxford University Press, 2005).
10. Jennifer Putzi and Alexandra Socarides, "Introduction – Making History: Thinking about Nineteenth-Century American Women's Poetry," in *A History of Nineteenth-Century American Women's Poetry*, Jennifer Putzi and Alexandra Socarides (eds.) (Cambridge: Cambridge University Press, 2017), 5.
11. See Vivian Pollak, "Dickinson and the Poetics of Whiteness," *EDJ* 9.2 (2000): 84–95; Wesley King, "The White Symbolic of Emily Dickinson," *EDJ* 18.1 (2009): 44–68; and Erica Fretwell, "Emily Dickinson in Domingo," *J19* 1.1 (2013): 71–96.
12. Wai Chee Dimock, "Introduction: Genres as Fields of Knowledge," *PMLA* 122.5 (2007): 1380.
13. Hassan's chapter addressing Iraqi/Arabic receptions of Dickinson joins, and expands the scope of, the essays collected in *The International Reception of Emily Dickinson*, Domhnall Mitchell and Maria Stuart (eds.) (London: Continuum, 2009); these essays address translation and readerships in many

European countries, including Ukraine, as well as in Brazil, Japan, and Australia, and there is a chapter on Hebrew translations.
14. See Virginia Jackson, *Dickinson's Misery: A Theory of Lyric Reading* (Princeton: Princeton University Press, 2005).
15. Wai Chee Dimock, *Through Other Continents: American Literature Across Deep Time* (Princeton: Princeton University Press, 2006), 5.
16. Dimock, 5, 3.
17. Ibid., 3.
18. Ibid., 8.

PART I

Poetics and the Imagination

CHAPTER I

Collaborative Dickinson

Alexandra Socarides

Ever since Emily Dickinson was first introduced to a reading public in 1890, she has been cast as one of the least collaborative of poets. The story of her aversion to people, friendship, and company was introduced by Thomas Wentworth Higginson in his "Preface" to the first volume of her poems, when he wrote: "A recluse by temperament and habit, literally spending years without setting foot beyond the doorstep, and many more years during which her walks were strictly limited to her father's grounds, she habitually concealed her mind, like her person, from all but a very few friends."[1] Critics were quick to pick up on this aspect of her life as a way to read her poems. As early as December 6, 1890, a critic for the *Literary World* wrote, in a particularly damning review: "Here surely is the record of a soul that suffered from isolation, and the stress of dumb emotion, and the desire to make itself understood by means of a voice so long unused that the sound was strange even to her own ears."[2] Here, the result of Dickinson's isolation is her semi-muteness. This is what it sounds like, the reviewer suggests, when one has no social intercourse. Less than two months later, a reviewer for the *Christian Advocate* took this logic to the next level by pathologizing Dickinson: "In reading her poems," he writes, "we cannot resist the impression that there is something unhealthy in a life of isolation. Perpetual introspection is the mother of melancholy, and melancholy the half sister of madness."[3] While later readers embraced a more benign story of Dickinson as an isolated writer, this became the dominant narrative through which she gained her enormous popularity.

And, of course, Dickinson herself contributed to this narrative. We can find evidence of this disposition in her poems themselves, for when she writes, in 1863, "In thy long Paradise of Light / No moment will there be / When I shall long for Earthly Play / And mortal Company –" (F1145), the appeal of heaven is firmly rooted not just in an image of isolation but in the absence of even the possibility to "long for" anything but. It is unsurprising, then, that very few twentieth- and twenty-first-century critics – myself included – have challenged the idea that underpins the image of Dickinson as a writer who undertook the project of making poems as a wholly solitary endeavor, for we have taken our cue from both the early critics and Dickinson herself. Given this, one might interpret the title of this chapter – "Collaborative Dickinson" – as a provocative one.

The other reason it might be read as provocative is that the very notion of women's literary collaborations has often been met with suspicion. Collaborations raise questions about the legitimacy of claims to authorship, a charge from which Dickinson has been largely sheltered. In *Writing Double: Women's Literary Partnership*, Bette London writes: "To study collaboration, then, [is] to study the conditions of its erasure. And these conditions [have] gender-specific connotations, reinforcing the idea that women were not 'real' authors."[4] Female collaborators, London goes on to argue, are often read as "amateurs," whose work is full of "adolescent experiments" in an early stage of development: "no matter how sustained these partnership ventures, there was a persistent undercurrent that collaborative writing was ultimately apprenticeship for some future apotheosis where the author would be singular."[5] What London registers here is the full force of twentieth-century assumptions about women's collaborations, assumptions that infantilize and domesticate women writers. Taking this one step further, Holly Laird, in *Women Coauthors*, has suggested that it is practically impossible to read collaborative writing as part of literary history precisely because of the ways in which it destabilizes authorship: "Despite contemporary demystification, a particular authorial life behind a work has long been an almost necessary adjunct both to a sympathetic reception and to the work's survival as an object of commentary. Not only has such an author been perceived as originator and authenticator, but she or he also has been perceived as validating a work, offering an individual human point of attachment for readers, enhancing even its aesthetic value."[6] Stripped of the authorial identity of "originator" or "authenticator," such collaborators, the argument runs, have made it difficult for readers to attach to them. In the absence of such attachment, readers are, according to Laird, encouraged to have a hostile reaction to collaborative writers.

London and Laird's assessments of how collaborations are viewed today makes it clear why even twenty-first-century critics might steer Dickinson clear of such readings. But if we read historically – if we take seriously the collaborative poetic culture in which Dickinson was steeped and begin to read her materiality within that context – then we might begin to see the collaborative underpinnings of this most retrospectively constructed solitary poet. Opening ourselves up to Dickinson's collaborative poetics, I want to argue, might help us rethink our investment in notions of solitary poetic genius and female lyric subjectivity more broadly – two issues that largely underpin twenty-first-century resistance to nineteenth-century American women's poetics.

In direct contradiction to the now-famous formulation espoused by John Stuart Mill that poetic utterance is solitary in nature, poets in the nineteenth century were actively engaged in the very kind of practices that reveal this solitude to have been an imaginative fiction of the genre.[7] Collaborative practices, most widely defined, included any of the following: influence, mentorship, editing assistance, consultation, inspiration, revision, mediumship, response, conversation, and cowriting. Many nineteenth-century poets treated the making of poetry as a collaborative act that often depended on more than one of these relations. We need only look at the most famous British examples to remind ourselves of this fact: the Brontë sisters, Elizabeth Barrett and Robert Browning, Dorothy and William Wordsworth, Wordsworth and Coleridge, Pound and Eliot, W. B. Yeats and Georgie Yeats, Katherine Bradley and Edith Cooper. And the list goes on. On the American side, we have fewer famous examples, although Eliza Richards' superb book on Edgar Allan Poe's poetic collaborations (again, widely defined) with Frances Osgood, Sarah Helen Whitman, and Elizabeth Oakes Smith opened the door for critics to think about how collaboration worked within the American context of periodical culture – a culture that supported the practices of, among others, mediumship and public conversations in verse.[8] Additionally, by now we know well the story of how Lydia Sigourney's readers supplied the details for the elegies that they requested her to write on the deaths of their children – a collaboration, in essence, between mourner and elegist.[9] And a close look at the midcentury anthologies of American women's poetry reveals several sets of sister-poets who were cast in different forms of collaborative relations: the Davidsons, the Carys, the Fullers, and the women known as "The Sisters of the West." What we have often regarded as a series of isolated incidents is in fact evidence of an American literary culture that was saturated by and invested in not only acts of collaboration but presenting the image of collaboration as integral to poetic culture. I have ever so briefly gestured to this context in order to show just how wedded readers of Dickinson must be to the idea of her as a non-collaborative poet to have assumed her non-participation in this culture.

While I say that Dickinson critics have not pursued the idea of her as a collaborative poet per se, I do recognize that many have mapped her echoes and allusions to other texts and writers; have scoured her correspondence, especially with key figures like Higginson and Helen Hunt Jackson, for evidence of an engaged and self-conscious poetic cross-pollination; and, following the hugely important work begun by Martha Nell Smith, have traced and analyzed her workshop practices with Susan Huntington Dickinson.[10] Such investigations have sometimes allowed for the emergence of a Dickinson different from the one presented by those late nineteenth-century reviewers. In *Emily Dickinson's Shakespeare*, for instance, Páraic Finnerty presents Dickinson as a poet who was "attentive to the possibility of indebtedness" and was "interested in the ways in which ideas and thoughts are shared."[11] Additionally, Dickinson's poems about Elizabeth Barrett Browning and Charlotte Brontë situate her as a poet who depended upon a form of communion with distant poets, and her reliance on correspondence about her own poetry that she initiated with friends and family reveals just how much she understood conversation and consultation to be an integral part of her process.

Each of our attempts to think about Dickinson in these ways produces a version of her that was engaged with others and that saw her poetry (and, in the case of her exchanges with Susan, the actual revisions of her poems) in conversation with writers and thinkers of her time. Yet even these instances of what we might call "collaboration" are often cast as exceptional moments, singular instances, or specific and personal engagements in an *otherwise* solitary woman's life. For example, in Smith's paradigm-shifting analysis of Dickinson's poems and letters to Susan, she refers to theirs as a "singular relationship."[12] In other words, one might argue that casting these relationships as somehow extraordinary or anomalous perpetuates the image of a non-collaborative Dickinson who had moments of collaboration or select people with whom she collaborated.

Dickinson studies has always benefited from turning to the places, networks, and methods that are not regularly associated with her and her poetry, and when it comes to thinking about Dickinson's relationship to collaboration I would argue that this again may be true. Along these lines, I would like to suggest that we take our cue from work done on the collection, curation, and preservation of writings that come out of specific communities, namely Alana Kumbier's work in *Ephemeral Material: Queering the Archive*, a study that maps the mass-produced ephemera that has been central to queer communities across America and theorizes everything from constructions of collective memory to the processes of archival labor. I turn to Kumbier not because she thinks explicitly about

Dickinson but because her reflections on material culture as a context for consideration are particularly suggestive when opened up to Dickinson.

In her final chapter on zines – small, low-budget magazines made by communities of feminists (among others) in the late 1990s that were not produced for profit – Kumbier writes that "the zines' materiality enables the production of embodied communities."[13] Whereas the typical way to understand the relationship between materiality and community is to say that communities enable the production of certain materials, Kumbier suggests instead that the makers of certain objects in fact produce the communities. The makers of these objects project themselves (and their texts) as agents of a collaborative enterprise – a process that depends on some imagined community's understanding of what the materials are and how they might be read.[14] The power of these texts, then, comes not just from the actual communities that produce, consume, read, and collect them but from the very production of those communities themselves. These communities, in other words, are constituted by both the creation and reception of specific materials. In this case one might say that the materiality of these zines embodies a collaborative logic in that it both imagines and produces not simply one reader, one "you," one historically-situated responder to the text, but whole communities toward whom the texts pitch themselves. Given that most considerations of Dickinson have posited any reception (real or imagined) of her poems as singular – she is writing either to herself or to a specific individual – Kumbier's connection between materials and communities allows us to resituate Dickinson's poetic practices within nineteenth-century cultures of collaboration.

Following from this logic, I would like to propose that we re-look at the dominant material structure of Dickinson's writing life – namely, the fascicles – and investigate them for the qualities that might allow us to read them as also embodying a similar collaborative logic. To do so is not to begin with the actual writers or readers with whom Dickinson was surrounded and clearly engaged but with the materials themselves, asking how they might have projected communities that were always present in her acts of making. Instead of highlighting Dickinson as a poet who wrote, copied, sewed, preserved, and revised these fascicles in isolation, we might foreground instead the materials themselves – and her particular processes with and uses of them – as objects that employ a fundamentally collaborative logic.

Often referred to as "enclosed textual space[s]," the fascicles have long been saddled with the story of their own discovery: objects found in a private trunk have become forty small private trunks of their own, never circulated (as far as we know), distinct from each other by the string that held the chosen sheets of stationery together.[15] Yet, as recent scholarship has shown, the fascicles were not objects of Dickinson's own invention. Because of the way they were constructed, the fascicles are related to commonplace books, autograph albums, and scrapbooks – all popular materials used by nineteenth-century Americans. Dickinson did not use already-bound blank books in which to copy her poems but instead took folded sheets of stationery, copied poems onto all four sides of each sheet, stacked completed sheets one on top of the other, and sewed between four and seven of them together with often red string, at the left-hand side of the page. Like the communities of women who made zines in the 1990s, communities of nineteenth-century women made, used, circulated, and kept such homemade objects. It was in these material objects that nineteenth-century women copied verses of their own and others, verses they often consulted in private but also shared with friends, family, and neighbors.[16]

When we think about the fascicles in relation to these other material objects, we are necessarily situating them within the context of gift exchange – one in which verses were written down, copied, and clipped into the private space of an individually made or owned book, with the intention that one's intimates would read them and sometimes even add to them. And it is this intention that matters – not only as it applies to Dickinson but as it applies to the materials themselves. As Paul Crumbley has written, "A central feature of gift culture is the collaboration of giver and receiver that takes the place of ownership."[17] Regardless of the fact that Dickinson probably never shared or circulated her fascicles – an act (or non-act) that we have long used to justify her privatization (and our re-privatization) of them – we might say that the specific materiality of the fascicles themselves posits a community of imagined receivers that they didn't constitute until long after Dickinson's death. Unlike writing that isn't framed by the material conventions allowing for the possibility of such exchange, Dickinson's fascicle poems foreground both their dependency on and their contribution to the construction of those communities.

We can see this collaborative logic at work in both the topics Dickinson takes up in her fascicle poems and in their embrace of certain poetic strategies. For instance, no topic was more thoroughly explored in women's commonplace and album books of the nineteenth century than that of death. Women shared such texts as part of mourning and consolation rituals. Dickinson's fascicle poems engage in every one of these texts' conventions, figuring specific deaths, asking questions about death and the afterlife, re-imagining particularly meaningful scenes from dead people's lives, and positioning Biblical and historical stories as a way to understand death. Regardless of whether Dickinson ever showed the fascicles to anyone, she made them knowing full well about the communities that were writing and sharing similar texts, communities that depended on such materials.

Let's look, for instance, at the first sheet of Fascicle 3, which opens with a poem that reads as a complex reflection on death's tendency to have bad timing, on the living's struggle to console, and on the notion of success or "victory" in this life:

> Delayed till she had ceased to know –
> Delayed till in it's vest of snow
> Her loving bosom lay –
> An hour behind the fleeting breath –
> Later by just an hour than Death –
> Oh lagging Yesterday!
>
> Could she have guessed that it w'd be –
> Could but a crier of the joy
> Have climbed the distant hill –
> Had not the bliss so slow a pace
> Who knows but this surrendered face
> Were undefeated still?
>
> Oh if there may departing be
> Any forgot by Victory
> In her imperial round –
> Show them this meek apparreled thing
> That could not stop to be a king –
> Doubtful if it be crowned! (F67)

Dickinson begins this fascicle sheet by invoking, and then responding to, many of her culture's ideas and questions about death. The poem speaks to those for whom these are pressing topics, figuring the singular dead woman as a stand-in for all the dead. "Show them this meek apparreled thing," Dickinson writes, as a way of both registering her anger at death and presenting a response to others' grief in this situation. It is also, though, a phrase that conjures the community that would read such a poem, for it is women mourners who would be engaged in this act of showing. When we read this poem as one that posits not just readers but participants – people on whom the poem's very existence depends but who are also themselves imagined in the process of the poem's creation – we can see the ways in which it is engaged in a kind of collaborative logic whereby the poem both illustrates and suggests answers to a situation that many face. It's not simply that Dickinson picks up on her culture's concerns and uses the poem to elaborate on them but that the poem materializes a community on which the fascicle depends.

By not nesting the individual fascicle sheets within one another and then copying poems onto pages in that order – a far more common practice when making homemade books – Dickinson invites later readers not to read all of the poems in a given fascicle in relation to each other and instead highlights the particular relationships of poems on a single sheet. In the case of the first sheet of Fascicle 3, Dickinson uses the poems that follow to employ and deepen into the logic that drives "Delayed till she had ceased to know –," all the while bolstering the very community of mourners that it posits along the way. In "Some things that fly there be –" (F68), Dickinson presents death as a riddle; in "Within my reach!" (F69), she abstracts lessons from the particular death of the particular woman in the first poem; in "So bashful when I spied her!" (F70), she explores the hidden aspect of the dead (both in their lives and in their deaths); in "My friend must be a Bird –" (F71), she asserts that death poses a problem for our understanding of permanence; and in "Went up a year this evening!" (F72), she celebrates the anniversary of Jesus' death. Throughout the poems she copied onto the first sheet of Fascicle 3, then, Dickinson conjures a community of mourners who depend on her poems and on whom her poems depend. By positing these dependencies, Dickinson reveals the collaborative logic that is at play: the poems can't exist without the community, and the community is brought into being by the poems.

The first sheet of Fascicle 16 makes a similar move as the first sheet of Fascicle 3 but this time in relation to a different community: those who are reading poetry about the Civil War. Critics have long noted that the years in which Dickinson made the fascicles largely coincided with the Civil War, leading many to read these poems as war poems.[18] But another way of thinking about this historical circumstance is to investigate the relationships among the materials Dickinson used to make the fascicles, the poems themselves, and the culture of contemporary Civil War poetry that Dickinson encountered in newspapers and magazines. Like attention to the context of mourning culture, focusing on the context of Civil War-era periodical poetry allows us to see the creation of the fascicles as informed by structures deeply ingrained in the reading habits of nineteenth-century Americans. For, as Faith Barrett has shown in her thorough analysis of periodical poetry, songs, and elegies from the war years, Dickinson was writing poems that respond to a variety of media in both reflective and radical ways.[19] Like Kumbier's zines of the 1990s, then, Dickinson's fascicles that address the war topically and thematically employ a collaborative logic.

Dickinson made Fascicle 16 in 1862, right at the height of the war and directly in the wake of Frazer Stearns' death. Paula Bennett has tracked the similarities in diction and syntax between the letters Dickinson wrote to her cousins about Stearns' funeral and the poems that appear in this fascicle, proving that, at the very least, these poems are engaged topically with the war and the war dead.[20] But in order to see how Dickinson positions the fascicle in a collaborative relationship with a community of imagined readers, we need to look at what kind of work the structure of the fascicle itself allows her to do here. The most striking thing about this fascicle – which Sharon Cameron accurately characterizes as one about "death, vision, and choice" – is that, unlike the first sheet of Fascicle 3, there is almost no coherence to be found among its voices, stances, or approaches to any of these topics.[21] But whereas Cameron reads this as the fascicle's continual contradiction of perspective, a move that obscures the relation of its terms, I want to suggest that Dickinson's engagement with wartime periodical poetry firmly situates the fascicle as part of a larger conversation about how to represent the crisis as it unfolds around readers and writers of poetry. In Eliza Richards' analysis of the wide variety of Civil War-era technologies for disseminating information about the war, she argues that a major concern of writers during this period was "early mass media's ability to transmit wartime impressions so forcibly that perception is permanently altered."[22] The fact that, as Cody Marrs has argued, Dickinson "shuttles between a dazzling array of viewpoints" and employs a "cacophony of perspectives" throughout her Civil War poems should come as no surprise, then, when we see that her engagement with the Civil War mimics and responds to the non-coherence produced by technological developments.[23]

The poem that begins "Before I got my eye put out –" appears first in Fascicle 16, foregrounding, as both Bennett and Cameron have noted, the vexed choice between sight and blindness:

> Before I got my eye put out –
> I liked as well to see
> As other creatures, that have eyes –
> And know no other way –

> But were it told to me, Today,
> That I might have the Sky
> For mine, I tell you that my Heart
> Would split, for size of me –
>
> The Meadows – mine –
> The Mountains – mine –
> All Forests – Stintless stars –
> As much of noon, as I could take –
> Between my finite eyes –
>
> The Motions of the Dipping Birds –
> The Lightning's jointed Road –
> For mine – to look at when I liked,
> The news would strike me dead –
>
> So safer – guess – with just my soul
> Opon the window pane
> Where other creatures put their eyes –
> Incautious – of the Sun – (F336)

This poem performs, in the first two stanzas, the problem of relative experience and the effect that deprivation has on our ability to make reasoned choices. While the poem is seemingly articulated by one who is blind, this poem can never say that outright, and the conditions under which this person struggles are made both gory and obscure: refusing terminology such as "to go blind," Dickinson writes that it is a singular "eye" that was, like a candle, "put out." Similarly, while we might expect the poem to position others as those "who can see," it imagines that community as those "that have eyes." Given this "eye" back, briefly and imaginatively, the poem revels in the temporary ownership ("mine" appears three times) of the details of the external world that would come along with this change. And yet, in the end, this has only been an exercise, as sight is deemed less "safe" and what is instead (and, I think, ironically) embraced is "just my soul." In many ways we might say that this poem encapsulates much of the tension that exists in Civil War poetry more broadly – the simultaneous obsession with and sidestepping of the details of physical brutality; the desire to return to (and revel in) a prior world, all the while knowing that return is impossible; and the creation of a natural landscape that is meant to counter the forces of darkness and death.[24] But the tension also exists in that one line "The news would strike me dead," which performs the poem's turn from a contemplation of sight to the choice of blindness. The "news," to Americans living in 1862, conveyed the names and the details of the dead, but to experience the news of the dead must have also felt, at times, like being struck oneself.[25]

This poem performs one version of what Civil War poetry was, one version that would have been, with the turn of both the newspaper page and the fascicle page, contradicted by another version. As American poets attempted to both get and render the news through poetry, as Richards has argued, they experimented with a variety of voices and perspectives, all of which produced anything but unity. While Bennett has pointed out that there are a number of poems narrated by soldiers, non-combatant observers, and the dead throughout this fascicle – a shift in perspective that, one might argue, is undergirded by the gaps between fascicle sheets – even looking at just the other poem on this fascicle sheet, "Of nearness to her sundered Things" (F337), shows the multiplicity of viewpoints on display. Whereas "Before I got my eye put out –" reflects on how one might digest the "news" of a changed world, "Of nearness to her sundered Things" displays a clarity (and confidence) about the difficult things that it sees. The poem is filled with images of the dead, and yet it renders them as "Bright Knots of Apparitions" that, when seen through this state of "Distinctness," seem more at peace in the world than the living. By mimicking the shifting stances that were an integral part of periodical poetry of the time, Dickinson employs a collaborative logic that relies on the mutually constitutive relations of poems and the communities produced through them. In the case of her Civil War poems, Dickinson is both writing in response to poems about the war and writing these poems in the context of poetry's accumulation and foregrounding of a diversity of perspectives on the war. Highlighting this collaborative logic allows us to push one step beyond Bennett's point that this fascicle creates empathy for its subjects, as we can now see how it also foregrounds those subjects as participants in the poetic culture that has sprung up around and through them.[26] The "other creatures" referenced in the first and last stanzas of "Before I got my eye put out –" may, on the surface, be there for comparative purposes, but they also gesture to all the other poems about all the other people and communities affected by the war.

Reading Dickinson's Civil War poems as part of a collaborative poetics that the fascicles participate in, undergird, and even at times set in motion allows us to come to a different conclusion about Dickinson's relation to that war. Whereas Marrs has argued that the war ultimately pushed Dickinson into greater privacy, that "the war, in short, disillusions Dickinson of the idea that poetry should be made public," my consideration of how the fascicles mimic the public structures and rhetorics of periodical publications leads us to see Dickinson facing outwards.[27] One of the things I have hoped to show here is that circulation need not be the primary way we think about Dickinson's turn toward the world outside of her home. As she modeled her fascicles on the kinds of materials that would have been made, read, circulated, and consumed by communities who depended on them for their very existence, Dickinson engaged with her culture in ways that have been largely invisible to us. This may be due, in part, to the fact that history is reticent to acknowledge the ways in which women writers are affected by the world of men, but it is also due to the perception that Dickinson in particular only registered the pain of the war in the most private of ways.

I want to close by turning to a poem that touches on the specific matrix of issues concerning mourning, news, and materiality that I have constellated in relationship to this question of Dickinson's collaborative poetics:

> The Birds reported from the South –
> A News express to Me –
> A spicy Charge, My little Posts –
> But I am deaf – Today –
>
> The Flowers – appealed – a timid Throng –
> I reinforced the Door –
> Go blossom to the Bees – I said –
> And trouble Me – no More –
>
> The Summer Grace, for notice strove –
> Remote – Her best Array –
> The Heart – to stimulate the Eye
> Refused too utterly –
>
> At length, a Mourner, like Myself,
> She drew away austere –
> Her frosts to ponder – then it was
> I recollected Her –
>
> She suffered Me, for I had mourned –
> I offered Her no word –
> My Witness – was the Crape I bore –
> Her – Witness – was Her Dead –
>
> Thenceforward – We – together dwelt –
> She – never questioned Me –
> Nor I – Herself –
> Our Contract
> A Wiser Sympathy   (F780)

Copied as the first poem on the third sheet of what we have come to call Fascicle 37 in late 1863, this poem highlights the variety of avenues that news traveled both toward and away from the poet. The first mode of communication is reporting, and this is one that the "I" of the poem rejects over and over again. No matter who or what this news comes from, the method is rejected outright, as she claims deafness, creates a physical barrier ("reinforced the Door"), and articulates her desire not to be "trouble[d]" by such information. But halfway through the poem a shift occurs as "Summer" becomes "a Mourner." Faced with someone "like Myself," the "I" approaches this transformed figure, although without the speech that the earlier part of the poem has revealed as undesirable and suspect. It is through the shared yet unarticulated experience of mourning (they know it by the physical details of dress and the psychic knowledge of the dead's presence) that communion occurs, until we learn that "Thenceforward – We – together dwelt –" without the burden of explanation or proof for such a "Contract." If Dickinson has an ars poetica of collaborative poetics, it might be this one, as here we can see the poem's rejection of a certain kind of sharing and its embrace of another. What ultimately works to console is the connection that is registered through a material artifact (the variant for "Crape" is "Black" on the manuscript) and through "Sympathy." Built into and constitutive of that material is the potential for communion with others, a dynamic that I hope to have shown is integral to the fascicles as Dickinson's cherished material objects.

Reading Dickinson's collaborative poetics allow us to read her poems in a different kind of dialogue, as they imagine a reader who is neither some version of lyric self-address nor a specific, identifiable, historically specific "you" (although there are also surely those throughout), but instead is a "you" who is everywhere on the horizon. Reading Dickinson in the act of putting her poems in a material position to be read – in the cases above, as a writer engaged in a collaborative poetics with women mourners as well as with readers of Civil War poetry – necessarily shifts our understanding of those poems from exceptional specimens of lyric isolation or one-on-one dialogue to those engaged in pervasive and widespread culturally embedded exchanges. When we begin by not assuming that Dickinson is talking to herself or to one other person, and when we take her choice of materials as an indicator that she was, instead, driven by a kind of collaborative logic that both depended upon and embodied the potential to constitute that community, then we can begin to see all of the ways that her fascicles position her as a collaborative poet.

In conclusion, the great contradiction that exists at the heart of Dickinson studies is that Dickinson stands in for *the* nineteenth-century American woman poet at the same time that she is cast as the very *opposite* of all other nineteenth-century American women poets. This contradiction asks us to vigorously recover the contexts in which Dickinson lived and wrote at the same time that it suppresses those contexts in the name of her exceptionality. I raise this critical contradiction in relation to a culture of collaboration with which other poets of the nineteenth century were deeply engaged in part to foreground the questions with which I am left: Even if we make the context of nineteenth-century collaborative poetics visible, could we bring this to bear on our study of Dickinson? Would we want to? Why or why not? What might it show us, and, inversely, why might it be particularly threatening to what has been the clearly popular and productive narrative of what we might call "Uncollaborative Dickinson"? For those engaged with the collaborative poetics of nineteenth-century American women's poetry, reading Dickinson's fascicles in this way may seem like an entirely natural undertaking. But we must remember that it is still the dominant inclination to treat all that is operative among Dickinson's contemporaries as absent from her life. In spite of all the work that has been done to recover her contexts, this is the one that may face the largest resistance.

Notes

1. Emily Dickinson, *Poems by Emily Dickinson*, Mabel Loomis Todd and Thomas Wentworth Higginson (eds.) (Boston: Roberts Brothers, 1890), iii–iv.
2. Quoted from "Emily Dickinson's Poems," Willis J. Buckingham, ed., *Emily Dickinson's Reception in the 1890s: A Documentary History* (Pittsburgh: University of Pittsburgh Press, 1989), 48.
3. Quoted from "Strange Poems," Buckingham, 107.
4. Bette London, *Writing Double: Women's Literary Partnership* (Ithaca and London: Cornell University Press), 9.
5. Ibid.
6. Holly Laird, *Women Coauthors* (Urbana and Chicago: University of Illinois Press, 2000), 2.
7. John Stuart Mill, "What Is Poetry?," quoted from *The Broadview Anthology of Poetry and Poetic Theory: Concise Edition*, Thomas J. Collins and Vivienne J. Rundle (eds.), (New York: Broadview Press, 2000), 566.
8. Eliza Richards, *Gender and the Poetics of Reception in Poe's Circle* (Cambridge: Cambridge University Press, 2004).
9. For a further discussion of Sigourney's collaborations with her readers, see Jennifer Putzi, "Remodeling the Kitchen in Parnassus: Lydia Sigourney's

Poetics of Collaboration," in *Lydia Sigourney: Critical Essays and Cultural Views*, Mary Louise Kete and Elizabeth Petrino eds. (Amherst: University of Massachusetts Press, 2018).
10. See Martha Nell Smith, *Rowing in Eden: Rereading Emily Dickinson* (Austin: University of Texas Press, 1992).
11. Páraic Finnerty, *Emily Dickinson's Shakespeare* (Amherst: University of Massachusetts, 2006), 85. In fact, he points to specific poems in which Dickinson "presents poetry as a collaboration between poets ... and later readers" (85–86).
12. Smith, *Rowing in Eden*, 33.
13. Alana Kumbier, *Ephemeral Material: Queering the Archive* (Sacramento: Litwin Books, 2014), 194.
14. My use of the term "imagined community," here and elsewhere in this piece, is obviously indebted to Benedict Anderson's use of this term in *Imagined Communities: Reflections on the Origin and Spread of Nationalism* (London and New York: Verso, 1983) but also to Michael Warner's crucial work on this concept, particularly in *Publics and Counterpublics* (Brooklyn: Zone Press, 2002).
15. Marta L. Werner, ed., *Emily Dickinson's Open Folios: Scenes of Reading, Surfaces of Writing* (Ann Arbor: University of Michigan Press, 1995), 12.
16. For more on how Dickinson made the fascicles and their relationship to other materials in nineteenth-century America, see Alexandra Socarides, *Dickinson Unbound: Paper, Process, Poetics* (Oxford: Oxford University Press, 2012), 20–48. The great irony of my analysis is that while the fascicles may have been the materials by and through which Dickinson indicates to critics today that she was engaged in a collaborate poetics, almost none of us gain access to her poetry through the fascicles. We read Dickinson through a variety of materials and in a variety of formats – in print, in variorums, in archives, on screens, in reading editions, in facsimile – but very rarely does anyone open a fascicle and begin to turn its pages. In other words, seeing Dickinson as a collaborative poet because of her fascicle-making project takes some imagination, since it is almost impossible for her present-day readers to simulate what it would have been like to hold them, and read them, and put them up against all of the other material objects that looked and felt like them.
17. Paul Crumbley, "Dickinson's Correspondence and the Politics of Gift-Based Circulation," in *Reading Emily Dickinson's Letters: Critical Essays*, Jane Donahue Eberwein and Cindy MacKenzie (eds.) (Amherst: University of Massachusetts Press, 2009), 33.
18. See Cody Marrs, *Nineteenth-Century American Literature and the Long Civil War* (Cambridge: Cambridge University Press, 2015), where he writes of "just how foundational that struggle was to Dickinson's conception of poetry itself" (124).
19. Faith Barrett, *To Fight Aloud Is Very Brave: American Poetry and the Civil War* (Amherst: University of Massachusetts Press, 2012), 161–180.

20. Paula Bernat Bennett, "'Looking at Death, Is Dying': Fascicle 16 in a Civil War Context," in *Dickinson's Fascicles: A Spectrum of Possibilities*, Paul Crumbley and Eleanor Elson Heginbotham (eds.) (Columbus: Ohio State University Press, 2014), 109.
21. Sharon Cameron, *Choosing Not Choosing: Dickinson's Fascicles* (Baltimore: Johns Hopkins University Press, 1990), 140.
22. Eliza Richards, "Correspondent Lines: Poetry, Journalism, and the U. S. Civil War," *ESQ: A Journal of the American Renaissance* 59.1 (2013): 147.
23. Marrs, *Nineteenth-Century American Literature and the Long Civil War*, 126.
24. Although Marrs doesn't reference this poem in particular, he writes, "The poems populated by soldiers, armies, and surgeries tend to focus on boundaries (both spatial and psychic), episodes of deafness and blindness, and various communicative failures that underscore the poems' distance from the very conflict that occasions them" (126).
25. See Vanessa Steinroetter, "'Reading the List': Casualty Lists and Civil War Poetry," *ESQ: A Journal of the American Renaissance* 59.1 (2013): 48–78, for a reading of how Civil War poets responded to both the culture and materiality of the published, public casualty list.
26. Bennett, "Looking at Death, Is Dying," 129.
27. Marrs, *Nineteenth-Century American Literature and the Long Civil War*, 152.

CHAPTER 2

Generic Dickinson

Michael C. Cohen

This essay proceeds from my belief that readers often over-invest in an idea of Emily Dickinson's originality in relation to nineteenth-century American poetry. I do not disagree that Dickinson was a daring, evocative writer, nor do I deny the pleasures of discovering in her poems the heterodoxy, skepticism, and irony that many have long enjoyed. Instead, I dispute the assumption that Dickinson's work is best understood when seen as antagonistic to the norms of her contemporary milieu.[1] There is no need, in my view, to consider it "disconcerting to find a poet of Dickinson's stature turning for sustenance to such second-rate romancers as Longfellow and 'Ik Marvel,'" as Paula Bennett, one of Dickinson's strongest readers, once wrote.[2] I will argue in contrast that Dickinson engaged actively with the poetry of her time, in ways that are better understood as emulation and play than as negation, critique, or subversion. Building on scholarship that has created a more specific understanding of Dickinson's relation to nineteenth-century poetics, my goal is to open our eyes to a literary culture capable of fostering Dickinson *through* its conventions, rather than in opposition to them.[3]

The tendency to value Dickinson as a poet of negation derives primarily from a twentieth-century standard of literary achievement, which cast American poetry in an antinomian mode, at its best when challenging or rejecting the commonplaces and complacencies of its time. A poet of "negation" is one who withdraws critically from her world, practicing an art of self-cancellation in line with Keats's famous sense of "negative capability" or Anne-Lise François's concept of recessive action as "the ethos of minimal realization" or "weightless experience" that insists "on *not* mattering."[4] The image of Dickinson as the reclusive "woman in white" has fueled this sense of her, of course, but so too have readers' desires to see themselves as her true poetic correspondents. "This is my letter to the World / That never wrote to Me," she puts it in a famous statement of assertion through withdrawal, her message "committed / To Hands

I cannot see" (F519). Imagining, as it is tempting to do, that such hands must belong to future readers – namely, us – places Dickinson outside her era, as though she were too modern for her own time. She did not write like other nineteenth-century writers, because she did not write for them; she writes more like we do, because she writes for us. Or so we might want to think. To read Dickinson this way is to envisage her transcending convention by refusing to be contemporary to her moment. "Before I got my eye put out," she writes in another poem, "I liked as well to see / As other creatures." The lost eye makes all the difference, though, since her blindness prompts a turning away: "were it told to me, Today, / That I might have the Sky ... The news would strike me dead." Much safer, she archly concludes, to look "with just my soul / Opon the window pane" (F336).

Even scholars who link Dickinson's work to nineteenth-century practices of reading and writing tend to emphasize her exceptionality, the ways in which her methods exceeded or diverged from those of her friends and fellow poets. Negation and withdrawal have been keys to unlocking her work: Dickinson "chooses not to choose" among variants within her poems, and she rejects publication so as to maintain indeterminacy in "a private space in which conventions could be revised without the revision's being contested"; her "liberties with poetic form and style assert ... her inalienable individual right to craft discordance, difficulty, and rarity out of common American materials"; "the visible handwritten sequence" of a Dickinson poem "establishes an enunciative clearing outside intention while obeying intuition's agonistic necessity," in which "free from limitations of genre Language finds true knowledge estranged in it self."[5] Clearly, many readers have productively idealized an Emily Dickinson who magisterially breaks the rules of language, style, genre, and media, in order to write poetry that later readers will finally know how to grasp.

By searching for a "generic" Dickinson, I do not mean that her work is somehow more formulaic or less interesting than previously believed. Nor do I intend to rehash the various genres (hymn, elegy, ballad, etc.) Dickinson could be said to have written in or against. To call a poem "generic" is not, in my vocabulary, an insult. Instead, by seeking the "generic" I insist that her poems take form inside a field of practices that constituted the meaning of poetic writing in midcentury America. *Dickinson did not dwell outside this field of meaning-making.* As I hope to show, some of Dickinson's most powerful poems draw their power from the play of conventions that defined how poetry was read and written in the nineteenth century. If we focus on the ways conventional thinking about poetry molded her, we can appreciate some under-recognized patterns in her work. Recognition renders genres generic; it is the gesture of relation that links readers, writers, reading, and writing. As Virginia Jackson has argued, controversies over reading and recognition have shaped Dickinson's poems (both figuratively and literally) since their initial publication in the 1890s.[6] In the "generic Dickinson" I hope to locate the powers of recognition that influenced her sense of what poetry was, thereby helping twenty-first-century readers better recognize the generic-ness of Dickinson's own notions of poetics.

The law that makes genres generic is circular: a poem is what readers read as a poem. The nineteenth century had rich and complex ideas of what poems were and how they could mold social and intellectual life, though much of that knowledge has been lost.[7] From her childhood, Dickinson was an energetic consumer of poetry, and she wove the pedagogical verses learned during her schooldays into her earliest extant letters, a practice of playful citation, combination, and exchange that continued throughout her life. Scholars have mapped with admirable precision the books she owned, accessed, and quoted, so I will not rehearse those details.[8] I am more interested in what Dickinson thought reading a poem could do. "If I read a book [and] it makes my whole body so cold no fire ever can warm me I know *that* is poetry. If I feel physically as if the top of my head were taken off, I know *that* is poetry" (L342a). So she told Thomas Wentworth Higginson in August 1870, though we have only his version of her words. At first glance, to describe reading a poem through the sensations of freezing or decapitation seems to fit the model of negation or cancellation that governs many accounts of Dickinson's poetics, as the imagined diminishment of embodied life initiates a far more expansive inward experience of the poetry. Some of her most quotable lines link aesthetic perception with bodily withdrawal:

> After great pain, a formal feeling comes –
> The Nerves sit ceremonious, like Tombs –
> The stiff Heart questions "was it He, that bore,"
> And "Yesterday, or Centuries before"? . . .
>
> This is the Hour of Lead –
> Remembered, if outlived,
> As Freezing persons, recollect the Snow –
> First – Chill – then Stupor – then the letting go –   (F372)

The formal feeling – the affect of form – becomes appreciable in the wake of a pain that deadens perception while enabling self-reflection, like having an eye put out in order better to see, so that the resulting loss of self-identity, marked here by the ceremoniously tomblike nerves, can prompt the Heart to question itself. The experience of poetic form (the metrical "feet" of the fifth line) is retrospective, conceived from the vantage of an imagined moment of "letting go" that comes in the wake of feeling "so cold no fire ever can warm me": "First – Chill – then Stupor – then the letting go." Moments of reading that can freeze or trepan thus seem akin to perceptions sharp enough to halt life at the limit of language. Such a sensibility requires a reader open to the encounter of the poem, but in a stance of extreme removal, which sounds like the familiar version of Emily Dickinson, nonconformist.

Except that this mode of understanding poetic form was, in fact, conventional to nineteenth-century poetics. Dickinson's way of threading together poetry and pain (and mutually unraveling them) strongly resembles the reading of reading a poem that Henry Wadsworth Longfellow models in "The Day Is Done" (1845).

> The day is done, and the darkness
> Falls from the wings of Night,
> As a feather is wafted downward
> From an eagle in his flight.
>
> I see the lights of the village
> Gleam through the rain and mist,
> And a feeling of sadness comes o'er me
> That my soul cannot resist:
>
> A feeling of sadness and longing,
> That is not akin to pain,
> And resembles sorrow only
> As the mist resembles the rain.
>
> Come, read to me some poem,
> Some simple and heartfelt lay,
> That shall soothe this restless feeling,
> And banish the thoughts of day. . . .
>
> Read from some humbler poet,
> Whose songs gushed from his heart,
> As showers from the clouds of summer,
> Or tears from the eyelids start . . .
>
> Such songs have power to quiet
> The restless pulse of care,
> And come like the benediction
> That follows after prayer. . . .[9]

Like Dickinson's poem, "The Day Is Done" cultivates a formal feeling through the desire to withdraw; the aesthetic melancholy of "sadness and longing" are linked to pain by an act of disavowal that seems to distinguish them but then fails to do so (lines 6 and 12 show that the differences between mist and rain are less than their shared capacity to elicit sorrow). Longfellow's sensibility also functions negatively: reading "from some humbler poet" soothes feelings and banishes thoughts, achieving the "letting go" sought for in Dickinson's poem but which Longfellow's humble poet never achieved amid "long days of labor, / And nights devoid of ease." That humble poet's double negation (his nights lack the lack of care nights should have) lies in the ongoing worldliness of his world, the condition from which reading his work will relieve his reader. If Longfellow thus desires poems capable of projecting a nature homologous to human feeling – poems that pour forth like rainfall or tears – such responsive-seeming verse must also cancel "the restless pulse of care" set racing by the "endless toil and endeavor" of modern life. Such an impossibly paradoxical letting-go comes only through hyperbolic self-cancellation. Don't let your footsteps echo through the corridors of time, poets, the poem seems to say, but listen instead to the wonderful melodies only your soul can hear. Give up even the choice of your text: "read from the treasured volume / The poem of thy choice," Longfellow tells his silent companion, "And lend to the rhyme of the poet / The beauty of thy voice." Whatever poem that reader finally chooses will be not the prayer but the benediction that *follows* prayer: what Longfellow seeks is not the ritual of praying but the affect of having prayed, a formal feeling of removal that comes, as it does in Dickinson's poem, after.

No poet was more conventionally nineteenth-century than Longfellow, and no poem more conventional than "The Day Is Done." Dickinson cites Longfellow in her correspondence as much as any other author, and his books featured among her favorites; there is no reason to assume that she ironizes his sentiments in her own work. Dickinson's modern readers should not be shy about claiming this affiliation. "After great pain" is neither a critique of nor a response to "The Day Is Done" but is instead a play upon the terms of meaning-making that Longfellow sets in motion in that poem. If we think of poems like "After great pain" as efforts to create "wonderful melodies" heard by way of the "restless pulse of care" that "long days of labor, / And nights devoid of ease" generate, then we can glimpse the poet I am calling the "generic Dickinson," who models even her posture of attenuated distance through close engagements with the poetry surrounding her.

Dickinson's accounts of reading, told in her letters and poems, offer many examples of a poet playfully inhabiting the conventions of poetic creativity that her century promulgated. The nineteenth century abounded in tropes and truisms regarding books and reading.[10] For example, in his 1858 essay "Books," Emerson writes how "in a library we are surrounded by many hundreds of dear friends, but they are imprisoned by an enchanter in these paper and leathern boxes," so many of which appear so similar from without that a good reader should read only "what is proper to him, and not waste his memory on a crowd of mediocrities."[11] Emerson's essay, like other didactic treatises about books, goes on to list the best authors that an aspiring reader should choose and concludes that "their communications are not to be given or taken with the lips and the end of the tongue, but out of the glow of the cheek, and with the throbbing heart," as intimate familiars.[12] The tropes of bookish friendship, intimacy, and enchantment, and the curricular suggestion to hold hands with great authors across time, make up the subject of a poem Dickinson wrote in 1862 or 1863.

> A precious – mouldering pleasure – 'tis –
> To meet an Antique Book –
> In just the Dress his Century wore –
> A privilege – I think –
>
> His venerable Hand to take –
> And warming in our own –
> A passage back – or two – to make –
> To Times when he – was young – . . .
> When Plato – was a Certainty –
> And Sophocles – a Man –
>
> When Sappho – was a living Girl –
> And Beatrice wore
> The Gown that Dante – deified –
> Facts Centuries before
>
> He traverses – familiar –
> As One should come to Town –
> And tell you all your Dreams – were true –
> He lived – where Dreams were born –
>
> His presence is enchantment –
> You beg him not to go –
> Old Volumes shake their Vellum Heads
> And tantalize – just so – (F569)[13]

This poem pushes Emerson's clichés about reading into a strange new place, as the Antique Book draws life out of death in a passage back to the "Times when he – was young," opening a moment when Plato, Sophocles, Sappho, and Dante and Beatrice live together with the equally vitalized, enchanted reader. As we might guess from "the glow of the cheek" that for Emerson marks the reading of good books, the "precious – mouldering pleasure" they elicit is weirdly, erotically generative. Far from working through the kinds of bodily negation in which reading takes off the top of the head or puts out an eye, this poem revels in the physical pleasures that an Antique Book can arouse. Dickinson does not read the Antique Book so much as she *handles* him, warming "his" personified hand in her own and passing with him from death into life. She returns to the time "When Sappho – was a living Girl" not through the book but in his company, as his guest. If the first option requires a phenomenology of reading that forgets the object held in the hands, so as to become "lost in a book" (more versions of self-cancellation), the second option – holding hands with the book – embraces its material life, "the Dress his Century wore." In this poem, "Vellum Heads" tantalize as much as "quaint opinions," and the joys of old volumes lie in their moldering rankness, out of which imagined life springs.

Cultural truisms about books abound in the poem: the book is a friend, a teacher, an enchanter, a dreamer, a portal. "The entranced and admiring reader runs to his favorite when he can snatch an hour from labor, society, or sleep," Noah Porter would write at the end of the decade in *Books and Reading*.[14] "No enchantment is so entire and delightful as that with which [novelists] invest the story which they recite"; "as we read ... we seem to be lifted above the actual solid earth ... to fly or float in a sort of cloud or enchanted land."[15] "Every author, whom we rake from oblivion, becomes to us, as it were, a personal friend," whose voice "speaks to us alone," says Oliver Wendell Holmes in an essay on "Old Books."[16] "Such intimacies may be formed by all," for "they ask not wealth to purchase, or flattery to retain," but instead offer "a solace in the humblest pages."[17] In a famous letter to Higginson written around the same time as the poem, Dickinson described her reading in similarly passionate, companionate terms:

> You inquire my Books – For Poets – I have Keats – and Mr and Mrs Browning. For Prose – Mr Ruskin – Sir Thomas Browne – and the Revelations. I went to school – but in your manner of the phrase – had no education. When a little Girl, I had a friend, who taught me Immortality – but venturing too near, himself – he never returned – Soon

after, my Tutor, died – and for several years, my Lexicon – was my only companion. (L261)

"A precious – mouldering pleasure" shares with this letter the experience of companionship, of being accompanied by books and enjoying the sociability they enable. But while the poem dovetails in certain ways with the letter's account of education (they share the sense of a reading curriculum, if not the same authors), there are important differences. Most notably, unlike the poem, where the aging materiality of the Antique Book revitalizes authors who had been "Facts Centuries before" but now live again in rereading, the letter's tale of companionate education illustrates Dickinson's tendency to meditate on the erotic passage of life into death: her friend and Tutor both "venture too near" immortality in the process of teaching her, which brings together education and death in a libidinal confluence that ultimately leaves Dickinson alone with her words. "My dying Tutor told me that he would like to live till I had been a poet," she explained in a subsequent letter, "but Death was much of Mob as I could master – then ... I felt a palsy, here – the Verses just relieve –" (L265). In words that echo Longfellow's desire for songs with the "power to quiet / The restless pulse of care," Dickinson's relief from palsy comes by way of verses that seem to lock hands otherwise separated – "the hand you stretch me in the dark," she quotes at the letter's conclusion, "I put mine in, and turn away" – offering lines from an early poem: "As if I asked a common Alms, / And in my wondering hand / A Stranger pressed a Kingdom" (F14; L265).

Metaphorical hands stretched together in epistolary exchanges forge the "as if" of the poem's first line, transforming a "common Alms" into a "Kingdom" all the more bewildering for being held in the hands, like a letter or a poem. "As if I asked a common Alms" and "A precious – mouldering pleasure" therefore reverse the eroticism of pedagogical death described in the letters by situating shared reading and writing as points of transfer into more fully vitalized life. In the context of its place in the correspondence with Higginson, "As if I asked a common Alms" becomes a statement of the fullness enabled by the conventions of manuscript verse cultures – poems freely given as gifts in writing beggar less imaginative notions of friendship, transmuting ordinary experience into something that can flood or shatter those who know "as if."[18] Higginson felt this clasping power of the hand (and the handwritten) when he held Dickinson's poems. "Sometimes I take out your letters & verses, dear friend, and when I feel their strange power ... I have the greatest desire to see you, always feeling that perhaps if I could once take you by the hand I might be something to you" (L330a). Holding the pages of her writings in his hand, Higginson desires to hold Dickinson by the hand, so that "I might be something to you." Their "strange power" is gripping and phantasmatic, or as Dickinson puts it, their "presence is enchantment," "familiar – / As One should come to Town – / And tell you all your Dreams – were true." In the nineteenth-century verse culture Dickinson and Higginson share, readers don't only read poems; poems also read readers. Poems that "lived – where Dreams were born –" reveal your inmost self to you, "just so –." The products of such readings are not idiosyncratic readers serene in their isolation, but readers tantalized, socialized, drawn out – in other words, *educated* in verse and the lives of sentiment and sensibility they make apprehensible.

The ways in which Dickinson plays with the conventions of her poetic culture attest to her thorough education in them. Yet deeply grounded as this education was, she tended to deflect attention from it. As Erika Sheurer argues, Dickinson's misleading claim to Higginson that she "went to school – but ... had no education" belies the ways in which her "originality as a writer was perfectly in keeping with the expectations" inculcated at the Amherst Academy, which she attended between 1840 and 1847.[19] Following scholars of composition studies like Jean Ferguson Carr, Sheurer contests the common assumption that nineteenth-century education consisted only of mechanical exercises in rote learning and Gradgrind-like recitations of facts.[20] Instead, Scheurer locates Dickinson's "distinctive style" in her early immersion in the developing composition pedagogy of the antebellum United States. While "the educational system Dickinson experienced was not the direct cause of her distinctive style," she concludes, "her experience in composition at the Academy enabled rather than hindered her gifts as a writer."[21] While Sheurer's essay focuses on the scholastic program in rhetoric and composition, I want to look more closely at how schooling in poetry shaped Dickinson's later writing. The literary curriculum of Amherst Academy emphasized the exemplary pedagogical texts William St. Clair has dubbed "the old canon," seventeenth- and eighteenth-century poems by John Milton, James Thomson, Edward Young, William Cowper, Robert Pollok, and Alexander Pope.[22] While biographers have mostly treated this education as a stultifying legacy the later poet would need to unlearn, I want instead to attend to the surprising ways it shaped her imagination.

Among the many sources that inflect her style, Edward Young's *The Complaint, or Night-Thoughts* (1745) stands out. Particularly in her teenaged correspondence with schoolmate Abiah Root, Dickinson used quotations from *Night-Thoughts*, and the orthodox, aestheticized Protestant piety they expressed, as compass points against which she began to chart her increasingly nonconformist views. Young's poem uses the naturalized setting of the night sky as a screen on which to project a series of metaphysical explorations on death and immortality, so that the content and blank-verse form of his poem function pedagogically as practices of reading and interpretation that the poem addresses thematically:

> O thou Great Jove unfeign'd!
> Divine Instructor! thy first volume, this,
> For man's perusal; all in capitals!
> In moon, and stars (heaven's golden alphabet!)
> Emblazed to seize the sight; who runs may read:
> Who reads, can understand. . . .
> A language, lofty to the learn'd; yet plain
> To those that feed the flock, or guide the plough . . .
> Which oft refers its reader to the skies,
> As presupposing his first lesson there,
> And Scripture 'self a fragment, that unread.
> Stupendous book of wisdom, to the wise!
> Stupendous book! and open'd, Night! By thee.[23]

This passage, from Night IX, "The Consolation," was a commonly excerpted "gem" from the poem, and as such appeared in numerous nineteenth-century anthologies, primers, and readers. It recasts the "book of nature" topos in scholastic terms, framing the poem as a set of exercises in being taught how to read: as Young puts it in Night II, "On this great theme kind Nature keeps a school, / To teach her sons herself," and again in Night IX, "stars teach, as well as shine."[24] Such schooling generates the poem's conclusion:

> Man's science is the culture of his heart;
> And not to lose his plummet in the depths
> Of nature, or the more profound of God.
> Either to know, is an attempt that sets
> The wisest on a level with the fool.
> To fathom nature, (ill attempted here!)
> Past doubt, is deep philosophy above;
> Higher degrees in bliss archangels take,

> As deeper learn'd; the deepest, learning still. . . .
> Teaching this lesson, pride is loth to learn –
> "Not deeply to discern, not much to know;
> Mankind was born to wonder and adore."[25]

Dickinson learned well Young's attention to the moments when the book of nature transforms wisdom into wonder and his consequent lesson on the limits of human knowing. Consider this poem of about 1862 (F435), which turns on a pedagogical comparison between worldly life and a child's primer, both of which, as Young would have it, shall be superseded by a superior spiritual literacy legible in the skies:

> Not in this World to see his face –
> Sounds long – until I read the place
> Where this – is said to be
> But just the Primer – to a life –
> Unopened – rare – Opon the Shelf –
> Clasped yet – to Him – and me –

Given the tutelary power granted to the night sky in *Night-Thoughts*, this poem could almost seem to be Dickinson's response, which is less a rejection of Young's natural theology than a thorough internalization of its conclusions on the ends of human knowledge. If the first stanza appears to explore faith and doubt – deferring until a future immortality the face-to-face meeting with God – the second stanza affirms a life lived fully in this world. Reversing the didactic reading in *Night-Thoughts* (and the didactic reading of that poem as well), the child's primer in Dickinson's poem mediates a transition from heavenly transcendence to non-transcendent worldliness, as its usage downshifts from being the preparatory volume in a program of spiritual literacy ("thy first volume . . . all in capitals") to the humdrum abecedary, like the *New England Primer*, familiar to generations of schoolchildren.[26] A world that is "just the Primer – to a life –" seems brief in comparison to the volume "unopened – rare – Opon the Shelf." This book, "Clasped yet – to Him – and me" is both open – held in a shared embrace between Him and me – and shut, like a family Bible sealed with metallic fastenings. Therefore its wonders are expansive to the extent they remain clasped, like His face, within a future that promises through withholding.

The turn in the second stanza rejects these promises of a future life as yet "Unopened – rare – Opon the Shelf" by literalizing the metaphorical Primer into "just my A – B – C –," a textbook that "suits me so / I would not choose – a Book to know / Than that." Unlike Young's "golden alphabet,"

"Emblazed to seize the sight ... In language universal," Dickinson's primer suits because the literacy it inculcates remains "sweeter wise," not venturing beyond the initial "A – B – C –" but as a result staying open. Far from rejecting Young's lesson, though, this conclusion seems to affirm his closing edict "Not deeply to discern, not much to know" so as to maintain the capacity "to wonder and adore." To choose "my A – B – C –" is to celebrate a literacy that refuses metaphor in favor of the "precious – mouldering pleasures" of the "sweeter wise," material reading and writing. "Not in this World" thus continues the legacy of Dickinson's training in poetic convention, in which reading matter enables her to exchange spiritual for worldly literacy.

To conclude, I want to consider one final example from around 1862 (F277) that also transacts the work of recognition inherent to mundane communication. This kind of knowing indicates the knower's training in the protocols that generate the communicative power of reading and writing.[27]

> Going to Him! Happy letter!
> Tell Him –
> Tell Him the page I did'nt write –
> Tell Him – I only said the Syntax –
> And left the Verb and the pronoun – out – ...
>
> Tell Him – it wasn't a Practised Writer –
> You guessed – from the way the sentence toiled – ...
> Tell Him – No – you may quibble there –
> For it would split His Heart, to know it –
> And then you and I, were silenter.
>
> Tell Him – Night finished – before we finished –
> And the Old Clock kept neighing "Day"! ...
> Tell Him – just how she sealed you – Cautious!
> But – if He ask where you are hid
> Until tomorrow – Happy letter!
> Gesture Coquette – and shake your Head![28]

This poem longs for a mode of understanding that can circumvent language and its forms. Young imagined the night sky speaking "A language, worthy the Great Mind that speaks," but here "Night finished – before we finished –," and thus the "Stupendous book of wisdom" that Night alone can open must be put aside. Without the "golden alphabet" and "language universal" of the stars, how can a reader recognize the emotional meaning inscribed into written words? The prosopopoeia invoked in the address to the letter – speaking to it so that it might speak to another – animates communication so as imaginatively to transcend the limits of connection between sender and recipient. By enabling the letter to express the surplus of meaning encoded in its material form but unspoken in its message, the incoherencies of writing are made to speak: "from the way the sentence toiled" the recipient will know "it wasn't a Practised Writer" who sent the letter, heightening emotional sincerity by way of contrast to the polished examples in manuals such as *Webster's Practical Letter Writer*. Such sincerity will be revealed in those non-semantic indications of "how the fingers hurried – / Then – how they waded – slow – slow" – inkblots, stains, and signs of haste or struggle in the handwriting. By asking the letter to "tell Him" all these things, the sender invokes both a fear of the communication's mute unresponsiveness – its inability to speak what the sender truly wishes to say – and its potential excess, revealing too much, "the page I did'nt write" as well as the page she did. Such a surfeit of emotive expression ironically threatens to overwhelm the communicative capacity of the mail: "Tell Him – No – you may quibble there – / For it would split His Heart, to know it – / And then you and I, were silenter."

"What would it hinder so – to – say?" the sender imagines the letter thinking of her. "You wished you had eyes in your pages" so as to see the force moving her writing fingers to such excessive speed or deliberation. The triangulation of address expresses the hope for an understanding between sender and recipient that will go beyond the letter's traditional communicative role. The poem is thus not about any failure of language but its supreme success: folding herself into the conventions of epistolary and poetic discourse, Dickinson activates the midcentury culture's desire for communication that speaks from some place deeper than the heart. Writing always says more than it says; this is how generic recognition cultivates literary force. "Happy letter!" The playful enthusiasm through which Dickinson addresses the protocols of writing reveal an author at home in the conventions that shape the meanings of her poetic world.

Notes

1. Arguments about Dickinson's poetry that proceed from this view include Roy Harvey Pearce, *The Continuity of American Poetry* (Princeton: Princeton University Press, 1961), 174–186; Sandra M. Gilbert and Susan Gubar, *The Madwoman in the Attic: The Woman Writer and the Nineteenth-Century Literary Imagination* (New Haven: Yale University Press, 1979), 581–650; Adrienne Rich, "Vesuvius at Home: The Power of Emily Dickinson," in

On Lies, Secrets, and Silence: Selected Prose 1966–1978 (New York: Norton, 1979), 157–183; and Shira Wolosky, "Emily Dickinson: The Violence of the Imagination," in *Cambridge History of American Literature*, Vol. 4 (Cambridge: Cambridge University Press, 2004), 427–480. Since several of these works are landmark feminist recoveries of nineteenth-century women's writing, it is important also to acknowledge the masculinism of twentieth-century accounts of sovereign, agonistic poetic achievement, which positioned the heroic, dissident poet against a field of feminized popular writers who capitulated to cultural conventions. Some of the most important such versions of American literature, including V. L. Parrington's *Main Currents in American Thought*, F. O. Matthiessen's *American Renaissance*, and R. W. B. Lewis's *American Adam*, hardly mention Dickinson at all.

2. Paula Bernat Bennett, *My Life, A Loaded Gun: Female Creativity and Feminist Poetics* (Boston: Beacon Books, 1986), 32. Bennett qualifies this embarrassment with the claim that "such poets provided Dickinson with the possibility of an alternate definition of self," but she is much happier noting how "later [Dickinson would] turn to such writers as Shakespeare to justify these same ideals" (ibid.).

3. This scholarship includes Ellen Louise Hart and Martha Nell Smith, eds., *Open Me Carefully: Emily Dickinson's Intimate Letters to Susan Huntington Dickinson* (Boston: Paris Press, 1998); Alexandra Socarides, *Dickinson Unbound: Paper, Process, Poetics* (Oxford: Oxford University Press, 2012); Cristanne Miller, *Reading in Time: Emily Dickinson in the Nineteenth Century* (Amherst: University of Massachusetts Press, 2012); and Eliza Richards, ed., *Emily Dickinson in Context* (Cambridge: Cambridge University Press, 2013).

4. Anne-Lise François, *Open Secrets: The Literature of Uncounted Experience* (Stanford: Stanford University Press, 2008), xviii, 133, 135.

5. Sharon Cameron, *Choosing Not Choosing: Dickinson's Fascicles* (Chicago: University of Chicago Press, 1992), 53; Mary Loeffelholz, *The Value of Emily Dickinson* (Cambridge: Cambridge University Press, 2016), 85; Susan Howe, *The Birth-Mark: unsettling the wilderness in American literary history* (Middletown: Wesleyan University Press, 1993), 136, 137. See as well Jen Bervin's introduction to *Emily Dickinson: The Gorgeous Nothings*, Marta Werner and Jen Bervin (eds.) (New York: Christine Burghin/New Directions, 2013), which begins with a discussion of "nothing" and "no" as keywords in Dickinson's lexicon (8).

6. Virginia Jackson, *Dickinson's Misery: A Theory of Lyric Reading* (Princeton: Princeton University Press, 2005).

7. Recent literary histories that examine the social roles of poems in the nineteenth century include: Paula Bernat Bennett, *Poets in the Public Sphere: The Emancipatory Project of American Women's Poetry, 1800–1900* (Princeton: Princeton University Press, 2003); Mary Loeffelholz, *From School to Salon: Reading Nineteenth-Century American Women's Poetry* (Princeton: Princeton University Press, 2004); Max Cavitch, *American Elegy: The Poetry of Mourning*

from the Puritans to Whitman (Minneapolis: University of Minnesota Press, 2007); and Michael C. Cohen, *The Social Lives of Poems in Nineteenth-Century America* (Philadelphia: University of Pennsylvania Press, 2015).
8. For good sources on Dickinson's reading, see Jack L. Capps, *Emily Dickinson's Reading, 1836–1886* (Cambridge: Harvard University Press, 1966), and the essays collected in the special issue on "Emily Dickinson's Reading," ed. Daniel L. Manheim and Marianne Noble, *EDJ* 19.1 (2010).
9. Longfellow, *Poems and Other Writings* (New York: Library of America, 2000), 48–49.
10. These tropes, which often pit the materiality of books against their content, literary or otherwise, form the subject of Leah Price's *How to Do Things with Books in Victorian Britain* (Princeton: Princeton University Press, 2012).
11. Ralph Waldo Emerson, "Books," *Atlantic Monthly* (January 1858), 344, 345.
12. Ibid., 353.
13. Franklin dates the poem to 1863, as does Cristanne Miller (*Emily Dickinson's Poems as She Preserved Them* [Cambridge: Harvard University Press, 2016], 259). Thomas Johnson and Richard B. Sewall each ascribe it to "about 1862": cf. Johnson, *The Poems of Emily Dickinson* (Cambridge: Harvard University Press, 1955), 1: 295; and Sewall, *The Life of Emily Dickinson* (Cambridge: Harvard University Press, 1974), 670.
14. Noah Porter, *Books and Reading; or, What Books Shall I Read and How Shall I Read Them?* (New York: Charles Scribner, 1872), 229. This volume of lectures was first published in 1870.
15. Ibid., 229, 128.
16. O.W.H. [Oliver Wendell Holmes], "Old Books," *New-England Magazine* (January 1832), 47.
17. Ibid., 49.
18. On nineteenth-century scribal cultures, poems, and gift-giving, see: Mary Louise Kete, *Sentimental Collaborations: Mourning and Middle-Class Identity in Nineteenth-Century America* (Durham: Duke University Press, 2000), 11–49; David M. Henkin, *The Postal Age: The Emergence of Modern Communications in Nineteenth-Century America* (Chicago: University of Chicago Press, 2006), 93–118; Leon Jackson, *The Business of Letters: Authorial Economies in Antebellum America* (Stanford: Stanford University Press, 2008), 89–141; Daniel Manheim, "'And row my blossoms o'er!': Gift-Giving and Emily Dickinson's Poetic Vocation," *EDJ* 20.2 (2011): 1–32; and Laura Zebuhr, "The Work of Friendship in Nineteenth-Century American Friendship Album Verses," *American Literature* 87.3 (2015): 433–454.
19. Erika Scheurer, "'[S]o of course there was Speaking and Composition –': Dickinson's Early Schooling as a Writer," *EDJ* 18.1 (2009): 1.
20. Jean Ferguson Carr, Stephen L. Carr, and Lucille M. Schultz, *Archives of Instruction: Nineteenth-Century Rhetorics, Readers, and Composition Books*

in the United States (Carbondale: Southern Illinois University Press, 2005).
21. Scheurer, "Dickinson's Early Schooling," 2.
22. William St. Clair, *The Reading Nation in the Romantic Period* (Cambridge: Cambridge University Press, 2004). Sewall recounts the curricula of Dickinson's schooling in *Life*, 335–367; see especially 349–353 for information about English literature. Also noteworthy is Dickinson's flirtatious 1852 letter to Susan Gilbert, which depicts "all the gallant men" of Amherst as old canon authors: "When I see the Popes and the Polloks and the John Milton-Browns, I think we are *liable*, but I dont know! I am glad there is a big *future* waiting for me and you" (L85).
23. Edward Young, *The Complaint, or Night-Thoughts* [1745] (Philadelphia: Griffith and Simon, 1845), 300.
24. Ibid., 36, 269.
25. Ibid., 306.
26. For much more on spelling books and their legacies in American culture, see Patricia Crain's incomparable *The Story of A: The Alphabetization of America from* The New England Primer *to* The Scarlet Letter (Stanford: Stanford University Press, 2000).
27. My sense of "protocols" comes from the discussion of the term in William B. Warner, *Protocols of Liberty: Communication Innovation and the American Revolution* (Chicago: University of Chicago Press, 2013), esp. 17–20.
28. There are at least three versions of this poem, each using different pronouns. Miller prints a version with "Her" as recipient (*Dickinson's Poems as She Preserved Them*, 529–530), which varies extensively from that reproduced in Franklin. An additional version, no longer extant, was sent to the Norcross sisters, with "Going to them, happy letter!" as the first line.

CHAPTER 3

"Success in Circuit lies": Dickinson, Media, and Imagination
Eliza Richards

In his essay "The Poet," Emerson stresses that it is "the quality of the imagination to flow, not to freeze." Imagination is a plastic, mobile force that relies on language as its vehicle:

> Here is the difference between the poet and the mystic, that the last nails a symbol to one sense, which was a true sense for a moment, but soon becomes old and false. For all symbols are fluxional; all language is vehicular and transitive, and is good, as ferries and horses are, for conveyance, not as farms and houses are, for homestead.[1]

If the poet wants to avoid losing track of sense, he must ride words like horses or ferries and never arrive at a particular location. This powerful emphasis on imagination as chronic motion and metamorphosis may emerge in part from a transatlantic shift in understanding that Michelle Kohler identifies: whereas Kant and his followers understood the imagination as an interior, mental force that could synthesize the faculties of Reason and Understanding, American Transcendentalists "began to theorize language in ways that transformed the subjective, creative figure of the *imagination* into the figure of an *eye* that could see poetic language manifest on the landscape."[2] In Emerson's "system," argues Kohler, "the trinity of Understanding, Reason, and imagination collapses into the single faculty of vision. In one act of apprehension, Emersonian vision incorporates the external world, consciousness, *and* their seamless unification all at once."[3] Externalizing mental processes, Emersonian vision may be more efficient, but it also places a tremendous burden on the eye: the poet's conscious, perceiving, and imaginative eye must somehow witness, comprehend, create, and convey ongoing transformations in the visible world. Such a charge requires constant mobility: imagination must rush to keep pace with the things that the roving eye sees. Emerson articulates this difficulty: "This insight, which expresses itself by what is called Imagination, is a very high sort of seeing, which does not come by study, but by the intellect being where and what it sees, by sharing the path, or circuit of things through forms, and so making them translucid to others. The path of things is silent. Will they suffer a speaker to go with them?"[4] The "sayer, the namer," the poet is the only speaker "they will suffer," and if he is to share their "path, or circuit," he must remain in motion.[5]

In spite of their substantial differences, Emerson and Dickinson share an urgent attention to imagination's "flow." Both wish to accompany "things" on their "path, or circuit"; both launch flurries of language in their attempts to align the imagination with vision and to keep pace with the shifting world. But while Dickinson's eye, like Emerson's, is often trained on nature, she also attends to cultural networks superimposed on, and sometimes entangled or fused with, nature. She focuses in particular on new communications technologies, wondering what their place in nature is and what sort of impact they might have on the imagination's form and velocity. If Emerson locates imagination in the eye, in some poems Dickinson suggests that the imagination moves through more radically externalized media pathways. Speaking for things on the move, the imagination in these poems negotiates between natural ecologies and communication technologies. In the process of "sharing the path, or circuit of things through forms," imagination assumes the qualities of the networks it traces. Rather than an interior, individual mental operation, poetry projects creative activity outward and tests the boundaries of individual vision; it becomes external, shared, and electrified by the same currents that drive mass media.

Dickinson's experiments with a networked imagination are situated in a broader culture shaped by what Paul Gilmore calls "romantic electricity." In the mid-nineteenth century, people experienced new forms of radical openness via mass information systems, frequently figured as a "nervous network" that linked together populations as if they were a single body. Speaking of mass communication during the Civil War, for example, Oliver Wendell Holmes Sr. declares that "the whole nation is now penetrated by the ramifications of a network of iron nerves which flash sensation and volition backward and forward to and from towns and provinces as if they were organs and limbs of a single living body."[6] Citing Holmes, Gilmore says that "the telegraph freed thought from space and time – the determinants of bodily existence – but simultaneously rendered mind and thought, or spirit, physical in the form of 'nerves' or wires criss-crossing and creating both the individual and the national 'body.'"[7] The sensation that the individual body is both connected to and subsumed within a larger body creates the conditions for figuring imagination as a fluidly circulating entity that passes through bodies even while belonging to a particular person. But the idea of the individual as one node in a larger complex, with a tenuous relation to individual agency, could make a person wish for self-enclosure and communication on a more intimate scale. Dickinson's poems figure the anxiety that attends a delocalized imagination, even as they celebrate the sense of expansive vision that attends such a configuration.

This essay suggests that Dickinson theorized about the forms that imagination takes when inspired by mass communications media, via which ideas circulate rapidly among people rather than centering in any particular individual. Aligning imagination's form with its focus, Dickinson counters romantic models of poetic inspiration. Instead of drawing environmental elements into the mind and transforming them through vision, the poems track the mind traveling outward and circulating in the external world, mapping mass-media circuitry in relation to natural elements. In the poems I analyze, Dickinson externalizes the imagination, casting the speaker as an observer of a spectacle rather than a creator. I argue that the resulting poetic environment, which blends natural and human-made media systems, offers a kind of imagination that envelops the reader, who shares an immersive experience with the speaker. Dickinson suggests that poems are not forms but environments that rely upon and interact with their mixed-media surroundings.[8]

The disorienting confluence of individual and mass is played out within "Myself" in poem F1049A, in which the speaker stops short of "sharing the path, or circuit of things through forms." The mind resists engaging with the information it receives, and imagination fails:

> Myself can read the Telegrams
> A Letter chief to me
> The Stock's advance and retrograde
> And what the Markets say
>
> The Weather – how the Rains
> In Counties have begun.
> 'Tis News as null as nothing,
> But sweeter so, than none.

"Myself" replaces the "I" as if the person needed to verify that she was self-possessed; and yet the substitution positions the subject as an object. Reading the Telegrams has generated uncertainty over whether she is an agent or a recipient of an action. The disorientation derives from and extends to the communication she has received, which could be a letter that resembles a telegram, a personal telegram, or telegrams published in the newspaper, which would specifically not be "chief to" her. (Many midcentury papers, including *The Springfield Republican*, which Dickinson read avidly, published telegraphic bulletins prolifically as a form of the most current news.) The poem's reader cannot determine the answer because the speaker conflates letters and telegrams, in the process conflating public and private correspondence, personal and impersonal forms of expression, and even singular and plural. (This confusion between telegrams and letters might be informed by the fact that the telegraph system was transferred to the postal service in 1845, becoming "the first electrical communications network to be open to the public on a fee-for-service basis."[9]) If it is a letter, public telegrams seem to have influenced it: it conveys nothing personal, and it emphasizes current events. If they are newspaper telegrams, which seems most likely, then the confusion of plural and singular, personal and public suggests that the reader within the poem has not fully grasped the nature of the medium. These circulating messages are themselves full of the news of circulation: market movements and weather systems. But rather than traveling with and through the information via the imagination, the speaker recounts the news in abstract generalities: "Weather" and "Markets." At the same time, though the "News" may be "null as nothing" to "Myself," the communication is "sweeter so, than none." The fact of circulation is pleasant and comforting, even if it has not afforded an occasion for creative expression. The "Telegrams" indicate a larger world's motions, life elsewhere, beyond the speaker's vision.[10] If, as Emerson says, the imagination is constituted by the poet "sharing the path, or circuit of things through forms," the speaker in "Myself can read the Telegrams" lacks imagination: she finds nothing to say about the "News as null as nothing" and fails to articulate a synthesis of natural and cultural media.

By bringing together the letter, the stock market, the weather report, and the telegram, Dickinson raises questions about the relation among these forms of mobile information. How does one imagine movements at a distance, beyond visual observation? How do we attend to telegraphic transport, which conveys information invisibly, in abstract, condensed form? Moreover, she asks, what is the relation between natural systems like the weather and human networks like the telegraph? Dickinson situates her study of mass media most notably in relation to what John Durham Peters calls "elemental media" ("the Weather – how the Rains/In Counties have begun"). In *The Marvelous Clouds*, Peters traces the etymology of the term "media" to its roots in the description of water, earth, fire, and air. He locates the "decisive break" from this understanding in the nineteenth century "with the slow turn of *medium* into a conveyance for specifically human signals and meanings." Peters asks us to consider the consequences of the way that "'media,' understood as the means by which meaning is communicated, sit atop layers of even more fundamental media that have meaning but do not speak." He insists that "we can learn much from a judicious synthesis, difficult though it be, of media understood as both natural and cultural."[11] Surprisingly, Dickinson's poems work through this idea, overlaying natural events with human media systems, producing a layered effect that poses questions about how or whether these elemental media will serve us once they are put to the task of fueling mass media.

Whereas "Myself" does not ponder these questions, other speakers pursue them. In dazzling visual figurations of elemental and cultural media that compensate for what cannot be seen in the physical world, Dickinson demonstrates the necessity of poetic imagination in adapting to media environments. In poem F595A, for example, the speaker attempts to speak for or with the "circuit of things," and she presents, if not "a judicious synthesis," then an odd bifurcation that allows us to think about electricity's manifestations both as lightning and as an invisible force that conveys news through telegraph lines:

> The Lightning playeth – all the while –
> But when He singeth – then –
> Ourselves are conscious He exist –
> And we approach Him – stern –
>
> With Insulators – and a Glove –
> Whose short – sepulchral Bass
> Alarms us – tho' His Yellow feet
> May pass – and counterpass –
>
> Opon the Ropes – above our Head –
> Continual – with the News –
> Nor We so much as check our speech –
> Nor stop to cross Ourselves –

The poem centers on motion and utterance, the attempt to share the circuit and speak for things. Though Peters stresses the voicelessness of elemental media in contrast to its cultural counterpart, "Ourselves" hear the lightning's voice: He "singeth" with a "sepulchral bass" when He grows more dangerous (He also "singes"). The speaker thus recognizes Lightning as an independent creative force, with a voice, a will, and musical talent, who asserts control over humans. Imagination resides in the Lightning's metaphorical being, which is observed by Ourselves, the poem's plural speaker, again an object pronoun deemed a subject, a recipient of action occupying the place of an agent. The fusion of subject and object reflects the speakers' role in both creating and receiving what they see and hear. Via this circuitous understanding, the lightning's song alerts Ourselves to danger and causes us to treat the natural, lethal force of electricity like a wild animal at the circus ("we approach Him – stern – / With ... a Glove").

Paradoxically, however, there may be more of a threat in the lightning we think we have already tamed, the electrical force that conveys verbal signals, reconstituted as "the News" once they arrive at the other end of the "Ropes – above our Head –." Mute, invisible, this seemingly innocuous force travels unnoticed; still, the imagination follows the telegraph's "path, or circuit" just as it traces the Lightning's. To do so, it makes the signals visible: "Yellow feet" that, like a gymnast's, "pass – and counterpass – / Opon the Ropes – above our Head –." The playful but ominous image of an electrical tightrope walker invokes an unremarked threat, which is not made "translucid" to Ourselves, who continue to speak freely, failing to "check our speech." Whereas "Myself" is an individual that the telegraph disorients and renders noncommittal, "Ourselves" is a distracted collective, unaware of the circumstances we are immersed in, oblivious to the electrical shock that may enlighten us in a gruesome, physical way. The "Yellow feet" may slip, and it may be too late for us to "check our speech," look up, and cross ourselves – too late to acknowledge the mighty force that is beyond human understanding, whether or not it manifests God's power. What are the consequences, the poem asks, of harnessing natural forces – nature's "voice" – in the service of human communication? Dickinson's circus metaphors show that imaginative play in the environment can generate such a question via spectacle.

Michelle Kohler's theory of Dickinson's metaphoric vision helps to underscore and elaborate on the poem's ending, which stresses asking, not knowing. In many of Dickinson's poems, according to Kohler, "metaphor derives from the experience of physical, disappointed, or otherwise limited vision, but it also constitutes a new epistemology, one contingent upon context ... and sustained activity rather than dependent on immutable, transcendent truths ... [F]or Dickinson, metaphorical prowess *increases* when visual access decreases. And she redefines metaphorical prowess as a provisional, ongoing visual activity rather than as a fixed apprehension of truth."[12] In "The Lightning playeth," Dickinson confronts the problem of

"Success in Circuit lies": Dickinson, Media, and Imagination

vision when taking up the question of electricity, which can assume different forms, has no essential shape, and cannot be touched or held: in one of the poem's images, it is kept, invisible, within an "Insulator"; in another, it travels unseen through a "Rope." Here electricity is understood as one entity that is also two, radically bifurcated into lightning in the sky and current traveling through a telegraph wire: elemental and cultural media. Dickinson nevertheless pulls them into a unity and makes them visible in the pair of circus images – a lion tamer and a tightrope walker. The two metaphors hold a common field in order to posit relations between two entities that are also one force. The comparison between the daring metaphors, as well as between tenors and their vehicles, raises the question of what electricity can do for human communication, without arriving at a "transcendent truth."

We have seen Dickinson presenting a figure – "Myself" – who fails to imagine the news, who can only summon a sense of the "nothing" that it brings. But once the imagination is projected into the landscape, so that it can travel alongside the movements of electrical forces, leaving "Ourselves" to watch, the circuitry comes alive via circus metaphors that are both playful and ominous. The poem's plural speaker is a spectator to their own fanciful, eerie creation, suggesting that the imagination has circulated beyond authorial control and has gained vivifying force through its identification with a combination of elemental and cultural media. Electricity's status as a crossover medium, one that flashes through natural environments and moves through human infrastructures – in this case the telegraph network – makes it a particularly productive focus for imagining connections between elemental and cultural media.

If poem 595A advises us to "check our speech" and "cross Ourselves" in acknowledgment of the potentially dangerous powers of the telegraph, a late poem that again relates lightning, electricity, and communication posits an unequivocally wondrous scenario of communal illumination. In poem F1665B, electricity's vital force brings people together through the miracle of light. Once again conflating lightning and human uses of electricity, the poem celebrates electrical force in both personal and communal terms:

> The farthest Thunder that I heard
> Was nearer than the Sky
> And rumbles still, though Torrid Noons
> Have lain their Missiles by –
> The Lightning that preceded it
> Struck no one but myself –
> And I would not exchange the Bolt
> For all the rest of Life –

Again, the metaphoric play opens possibilities rather than disclosing truth. At first the speaker seems to refer to a literal storm in metaphoric terms: warring weather stores its "Missiles," even as thunder continues to rumble. But metaphoric and not literal lightning must have hit the speaker, since she has not died from it. To the contrary, the "Bolt" illuminated her. Personal enlightenment, figured as a physical event, is then cryptically hooked into networks of light, as Dickinson returns to the literal subject of electricity, this time transmitted through wires:

> Indebtedness to Oxygen
> The Happy may repay –
> But not the obligation
> To Electricity –
> It founds the Homes and decks the Days
> And every clamor bright
> Is but the gleam concomitant
> Of that waylaying Light –

This homage celebrates the joys of electrical lighting as a literal instantiation of poetic inspiration. R. W. Franklin assigns 1884 as the poem's composition date, the year the Amherst Gas Company moved into the electricity business; in 1888, they discussed entering the electric lighting business. The Thomas-Houston Company beat them to it and began putting up poles and stringing wires in 1889.[13] Jane Wald, the executive director of the Dickinson Museum, says "architectural evidence suggests" that The Evergreens acquired electric lightning between 1890 and 1895, the Homestead in 1916.[14] In a "gleam" almost "concomitant" with the advent of electric lighting in Amherst, then, Dickinson imagines the power of electric lighting as a unifying medium that "founds the Homes" as well as larger communities held together by a shared "clamor bright." In this deeply optimistic poem, Dickinson connects through an electrical current her own illuminated state, brightly lit homes, light-filled days, and ubiquitous joy: she evokes simultaneously elemental, cultural, and poetic media environments. This vision is more a physical experience than one that can be expressed in speech:

> The Thought is quiet as a Flake –
> A Crash without a sound,
> How Life's reverberation
> It's Explanation found –

"Success in Circuit lies": Dickinson, Media, and Imagination 57

Electrical force cycles through the poem's I and broader communities, binding them together with a "Life[]" that is both a common and a profound "reverberation." Dickinson's "Explanation" is not a transcendent truth but an immanent one, a feeling in the body that pulls all entities together into a circulatory system. The electrical suspension of the individual in the larger whole generates an understanding of the poem itself as an environment, one that encompasses as well as emerges from the speaker's imagination.

According to Gilmore, "metaphors of aesthetic electricity ... were outgrowths of residual and emergent literary, popular, and scientific understandings of electricity, and these sources for aesthetic electricity point to the attempt of many to imagine aesthetics as a sensuous experience of the individual body embedded in specific social situations that somehow led to the momentary suspension of the individual in a sense of a larger whole."[15] Gilmore goes on to say that "metaphors of electrical effect and affect were more than just metaphors. Figures of electricity were not simply used to conjure some analogous relationship between aesthetic experience and electrical phenomena. Rather, aesthetic experience itself was often imagined to be, in fact, electrical itself, as the product of nervous impulses viewed as electrical, or the result of words or thoughts conveyed through electrical technology or through a spiritual medium itself envisioned as electric."[16] Dickinson's vision of an electrical infrastructure that fuels imagination, turns houses into homes, and makes each day a celebration exemplifies this understanding of electricity as a force that interpenetrates and connects insides and outsides, minds and their environments.

"The old idea that media are environments can be flipped: environments are also media," Peters says, since at this point all media "are ensembles of natural element and human craft."[17] Dickinson signals concordance with this formulation by foregrounding the imagination's blending of natural systems and cultural circuitry, creating ensembles within the environment of the poem. The play of metaphor and observation in poem F1152A offers such a study, presenting a wind that does impossible things, even as it inhabits the same landscape as, but is distinguished from, "nature":

> The Wind took up the Northern Things
> And piled them in the South –
> Then bent the East unto the West
> And opening it's mouth
> The Four Divisions of the Earth
> Presumed as to devour
> While everything to corners slunk
> Behind the awful power –

> The Wind unto his Chamber went
> And nature ventured out –
> Her subjects scattered into place
> Her systems ranged about
>
> Again the smoke from Dwellings rose
> The Day abroad was heard
> How intimate, a Tempest past
> The Transport of the Bird –

If we take the subject literally, we understand that the observer describes a hurricane-like wind, stressing its force through hyperbole. The level of exaggeration, however, summons a "Tempest" of unimaginable proportions that strains the reader's capacity for belief – why describe the Tempest in terms that render it unbelievable?

The exaggerated description begs for allegorical or metaphorical interpretation: what sort of force can take up things at one point of the compass and "pile[]" them at the opposite point? The indefiniteness of the scene – that "Things" are piled in an abstract, non-specific location – increases the reader's doubt that the poem describes an observable phenomenon, as does the knowledge that no human observer could witness such a vast, global movement. Cody Marrs has identified this as a Civil War poem, interpreting the apocalyptic quality of the scenario as a sign of the immensity of the conflict between the Union and the Confederacy; the poem supports this reading, with its account of the wind violently putting "Northern Things" in the South.[18] But the folding of East to West moves beyond North–South violence, and the ravenous consumption of "The Four Divisions of the Earth" is weighted equally, locating the catastrophe nowhere in particular. The geographical enormity and dislocation exceeds the historical tragedy of the Civil War – if, again, we don't accept the explanation of hyperbole as a strategy to underscore catastrophe.

The poem asks us to understand the Wind as both literal and figurative; this becomes definitive once it is said that "nature ventured out" when the Wind retreated. Why separate the Wind from nature, when it shares the same scenario? One response would be that the poem is neither fully metaphorical nor fully empirical because it is exploring the impact of human media environments on elemental media environments: the relation between a human "wind" and a natural wind. The poem juxtaposes systems of different scales: it envisions a future when mass media will encompass the "Four Divisions of the Earth." While the poem's Wind circulates on a global scale, the scene shrinks back to a human scale once the

"Success in Circuit lies": Dickinson, Media, and Imagination 59

storm has returned to his "Chamber." With the Wind calm, nature's "systems ranged about" methodically, like a planned community: everything has its "place." If we want to understand the unnatural Wind as a human-constructed, overawing force, the poem inverts the idea of natural wilderness and human civilization. The poem juxtaposes the mass media's potential to bring the four corners of the earth together – in a time "when every Man / Shall comprehend as one," as Dickinson says of the power of the news "traveling" in another poem – against the more "intimate" possibility of nature (which includes human "Dwellings") relieved of the Tempest (F1379A). The consuming force's displacement of local "systems" suggests a fundamental incompatibility between smaller, settled interactions and a larger, ravenous power. Unlike the other poems I've discussed, here elemental and mass media environments are incompatible, even if "Tempest" serves as the most suitable metaphor for a cultural form of transport and mobility. A common figure of poetic inspiration, the Wind here moves beyond the capacity for imagination to share its path; the movements are less circulatory than annihilating. What remains is a bifurcated poem with an imagination, stranded between frenetic, violent activity and overly tame "systems," which retroactively and inadequately describes the Tempest as the "Transport of the Bird."

While poem 1152A infuses an elemental media environment with the metaphoric implications of cultural media environments, poem F1127A intensifies local forms of human communication with the qualities of mass media:

> After the Sun comes out
> How it alters the World –
> Wagons like messengers hurry about
> Yesterday is old –
>
> All men meet as if
> Each foreclosed a news –
> Fresh as a Cargo from Balize
> Nature's qualities –

After a storm, people emerge and repopulate their town with an energy derived from the Sun, which serves as a sort of current that animates both the Wagons and the men. The poem describes a bustling town: men gather to converse, and Wagons drive around, perhaps making deliveries. But the scene has a frenetic urgency in excess of the occasion: Wagons rush about "like" messengers. The simile is strange: first Dickinson erases the people driving the Wagons, and then she attributes the qualities of people to the vehicles. This double transformation makes the messenger-Wagons seem automated: they transmit information without human aid, almost like a telegraph wire. The men are equally estranged from the information they seem to be transmitting. They "meet as if / Each foreclosed a news" – the singular use of a mass noun separates the messages and distorts the idea of a conversation among people. Rather than exchanging information, each man arrives with his news and delivers it to the others: again, with a machine-like quality. Even stranger, they meet as if they "foreclosed" rather than "disclosed," making gestures of expressive transmission that suggest to the observer that they are shutting down that transmission. The information that they do or do not share is "Fresh as a Cargo from Balize," suggesting long-distance transit while the simile negates actual distance. The speaker posits theories about what she observes, qualifying her comments by making them similes. She doesn't really know what the Wagons or the men are doing, which is odd in itself, since they are engaged in such quotidian activities. But in estranging a scene of daily activity resumed after a storm, the poem presents an environment in which "Nature's qualities" are informed by, and therefore made strange by, mass media communications. In the poem's environment, "Nature's qualities" fuel cultural media transactions; the spatialized imagination offers a scenario that renders mysterious familiar scenes of transport and human exchange.

Via an environmental imagination – by which I mean an imagination that serves as an environment for both speaker and reader – Dickinson shows us that elemental and human media can become indistinguishable or interpenetrating, in part via an insistent mixing of modes. In one early poem, for example, "Butterflies from St Domingo," "Cruising round the purple line," enact mass media transport akin to a telegraph system in their natural migrations (F95B). These butterflies' superior "system of aesthetics" is figured in terms of electric or steam-powered movement: they cruise like steamships; they follow the "purple line" as if moving through a telegraph line. Like the cruising butterflies, in F1213A steam-powered bees make their circuit from flower to flower "Like Trains of Cars on Tracks of Plush." Elsewhere, sleds operate like electrical signals, "Shod vibrations / Emphacized and gone" (F1518A). In another poem, "Hope," a "strange invention," is a perpetual motion machine, "In unremitting action / Yet never wearing out" (F1424A). An "electric adjunct" with a "Patent of the Heart," Dickinson's Hope exists as a possibility that electricity, mass infrastructure, and mechanical reproduction make possible. Dickinson shows us a nineteenth-century worldview actively blending technological and elemental systems via metaphor, asking us to imagine mixed media

"Success in Circuit lies": Dickinson, Media, and Imagination 61

environments in which it is difficult or impossible to determine where human technologies leave off and natural entities begin.[19]

These visions of sleds powered by electricity or Hope perpetuated via a psycho-prosthetic device pull the future toward the present. Dickinson's mediated imagination posits visions on the verge of instantiation. Poem F638B imagines such a temporal transaction:

> The Future never spoke –
> Nor will he like the Dumb
> Report by Sign a Circumstance
> Of his profound – To Come –
>
> But when the News be ripe
> Presents it in the Act –
> Forestalling Preparation –
> Escape – or Substitute –
>
> Indifferent to him
> The Dower – as the Doom –
> His Office but to execute
> Fate's Telegram – to Him –

Juxtaposing two signaling systems, sign language and the telegram, the poem identifies the latter as more appropriate for the future's appearance in the present. Sign language is embodied and intimately communicative. A language shared under specific conditions, signing makes one part of a small and close-knit group. Telling in sign language unfolds over time, via a person, which is why the figure is unsuited for this poem's vision of the future's arrival. The telegraph is more suitable because the carrier is impersonal, "indifferent," and disembodied. Dickinson imagines a system that goes beyond the capacities of the telegraph but retains its properties. Rather than conveying news as soon as it happens, it "Presents it in the Act": news is shown *in medias res*, as if it were filmed. Portraying the Future becoming the present, Dickinson imagines a circuitry that is both completely closed and utterly open: Present and Future are unknown to each other, even as the Future delivers the Present to itself. Only Fate, the sender, knows what the Telegram holds. By extending telegraphic capacities to the edge of now, taking its exaggerated reputation for instantaneous transmission literally, Dickinson shows how the telegram reconfigures ideas of time itself via the mediated imagination. That imagination is both shaped by communication technologies and not restricted to them. Fate's telegram, unopened, carries future possibilities into the present, leaving poets to remediate new forms of mediation.

In *A New Theory for American Poetry: Democracy, the Environment, and the Future of the Imagination*, Angus Fletcher says, "If we identify coherence with a loose and notably inconsistent completeness, we reach the artistic representing of environments, by a representing pressed so far that the poem actually *is* an environment."[20] By asserting that the poem is not "about" but is itself an environment, Fletcher hopes to break down the distinction between "the world within and the world 'out there,' outside the poem."[21] This essay has sought to show that Dickinson writes such "environment poems" by conceiving of a mediated imagination. These poems question the relation between observation and invention, object and subject, and elemental and cultural environments. Inspired by and through mass media networks, Dickinson figures poetic imagination as part of a circuitry that connects the world within and the world without while foregrounding the porous relation between them. Offering "the experience of an outside that is developed for the reader inside the experience of the work," Dickinson's environment poems attend to acts of transition, modes of imagining media's capacities for shifting the terms in which we interpret nature and culture.[22] While for Fletcher, "the environment poem seeks symbolic control over the drifting experience of being environed," Dickinson captures that drifting experience without asserting control, perhaps because she believes control is impossible.[23] What is possible is an orientation toward disorientation and an ability to use the imagination to inhabit capacities and potentialities. In Dickinson's poems, mass media can threaten nature or bring it closer. Our experience with electrical wires can connect us to nature's, or God's, or human electricity. Sharing lightning's force, Dickinson "dazzle[s] gradually," for "Success in Circuit lies." That circuitry is not only "within": it surrounds us in poems that are open to both human and natural media. Dickinson helps us negotiate shifting, often drastic changes in our environments and to understand that imagination itself is never just "within."

A host of recent publications indicates that Dickinson studies have taken a decidedly environmental turn. This essay itself takes such a turn by embracing Peters' insistence on the continuities between elemental and cultural media. Via animalization, anthropomorphism, and technomorphism (in the case of the steam-powered bee or the driverless wagons, for example), Dickinson plays out lively scenarios in external environments through the mental imaging of her poems. The process, while open to the elemental and sentient world, remains fundamentally anthropocentric, a mode frequently identified as "utilitarian, exploitative, [and] destructive" in environmental and ecological studies.[24] Rather than fearing its destructive powers and trying to safeguard nonhuman environments from mental invasion, Dickinson foregrounds the mind's power to figure its surroundings in ways that allow readers to question the human's place in the world. Without the mediated imagination, for example, the stunning consequences of harnessing electrical forces for human ends would not be thinkable. Theo Davis has recently identified "an overarching trend in the humanities to perceive the existence of human thought and perception as an interference in the world."[25] For Davis, in contrast, "the mind doesn't need to be abolished or redeemed, because its presence in the world not only isn't a problem, it isn't up to us": human thought exists.[26] Davis claims that Dickinson also thinks of thinking as part of reality, and for this reason "the differences between material and mental phenomena, or between inner and outer phenomena, do not greatly concern" her.[27] With Davis, I find that Dickinson believes in thought's reality, but I suggest that there is a historical specificity to the relation of mind and elemental and cultural environments that foregrounds questions about "inner and outer phenomena," imagination, mass media, nature, and poetry. Human thinking exists, and perhaps thinking's human-centrism cannot or even should not be evaded; what is important, then, is how we think and what we think about. The "newness" of this essay may lie in the suggestion that Dickinson's poetry calls for an ethical anthropocentrism, based on a renewed attention to imagination after the environmental turn.

Notes

1. Ralph Waldo Emerson, "The Poet," in *Essays and Lectures* (New York: Library of America, 1983), 463.
2. Michelle Kohler, *Miles of Stare: Transcendentalism and the Problem of Literary Vision in Nineteenth-Century America* (Tuscaloosa: University of Alabama Press, 2014), 4.
3. Ibid., 23.
4. Emerson, 459.
5. Ibid., 449, 459.
6. Oliver Wendell Holmes Sr. "Bread and the Newspaper," *Atlantic Monthly* (September 1861), 346–352.
7. Paul Gilmore, *Aesthetic Materialism: Electricity and American Romanticism* (Stanford: Stanford University Press, 2009), 54.
8. This idea resonates with two recent theorizations of American poetry. Angus Fletcher describes what he calls "the environment poem": "Supposing then that such poems are intended to surround us in exactly the way an actual environment surrounds us, there will occur a breakdown of the old distinction …

between the world within the poem and the world 'out there.'" Angus Fletcher, *A New Theory for American Poetry: Democracy, the Environment, and the Future of Imagination* (Cambridge: Harvard University Press, 2004), 227. Theo Davis explores "the possibility of thinking of poetry as a way of relating to the world, rather than as an expressive object." *Ornamental Aesthetics: The Poetry of Attending in Thoreau, Dickinson, and Whitman* (New York: Oxford University Press, 2016), 11.

9. Richard R. John, *Network Nation: Inventing American Telecommunications* (Cambridge: Harvard University Press, 2015), 25.
10. Shannon Thomas argues that Dickinson defends and claims interpersonal relations and individualistic forms of creation when confronted by the threat of debilitating mass media forms. I argue instead that Dickinson explores the shifts in subjectivity and poetic creation that the emergence of mass media demands. Shannon L. Thomas, "'What News must think when pondering': Emily Dickinson, *The Springfield Republican*, and the Poetics of Mass Communication," *EDJ* 19.1 (2010): 60–79, 70. See also Eliza Richards, "'How News Must Feel When Traveling': Dickinson and Civil War Media," in *A Companion to Emily Dickinson*. Martha Nell Smith and Mary Loeffelholz (eds.) (Malden, MA: Wiley-Blackwell, 2008), 157–179. On Dickinson and the telegraph, see Jerusha Hall McCormack, "Domesticating Delphi: Emily Dickinson and the Electro Magnetic Telegraph," *American Quarterly* 55.4 (2003): 569–601.
11. John Durham Peters, *The Marvelous Clouds: Toward a Philosophy of Elemental Media* (Chicago: University of Chicago Press, 2015), 2, 47, 2.
12. Kohler, 125–126.
13. Edward W. Carpenter and Charles F. Morehouse, *The History of the Town of Amherst, Massachusetts* (Amherst, MA: Press of Carpenter, 1896), 418.
14. Jane Wald provided the information about the Homestead and Evergreens in an email exchange (11/27/2017).
15. Gilmore, 6.
16. Ibid., 7
17. Peters, 30, 3.
18. "Reflecting on what the war has wrought, Dickinson describes the conflict as a terrible storm that has nearly swallowed up the earth." Cody Marrs, *Nineteenth-Century American Literature and the Long Civil War* (Cambridge: Cambridge University Press, 2015), 139.
19. In *A Cyborg Manifesto*, Donna Haraway identifies such fusions with a twentieth-century culture of informatics, but Dickinson's work shows that fusions of animal and machine arise from nineteenth-century communication systems as well. "Contemporary science fiction is full of cyborgs – creatures simultaneously animal and machine, who populate worlds ambiguously natural and crafted." Donna Haraway, *Manifestly Haraway* (Minneapolis: University of Minnesota Press, 2017), 6. For Haraway, these fusions are full of both radical political potential and the capacity for political

oppression. For Dickinson, the cyborg holds threat and possibility for experiential being, shaped more by ontological than political questions.
20. Fletcher, 227.
21. Ibid.
22. Ibid.
23. Ibid.
24. Christine Gerhardt, "Emily Dickinson Now: Environments, Ecologies, Politics," *ESQ* 63.2 (2017): 329–355, 346.
25. Davis, 110.
26. Ibid., 112.
27. Ibid.

CHAPTER 4

"*Criterion for Tune*": *Dickinson and Sound*

Christina Pugh

Throughout Emily Dickinson's poems, we hear hefty cathedral tunes, talking cornets, and bells of every aural stripe. The significance of these sounds, with their variegated pitches, must not be lost as we begin to limn a "new" Dickinson, as it is impossible to overstate the role that sonic values play in the genesis and instantiations of her poems. Yet even though twenty-first-century American culture has seen an explosion of poetry readings, slam competitions, and hip-hop music, there remains a significant chasm between such sound-based culture and the focus of much of the most celebrated scholarship treating Dickinson's work.[1] In many cases, Dickinson's complex relationship to sound has been downplayed in favor of a more sustained attention to the visual, orthographic, or epistolary aspects of her manuscripts. The work of Marta Werner, Jen Bervin, Virginia Jackson, and other manuscript scholars has made groundbreaking gains with respect to Dickinson's manuscript materials; and the popularity of the recent facsimile collections *The Gorgeous Nothings* and *Envelope Poems* shows that the reading public shares such fascination with what Susan Howe has called the "visual productions" of Emily Dickinson's poetry.[2] This focus on the visual aspects of Dickinson's poems has also been encouraged by the digital media that has disseminated her archival materials to more readers than ever before.[3]

The fascination with these manuscripts is understandable. As Werner says of Dickinson's poems written on envelopes, which are reproduced in facsimile in *The Gorgeous Nothings*, "[o]nce we have seen these documents, it becomes difficult to dissociate the texts from their carriers."[4] The facsimile editions do often seem electrically charged as relics. But on the other hand, a microscopic attention to handwriting, folds, and stitches doesn't always allow room to consider the sonic and lyric values that were, and remain, crucial to Dickinson's output as a poet. Moreover, Jackson's argument against a monolithic "lyric reading" of Dickinson's poetry, while globally concerned with the "ahistoricism of the lyric genre itself," has distanced Dickinson from the sonic concerns that characterized an older, yet still vital, conception of the lyric poem.[5]

In our moment in the twenty-first century, recovering the role of sound in Dickinson's work requires balancing the visual aspects of the manuscripts with a renewed and energetic listening: we must listen intently, and differently, to the poetic and extra-poetic sounds that inform her poetry, much as Cristanne Miller has done in her recent *Reading in Time*.[6] As we'll see by looking closely at several of her poems, Dickinson employed the shorter English meters not only for the musical pleasures they afforded but also to critique our sense of extra-poetic sound writ large. In both celebrated and lesser-known poems, Dickinson at once succumbs to and critiques the ubiquity of sound in everyday life; this critique also warns her readers that less creative approaches to prosody may be stultifying and even deadening. And although Dickinson relishes even the most infinitesimal grace notes in sonic experience, she also finds cautionary tales hiding in musical instruments, nineteenth-century mechanization, and even silence itself.

To critique sound, as Dickinson knew, is to critique the very seed of lyric utterance. Since its association with the lyre in ancient Greece, the lyric poem has arguably engaged sound more than any of the other human senses; as Susan Stewart writes, "In classical practice, and classical criticism, the bond between music and lyric is paramount – nonnarrative and nondramatic poetic genres were intended to be sung, chanted, or recited to musical accompaniment."[7] Of course, Dickinson maintained her own relationship to musicality since she wrote her poems against the backdrop of, and in dialogue with, the most musical of English metrical forms: common meter and short meter, which are the measures of the ballad, the hymn, and the nursery rhyme. As Derek Attridge has shown, the tetrameter line, which was the baseline of Dickinson's folk-influenced meters, constitutes "the most common underlying rhythm in English popular verse."[8] As a measure that attaches almost organically to end-rhymes and often tends to gather in quatrains, tetrameter is more melodic, and often less discursive, than the pentameter line. But Dickinson's poems don't always conserve the exactness of these shorter forms. Her poems often diverge from these forms by torquing, stretching, and truncating the tetrameter line, as well as the trimeter (three-beat) line and its "unrealized beat" that pairs with tetrameter in both common meter and short meter. Dickinson also thwarts melodic sound by "tell[ing] it slant" with cannily imperfect rhymes that foil the perfect masculine rhyme that her work never ceases to employ (F1263).

The effect of these formal changes, which added an element of unpredictability to popular poetic forms and to the aural expectations attendant upon rhyme, was to transfer the metrical patterning associated with narrative and prayer – the folk ballad and the hymn, respectively – to a soundtrack inextricable from the "nimble believing" that James McIntosh finds in the work of this poet who "prefers not to adhere for long to any preconceived religious or philosophical doctrine."[9] So-called irregularities of rhyme and meter serve, then, to underline Dickinson's continuous experience of emotional and ideological flux: the musical score of her prosody often suggests a searching – and poetically fruitful – experience of philosophical and theological instability.

Dickinson's readers and critics have long been grateful that she resisted taming the "spasmodic" gait that Higginson had critiqued in her meter and rhyme.[10] In 1925, Susan Miles argued that Dickinson's formal irregularities signaled "a cleft and unmatching world"; Miles' opinion would be shared by readers who found Dickinson's irregular prosody to be an appropriate expression of her poems' most extreme emotional content.[11] But Miller suggests that Dickinson's reconfiguration of these shorter meters was less revolutionary, and more a product of her time, than scholars have traditionally thought:

> [A]ntebellum American verse cherished originality, often described as wildness, and encouraged what we might call a fluid relationship between European or traditional forms and innovative poetic practice. Dickinson grew up reading poetry of (for that time) experimental and at times markedly irregular forms; her own numerous variations from standard ballad and hymn meter are in tune with this aspect of her contemporaries' poetry, although they push farther in the degree and frequency of the irregularity and combine these features with a strikingly original compression of syntax and meaning.[12]

Such "strikingly original compression" of meter and rhyme enabled Dickinson to showcase what I've elsewhere described as "the legitimately destabilizing potential that resides within the confines of the metrical project itself"[13] – that is, the way that regular rhyme and meter, often considered a predictable and even staid approach to poetic form in our day, can pursue the unforeseen.[14] And yet, as Miller shows, the practice of metrical substitution and variation was a common strategy for antebellum American poets. It follows that although Dickinson's now-memorable formal irregularities were initially too pointed for Higginson's taste, they were also not, in spirit, "sovereign" with respect to these forms.

Dickinson's metrical choices were not made in an intellectual or cultural vacuum. Her poems were crucibles that brilliantly refracted not only the prosodic but also the historical and philosophical issues of her era, including those encapsulated in – and as – sound. Some recent Dickinson scholarship has supported similar notions of a more culturally and socially engaged Dickinson. For example, Alexandra Socarides has argued that Dickinson's seemingly singular manuscript practices were "influenced by nineteenth-century material culture, women's copying and bookmaking practices, familiar epistolary networks, and contemporaneous poetic discourse."[15] And in its use of twenty-first-century diction, the very title of *The Networked Recluse: The Connected World of Emily Dickinson*, a catalogue accompanying the 2017 exhibit of Dickinson manuscripts and memorabilia at New York's Morgan Library, highlights the poet's sociability.[16] In fact, a "networked recluse" could easily refer to a twenty-first-century woman who never leaves her house but has thousands of Facebook friends.

While many of Dickinson's networks were certainly epistolary – formed and maintained by the sociable exchange of written words – the "networked" aspect of her quotidian experience also had to include extra-poetic sound both nonverbal and ambient. This is what Mark Doty has discussed as a poet's experience of a "sensorium," or "that continuous, complex response to things perpetually delivered by the senses, that encompassing sphere that is such a large part of our subjectivity."[17] While Doty defines the sensorium as a combination of all the human senses, he uses a specifically sonic metaphor to describe it further: "The word always makes me think of a label invented to describe the totalizing experience offered by a kind of movie speakers, Sensurround."[18] In this way, Doty suggests that sound – in this case, sound that is amplified by a movie speaker – becomes synecdochal of sensory experience more globally.

Such a synecdoche may have been especially acute for Emily Dickinson, for whom the sense of sound was paramount in poetry and in life. As Miller has noted, emphasizing "the huge popularity of music, in and out of the home" during nineteenth-century America, sound was a crucial aspect of Dickinson's social and domestic culture.[19] At this time, one would have heard the tentative notes of girls learning to play the piano (including, of course, Dickinson herself), army regiments singing, and songs in theatrical productions.[20] Imagining Dickinson in the midst of, and buoyed by, such music should correct any earlier views of the poet as silent and solitary. For Dickinson, seeing "New Englandly" also necessitated a synesthetic listening – not only to the robin as a "Criterion for Tune" but to the great influx of popular song and music that permeated upper-middle-class life during the Civil War period (F256).

Moreover, as Miller writes, "[a]rmy music, parlor songs, hymns, and poems were not strictly separable" in the nineteenth century.[21] Such permeability between poetry and popular music only underscores the cultural weight carried by particular meters, especially the shorter and more populist ones. Annie Finch has suggested, for example, that Dickinson's resistance to the pentameter line was, in effect, a resistance to patriarchy: "Iambic pentameter codifies the force exerted on Dickinson's poetry by patriarchal poetic tradition (she associates the meter with the power of religion and public opinion, with formality, and with stasis)."[22] Though it is often ignored in cultural investigations into poetry, then, meter is no less culturally influenced than diction, metaphor, or any other aspect of verse; its strong relationship with music in antebellum America only underscores this fact.

Other recent historical and materialist studies have shown industrial and conversational sound to be important aspects of Dickinson's quotidian experience, potentially influencing her prosody and other aspects of her compositional process. As Daneen Wardrop writes, "Emily Dickinson was more or less born at the transition from handmade to machine-made economy."[23] Such a transition necessitates an increase in industrially generated ambient noise, such as the whistles Dickinson would have heard summoning the workers to the hat factory near her home in Amherst. Along these lines, Wardrop quotes Hills family historian Ruth Pratt, who says that Dickinson "heard the whistles that sounded 'six mornings a week at 6:00 a.m.' as well as five other times throughout the day; she adds that Dickinson heard the train whistles four to six times a day, and the banging of trains in the shuttle yard."[24] Aífe Murray has also studied how the Dickinsons' domestic workers' dialects came to inflect diction and cadence in the poet's lines. Murray calls Dickinson's quotidian conversations with these workers "the hum of the kitchen," thus turning to the metaphor of music to describe speech and also putting a dialogic spin on poems that can sometimes seem the pinnacle of self-containment.[25]

While I wouldn't want to limit Dickinsonian sounds to the role of decoding her biography or her demographic, investigations such as Wardrop's and Murray's shed more light on Dickinson's multifaceted relationship to the sonic. As we'll see in the poems that follow, her poetry shows her ambivalence not only toward industrial sounds but also toward the prevalent musicality within everyday "New Englandly" life. Moreover, while we can underline that the drive animating Dickinson's prosodic innovation was not unique, her particular approach enabled her to critique the relationship between formal poetry and extra-poetic sound.

Dickinson's relationship to her sound-saturated environment was fraught with paradox and contradiction. On the one hand, as Katie Peterson has discussed in her aptly named "Surround Sound: Dickinson's Self and the Hearable," Dickinson celebrates the thrall that hearing a bird call, or human-made music, can afford: "When Dickinson gives herself over to an act of attention, she fruitfully neglects herself for the purpose of recording the presence of another being. In the auditory realm, she often concerns herself not with singing her own songs but with hearing the songs of others."[26] Dickinson does often wish to be captured by a sound whose amplitude would be great enough, or beautiful enough, to absorb the self and to obliterate thought. On the other hand, however, Dickinson rejects – and sometimes fears – such captivating sound. We can see this contradiction in the deliberative "I would not paint – a picture –," whose second stanza considers the sense of sound. Here, Dickinson rejects communicability for an ecstatic absorption in the notes of a wind instrument. Yet the choice is not as euphoric as it initially seems:

> I would not paint – a picture –
> I'd rather be the One
> It's bright impossibility
> To dwell – delicious – on –
> And wonder how the fingers feel
> Whose rare – celestial – stir –
> Evokes so sweet a torment –
> Such sumptuous – Despair –
>
> I would not talk, like Cornets –
> I'd rather be the One
> Raised softly to the Ceilings –
> And out, and easy on –
> Through Villages of Ether –
> Myself Endued Balloon –
> By but a lip of Metal
> The pier to my Pontoon –
>
> Nor would I be a Poet –
> It's finer – Own the ear –
> Enamored – impotent – content –
> The License to revere,
> A privilege so awful

> What would the Dower be,
> Had I the Art to stun myself
> With Bolts – of Melody! (F348)

Many readings of this poem's second stanza echo Sharon Cameron's, who notes that Dickinson "produces an impression of her own relationship to the music that is essentially equivalent to producing the music ... [T]he claimed incapacity reveals capacity."[27] According to such an interpretation, Dickinson's use of *negatio* suggests the ironic opposite of what the poem actually says: in other words, the reader is meant to believe that Dickinson (figuratively) *does* paint pictures, talk like cornets, and stun herself with bolts of melody. Despite the poem's anaphoric insistence on the subjunctive wish, I'd also like to suggest that this sonic transport is strongly countervailed by Dickinson's suspicion and even dread of the sonic as such. First, as Dickinson charts her preferences in a progression of painting, music, and poetry, the speaker is more physically acted upon – "moved," in a literal as well as figurative sense – by the musical "talk" of cornets than she is by either the arts of painting or of poetry. Rather than actively "dwell[ing]" on the impossibility of the painted picture, or "Own[ing]" the ear, she is passively "Raised" up by sound itself in the poem's geographical center. So the most concrete of the three verbs at issue, and the one that spatially elevates the speaker's station ("to raise"), is also the one that grammatically deprives her of agency. In this way, Dickinson suggests that music spirits one away in a manner that the other arts do not.

The poem insists, of course, that such ravishing of self is an experience devoutly to be wished for. Yet its quick figurative leaps, lighting momentarily at the crucial "lip of Metal" that is synecdochal of the cornet, clears space for a multitude of ambivalence. Almost as soon as it is mentioned, this "lip" is recast as the "pier" from which the balloon-speaker departs. Thus the act of listening to the cornet's music, already personified as "talk," releases a dizzying stream of metaphors in which the poem's speaker becomes a balloon that then transforms to a pontoon, or boat. This balloon floats within ether that soon forms "Villages" but then resolves as implicit waves in the sea that the boat must navigate; these waves are only metonymically represented by the pier that limits them.

While this progression is appealingly hallucinogenic, and certainly performs the self-scattering that Peterson discusses, on the other side of the proverbial coin lurks a cautionary tale. Sound is not only more powerful but also more ominous than the sight of a picture. There is, in fact, something dangerously stultifying about the "lip of Metal" that gives rise to such multifarious transport. We see this further as the speaker is jounced by the rhyme between "Balloon" and "Pontoon" at the very moment the poem shows her to be the most compromised. There is a certain aural relief that attends the perfect masculine rhyme here; yet, given Dickinson's consistent use of slant rhyme up until this moment in the poem, its airtight quality seems to take the wind out of the speaker's sails. The rhyme aurally "flattens" this formerly weightless balloon into the paradoxically water-grounded "Pontoon." Again, Dickinson's speaker-pontoon is launched by the "lip of Metal" that hovers between human and nonhuman, mechanical and subjective. While such oscillation of trope is nothing new in poetry – one need only remember, for example, John Donne's "stiff twin compasses" figuring lovers in "A Valediction Forbidding Mourning" – it may register Dickinson's ambivalence toward the sounds of encroaching industrialization in nineteenth-century New England, in which a human worker becomes synonymous with, or joined to, industrial materials such as metals. These are tools that, from her perspective, can numb personhood just as "Ether" does.[28]

This "lip" fused of "Metal" and personhood may also speak to Dickinson's suspicion of overly regular meters: if meter becomes too regular, it elides the human in favor of the mechanical or petrified, thereby rejecting spontaneity in favor of the more calculated approach to form described in Poe's "Theory of Composition."[29] "I would not paint – a picture" itself is predominantly trimeter, and its brief forays into the tetrameter lines used by common meter ("And wonder how the fingers feel"; "Had I the Art to stun myself") are feints rather than true inaugurations of that metrical form. If viewed – or listened to – capaciously enough, then, this "Metal" trope can collapse the distinction between intra-poetic and extra-poetic sound: both are served by irregularity. We can find another example of such convergence in the "horrid – hooting stanza" that is emitted by the locomotive in "I like to see it lap the Miles" (F383). While it may not be automatic, the train whistle is nevertheless not humanoid or even humanist; while the speaker claims to "like" the *sight* of the locomotive lapping the miles, its hooting sound transforms the train to a stanza that, while mobile, also lacks the nuance, hesitation, and variation that she loves in lyric poetry.

Dickinson's ambivalence about the sonic realm, even as "I would not paint – a picture" fairly aches for the transport that music affords, is significant in "painting" her complex relationship to historically familiar meters and to the sounds of historical change. Our major paradox remains, however: by retaining common meter and short meter formats – even their fragments or remnants, as in "I would not paint – a picture" – Dickinson is able to use the most musical of poetic structures in order to articulate ambivalence around sound as such. We can find a more sinister critique of sound and of over-regular meter in the first two quatrains of her celebrated "I felt a Funeral, in my Brain" (F340):

> I felt a Funeral, in my Brain,
> And Mourners to and fro
> Kept treading – treading – till it seemed
> That Sense was breaking through –
>
> And when they all were seated,
> A Service, like a Drum –
> Kept beating – beating – til I thought
> My mind was going numb –

Much like "I would not paint – a picture," the poem describes an aural takeover; but here we have nary an inkling of euphoric reception. Instead, the repetitive "beating" numbs a mind that is no longer capable of transforming itself to escape "Villages of Ether." The repetition of "beating" occurs at the moment that the poem switches from common meter to short meter format, thus calling attention to the deceptively "misplaced" length of its tetrameter line in the second quatrain: at that moment, repetitiveness ("beating – beating") is inseparable from (metrical) variation.[30] Yet metrical "beating" becomes more powerful than ether: it can numb the mind and "wreck" both persons and personifications, or the "Race" of silence. Here, Dickinson subtracts the non-synecdochal senses from the sensorium, imagining what would happen if subjectivity were governed entirely by the ear or listening – if "all the Heavens were a Bell, / And Being, but an Ear." In the near-homophony between "beating" and "Being," she suggests the unexpectedly ominous capacity of overly predictable sounds, including unsubstituted metrical lines. Hearing such lines must endow the ear with too terrible of a power, Dickinson suggests. Becoming nothing but a vessel for "beating" (or perhaps a vessel for too-regular poetic beats) is a way to abolish the complexity and variance of subjective "Being." This is also accomplished by the "Boots of Lead" later in the poem – the "lead foot" whose horrifically adamantine humanness recalls the "lip of Metal" and its risk of petrification (as well as the "Hour of Lead" in "After great pain, a formal feeling comes," when "The Feet, mechanical, go round" in "A Wooden Way" [F372]).

The unvaried beating in "I Felt a Funeral, in my Brain" goes on to wreck silence, thus suggesting sound's ultimately destructive capacity: "I, and

Silence, some strange Race / Wrecked, solitary here –." For Dickinson, silence can be both an abstraction and a nearly spatial articulation; it can be mapped with coordinates and endowed with a weight that both rivals and foils the value of music or the palpable "Heft / Of Cathedral Tunes" (F320). Thus to wreck silence is not simply to wreck the absence of sound but to ruin an entity that is, in itself, "positive, as Sound" (F373).[31] While the greater import of "I felt a Funeral, in my Brain" cannot be limited to the role of an ars poetica, it does register sizable ambivalence about the "tolling" and deadening effects of non-Dickinsonian approaches to meter and rhyme – approaches that may be too regularized and predictable, much like factory whistles.[32] Of course, as Miller has reminded us, Dickinson was not the sole author of variations within the shorter meters and within rhyme; in this particular case, we may need to redefine the adjectival "Dickinsonian" so as to suggest as much solidarity as singularity.

If the "beating" of overly regular lines wrecks silence, then a more creative prosody might conserve it. Yet Dickinson also shows considerable ambivalence about silence itself. We can see this in the following infrequently anthologized poem:

> All the letters I can write
> Are not as fair as this –
> Syllables of Velvet –
> Sentences of Plush,
> Depths of Ruby, undrained
> Hid, Lip, for Thee –
> Play it were a Humming Bird
> And just sipped – me –   (F380B)

As Judith Farr notes, Dickinson sent this poem with a rose to her cousin Eudocia Flynt.[33] For that particular occasion, the second line's "this" was deictic, pointing to its accompanying epistolary flower. For Farr, the poem employs the literal rose as a simile for itself, maintaining an equivalence between the flower and the poetic words that describe it: "Like a good poem, it hides its softest velvets or deepest, most intimate petal-sentences for the one who appreciates it."[34] While this interpretation is compelling and useful, the poem's figurative relationships also embed a stringent critique of such privacy and silence, even if the poem is read as fundamentally epistolary.

First, Jackson has memorably described the "inhuman lyricism" attendant upon nineteenth-century poets' idealization of birdsong as "Criterion for Tune"; as she notes, many poets in Dickinson's time wished to emulate a bird's pure, nonverbal musicality.[35] Surprisingly, however, this particular poem embeds a bird in order both to idealize silence and to critique that very idealization. The penultimate line's hummingbird is quieted, becoming metaphoric of a flower that is described as both language (syllables and sentences) and fabric (plush and velvet). In this way, syllables are cushioned at an exponential remove from the linguistic, making them even more "inhuman," as figurative language transforms aural and verbal experience into the silences of fabric.

From the content of numerous poems, we know that Dickinson was attuned to the smallest aural components of words; this attunement translates into claims about the impossibility of separating "Syllable from Sound" (as in "The Brain – is wider than the Sky" [F598]) and also serves to illuminate Dickinson's copious use of feminine rhymes: when more than one syllable rhymes, rhyme itself redoubles its emphasis on sonic resemblances. In "All the letters I can write," however, both alphabetic and epistolary "letters" are found dramatically wanting, in favor of velvet and plush. Does Dickinson mean that she values clothing and ornament over writing? On the one hand, the formulation allows Dickinson to use meiosis, or self-diminishment, in order to posit a hypothetical silencing; on the other hand, however, the very hyperbole within the claim ("All the letters I could write could never be as beautiful as a flower, or as velvet or plush!") calls self-diminishment into question.

Such questioning is also encouraged by the poem's approach to meter and to perfect, or near-perfect, rhyme. Its common-meter opening reduces to an almost uniform trimeter after its first two lines, increasing the poem's pace and thereby allowing it to "outrun," metrically, the platitude of its first clause. Concurrently, the "lip of Metal" belonging to the cornet here transforms to the silent, drinking "Lip" that almost rhymes – internally – with "sipped." This near-rhyme, however, does not deliver on the sonic fit it almost-promises: the "Hid" and "undrained" materials – now reconfigured as flower-food for hummingbirds – cannot viably be compared to the potentially infinite "*All* the letters I can write," as Dickinson surely knows. Here, near-rhyme will not buttress the poem's content, in which epideixis – the heightened praise of the flower – must be built by the meiosis of Dickinson's self-diminishment. And while the perfect rhyme between "me" and "Thee" also suggests an aural closure that lends authority to Dickinson's diminution of her writing, this, too, is deceptive: the mathematically sublime "All the letters I can write" is potentially infinite and thus beyond discrete comparison. Here, as we also often see in her correspondence, Dickinson "protests too much" by insisting on her own hyperbolic smallness. While Dickinson may fetishize the silencing of sound – and at times, like Keats, finds the unheard melody to be sweeter – the poem guarantees that we see the fetish as a rhetorical flourish, a tip of the hat to the poem's (and letter's) addressee.[36] Dickinson reveals silence as both a wish and a posturing; she shows the wish for silence as itself a rhetorical posture, particularly when it is voiced by a poet. In this way, she critiques her own edification of silence as a value.

Although it would be a mistake to read her work proleptically too often, Dickinson's poems sometimes show remarkable foresight with respect to her future critical reception. Her reduction of heard syllables to clothed silence in "All the letters I can write" could ultimately critique many recent readers' attention to the textures of her writing materials rather than her poems' sounds. And in an even more powerful dramatization of what's missing from much manuscript criticism in the twenty-first century, let us consider "As Sleigh Bells seem in Summer," as presented in the facsimile edition of *The Gorgeous Nothings*. Lettered on in its envelope "carrier," in Werner's words, the poem reflects movingly upon the disappearance of Dickinson's sounds from much of our current critical context:

> As   Sleigh Bells
>   sound
> seem   in   Summer
> Or   Bees,   at
> Christmas   show –
>   foreign
> so   fairy –   so
> fictitious –
> The   individuals
> do
> Repealed   from
> Observation –
> A Party that   we
>   whom
> knew –
> More   distant in
>   an   instant
> Than   Dawn
> in Timbuctoo –
> on[37]

Here, in a manner not universally found in her "envelope" poems, Dickinson's lettering creates a poignant relationship to her poem's content. Much as her lines scatter across the envelope's shape, the poem compares the disappearance of persons, or a specific person, in death ("A Party that / whom we knew") to the ephemeral nature of sounds in the world ("Sleigh Bells / ... in Summer"). What is striking, though, is the poem's insistence that these "repealed" individuals are more than just ephemeral in a phenomenological sense: their deaths also cause them to be as "out of context" as it would be to hear sleigh bells in the summer or bees at Christmas. Thus Dickinson uses similes to suggest not only that living and breathing take place in a seasonal (and occasional) context but that the specific sense of hearing does, too. Rather than a music that endures, or "vibrates in the memory" when soft voices die, as Shelley would have it, Dickinson shows the opposite: that memory necessarily makes music "distant" because it cannot reconstruct the immediate context in which sounds are both sounded and heard.[38] In other words, the reception of sound is indivisible from the ontology of sound; for Dickinson, no tree can fall in the forest without specific human ears to "catch" it. In that sense, the sound of the bell must always be "re-pealed," or pealed again, in a continuous present; without such an enduring context, the life of a sound will be repealed, in the legalistic sense.

While a metaphor's vehicle often helps us better understand the tenor to which it corresponds, my focus on sound provokes an opposite attention here: the portrayal of human death as sonically "out of context" makes us realize the fragility of (in this case, nonhuman) sound because it, too, is dependent upon context for its phenomenological "life."[39] Without ears that are attuned to hear the sonic Dickinson – and in many cases, this means the prosodic sounds of rhyme and meter – we might well miss myriad implications; if we only stop to marvel at the shape of Dickinson's lettering on its envelope, we may miss the warning note that the *Gorgeous Nothings* poem also offers. Sound needs context in order to be heard, and this includes a critical context that recognizes its enduring role in poetry; otherwise, sound will recede, only to become as "fictitious," and perhaps as irrelevant, as fairies. The urgent task of creating a contemporary Dickinson, then, is not to forget what limned the "old" one; we must supplement important visual information with the equally invaluable role of sound.

In her poems, Dickinson not only thinks through sound but also thinks *about* sound – not only the sounds governing rhyme and meter formats, but also the sounds of the sensory and social worlds. That she cannot make a lasting decision about sound – that she wishes both to be enthralled by it and to critique it – is in concert with the "nimble believing" that McIntosh has noted in her poems and with the "choosing not choosing" that Cameron has described in her fascicle organization. Dickinson shows herself alive to infinite sounds – musical and industrial, verbal and nonverbal – that become the genesis and foil for these poems' remarkable sonic containments. To hear her poems as lyric is not to interpret them as sound-celebrations only but instead to know that an embrace of sound can also act as a critique. To discount the second part of this equation would be to deny the deeply self-critical strand that animates lyric poetry in general and Dickinson's work in particular.

Notes

1. For a further discussion of how these phenomena, especially hip-hop, have influenced poets and poetry, see David Caplan, *Rhyme's Challenge* (New York: Oxford University Press, 2014).
2. Susan Howe, quoted by Jen Bervin, "Studies in Scale," in Emily Dickinson, *The Gorgeous Nothings*, Marta Werner and Jen Bervin (eds.) (New York: New Directions, 2013), 10. Also see Emily Dickinson, *Envelope Poems*, Marta Werner and Jen Bervin (eds.) (New York: New Directions, 2016).
3. See especially *The Emily Dickinson Archive*, www.edickinson.org.
4. Dickinson, *Gorgeous Nothings*, 207.
5. Virginia Jackson, *Dickinson's Misery* (Princeton: Princeton University Press, 2005), 93. For a study of the historical relationship between lyric poetry and musical performance, see C. Day Lewis, *The Lyric Impulse* (Cambridge: Harvard University Press, 1965). For a critique of Jackson's historicist reading of the lyric genre, see Jonathan Culler, *Theory of the Lyric* (Cambridge: Harvard University Press, 2015), 83–85.
6. Cristanne Miller, *Reading in Time: Emily Dickinson in the Nineteenth Century* (Amherst: University of Massachusetts Press, 2012).
7. Susan Stewart, *Poetry and the Fate of the Senses* (Chicago: University of Chicago Press, 2002), 68.
8. Derrick Attridge, *The Rhythms of English Poetry* (New York: Longman, 1982), 81.
9. James McIntosh, *Nimble Believing: Dickinson and the Unknown* (Ann Arbor: University of Michigan Press, 2000), 35.
10. Emily Dickinson, *Selected Letters*, Thomas H. Johnson (ed.) (Cambridge: Harvard University Press, 1986), 174.
11. Susan Miles, "The Irregularities of Emily Dickinson," *London Mercury* 13 (1925): 158. In *Positive as Sound* (Athens: University of Georgia Press, 1990), Judy Jo Small takes issue with the neatness of matching Dickinson's slant rhymes to themes of instability (see especially 7–8).
12. Miller, *Reading in Time*, 20.
13. Christina Pugh, "Ghosts of Meter: Dickinson, After Long Silence," *EDJ* 16.2 (2007): 1–24, 2.

14. In *How Poems Think* (Chicago: University of Chicago Press, 2015), Reginald Gibbons has also discussed how poetic form, especially rhyme, is an explorative modality. See especially 58–86.
15. Alexandra Socarides, *Dickinson Unbound* (New York: Oxford University Press, 2012), 5.
16. Mike Kelly et al., eds., *The Networked Recluse: The Connected World of Emily Dickinson* (Amherst: Amherst College Press, 2017).
17. Mark Doty, *The Art of Description* (St. Paul: Graywolf Press, 2010), 3.
18. Ibid. Doty's thoughts on sound are conversant with seminal work in the area of sound studies, such as R. Murray Schafer, *The Soundscape* (New York: Simon & Schuster, 1993), and Jonathan Sterne, ed., *The Sound Studies Reader* (New York: Routledge, 2012). Marta Werner is also currently studying nineteenth-century soundscapes in Amherst during Dickinson's lifetime.
19. Miller, *Reading in Time*, 53.
20. Ibid.
21. Ibid., 54.
22. Annie Finch, *The Ghost of Meter* (Ann Arbor: University of Michigan Press, 2000), 13.
23. Daneen Wardrop, *Emily Dickinson and the Labor of Clothing* (Durham: University of New Hampshire Press, 2009), 178.
24. Ruth Pratt, cited in ibid., 99.
25. Aífe Murray, *Maid as Muse: How Servants Changed Emily Dickinson's Life and Language* (Durham: University of New Hampshire Press, 2009), 100.
26. Katie Peterson, "Surround Sound: Dickinson's Self and the Hearable," *EDJ* 14.2 (2005): 78.
27. Sharon Cameron, *Choosing Not Choosing* (Chicago: University of Chicago Press, 1992), 167. For similar readings, see Miller, 37, and Helen Vendler, *Dickinson: Selected Poems and Commentaries* (Cambridge: Harvard University Press, 2010), 148–150.
28. John Donne, "A Valediction Forbidding Mourning," in *Seventeenth-Century Prose and Poetry*, 2nd enlarged ed., Alexander M. Witherspoon and Frank J. Warnke (eds.) (New York: Harcourt, 1982), 747.
29. Edgar Allan Poe, "The Philosophy of Composition," in *The Norton Anthology of Theory and Criticism*, 2nd ed., Vincent B. Leitch (ed.) (New York: Norton, 2010), 639–647.
30. In *Dickinson*, Vendler emphasizes that this metrical switch is the only variation from common meter in the entire poem, adding that "if Dickinson had not made the meter so insistently percussive, we would not 'feel' the Funeral she 'felt'" (143).
31. Vendler also describes Silence as Dickinson's "companion" in this line (143).
32. My readings here of "I would not paint – a picture" and "I felt a Funeral, in my Brain" draw on aspects of my previous examinations of these two poems in "Dickinson's Ambivalence: Lyric Resistance to Rhyme," in *On Rhyme*, David Caplan (ed.) (Liège: Presses Universitaires de Liège, 2017), 143–160.

33. Judith Farr, *The Gardens of Emily Dickinson* (Cambridge: Harvard University Press, 2004), 188.
34. Ibid., 189.
35. Jackson, *Dickinson's Misery*, 27.
36. John Keats, "Ode on a Grecian Urn," in *The Norton Anthology of Poetry*, 4th ed., Margaret Ferguson, Mary Jo Salter, and Jon Stallworthy (eds.) (New York: Norton, 1996), 848–849.
37. Dickinson, *The Gorgeous Nothings*, 34–35.
38. Percy Bysshe Shelley, "Music When Soft Voices Die" at poetryfoundation.org (www.poetryfoundation.org/poems-and-poets/poems/detail/45132).
39. Cameron also notes that the "principle of exchange" animating Dickinson's work sometimes results in the fungibility of literal and metaphoric elements (*Choosing Not Choosing*, 185–188).

PART II

Theoretical Frameworks

CHAPTER 5

Dickinson's Object-Oriented Feminism
Michelle Kohler

Feminist theory was at the heart of the robust community of Dickinson scholars who began to coalesce in the late 1970s and ultimately established the Emily Dickinson International Society in 1988 and the *Emily Dickinson Journal* in 1991. In the immediate wake of now-classics like Adrienne Rich's 1976 essay "Vesuvius at Home: The Power of Emily Dickinson" and Sandra M. Gilbert and Susan Gubar's 1979 chapter on Dickinson in *The Madwoman in the Attic*,[1] a remarkable number of groundbreaking feminist studies of the poet emerged during the 1980s and early 1990s from this community of scholars.[2] There is not space here to do justice to this scholarship's nuances, but together these studies fundamentally reassessed a poet whose gender had long been either pathologized or ignored.[3] Whether they find rage, anxiety, comedy, or critique in her poems, they tell the story of a Dickinson "who would assert [her] own power" as a woman poet in a male-dominated society and literary tradition.[4] As Suzanne Juhasz argues in the introduction to her 1983 collection *Feminist Critics Read Emily Dickinson*, what brings these critics together is the sense of a Dickinson who developed a "process of power" that begins with defiance of gendered constraints ("*critique, strategy, subversion*") and leads to a sovereignty that transcends those constraints ("*transformation, control, possibility*").[5]

Dickinson scholarship today is unimaginable without the research of these scholars, who continue to produce excellent new work on the poet. Their reassessments of Dickinson as a woman poet in control of her art established Dickinson studies as an esteemed field and made it possible to then recognize her critical engagement with myriad cultural contexts from which she had been excluded. Moreover, this trove of explicitly feminist scholarship in the twentieth century codified a recognition of gender politics that implicitly informs much twenty-first-century work on Dickinson. But if gender has sometimes come to the fore in recent work,[6] feminist theory has not been at the center of any book-length study of Dickinson since the first half of the 1990s; there are vital new developments in feminist theory that have not yet been brought to bear on Dickinson's writing. Among these developments are emergent feminist interventions in speculative realism, new materialism, and object-oriented ontology – philosophical discourses that variously take *matter* as primary while dismantling the notion of a sovereign humanist subject. Feminist theorists in these fields aim cautiously to restore a concern with matter and embodiment to feminist discourses that have privileged individual subjectivity and embraced linguistic constructionism's salvo against biological essentialism. The turn to material feminisms recalibrates the politics of subjects and objects, of minds and matter; it changes the questions one can ask and the stories one can tell about objectification, subjectivity, transformation, and power. In what follows, I bring a new feminist lens to Dickinson, beginning with a reading of "Dont put up my Thread & Needle" that looks to object-oriented feminism to understand the speaker's emphatic desire to keep hold of her objects – and to understand our repeated attempts to make her transcend them. I then turn this framework onto other poems that might seem to tell familiar narratives of transcendence; I ask how a feminism oriented around objects might constellate these poems anew and point us toward new ways of intersecting Dickinson with feminist theory.

Let's consider the way we have read "Dont put up my Thread & Needle" (F681), a poem ostensibly about a stymied craftswoman – a seamstress and gardener – who will, she promises, produce better work in time and so pleads with her interlocutors not to take away her tools:

> Dont put up my Thread & Needle –
> I'll begin to Sow
> When the Birds begin to whistle –
> Better Stitches – so –
>
> These were bent – my sight got crooked –
> When my mind – is plain
> I'll do seams – a Queen's endeavor
> Would not blush to own –
>
> Hems – too fine for Lady's tracing
> To the sightless Knot –
> Tucks – of dainty interspersion –
> Like a dotted Dot –

> Leave my Needle in the furrow –
> Where I put it down –
> I can make the zigzag stitches
> Straight – when I am strong –
>
> Till then – dreaming I am sowing
> Fetch the seam I missed –
> Closer – so I – at my sleeping –
> Still surmise I stitch –

We have been inclined to read the poem's thread, needle, zigzag stitches, furrow, and other objects as parts of an extended metaphor for poetic creativity, a subjective faculty put on hold until the woman artist is well again. Accordingly, readers have also variously recast the poem's objects as metaphors for other objects: the needle is a pen; the thread is a dash; the stitch is a *stich*; the furrow is a fold in the fabric for sewing, not a trench in the ground for sowing (and, ultimately, the furrow is neither fabric nor soil but a line of poetry).[7] Thomas H. Johnson even replaces line 2's punning use of "Sow" with "Sew" (and line 17's "sowing" with "sewing"), arguing in his variorum that *sow* "is undoubtedly a [spelling] mistake."[8] In these several ways, we have looked past the objects in the poem, usually in order to say something about a woman poet-speaker who has fallen short of her artistic power because of mental and physical weakness and who longs for recovery, for the "dotted Dot" and "dainty" "Tucks." Sometimes the story has been about a coy, already-sovereign poet-speaker who surreptitiously values her own zigzag poetics. Or, as Gilbert and Gubar argue, it is a story about Dickinson herself, whose manuscript dashes and script are not zigzag at all: "Tiny and clear, they are elegant as 'Tucks – of dainty interspersion.'"[9] In any case, we have read for a story about female subjectivity (in triumph or deprived of triumph) at the expense of the poem's particular set of objects. For the speaker, who pleads "Dont put up my Thread & Needle," this would seem to be a dear expense.

What does it mean that we have been so quick to take away the thread and needle in various ways when the poem so explicitly directs us to do otherwise? How does our understanding of the poem shift if we heed its focus on objects – and if we tend to its adamant focus on *these* objects? These objects as opposed to the better, daintier objects imagined in the second and third stanzas; as opposed to poetics or poetic objects; as opposed to a sovereign subjectivity that will one day be free from their restraints?

To begin answering these questions, an initial detour through "I cannot dance opon my Toes" (F381B) may be useful, for it is a striking counterpoint to "Dont put up my Thread & Needle." "I cannot dance" features another apparently deficient woman artist – this time a dancer – whom we likewise often read as a figure for the woman poet. But these two poems differ in crucial ways that crystallize the decidedly converse way "Dont put up my Thread & Needle" asks us to read it.

> I cannot dance opon my Toes –
> No Man instructed me –
> But oftentimes, among my mind,
> A Glee possesseth me,
>
> That had I Ballet Knowledge –
> Would put itself abroad
> In Pirouette to blanch a Troupe –
> Or lay a Prima, mad,
>
> And though I had no Gown of Gauze –
> No Ringlet, to my Hair,
> Nor hopped for Audiences – like Birds –
> One Claw opon the air –
> . . .
>
> Nor any know I know the Art
> I mention – easy – Here –
> Nor any Placard boast me –
> It's full as Opera –

Here, the dancer itemizes the things she lacks ("No Man," "no Gown," "No Ringlet," "Nor . . . Audiences"), only to insist at the end that such limitations are not limitations at all: "It's full as Opera." Much of the poem is in the subjunctive: the speaker imagines how well she would dance *had she* instruction despite still lacking these ballet objects. But this final line – "It[*is*] full as Opera" – declares artistic victory in present tense. The story this poem ostensibly tells about the dancer is that ballet objects are appurtenances that precisely don't matter. This female subject would be, and is, a supreme artist precisely because she sets these objects aside. She even sets aside ballet for a reference to "Opera" in her final line.[10] And as readers we, in effect, follow her lead, further setting aside the ballet objects by recasting them as metaphors for conventional poetics and publication. Her victory here tells a story of transcendence and female subjectivity beholden to "No Man" and no thing.

If "I cannot dance" invites us to dismiss its objects to focus on its woman artist-speaker's sovereignty, "Dont put up my Thread" explicitly tells us, from its very first line, not to set its objects aside: "Dont put [them] up" (or "down," a variant Dickinson includes, as if to cover her bases). The speaker wants not only her sewing tools but also the out-of-place furrow and the less-than-perfect "zigzag stitches" she's already made. "Leave my Needle in the furrow / Where I put it down," she specifies, as if to acknowledge that we might not think needles go in furrows; "Fetch the seam . . . / Closer," she insists warily. While the speaker details both her weakness and the exquisite work she'll do "when . . . strong," it is this repeated urgency about retaining her sewing/sowing objects – not transcending them, nor rendering them figurative – that motivates the poem. Tempted by our favorite narratives about Dickinson's poetic sovereignty, we have not always recognized just where the poem's note of urgency lies.[11]

Given that we have indeed been so eager to displace the thread and needle for a reading that focuses on either poetics or an artist's potential for transcendent subjectivity, it is no wonder the poem is so insistent. It is not quite my intention to suppress a figurative reading of the poem, but, given the poem's own urgency about retaining its specific things, it is worth asking whether we have been right to turn the speaker's objects into a poet's oeuvre and style, putting up the thread and needle for pen and dash. Even if one finds that the poem values zigzag poetics, rather than longing to transcend them in favor of something more exquisite, such a reading would still displace the specific things the speaker is so focused on retaining by casting them as subordinate vehicles in a metaphor for Dickinson's slant artistry. "I cannot dance upon my Toes" insists on such a triumphant reading of the woman artist's subjectivity overcoming the pull of mundane objects. "Dont put up my Thread & Needle" precisely does not.

This poem's unrelenting, canny resistance to one of our strongest critical tendencies provides a road map for telling new stories about Dickinson and for rethinking the feminist stakes of these stories. To think through these concerns – and ultimately to consider what might be the value in turning our attention from subjects to objects (and, as we'll see, in turning subjects into objects) – I enlist the emerging discourse of object-oriented feminism, informally called so to signal its simultaneous interest in and critique of object-oriented ontology, a philosophy that posits a world made exclusively of objects ontologically (not just epistemologically) withdrawn from us and from each other, never fully accessed by our, or anything's, use of them.[12] Object-oriented ontology, often termed OOO, not only stresses the importance of objects as things-in-themselves but also dismisses the humanist subject. The human becomes simply another object with no special status, a material object among other material objects. There is an ontological claim here (this is the way things are), but there is also a political motivation — a desire to find more sustainable ways to conceptualize the nonhuman world and the human's place in it, to level the anthropocentric distinction between humans and nonhumans. Object-oriented feminists (who wryly adopt the acronym OOF) see potential value in thinking about, through, and as objects, but they also see risks, given the deep and tangled problem of objectification.[13] Object-oriented feminists variously ask (1) what it means, in effect, to *objectify objects*, to make them suddenly our tools of ontological and political thought, to interrogate them as "things-in-themselves" ("what do they do for us that we have turned to them right now?" asks Irina Aristarkhova[14]; is there a colonial motive underlying the claim to what Levi R. Bryant calls a "democracy of objects"?[15]); and (2) what it means to *objectify human subjects*, especially those who have historically been objectified, deprived of the very subjectivity object-oriented ontologists are so elated to give up. As Katherine Behar notes, "OOO seems to relish ... a sense of liberation from the shackles of subjectivity"; object-oriented feminism is a reminder "that all too many humans are well aware of being objects, without finding cause to celebrate that reality."[16]

Nonetheless, Behar finds feminist possibility in object-oriented thinking, proposing a kind of solidarity in which we "rally around objects, not subjects":

> While at first such a move may seem to risk abandoning the concerns of real human subjects (i.e., women), the object world is precisely a world of exploitation, of things ready-at-hand ... This world of tools, there for the using, is the world to which women, people of color, and the poor have been assigned ... throughout history ... Perceiving continuity with other objects in the world, not as subjects but as subject to subjects' dominion, allows us to rework assumptions about feminist political priorities ... Object-oriented feminism's intervention is to approach all objects from the inside-out position of being an object, too.[17]

Feminist thinking has long fled objectification and sought instead to make objects into subjects, to distinguish women from "things ready-at-hand." What happens if we do not take this set of priorities for granted? Aristarkhova cautions that it would be naive to assume that such thinking changes the very real context of hierarchical relations between human subjects and human or nonhuman objects. Behar makes a similar point, but with more optimism, when she asks: "What is the transformative potential for a feminist politics that assumes no transformation, when all things are and remain objects?"[18] Behar's question is sincere, not rhetorical. At the core of feminist considerations of object-oriented ontology are both wariness toward objectification and a sense that there is critical potential in all of this fresh thinking about objects. What happens if we turn against the grain of valuing subjects and subjectivity, if we attune ourselves to objects, not as things to avoid being, nor as things from which to distinguish ourselves, nor as things ready for our use, but as entities that both are with us and *are* us?

Crucial to this twinned wariness and optimism is a resistance to OOO's focus on making truth claims about what things are. Instead, object-oriented feminism strives for a focus on experimentation (indeed, is itself a series of experiments rather than a set of claims). The goal is, as Behar argues, to find diverse ways of "being with things" or ways of "being things."[19] Ultimately, what's "methodologically necessary" is "insistent self-implication and meticulous modesty": in this humility, the hope is "to be objects, generously and generatively, together; to recognize how fraught that position is, always for all parties, as power articulates itself through each and every arrangement of objects; and from this recognition about objecthood . . . to cultivate a praxis of care."[20] This experimental framework of care for and with objects in the face of power might give us a way to approach female subjectivity in "Dont put up my Thread & Needle." To rephrase Behar's question, we might ask: What is the transformative potential of a poem that pays lip service to transformation but is more urgently focused on remaining next to its (clumsy, untranscendent) objects?

In opposition to readings of this poem that seek to tell a story of subjective transformation (even if a failed one), Dickinson posits a camaraderie between the poem's female subject and its various nonhuman objects. The speaker not only asks us to leave them alone; she also distinctly, materially, wants to be with the tools, furrow, and stitches, however zigzag ("Fetch the seam I missed – / Closer," she insists). By contrast, the speaker is much less taken with the imagined "sightless Knot" and "dotted Dot" than readers have tended to be. This disinterest is evident in the poem's structure, as it shifts forcefully at the fourth stanza from its apparently exquisite "dotted Dot" right back to the speaker's focus on her actual things, this time her urgent order to leave her needle in the furrow. Her disinterest is also evident in her descriptions of the imagined stitches, which seem overwrought and at the same time underwhelming and immaterial. They are presented in the subjunctive and thus don't exist, and if they were to exist they would barely be there: the hem would be "too fine" to "trac[e]"; the "Knot" is "sightless" (a pun on *nought*, suggests Daniel Manheim)[21]; and in the "dotted Dot," the dot that dots the Dot is invisible, indeed ostensibly valued for its invisibility.

Thus, when the poem shifts from the dotted Dot to the needle in the furrow, it is a shift from subjunctive to actual, and from immaterial to material, from invisible to visible – from a pair of objects that quietly erase one another (dot and Dot) to a pair of objects (needle and furrow) that are jarring enough in juxtaposition to have driven editors to insist she surely must have meant otherwise. And it is here – with the needle strangely in a furrow, with the crooked stitches, and with the repeated commands to leave all of these things with her – that the poem spends its final two stanzas. The poem works quite hard to keep this speaker in the company of her objects and to do so in the face of forces that would pull them apart. Such forces include both those implied within the poem's narrative (perhaps a doctor ordering a rest cure à la "The Yellow Wall-paper") and those of us who interpret or edit the poem in the various ways I have outlined above.

By pointedly resisting such forces, the poem seems primarily invested in something like Behar's notion of an object-oriented "praxis of care," a praxis of solidarity. For Behar, recall, this praxis of care derives from recognizing how fraught objecthood is and the way "power articulates itself through each and every arrangement of objects." The speaker here seems to act on this recognition, as she not only resists an objectification that would render her a patient therapeutically isolated from her things but also resists an eventual "subjectification" that would render her a craftswoman/gardener who transcends her clunky things (or a poet who transcends sewing things). Instead, this speaker would like to hold on to her stuff, to sit and rest and sleep among it, whether she is lying in a bed or in a ditch. She does not even seem poised to use the objects anytime soon – they matter as things to be cared for. (Indeed, she seems to have sown the sewing needle in a garden row, where it is decidedly not useful.)

What, then, is the transformative potential for a feminist politics that assumes no transformation, when all things remain objects? While the speaker gives a hyperbolic nod toward transformation – yeah, sure, I'll become the most extraordinary seamstress ever – she then ardently leaves transformation behind to tend to the more pressing matter of keeping track of her ordinary things. Further, she argues *against transformation* by telling her interlocutor to leave things as they are. In striving primarily to be with her objects rather than to subordinate or overcome them, the speaker refuses a transformation that relies on the conventional hierarchy of subject and object. The transformative potential for feminist politics here, then, rests not in the female speaker's reaching proleptically toward triumph over bad stitches but in a deeper revision of how one values what has been objectified. Rather than reaching for triumph over objects, the speaker reaches for the objects themselves, and she does so in part in order to rescue them, and herself, from unfriendly circulations of power. The transformation this poem suggests is an object-oriented one – from a model of sovereignty-over to a model of camaraderie-with. Let's sit with these objects, pleads the speaker, as her interlocutors within and without the poem try to make them go away.

I noted earlier that object-oriented feminists are keen to replace ontology with experimentation, to resist being right about what things are in favor of trying out ways of being with things, or ways of being things. This turn to experimental thinking is an ethical turn: "Only in willingness to be all kinds of wrong can we arrive at being in the right, in the ethical sense ... [V]ariance in truth claims produces varying worlds, which is to say, an array of differing political arrangements."[22] I would like to return, then, to "I cannot dance opon my Toes," which I glanced at earlier as a foil for my reading of "Dont put up my Thread." If the former is a foil for the latter, the reverse is also true. And the fact that "I cannot dance" in many ways diametrically opposes her stance in "Dont put up my Thread" suggests I might be "all kinds of wrong" when I insist that Dickinson eschews transformative subjectivity in favor of companionship with objects, for there is no reason to suppose she preferred one over the other. But I would also like to consider whether our object-oriented pathway through "Dont put up my Thread" might alter our way of reading "I cannot dance." Like Behar, I would suggest that such variations in Dickinson's stories and in our methods for reading them comprise a productive epistemological, and feminist, praxis that can estrange us from well-worn ideas about subjectivity, objects, and objectification.

The narrative I've insisted Dickinson resists is one she embraces in "I cannot dance." Dismissive of, even hostile toward, objects, the dancer needs only to dance "among [her] mind." What's more, the speaker scorns the things the other women dancers keep hold of, even derides the dancers for keeping hold of them: the "Gown of Gauze," the "Ringlet," the duck feathers ("Eider Balls"), the "Placard." She also casts other women dancers as objects – they are birds hopping with "One Claw opon the air" or mechanical "wheels of snow," clusters of gaudy things rendered distinctly absurd by their thing-ness, in contrast to the speaker's transcendent, "easy," "full" artistry. Where we find caretaking in "Dont put up my Thread," we find derision here, directed at everyone and everything except for the triumphant artist-speaker herself.

This is another version of our favorite story: a demure Dickinson feigns helplessness only to emerge triumphant, having been in control all along. The fact that Dickinson included this poem in one of her earliest, coyest letters to Thomas W. Higginson, asking him to instruct her in the face of her own "Wayward[ness]," has heightened our sense that the poem's wry spurning of (male) instruction and objects is Dickinson's own story (L271). There is no question that this narrative of the transcendent woman isolate is in play, nor that it is an important one for understanding Dickinson. However much I insist above that Dickinson eschews triumph, it is everywhere in her poetry.

Nevertheless, we might look at this story with fresh eyes. What happens if we reread this poem's narrative of transcendence through the lenses of "Dont put up my Thread" and a feminist politics that asks us to see objects and subjects anew? We might first note that, however much the poem dismisses things, it is itself full of things. If the poem showcases a transcendent subject, it also wades through, rather than simply transcends, objects: it thinks through the fraught arrangements of objects and objectification entangled with women's action in the world, as students and artists; and it takes an interest in what kind of subject remains if these object(ifying) arrangements could be stripped away. And what does remain? Ostensibly a "full," transcendent subject, unbound by objects and figured as operatic voice rather than dancing body. But isn't there, too, some irony in the poem's final line? After several stanzas of stripping the "I" of objects, and distinguishing the "I" from women-as-objects, the "I" abruptly becomes an "It[]." This is an It cleared of ballet objects, yes, but It is nevertheless "full," like opera is full. *Full* might refer here to opera's sonority and conceptual scope, but an opera is also quite literally full of stuff – fuller of stuff than ballet (and in fact operas often included ballet interludes). To note the poem's movement from an emptied "I" to a full "It" is not so much to say that the ending fails to establish the speaker's artistic power, or that the "I" is lost, as it is to suggest that the speaker perhaps wryly finds that the female subject, instructed or no, derisive or no, is ineluctably mired in objects, indeed is an object. Or perhaps it's to suggest that if the speaker doesn't recognize this, *we* might do so – for we have only the speaker's word that she has the situation, and story, under control. Like me, she might be "all kinds of wrong."

Something similar happens with the "it"s that accumulate alongside the "I" in "A solemn thing – it was – I said" (F307), another poem that wades through conventional gendered constraints, other women, and male authority to reach its transcendent climax:

> A solemn thing – it was – I said –
> A Woman – white – to be –
> And wear – if God should count me fit –
> Her blameless mystery –
> . . .
>
> I pondered how the bliss would look –
> And would it feel as big –
> When I could take it in my hand –
> As hovering – seen – through fog –
>
> And then – the size of this "small" life –
> The Sages – call it small –
> Swelled – like Horizons – in my vest
> And I sneered – softly – "small"!

The "I" conceptualizes wives and wifehood as objects and supposes what it would be like to yield to "it." The poem uses "thing" twice and "it" five times as the speaker considers what kind of "thing – it" is, how "it" would feel. From this process, the speaker shrugs off wifehood and emerges transformed with a quietly sneering "I" whose expansion is hers alone. There is derision here: she sneers at, and transcends, not only Sages, husbands, and gender conventions but also women who are wives. The sneer relies on the sneerer not being a wedded thing like other women are.

But here again, as this poem imagines what kind of subject remains if these fraught, objectifying arrangements are stripped away, the concluding triumph does not leave objects behind. There is the sneering "I," but there is also the speaker's "life," which has a size, is in her vest, and is regarded by Sages as an "it" – they "call it small." In the final line, while she sneers at "small," she doesn't necessarily sneer at her life's *it*-ness but rather lets her own "it" be added to the poem's four previous uses.

And the sneer itself is not just a triumph. A sneer is an *embodiment* of triumph, a turning of the body into a body that sneers rather than a body that wears white or puts marital bliss in its hand. Perhaps there is some camaraderie in sharing this embodied thing status with the wives. The poem might accumulate objectified women's subjectivities – wedded *it*s and sneering *it*s – in order to gather them up in contemptuous solidarity against those who would circumscribe women's experiences. The sneer, and its transformative potential, comes perhaps not from isolated transcendence but from the canny subject projecting itself as an object, too. That "too" is grammatically multivalent: the sneering subject is both subject and object; and the sneering subject is an object like other objectified subjects, like the wives. Perhaps this "too" is a way of, in Behar's terms, "[p]erceiving continuity with other objects in the world."[23] This is akin to the "too" Sara Ahmed enlists to describe the exchanged glances of women as they witness one another's marginalization in public spaces: "you too, me too, she too, we too."[24] Perhaps the sneer, then, which may also emerge as a glance, is a crucial tool in an object-oriented feminist praxis, not of transcendence but of care.

However, if we want to consider such camaraderie among humans who are objects, there is much more thinking we must do to understand who is and is not included in Dickinson's "too." I have, for example, been treating the reference to "Woman – white" as though it indicated a "Woman [in] white," but "[white Woman]" is a more direct reading of the phrase. If the poem gathers up objectified female subjectivities in camaraderie, it is arguably a gathering-up only of white women. Or, if the poem sneers at the expense of "Wom[e]n – white," does that mean, as Vivian Pollak has suggested, that Dickinson's speaker sneers at not just wifehood but white womanhood?[25] Aífe Murray, in her book *Maid as Muse: How Servants Changed Emily Dickinson's Life and Language*, makes some strides in mapping out the complex scope of Dickinson's relationships with and treatment of people of color and those outside her social class, especially those who worked in her home[26]; there is more such work to be done if we hope to have a fuller understanding of the ways Dickinson and her poems are in camaraderie, or not, with other women.[27] An intersectional object-oriented feminism would need to account for the fact that thing-status with regard to race is akin to but not the same as thing-status with regard to gender, and for the fact that thing-status has particular weight in the context of chattel slavery.

What I hope to have offered through this series of readings are not only new interpretations of these poems but also starting points for new feminist approaches to Dickinson. Object-oriented feminism offers one pathway: even as it intervenes in emerging theories of materiality and subjectivity, it also recalibrates our most beloved feminist narratives, and its experimental method invites us to toggle our lenses so that old stories might constellate differently and new questions can emerge. We might suddenly see a seamstress supine in a ditch beside her needle,[28] or a breezy operatic poet who, it turns out, is unwittingly still full of gaudy stuff, or we might see a sneer whose multivalent status as subject and object, and whose multivalent gestures of exclusion and inclusion, urge us to ask where we have been "all kinds of wrong," so that we might, as Behar suggests, "arrive at being in the right, in the ethical sense." There is potential for radical political work in thinking through these surprising figures, for they break our narratives of transformation and control, of subjects mastering objects, in favor of camaraderies and entanglements that reorganize our understanding of the way power laces through subjects and objects.

Notes

1. Adrienne Rich, "Vesuvius at Home: The Power of Emily Dickinson," *Parnassus* 5.1 (1976): 49–74; and Sandra M. Gilbert and Susan Gubar, *The Madwoman in the Attic: The Woman Writer and the Nineteenth-Century Literary Imagination*, 2nd ed. (New Haven: Yale University Press, 2000), 581–650.
2. See, for example, *Feminist Critics Read Emily Dickinson*, Suzanne Juhasz (ed.) (Bloomington: University of Indiana Press, 1983); Vivian R. Pollak, *Dickinson: The Anxiety of Gender* (Ithaca: Cornell University Press, 1984); Susan Howe, *My Emily Dickinson* (New York: New Directions, 1985); Joanne Feit Diehl, *Women Poets and the American Sublime* (Bloomington: Indiana University Press, 1990), 26–57; Mary Loeffelholz, *Dickinson and the Boundaries of Feminist Theory* (Urbana: University of Illinois Press, 1991); Martha Nell Smith, *Rowing in Eden: Rereading Emily Dickinson* (Austin: University of Texas Press, 1992); Suzanne Juhasz, Cristanne Miller, and Martha Nell Smith, *Comic Power in Emily Dickinson* (Austin: University of Texas Press, 1993); and Karen Jackson Ford, *Gender and the Poetics of Excess: Moments of Brocade* (Jackson: University Press of Mississippi, 1997), 25–74.
3. See, for example, John Cody, *After Great Pain: The Inner Life of Emily Dickinson* (Cambridge: Belknap Press of Harvard University Press, 1971); David Porter, *Dickinson: The Modern Idiom* (Cambridge: Harvard University Press, 1981); and Sharon Cameron, *Lyric Time: Dickinson and the Limits of Genre* (Baltimore: Johns Hopkins University Press, 1979). Cameron addresses a number of concerns shared by Dickinson's feminist critics, but she almost never frames her discussion in terms of gender.
4. Feit Diehl, xi.
5. Juhasz, "Introduction," in *Feminist Critics Read Emily Dickinson*, 18.
6. Gender emerges as an important category in scholarship that places Dickinson in the context of other women poets. Such work includes Elizabeth Petrino, *Emily Dickinson and Her Contemporaries: Women's Verse in America, 1820–1885* (Hanover: University Press of New England, 1998); Mary Loeffelholz, *From School to Salon: Reading Nineteenth-Century American Women's Poetry*

(Princeton: Princeton University Press, 2004), 131–161; Vivian R. Pollak, *Our Emily Dickinsons: American Women Poets and the Intimacies of Difference* (Philadelphia: University of Pennsylvania Press, 2017).
7. See Gertrude Reif Hughes, "Subverting the Cult of Domesticity: Emily Dickinson's Critique of Women's Work," *Legacy* 3.1 (1986): 19; Gilbert and Gubar, *The Madwoman in the Attic*, 639–641; Bob Perelman, "So," *EDJ* 15.2 (2006): 22–33; Susan Stewart, "Some Thoughts about Dickinson's 'Dont put up my Thread & Needle,'" *EDJ* 15.2 (2006): 58–65; Daniel Manheim, "'And row my blossoms o'er!': Gift-Giving and Emily Dickinson's Poetic Vocation," *EDJ* 20.2 (2011): 25; and Adam Katz, "Deconstructing Dickinson's Dharma," *EDJ* 22.2 (2013): 59–61.
8. Thomas H. Johnson, ed., *The Poems of Emily Dickinson; Including Variant Readings Critically Compared with All Known Manuscripts*, 3 vols. (Cambridge, MA, and London: The Belknap Press of Harvard University Press, 1955), 475.
9. Gilbert and Gubar, 641.
10. Dickinson may also be thinking about opera traditions that incorporated ballet and other forms of dance.
11. Adam Katz, for example, describes the zigzag stitches as "a symptom of an illness from which the poet dearly wants to recover"; he finds a "painfully sincere" longing to perform dainty stitches. Katz rightly picks up on the poem's pleading tone, but I argue the urgency is directed elsewhere (Katz, 60).
12. There is not space here for a full account of object-oriented ontology (nor are its nuances immediately essential for understanding the object-oriented feminism framework I enlist here). Elsewhere, I consider Dickinson's poems more directly in relation to both object-oriented ontology and new materialism ("Ancient Brooch and Loaded Gun: Dickinson's Lively Objects," *ESQ* 63.2 [2017]: 79–121). On object-oriented ontology, see Graham Harman, *Tool-Being: Heidegger and the Metaphysics of Objects* (Chicago: Open Court, 2002); Levi R. Bryant, *The Democracy of Objects* (Ann Arbor: Open Humanities Press, 2011); Rebekah Sheldon, "Form/Matter/Chora: Object-Oriented Ontology and Feminist New Materialism," in *The Nonhuman Turn*, Richard Grusin (ed.) (Minneapolis: University of Minnesota Press, 2015), 193–222; and Jane Bennett, "Systems and Things: On Vital Materialism and Object-Oriented Philosophy," *The Nonhuman Turn*, 223–239.
13. According to Katherine Behar, the foundations of OOF took shape during four years of panels at the Society for Literature, Science, and the Arts conference, first emerging as a response to OOO's sexist underpinnings; Behar collects the fruits of this feminist intervention in *Object-Oriented Feminism* (Minneapolis: University of Minnesota Press, 2016).
14. Irina Aristarkhova, "A Feminist Object," *Object-Oriented Feminism*, 51.
15. Bryant, *The Democracy of Objects*, 19.
16. Behar, "An Introduction to OOF," *Object-Oriented Feminism*, 5.
17. Ibid., 7–8.
18. Ibid., 9.

19. Ibid., 13.
20. Ibid., 19.
21. Manheim, "Gift-Giving," 25.
22. Behar, 18.
23. The "too" here is akin to the feminist "too" of the #MeToo movement, which began in 2006 under Tarana Burke's leadership as a way to create solidarity among sexual abuse victims, particularly those of color; it went viral on social media under the hashtag #MeToo in 2017.
24. Sara Ahmed, *Living a Feminist Life* (Durham: Duke University Press, 2017), 215.
25. Pollak argues that Dickinson treats whiteness in this poem as a burden she throws off, eschewing fixed categories, akin to the way she's resisting gender constraints here ("Dickinson and the Poetics of Whiteness," *EDJ* 9.2 [2000]: 84–95).
26. Aífe Murray, *Maid as Muse: How Servants Changed Emily Dickinson's Life and Language* (Durham: University of New Hampshire Press, 2009).
27. Betsy Erkkila, in *The Wicked Sisters: Women Poets, Literary History, and Discord* (Oxford: Oxford University Press, 1992), especially 17–54, argues that however much Dickinson lived an unconventional life as a woman, it was a life in which economic privilege enabled her *not* to join with other women. Erkkila reminds us that Dickinson's conservative family resisted political transformations and that Dickinson herself could be derisive toward other women.
28. Thanks to Eliza Richards for this formulation.

CHAPTER 6

"The Vision – pondered long": Dickinson, Chronic Pain, and the Materiality of Figuration

Michael D. Snediker

This is an essay about suffering as a means of feeling time in the figurative gestures of pain's perdurance. While its immediate subject is the corpus of Emily Dickinson and the figuration of suffering therein, its exploration cannot help but occur in the sidelight of my own experience with something similar, so I let myself imagine. I would like, along these lines, to propose a variation in our customary thinking about the relation between the notion of Dickinsonian pain and the epistemologically deceptive undertow of vantage as it shapes those elements of inquiry it professes only to stage. For instance, when it comes to those poems that seem most keenly moored in pain, to what extent is our impression of their difficulty informed by some inkling of an ulterior distance – in Sharon Cameron's words, the "outlandishness of their extremity"[1] – from which the affliction at hand seems to operate? To what extent, that is, does our appraisal of these textuary scenes of hurt presuppose an understanding of inscrutability's distancing retreat from the ordinary?[2] In contrast to the implied terrain of these questions, this essay is premised on a belief in the peculiar responsiveness of Dickinsonian pain, however biographically or otherwise understood, to being thought *with*, alongside.[3] Frequently as critics have interpreted Dickinson's elliptically harrowing texts along the lines of grief, distress, and loss, fewer have been drawn in any sustained way to the affinity between the specifically figurative dimensions of this psychical archive and those aspects of suffering associated with (if not summarily reduced to) autobiography's physical object-world. It is in the face of this disparity that I have come to understand Dickinson's intimacy with chronic pain – its fitful hydraulic between the wakefulness of poetic aperture and an unreliable body's arresting attention – as that which catechizes her feel for the rich, unremitting breakage by which her poetry's figurative universe is drawn.[4]

Lest one assume more broadly that pain's intimacy with a figurative lexicon is only an effect of its subsidiary inscription in poetry, allow me to clarify my speculative sense that a figurative idiom as vividly mercurial as Dickinson's might be uniquely suited to articulating chronic pain's phenomenal field to the extent that her experience of the latter is shot through with a figurative capacity in its own right. From the shadows of foreboding to an aftermath never quite distinct enough from the event itself, the murkiness of this interval is stitched into Dickinson's life as a poet, an unsettled sharpening of awareness that spurs no less than interrupts her most moving work. And yet critical disinterest in this twin figuration of pain's psychical and physical registers is such that explorations of Dickinson's remarkable industry across this period of duress usually depict it – more glancingly, as it were, than not – as "eye trouble" and leave it at that. As Thomas H. Johnson writes in his 1955 biography, "In the autumn of 1863 began the trouble with her eyes, which bothered her to such an extent that by late April 1864 she was compelled to spend some weeks under a physician's care in Boston . . . . The condition of her eyes made imperative her return to Boston for a similar period of time in the following year."[5] Both Johnson and subsequent critics rely on what scant textual evidence may be found, but there is less material than one might hope, not least because the strain on her eyes increasingly leaves Dickinson unable to read or write with her accustomed fervor. In an oft-cited June 1864 letter to T. W. Higginson, Dickinson writes, "I was ill since September, and since April, in Boston, for a Physician's care – He does not let me go, yet I work in my Prison, and make Guests for myself." She ends the letter, asking if Higginson "[c]an . . . render [her] Pencil," as "the Physician has taken away my Pen" (L290). The anguish running through her Boston correspondence embellishes and refracts the nonplussment inherent to the ailment itself. In the spiral of poetic industry giving way to a malady experienced as writing trouble, the uncanny doubling of writerly distress and ongoing affliction pressures us to reassess as constitutive what would otherwise seem merely coincident.

As Donald L. Blanchard notes in an article for the American Medical Association, "no record survives of any diagnosis of her condition during her lifetime."[6] However Dickinson's ailment is imagined (let alone named), her Boston correspondence proves a stark measure of its debilitating effects, an eloquence all the more ironically striking in the record's paucity. "I have been sick so long," Dickinson writes, "I do not know the

Sun" (L296). It's practically impossible to know whether or not surgery was performed on Dickinson's eyes,[7] just as it is impossible to rule out for how many years complications may have followed. One is left wondering for how long her physician ordered Dickinson to wear blindfolds in bright light when, spending so much time in the dim indoors, she writes to Susan in June 1864, "I knew it was 'November,' but then there is a June" (L292). And one can only guess for how long Dickinson needed to be led by the arm when she writes in another letter that "the Doctor says I must tell you that I 'cannot walk alone'" (L295). When it comes to these and related matters, saying that the correspondence won't tell is an understatement. After all, one acclimates to chronic pain, however ambivalently; whether therapeutic hook or crook avails any form of relief, one unwittingly ceases to remark upon what no longer seems remarkable. Notwithstanding the lesser portion of her Boston correspondence, the quotidian of Dickinson's epistolary practice occupies her days regardless of questions of travel. The relative volume of this archive is critical to understanding the scale of the challenge of distinguishing how little Dickinson's letters reference pain on account of its invariant intensity from how little pain is referenced because of its remission.[8]

I raise this point as a way of forestalling the assumption that when Dickinson returns from her second trip to Boston in October 1865 her subsequent epistolary quietness on the matter necessarily means her eyes are cured. In the absence of further evidence, it's unclear as to whether she felt "healed," then or ever, or able to return to the industry of poetic insight without enduring it – simultaneously, anxiously – as a pang. After such excruciating, extended worry over the possibility of losing sight altogether, after how long is one able to see again without needing to stifle the former, habitual apprehension that one is going blind, that the blindness so often worried about would permanently return? While the absence of a diagnosis isn't equivalent to there having been none, it's reasonable to surmise that for at least some span of time, Dickinson's debility would have eluded both her doctor's interpretive efforts and her own. Without a sense of either its internal principle or the chance of its eventual subsiding, how could Dickinson not experience the crisis of her ailment as a hermeneutic no less than corporal conundrum? In this sense, her life writ large comes to resemble a puzzle in the grain of her poetry's major idiom. I mean in particular to suggest a kindred material shared between the lived deliberations of chronic illness and the figurative brilliance that unfurls, wavelike, from her effort to cozen into further being – resolving, calibrating, if not stopping (in the manner of a photographic bath) – the event with which her lyric experiments are obliquely continuous. From where "formula had failed" to this latter "formal feeling," figuration halts somewhat between pain's own dispositional means and our exasperating effort to better, less painfully, habit it.

Taken together, the above claims point to a simple but defining aspect of Dickinson's experience of this wearing, elonging event: her eye trouble renders vision and pain coincident. Whereas the frisson of Emerson's fantasy of becoming a "transparent eyeball" is predicated on the vanishment of the body and its attendant, obtruding egotism, Dickinson's ocular impingements intimate an erethism toward the body's vulnerability to the world the eye lets in[9] – unless so indurating a pain simply leaves the body merely, ancillarily, dumb. The latter scenario complicates the titular premise of Elaine Scarry's *body in pain* – i.e., that pain resides in the body, or, at least, that the body is where pain is felt to occur – by positing the "body" as the unvibrant matter of whatever pain happens *not* to touch.[10] The longer one experiences ordinary vision as this vibratory, collateral damage, the more likely the eye will come to be conceived as a frangible opacity, disrupting the effortless lubrications by which ordinary vision all but vanishes into sight. So exasperating an encounter proliferates epithets, tributes of infelicitous grappling (willful, recalcitrant, unreliable) that render vision a threshold for epistemology's re-inscription as a wrinkle or tear in embodiment: to paraphrase Jean-Luc Marion, as the flesh of the eye impinging on the eye's experience of the world, the pink blur of an immoveable, un-comic thumb at the edge of every photograph.[11]

In addition to the normatively physical aspects of her optical condition, the subject-object of Dickinson's chronic pain thus signifies pain's own expression of and propensity toward a specifically figurative capacity consubstantial with (rather than predicated on) the figurative dimensions of her writing. So semiotically complex a model of duress compels a phenomenological conception of pain's figurative moorings that neither Dickinson criticism nor disability theory has yet quite to articulate. When it comes to theories of pain more generally, the timeliness of this undertaking may be all the more felt in terms of the continued influence of Scarry's near-exclusive alignment of chronic pain with narrative theory and tropes of narration. If the figurative gestures of Dickinson's chronic pain have been biding in her poems all this time with the ongoing urgency of lyric triage, the makings of a criticism adequate to them is nevertheless perceptible at the edges of the criticism we have. Like a premonition in the wings, a critical account of chronicity's logic of figuration beats into interstitial perceptibility, for example, in the foundational readings in Sharon Cameron's in *Lyric Time*. "As most critics agree," Cameron writes, "there is no development in the canon of poems. The experiences recorded by these poems are insular ones, subject to endless repetition. Indeed it sometimes seems as if the same poem of pain or loss keeps writing itself over and over."[12] Shifting quietly between substance (the haecceity of what is recorded) and form (sharpened into being as later poems repeat what has been recorded in the latter's idiom), Cameron's account of poetic inertia suggests that experience is not only reported by the poems but also made to fit inside them. Chronic pain interrupts this aesthetic ratio, in that its temporality can be represented by a single poem but not "recorded," per se. To "fit" a single poem, the essential persistence of duress would have to be shrunk in a manner at odds with the fidelity we've come to expect of Dickinsonian rigor.

This effortful conformation of single poems to single experiences is complicated by the further puzzlement of distinguishing the substance of a poetic self's experiences, "over and over," from the lyrical matter it becomes; an analogous texture informs Cameron's collation of the canon's apparent lack of development with the hectic industry sounded in the compulsive auxiliary verb "keeps." In an endnote following the text's invoking of "endless repetition," Cameron cites David Porter's claim that "[p]erhaps the principal reason for [Dickinson's] early success is that she addressed herself again and again to a single theme."[13] In the seeming equivocation between Porter's account of iterative "theme[s]" and Cameron's revision of the latter as "insular" experiences "subject to endless repetition," we find a shared, lingering presentiment over experience's rapport with poetic substance expressed in the crosshairs of ongoingness and figurative miscibility, to the extent that figuration approximates the sphere of activity by which Porter's notion of the thematic is comprised. Notwithstanding Cameron and Porter's alignment of poetic substance with the unporous privacy of what Cameron calls the "insular[ity]" of a lone poem's autonomy, the refrains of "over and over" and "again and again" symptomatically gesture toward an experience of chronicity exceeding a single poem's means. The textual scenes toward which these descriptions of iterance correspond draw us toward a sense of the chronic figured in no small part – that is to say, experienced – as an injury to just this autonomy. Whether taken as "experience" or "theme," chronic pain's subject-under-duress demands some shift in the poetic machinery: an impoverishment of the single poem's phenomenal unity, redistributed across the accumulative breadth of some larger poetic assemblage's pulsations. Where before had been suggested the same poem repeated indefinitely, we find the reverberating fractal of a pain-frequency not reducible to synchronic or diachronic substance alone. Beyond the glimmer of sequence and amplification teased in the curated shapes of Dickinson's fascicles, a bewitchment occurs in the temporal grain of a poem's absorbing participation in some larger textual constellation, cooperatively invested in the borealis of pain-across-time.

"Again and again," Cameron writes, Dickinson "tells us that pain is atemporal."[14] This may sometimes be true, but the poems no less frequently communicate that the medium of pain is time itself, even or especially stretched past recognition. "'Twas like a Maelstrom, with a notch," for example, narrates an oneirically indeterminate scene of torture in which the glitch-like sharpness of a partially recollected gauntlet belies the speaker's founding exposure to the horror of time itself (F425). This uncharacteristically long poem (by Dickinson's standards) posits a series of macabre metaphors, each of which amplifyingly substantiates the opening figure of the maelstrom and its notch, a "synecdochic distortion [whose] isolat[ion] and magnifi[cation] is frightening," Cameron writes, "precisely because it lacks a context."[15] In its sharply carved interruption of the maelstrom's spiraling circuit, however, the notch allows for the chronicization of otherwise undifferentiated space. That time proves markable (and, in its persistence, remarkable) while making its own unremitting impression subtends the lyric apparatus by which a world of limitless feeling can be delineated at all, calibrating nothing less than the speaker's experience of herself at the shifting brink of a universe felt otherwise as blindness. The speaker of the poem comes into being as an effect of a pain that (the poem all but imagines) precedes her, into whose vortex she is roughly asserted. Just enough climbing out of her pain to be interpellated as its residue, the queer resolve of the speaker's utterance lies somewhere between Hawthorne's "I am a citizen of somewhere else" and Melville's "I only am escaped alone."

A value collects in the poem's figurative accretions beyond the comparable reductions of diegesis, a testament to the frequency with which Dickinson's writing cultivates a figurative thickness that isn't impenetrable so much as operates beyond translation. As with "I felt a Funeral, in my Brain," "'Twas like a Maelstrom" exploits stanzaic length less for the sake of developing a narrative over time than populating the chronicity signaled in the poem's multiple aspectual gerund forms – "kept narrowing," "kept measuring" – and temporally inflected conjunctions: "And you dropt," "and let you from a Dream," "And not a sinew stirred," "And sense was setting numb." The sheer accretiveness of the poem's articulation of pain-in-time counters Cameron's suggestion that "the impulse to tell and retell the same story has a quality of hysteria to it,"[16] or the like-minded insinuation of a Freudian compulsion-to-repeat in Helen Vendler's sense that "the insufficien[ce]" of the first simile's "two-stanza span" prompts the further clarifying efforts of the second simile and, in turn, the third.[17] Even as the poem's exacting rigor can be said to yield a series of figurative displacements, it is no less arguably invested – like the "Goblin with a Guage [sic] – / ... measuring the Hours" – in the waxing, phenomenological density of figurative occurrence for its own sake. The poem's recitation of preterite analogies doesn't belong to a speaker, per se, so much as a style of vocal effects. Whatever self precedes the event being relived while being pieced together – that is, a self in keeping with even the minimal assumptions of lyric voice – is at best holographed through the machine of a poem it cannot without doubt be said to survive: hence the speaker's self-ventriloquized "you" where we might expect an "I." Somewhat differently put, the breakage that the poem describes collectively can be said to roughly analogize the breakage of a lyric self incompletely memorialized in the text's friable parts. To imagine otherwise prematurely assumes that the fission of which the "you" is remaindered is reversible, that a lyric self thus strewn across time is anything but lagan. Just past the parallax of pain's own industrious scriptorium, the self hovers as an impression of stillness.

Sinking into itself – digging in its heels as though to reckon a ground for counter-acting the queasy weightlessness of the last stanza's questioning, gasping air – the generative heft of "'Twas like a Maelstrom, with a notch," insists on figuration as quasi-entelechial force, self no more winnowable from world than tenor from vehicle, form from power. It's along these lines that the substance of chronic pain may be understood not only as liminal but indivisible, speculatively adumbrating and exceeding the gentrified force of metaphor and simile's component parts. Even as its accounts of metaphorical coupling depend on the centripetal break around which our own stabs at cohesion dehiscingly collect, *Lyric Time* also invokes a conception of figurative difficulty's unified stuff consonant with my sense of chronic pain's aesthetic medium. For example, Cameron hypothesizes that the remediating value of similes lies in their crystallization of space between oneself and those things that seem most to resist one's pains to hail or otherwise bring them within one's ken. "Similes," she writes, "are both the acknowledgement of this space and, since it cannot be overcome, the effort to make connections within it." Cameron's suggestion that "such connections are painful, for they remind us that each of us is neither identical to nor opposite of any other," echoes her earlier claim that metaphor "is a response to pain in that it closes the gap between feeling and one's identification of it."[18] In the first statement, connection's consciousness of itself – like an eye made to feel aware of its seeing – is felt as the painfulness of a simile, as though in its awareness of imperfect alchemy a self were being carved out of what didn't hurt long enough to feel the hurt return; hence simile's mnemonic structure, both awakening painful recollection and analogizing pain's own self-recursive matter. In the second statement, by contrast, pain isn't a response to figuration (momentarily following *Lyric Time's* lead, here, in treating figuration as synonymous with either metaphorical or similetic rapport); figuration is itself a response to pain. Taken together, these claims conjure pain and figuration as so nearly at each other's heels as to comprise a single entity. Pain emanates from the hollows and rifts between self and the affective weather to which it is exposed, even as it names the bone-chilling, alien affect by which a self is "frozen led [/lead]," reduced to the implement that could render pain's inscriptive force pronounced, if not processed or understood. In both cases, the matter of figuration serves as a proxy expedient, epoxy for filling the cavity of pain it has itself hollowed. As these attempts to represent figuration's relation to pain bend in on themselves – simile's figuration-as-distress grown indistinguishable from the substance that metaphor's capacity for connectivity would seem to allay – we are left with a chiastic sense of figuration not only on both sides of a divide but washing over it, nimble submergence.

The simultaneously pernicious and seductive ease of figuration's uncannily looming resemblance informs the following late text, "We send the Wave to find the Wave" (F1643A). That it is not a poem about pain, per se – that pain is not *named* in its lines – says less about its thematic content than the manner in which its notionally governing self is dispersed within the poem's atmosphere, obsolescing the naming function found at the persistent, bruising heart of "Maelstrom." In its place we find an attention to conspicuity all but submerged in the haptic – call it sea, call it pain – loosely shaped around the latter's only apparently discrete principle of attraction:

> We send the
> Wave to find
> the Wave –
> An Errand so
> divine,
> The Messenger

> enamored too,
> Forgetting to
> return,
> We make the
> wise distinction
> still,
> Soever made in
> vain,
> The sagest time
> to dam the sea
> is when the
> sea is gone –

Figuration is to pain as wave to wave. Whereas *Lyric Time* evokes such transactions from the perspective of a self in pain, "We send the Wave" vitally dramatizes the work of figuration from the vantage of figuration itself, the difference between viewing a ship from land and straining to see the land from sea.

"A Pang is more conspicuous in Spring" is another late text invested in dissolving the dream of visualizable feeling in the divagating entropy of felt intensity (F1545B). Its phenomenological field is shared only contingently with its notional speaker:

> A Pang is more
> conspicuous in Spring
> In contrast with the
> things that sing
> Not Birds entirely – but
> Minds – Minute Effulgen-
> And Winds –   -cies
> When what they sung
> for is undone
> Who cares about
> a Blue Bird's Tune –
> Why, Resurrection
> had to wait
> Till they had moved
> a Stone –

Contra Dickinson criticism that would posit pain as a central, ontological wound, this poem's rhizomatic movement through itself imagines pain's semi-autonomy, and the speaker's capacity, if only within the apparatus of the poem, to reconceive her hurt as from its nebulous perimeter – or, as the poem's figurative impactions suggest, suspended between too close and too far away. As often is the case in Dickinson's poems, "A Pang is more conspicuous" ventures an opening claim about sharpened perception quickly enough overtaken or undermined by the subsequent lines' real-time, muddling enactment of pain's affective impingement. Like that of "Further in Summer than the Birds," this opening statement treats as self-sufficient a phrase that seems to signal incompletely just half of an argument. Further than the birds from what? More conspicuous than what? To be sure, to understand "in contrast with" as synonymous with "than" suggests that the first two lines solicit the next ones. Notwithstanding the comparison's strain to treat the visible and audible as synaesthetically congruous, what would it mean for "[a] Pang" to be "more / conspicuous ... [than] / the things that sing"? Even as the "ng" digraph's perseverating jingle eases us into taking birdsong as the pang's term of comparison, these opening lines and the "s[o]ng" they mechanically emulate collate the pang, in fact, to the birds themselves; or more precisely, a category of "things" recalling Dickinson's earlier definition of hope as the "thing with feathers."

In such moments of figurative interruption and fragmentation, the text expresses (as though for our own empirical regard) something intrinsic to the experience of pain it describes. The resulting description isn't abstruse; there is no more accessible version of the pang than what is presented. To a certain extent, this reading can't help but dovetail with Virginia Jackson's delineation of "sentimental poetry's stress on an unrepresentable embodiment, on a historicity threatened by the elevating aims of figuration."[19] Whereas Jackson, however, laments the "rhetorical difficulty of pointing to an experience ... before it becomes a metaphor,"[20] I am drawn to figuration not where it threatens historicity – specifically, the historical textures of chronic pain – so much as indicates it. Whether or not any given experience can be rescued from the metaphor into which our deictic apperception converts it, there is no version of Dickinson's ocular duress that isn't figurative (rather than metaphorical), in part because there is no "original" version of something so ontologically accruing. Somewhere between entropy and ecology, the figurative commotion of these lines doesn't "elevate" some truer, less ideational experience of pain: it comes as close to pain as Dickinson, or we, can get. Our shared experience of the pang – experience *as* pang – is one of lived impediment, crystallizingly suspended in or sutured to the poem's experience of time. These moments of suspension impress upon us the pause of temporally being in or as the absence of an understanding that might otherwise propel us through it.

No matter how long it is suffered, how much it comes over time to feel like an actual, thing-like object, pain remains devoid of intrinsic qualities since our experience of it as sharpness, aching, or throbbing conveys nothing properly its own so much as our relation to it. Unlike a leaf or a cloud, pain is *ontologically relational*. That we call it physical says less about its substance than our own, about where or how it is felt. And at the same time that we come to understand and thereafter feel physical pain as if it were more material than feeling or thought, it seems to lack emotional or intellectual content of its own, bracketing the extent to which it is felt as infuriating, beleaguering, et cetera. One of the relatively few things we may know for certain about chronic pain is that it *lasts*. Another is that no matter its felt intensity or duration, it is experienced not only as an epistemological impasse but as a crisis of impeded vision. How to arrive at or refine an idiom for a phenomenon incapable of being perceived (like things of the world) or internally envisioned (like things of the mind)? How to accomplish this when pain's phenomenality seems so neatly aligned with the organ of vision it eludes, as though pain, in Dickinson's case, were in the arduous process of translating sight into another system entirely? Figuration comes closer than other modes of language to doing justice if not to what chronic pain is then to how it operates. Freed from or simply heedless of the constative allure of the present, it magnetizes as it finds its way as by a different name. In the groove its temporal orbit forges with our own, an absorbing, sometimes transmuting difficulty emerges as without being equivalent to the stuff of poetic expression. The taxing excrescence of its pivots informs the vivid difficulty of the following, late Dickinson text; one may along these lines hear the influence of the Latin root, *pluere* – to make to flow, a flowing outward – on the "Plush" of its exploratory syncopations:

> Opon a Lilac
> Sea
> To toss
> incessantly
> His Plush
> Alarm
> Who fleeing
> from the
> Spring
> The Spring

>   avenging
>   fling
>   To Dooms
>   of Balm – (F1368)

This strange little text serves as the opening for the insightful Dickinson chapter of Theo Davis's monograph *Ornamental Aesthetics: The Poetry of Attending in Thoreau, Dickinson, and Whitman*. Cutting to the chase, Davis characterizes these lines as "a poem about a bee who is said 'Opon a Lilac Sea / To toss incessantly.'"[21] For better or for worse, to speak in this way of what the text is "about" scenically accords to its material an intelligibility exceeding or external to what the text presents, implicitly designating this instance of figurative complexity as extraneous or ancillary to the matter at hand. That figurative difficulty poses a challenge to the economy of paraphrase's will-toward-transparency is true enough. Treating its interference, however, as eschewable bristles against the text's perceived resistance to paraphrastic resolution, not to mention the attentiveness invoked in Davis's title.

To frame "Opon a Lilac/Sea" in terms of a bee imparts the foreclosing clarity of a subject merely absented, reducing the poem's luxuriating ungainliness to the thrift of a riddle. On the contrary, this perverse lushness posits the poem's tergiversations as proscenial rather than remedial: suspended between outer and inner, material and abstraction, their figurative indetermination is less solipsistic then shared between world and self as that which neither can completely metabolize nor jettison. In the context of a related set of Dickinson poems, Gillian Osborne notes that "the mechanism of the poem ... has led the collapsed subject ... to suffer the pain of misplaced and presumptuous identification."[22] Osborne's account of pain in the ligatures between collapsed subject and poetic mechanism articulates at a wider optic a kind of intrigue that the figurative iridescence of "Opon a Lilac/Sea" at most implies. The latter's impactions neither metaphorize nor bear witness from any single, guarded vantage, and in this respect their peculiar disorientation recalls the anti-narrative subversion of perspective found in late Assyrian palace reliefs.[23] Rather, they pulse minutely between something like pain as though viewed from a poetic perimeter and a poem that is *pained*, as Bartleby's lawyer might say, perceived from (and simultaneously *as*) pain's own core: J. W. M. Turner lashed to the mast of a steamship for the sake of experiencing a storm from the storm, solitary perspective emptied into the weather. In their asymptotic resistance to the poetic repertoire of symbolic/representative/personified, the optical rhythms of "Opon a Lilac/ Sea" evince a textual passion that "never quite arrive[s]" where we await them. However we understand the grammatical subject of these lines – whether bee, or Being, or what Osborne, discussing "The nearest Dream recedes – unrealized" calls "the bee in the brain" – it is always already submerged in the poem's nebulous medium.[24] So dissolvingly enveloped is this textually brilliant scene that it's difficult to see within it anything but the "Sea" itself.

We may glean in the unfamiliar literacy of this textual liquefaction several things. First, its impersonal infinitive, "to toss," refers alike to both textual solution and the subject of its apparent obscuration. The verb form takes the lurching movement of the sea and pauses it at the same time that it indefinitely projects it beyond itself, the temporal singularity of a wave at once disrupting and coalescing in the sea's endlessly oscillating surface. Deleuze helps us conceptualize this simultaneously frozen and recursive impact: "When a body combines some of its own distinctive points with those of a wave, it espouses the principle of a repetition which is no longer that of the Same, but involves the other – involves difference, from one wave and one gesture to another, and carries that difference through the repetitive space thereby constituted."[25] The vibrant, claustral space that the poem seems to enact likewise extends to our experience of reading as the sensation of being held too close to see what it is we are seeing. Deleuze continues:

> We are right to speak of repetition when we find ourselves confronted by identical elements with exactly the same concept. However, we must distinguish between these discrete elements, these repeated objects, and a secret subject, the real subject of repetition, which repeats itself through them.... As a result, rather than the repeated and the repeater, the object and the subject, we must distinguish two forms of repetition.[26]

As corrective to the flattening production of a truant subject (not least to the extent that this operation treats as recoverable the corresponding vantage that it is the accomplishment of the poem to have reformulated) or the analogously enforced realism that transforms the lilac sea into a hedge of lilacs, Deleuze's account of the wave enriches our encounter with what in the poem pushes past the datum of mise-en-scène, sharpening, in turn, our attention to the perhaps surprising specificity of another word without physical correlative and not coincidentally, largely impervious to our simplifying handling: incessantly. Even graphically, the conceptual allure of the word is marked in its syllables, taking up as much metrical space as the first two lines combined. Although an uncommon word in her corpus (it appears in just one other late poem), "incessantly" names all the same a temporal milieu found throughout Dickinson's oeuvre. A far more frequent word, for example, corresponding to a nearly equivalent experience of time, is "Perpetual." Consider this second stanza of a late fragment beginning "A not admitting / of the wound":

> A closing of the
> simple (Gate) lid that
> opened to the sun
> Until the (unsuspecting Carpenters) (sovreign) tender
> Carpenter
> Perpetual nail
> it down –   (F1188)

Bearing in mind Allen Tate's account of the absorption of Dickinson's poetry's less in Calvinism than the latter's desuetude illuminates a perpetuity pried from its religious aspect, leaving in its place a sense of pain's ongoingness as an afterlife stripped bare of redemption.[27] Dickinson's captivation with the possibility of sensorial consistency on both sides of the afterlife not only posits immortality as the tenor that figuration vehiculates but can't quite reach but also subjects it to the more finely searching analysis of a metaphorical vehicle in its own right, the "remnant" reliquary material of time without interruption by which one might come to fathom pain's own enigmatic chronicity. If, as with "Opon a Lilac / Sea," the speaker's experience of visual obstruction comes to reverberate as our own, the stanza's last lines reorient this ocular relation as an haptic vulnerability, the carpenter's "tender[ness]" distributed through the poem as that which belongs to neither wound nor wounded self so much as the fiber of the poem writ large. As the lid is secured and we too are left in darkness, the bruising delicacy of the carpenter's calling converges with the tenderness of the "simple lid," a transmutation of the first stanza's hurt into a vision of the lid's own experience of impingement, one nail at a time. Up until this point, the predominant temporal mood of the poem had moved between the gerunds at the start of each stanza (a not admitting, a closing) and the deep bass note marking the pluperfect submergence of the speaker's Life – "the wound / … gr[own] so wide / … my Life had entered it" – into pain's wake. In this light, the present tense of the poem's last lines, "Perpetual nail / it down," grows all the more jarring: the urgency of a command, no matter the difficulty of saying to whom it is directed or by whom or what it is spoken. If only in the figurative florescence of the text, the speaker's excruciation gives way to the horror of an abstract, "Perpetual" crucifixion. The haeccity of a single nail driven into the poem's tender surface multiplies with every stroke the nail receives from the poem's absent hammer, further kaleidoscoping into however many nails are needed to secure such a lid against the sun to which in some dream of a prior life it had opened: exponentially multiplying unto perpetuity, sharp waves of pain vanishing into the sea's horizon, far as Dickinson's figurative eye – its own tender lid always on the verge of closing – can see.

Notes

1. Sharon Cameron, *Lyric Time: Dickinson and the Limits of Genre* (Baltimore: Johns Hopkins University Press, 1979), 23.
2. This movement away from an hermeneutically overfamiliar relation to Dickinsonian unfamiliarity follows the bracing *bon voyage* of R. P. Blackmur's 1954 proposal "first to examine a set of prejudices which are available as approaches to Emily Dickinson, and then to count – and perhaps account for – a few staring facts: obvious, animating, defacing facts about the verses as they now appear," since "depend[ing] on prejudice for the nature of time or poetry . . . allows for mistakes, and in the present condition of Emily Dickinson's poetry, it is imperative to allow for continuous error, both in the facts and . . . in the prejudices by which we get at them" (26–27).
3. This project's interest in pain's seeming responsiveness to our attention to it arises in part from a dissatisfaction with extant critical descriptions of pain's place within the Dickinson canon; I address a related set of concerns in *Queer Optimism: Lyrics Personhood and other Felicitous Persuasions* (Minneapolis: University of Minnesota Press, 2009), 79–125. Consider Marianne Noble's suggestion that "the experience of affliction . . . is intrinsically transgressive. While contentment quietly remains within the confines of the law, pain will not stay in its place. It defies laws and the boundaries that regulate them and (as Scarry demonstrates) the language that articulates them" (161). Noble is able to insist on pain's juridical abruption because pain, for Noble, has no laws of its own. Noble's paraphrase of "A nearness to Tremendousness" turns pain into something more Byronically roguish than what the poem examines. After all, pain doesn't "def[y] laws" (a pun on loss, to be sure), but lies in *vicinity* to them; its closeness to explanation or principle – and it's worth noting that the third and fourth definitions for "vicinity" in Dickinson's 1844 *Webster's Dictionary* are "obedience; compliance" – invokes far more subtle a quandary. Similarly, to my eye, "It's location/Is Illocality" doesn't quite mean it "will not stay in place," but that *where* it lives seems to exist as a cartographic blur or sylph,

innavigable (rather than merely piratical) in the manner of Emerson's enigmatically intercalated days. As Dickinson (and anyone, for that matter, living with chronic pain) would know all too well, pain frequently *does* stay in place, like a ghost in the bone no technology or procedure can deliver, let alone resolve.
4. My understanding of Dickinson's figurative practice is admittedly idiosyncratic, not least in its effort to distinguish figurative difficulty's propulsive density from the comparably static visual lure of metaphor. Whereas metaphorical meaningfulness is tethered to an expectation of objectual intelligibility, Dickinson's most autonomous figurative gestures are neither scrutable nor inscrutable so much as semi-charismatically transcrutable (impacted and impacting). It's along these lines that I think of figuration's suspensive substance as *transmaterial*. While I admire Nathan Brown's recent exploration of materialist poetics, and don't disagree with its suggestion that poetry may need to "acknowledge the diminished power of its privileged capacity to present the unpresentable by producing *figures* of invisible worlds" (Nathan Brown, *The Limits of Fabrication: Materials Science, Materialist Poetics* [New York: Fordham University Press, 2017], 19), I'm also inclined to think the knell for figuration *tout corps* is premature. This present sense of figuration's phenomenological pressure resonates hopefully with Dana Luciano's claim that "the point of historicizing materiality, and the range of responses thereto, would ultimately be to question our own assumptions about what qualities count as 'material,' what the purpose of transmateriality or transobjectivity might be, why we have come to equate vibrancy and activity with agency, and what we might do when things don't work out that way" (Dana Luciano, "Sacred Theories of Earth: Matters of Spirit in *The Souls of Things*," *American Literature* 86.4 [December 2014]: 730). See also Daniel Tiffany's indispensable *Toy Medium: Materialism and Modern Lyric* (Berkeley: University of California Press, 2000).
5. Thomas H. Johnson, *Emily Dickinson: An Interpretive Biography* (Cambridge, MA: Belknap Press of Harvard University Press, 1955), 124.
6. Donald L. Blanchard, "Emily Dickinson's Ophthalmic Consultation with Henry Willard Williams, MD," *Archives of Ophthalmology* 130.12 (2012): 1594.
7. Following Richard B. Sewall's 1974 *The Life of Emily Dickinson*, Kerry McSweeney notes that while it "is not clear whether during these stays [Dickinson] was operated on," surgery was "the standard treatment in severe cases" (*Language of the Senses: Sensory-Perceptual Dynamics in Wordsworth, Coleridge, Thoreau, Whitman, and Dickinson* [Montreal: McGill-Queen's University Press, 1998], 148). In the absence of corroborating sources, Diana Fuss's claim that Dickinson was "eventually cured ... of her temporary blindness" (21) seems less authoritative than wishful (*The Sense of an Interior: Four Writers and the Rooms that Shaped Them* [New York: Routledge, 2004], 21).
8. This is contra James R. Guthrie's more sanguine assessment of the scarcity of this pain dossier: "Although references to her optical illness faded away from letters and poems written after 1866, some of the tropes Dickinson had adopted

perhaps are a result of having been ill persisted, yet in contexts that are distinctly more positive. For example, the carcerative images we saw her associate in her poems with sickroom confinement reappear in her communications with Judge Lord in a completely different guise, as a form of erotic play" (*Emily Dickinson's Vision: Illness and Identity in Her Poetry* [Gainesville: University Press of Florida, 1998], 155). Suffice it to say that I find Guthrie's heterosexualization of Dickinson's chronic illness – here and elsewhere in his investigation – puzzling to say the least. That Dickinson's duress might spur in the critic a homophobic discomfiture soothed only by heterosexuality's appearance on the horizon of pain's abatement speaks to the occult intervolutions between queerness and chronic pain traced in *Contingent Figure: Aesthetic Duress from Emerson to Eve Kosofsky Sedgwick* (under contract, University of Minnesota Press), of which this essay is an excerpt.

9. Michelle Kohler's monograph *Miles of Stare: Transcendentalisn and the Problem of Literary Vision in Nineteenth-Century America* analyzes a Dickinsonian ocular poetics that in many ways overlaps with my own concerns. Notwithstanding her investment in how Dickinson complicates Emerson's fugue on the transcendent eyeball, Kohler's attraction to the epistemological orientation of Dickinson's metaphors frames as elevated intention what, in the clutch of chronic pain, Dickinson both experiences and chronicles as agential vertigo. For instance, Kohler is right to note those poems "that engage the transcendentalist figure of literary vision in order to disable or reframe the figure itself, as well as to redefine what sort of metaphors might derive from vision – moves made in part by her efforts to resee the American landscape in light of the Civil War" (106) – after all, Dickinson's poems from this period *do* conjure scenes of lurid ocular instability, to no small degree because the poetic eye (impeded or not) comes to see carnage wherever it turns. At the same time, however, the optical crisis effected by the war is inseparable for Dickinson from a coterminous ocular distress (coincidence of which raises unsettling questions about queer synchrony and the self's endfoldment in a universe the war illuminates as, if not renders, all too harrowingly pervious). And so if Kohler reckons that the "landscape, estranged and incomprehensible, becomes in this context a dismembered stranger, a distant superior, or an oversize, fatal threat to the body's integrity," I would add that in the same or at least a contiguous context, chronic pain becomes a stranger/superior, too. Except that in its keenest throes, pain's ongoingness may feel less like either a threat against the body's integrity or the awfulness of the self under the self's own siege then the sundered field. For another phenomenologically attuned account of Dickinson's vision, see Marianne Noble's "Dickinson on Perception and Consciousness: A Dialogue with Maurice Merleau-Ponty" in *Emily Dickinson and Philosophy*, Jed Deppman, Marianne Noble, and Gary Lee Stonum (eds.) (New York: Cambridge University Press, 2013), 188–206. See also Jed Deppmann's *Trying to Think with Emily Dickinson* (Amherst: University of Massachusetts Amherst Press, 2008), 71–74; Joanne Feit Diehl's

Dickinson and the Romantic Imagination (Princeton: Princeton University Press, 1982), 10; and Guthrie's *Emily Dickinson's Vision* (discussed above).

10. To be sure, Scarry herself is deeply interested in pain's extra-somatic life, the ways its "felt-characteristics – one of which is its compelling vibrancy or its incontestable reality or simply its 'certainty' – can be appropriated away from the body and presented as the attributes of something else" (Elaine Scarry, *The Body in Pain: The Making and Unmaking of the World* [New York: Oxford University Press, 1985], 13–14). The genres at the heart of *The Body in Pain* may be prose, but that Scarry theorizes pain's centrifugal vibrancy in terms of "*analogical verification*" (italics in original) suggests a figurative principle at play above and beyond literature's mimetic terms.
11. Jean-Luc Marion, *In Excess: Studies of Saturated Phenomenon* (New York: Fordham University Press, 2002), 92.
12. Cameron, 14.
13. Ibid., 262 n. 31.
14. Ibid., 27.
15. Ibid., 95.
16. Ibid.
17. Helen Vendler, *Dickinson: Selected Poems and Commentaries* (Cambridge: Harvard University Press, 2012, 198–199.
18. Cameron, 53, 28.
19. Virginia Jackson, *Dickinson's Misery: A Theory of Lyric Readings* (Princeton: Princeton University Press, 2005), 219.
20. Ibid.
21. Theo Davis, *Ornamental Aesthetics: The Poetry of Attending in Thoreau, Dickinson, and Whitman* (New York: Oxford University Press, 2016), 90.
22. Gillian Osborne, "Dickinson's Lyric Materialism," *EDJ* 21.1 (2012): 57–78.
23. Leo Bersani and Ulysse Dutoit, *The Forms of Violence: Narrative in Assyrian Art and Modern Culture* (New York: Schocken Books, 1985), 46.
24. Osborne, 71.
25. Gilles Deleuze, *Difference and Repetition*, translated by Paul Patton (New York: Columbia University, 1994), 23.
26. Ibid.
27. Allen Tate, "New England Culture and Emily Dickinson," in *The Recognition of Emily Dickinson*, Caesar R. Blake, and Carlton R. Wells (eds.) (Ann Arbor: The University of Michigan Press, 1968), 153–167.

CHAPTER 7

Emily Dickinson's Posthuman Worlds: Biopoetics and Environmental Subjectivity

Colleen Glenney Boggs

Michelle Kohler notes in her Introduction to this volume that we have come to understand Dickinson as being "firmly *in* the world." But given the philosophical range of the term, we may ask *which* world Dickinson inhabits, and how. "World" itself poses a challenge to our engagement with Dickinson, since, in her poems, worlds are themselves the things we make and that make us. As Kohler puts it in the Introduction, "while the attention to [Dickinson's] intellectual sovereignty [*in* the world] has given us a more sophisticated, saner Dickinson, it also to some extent perpetuates a notion of bounded, controlled selfhood and authorship that we resist (indeed, deconstruct) in many other critical contexts in the wake of post-structuralism."[1] Dickinson herself performed such resistance from the moment she emerged as a poet. The long "wake of post-structuralism," which Jacques Derrida's late work extended into posthumanism, enables us to see a new Dickinson, one whose notions of self are not bounded by "the human" but engage other species.[2] Staging forms of selfhood that are cocreated in relationships between species and environments, Dickinson experimented with poetics – reconfigured as biopoetics – that push beyond the kind of world-making Martin Heidegger defines as the essence and prerogative of the human.[3]

According to R. W. Franklin, Emily Dickinson's first poem dates back to March 4, 1850, and is "Awake ye muses nine, sing me a strain divine." Setting aside our expectations of what poetry is and does, we might select a verse written the previous month as Dickinson's inaugural poem: "his mistress's rights he doth defend – although it bring him to his end – although to death it doth him send!" (L34) These lines appeared in a fanciful Valentine's letter addressed to George H. Gould and were published in *The Indicator* (Amherst College) of February 7, 1850. They are usually not counted among the few poems Dickinson published during her lifetime, and perhaps no wonder, since they are what we think of derisively as doggerel. But they are also doggerel in a more literal, and more significant, sense, for they explicate what Dickinson means when she writes earlier in the same letter that her dog Carlo "is the noblest work of Art."[4] Despite the marked levity of these lines, and my own playful reading of them as doggerel, I want to take seriously the entanglement of doggerel and dog, of poetry with animal, for expressing what would become a key preoccupation as Dickinson matured as a poet, namely the question of how relationships to the nonhuman world shape subjectivity and make meaning.

The larger passage in which Dickinson includes her doggerel is worth a look for the way it stages poetry's ability to move fluidly between figurative and literal meanings as it engages in a collaborative process of world-making. She playfully performs relationships that span biblical allegory as well as national metaphor to end, crucially, on a note of animal companionship that is also a form of artistic superlative:

> We will be David and Jonathan, or Damon and Pythias, or what is better than either, the United States of America. We will talk over what we have learned in our geographies, and listened to from the pulpit, the press and the Sabbath School. This is strong language sir, but none the less true [...] All choice spirits however distant are ours, ours theirs; there is a thrill of sympathy – a circulation of mutuality – cogntionem inter nos! I am Judith the heroine of the Apocrypha, and you the orator of Ephesus. That's what they call a metaphor in our country. Don't be afraid of it, sir, it won't bite. If it was my *Carlo* now! The Dog is the noblest work of Art, sir. I may safely say the noblest – his mistress's rights he doth defend – although it bring him to his end – although to death it doth him send! (L34)

Dickinson's movement between the figurative and the literal is dizzying. Jumping from one pairing (David and Jonathan) to another (Damon and Pythias) and another (Judith and the orator of Ephesus) and yet another (Dickinson and her dog Carlo), she obsessively performs what she calls "a thrill of sympathy" and a "circulation of mutuality" which the final pairing extends across species lines. Pointing out that this mutuality depends on "what they call a metaphor," she then goes on to unsettle the abstraction she produces when she playfully suggests that metaphors won't bite though her dog Carlo will. The notion that a metaphor could bite seems utterly absurd. But that absurdity itself depends on limiting metaphor's reach – that is, on confining metaphor's power only to the figurative at the cost of the literal references Dickinson invokes by introducing her dog Carlo. The dog does not merely become the literal object against which figurative meaning is played off: he also enters into the figurative realm as a "work of

Art." Moving between "what they call a metaphor" and "Carlo," the passage unsettles the distinctions between figurative devices and literal beings. Through these staged relationships, Dickinson creates a "circulation of mutuality" in which metaphor and animal encounter one another. Putting in play metaphor's "bite" and the dog's "Art" enables Dickinson to stage a "mutuality" that connects the human with the other-than-human. Insisting that the "Dog is the noblest work of Art," she humorously uses her doggerel to perform relationships that extend art itself beyond human subjectivity, producing in the process what I will describe as biopoetics. Thereby, she indicates that rethinking subjectivity so as to include nonhuman beings opens up poetry's parameters and extends it to structures of meaning-making that are not (or not only) abstractly metaphoric but also concretely animal.

A "circulation of mutuality" informs Dickinson's poetic enterprise and her reconfiguration of subjectivity along lines that we might call, anachronistically, posthuman in method and, playfully, doggerel in form. In what follows, I situate Dickinson's conception of relational subjectivity – in familiar poems such as "One Sister have I in the house" – within contemporary conversations about posthumanism and biopoetics (F5). As she exemplifies in "The Robin's my Criterion for Tune" (F256), extending the boundaries between the figurative and the literal dimensions of poetry enables Dickinson to engage in cross-species relations that reorient her and our understanding of poetry's ability to generate environmental subject-worlds.

Posthuman Dickinson

Two developments have put the term "posthuman" at the forefront of current scholarly discussions, namely the study of new technologies that challenge previous forms of subjectivity and the rise of animal studies as a field that expands notions of subjectivity beyond anthropocentrism to other species. Brought to prominence in the work of N. Katherine Hayles, the term "posthuman" traced modern technology's departure from liberal humanism.[5] Whereas this version of posthumanism focused on the challenges technology posed to definitions of the "human," Cary Wolfe used the term to examine cross-species relationships. Instead of expanding historically available forms of anthropocentrism so as to become more encompassing of nonhuman beings, this project of imagining posthumanism, argues Wolfe, "poses fundamental challenges ... to a model of subjectivity and experience drawn from the liberal justice tradition and its central concept of rights, in which ethical standing and civic inclusion are predicated on rationality, autonomy, and agency."[6] Because the term "posthumanism" still carries traces of the history from which it departs, one of its key theorists, Donna Haraway, has come to reject the term altogether, preferring instead the notion of what she calls companion species, "which is less a category than a pointer to an ongoing 'becoming with,'" in which the "partners do not precede their relating" – or, in Dickinson's words, in which they experience "a thrill of sympathy – a circulation of mutuality" that profoundly shapes them.[7]

Whatever we want to label this way of relating, Theo Davis has recently enabled us to see that in Dickinson, it amounts to a "mode of aesthetic attending to the *world*" [emphasis added].[8] In referring to "the world," a philosophical term she draws from Martin Heidegger, Davis intends

> both the sense of what appears to us in our sensory experience, and also the underlying sense of Being, an ontological condition that makes the existence of any particular moment or encountered thing possible.[9]

Redirecting our attention, then, Davis enables us to see Dickinson's "circulation of mutuality" as one that does not only occur on an affective level (as the "thrill of *sympathy*" might indicate), but that also functions to relate sensory experience to Being (as the *"thrill* of sympathy" suggests).

The "world" Davis references is specifically that of Heidegger's philosophy, with which she engages critically while ultimately sharing Heidegger's investment in a particular mode of humanism from which Dickinson's poems often stray. In defining beings via their relationship to world, Heidegger argued for three distinctions, namely that material objects are "*worldless*," that "the animal is *poor in world*," and that "man is *world-forming*."[10] Arguing that animals have their "*own relation*" to their surroundings in ways that material objects do not, Heidegger nonetheless saw that relationship as fundamentally about accretion and not creation, which he attributed to the human's special ability to be both "master and servant of the world."[11] For Heidegger, the ability to relate to and form a sense of world, of being rich in world, is ultimately a prerogative that defines the human as human in distinction from material and biological others. But Emily Dickinson rejects such demarcations. She explores changes in subjectivity, moving fluidly among objects, animals, and human beings and variously imagining what it means to be worldless, poor in world, and world-forming. Most crucially, she experiments with creating subject–world relations that posit being (or becoming) poor in world as a mode of deeper engagement and a means of forging complex subjectivities.

Dickinson stages withdrawals from the world that more closely align her subject position with that ascribed by Heidegger to animals and material objects. While Heidegger attributes a reduced and reductive sense of "world" to animals and material objects, Dickinson performs such reductions as constitutive of subjectivity, which for her is not limited by species but emerges in cross-species relationships. Those positions, which according to Heidegger are reductive or even antithetical to subjectivity, in Dickinson intensify subjectivity. Being poor in world for Dickinson thus does not amount to a reduction in world but to world's more intensified value and meaning. Important work has previously taken up this issue as one of renunciation. Whereas Sandra Gilbert and Susan Gubar argued that Dickinson chose to "avoid the necessity of renouncing her art by renouncing, instead, that concept of womanliness which required self-abnegating renunciation," Wendy Martin reread Dickinson's seeming "renunciation or denial" instead as a "measure of her autonomy and determination."[12] As we'll see, shifting our attention from renunciation to what I will characterize as selectivity enables us to reframe Dickinson's "autonomy" as a form of worldly relationality. To the extent, then, that being poor in world reflects on subjectivity, it is for Dickinson not reductive of but intensifying to subjectivity in ways that also push the parameters of the human into the realm of the posthuman. Dickinson theorizes posthumanism – in the sense of post-Heideggerianism – when she stages being poor in world as a condition of subject formation in general and poetic subject formation in particular.

Before I develop this theoretical claim more fully, let me offer one brief example of how Dickinson concretizes a subject formation that is poor-in-world in "Some keep the Sabbath going to Church":

> Some keep the Sabbath going to Church –
> I keep it, staying at Home –
> With a Bobolink for a Chorister –
> And an Orchard, for a Dome –
>
> Some keep the Sabbath in Surplice –
> I, just wear my Wings –
> And instead of tolling the Bell, for Church,
> Our little Sexton – sings.
> [...]   (F236)

Juxtaposing formal church service with nature, she rejects the notion that the word of God is tied to human logos. Instead, she posits a wor(l)d-of-God that has its own superior meaning: the "Bobolink" functions as a "Chorister" and a "Sexton" who "sings" in a way that makes "Heaven" imminent and immanent (in the last stanza, she is "going, all along"). Punning on "Surplice" as "surplus," and rejecting such excess when she decides to "*just* [emphasis added] wear my Wings," Dickinson creates a sense of diminution, of being poor in world. That diminution amounts to her becoming the bobolink: the speaker, "I," is now the winged creature that keeps the Sabbath staying at Home. The bobolink that was singing in the first stanza is supplemented in the second verse by the "I" of the speaker. And then both seem to enter a relation of mutuality when "*our* [emphasis added] little Sexton – sings." The formation of world here is premised both on a reduction of world – a "staying at home" rather than "going to Church," a selection of *just* wings – and on a relationship with other subjectivities. Those relationships to nonhumans reshape the poet's own subjectivity via her ability to participate in cross-species meaning-making that exceeds the limitation of casting the word of God as reflected (only) in human speech. In "Some keep the Sabbath," we see a strategy of using relational subjectivities to push into a natural space that is configured at once as symbolic *and* material. The birds enable a relational poetics that reshape the poet's sense of self and semiosis.

Biopoetics and Environmental Subjectivity

This theorization and emphasis on the surrounding natural world aligns Dickinson's work more closely with Jacob von Uexküll's than with Heidegger's. Long known only as the biologist who most influenced Heidegger, Uexküll's work has recently appeared in a new translation that allows English readers to understand how he theorized the concept of *Umwelt* – that is, of environmental relations as subject-forming. As his modern translator Joseph D. O'Neil notes, the term *Umwelt* is notoriously difficult to translate in that it means both "world" ("Welt") and "environment," or immediate surroundings.[13] Whereas the latter is "the literal translation of *Umwelt*," the former, despite its expansiveness, "accurately reflects a key aspect of the term *Umwelt*, if one assumes that 'world' is always the world of or for some subject."[14] As I will explain in a moment, Dickinson delights in playing these meanings against each other.

Because *Umwelt*, whether world or environment, is "always . . . of or for some subject," different beings have complex ways of meaning-making.

As Dorion Sagan writes in his assessment of Uexküll, "within a given animal's perceptual life-world, [or] *Umwelt*, signifying things trigger chains of events, sometimes spelling the difference between life and death."[15] For Uexküll, this process of "meaning-making [...] evolves between organisms and their environments, among organisms of the same species and across species, and within individual organisms such as humans attempting to understand the symptoms of their bodies."[16] Sagan says that Uexküll summarily conceptualizes these processes as "biosemiotics," but that he does not fully theorize the term. For such a theorization, we might productively turn to Dickinson, who thinks about "signifying things" in both literal and symbolic ways – as objects as well as symbols. Dickinson gives these options for meaning-making full play across her poetry, often making it difficult for readers to assess what the parties are that she relates to one another.

We have seen her playfully stage such relations in the doggerel of her early letter, where she indicates that poetry is not just situated in relation to an external *Umwelt* (captured by her reference to the "United States" as well as textbook "geographies") but can itself function as an environment in which beings encounter one another. Whereas doggerel enacts these associations on the formal level, "Some keep the Sabbath" brings materiality and abstraction into a direct connection that hinges on symbolization (the church mass) as well as embodiment (the bobolink and the speaker's own "wings"). The subjectivity Dickinson envisions emerges where the being experiencing a "perceptual life-world" becomes formed by that experience.

In several poems, Dickinson plays the meanings of *Umwelt* as "world" and "environment" against each other. A poem such as "The Robin's my Criterion for Tune" creates what we might characterize as a transatlantic imagination of worlds elsewhere and yet balances that sense of world against an understanding of subjectivity as tied to the *Umwelt* of the specific local environment.[17] Turning a transatlantic gaze toward Britain, Dickinson paradoxically uses that perspective view of the larger world to develop a regional sense of what it means to see "New Englandly." Dickinson's poem arrives at a local environmental perspective of *Umwelt* from the poem's wider worldview. Dickinson creates a biopoetics that is specific in its manifestations and yet (or: therefore!) worldly. That process hinges on the literal and symbolic meanings of birds, namely robins and cuckoos, in a poem that produces subjectivity via biopoetics:

> The Robin's my Criterion for Tune –
> Because I grow – where Robins do –
> But, were I Cuckoo born –
> I'd swear by him –
> The ode familiar – rules the Noon –
> The Buttercup's, my whim for Bloom –
> Because, we're Orchard sprung –
> But, were I Britain born,
> I'd Daisies spurn –   (F256)

Making the robin her "Criterion for Tune," Dickinson justifies that choice by attributing the natural habituation of her "I" to the Robin's singing.[18] That habituation depends on having "grow[n]" in a place marked by seasonal change: the poem portrays robins as migratory birds whose return heralds spring, and the poem progresses from spring (the robin) through summer ("the Noon" of "Bloom" and "Orchard") to fall ("October") and "Winter."[19] The poem thus ties subjectivity to nature, but that also means that subjectivity is not natural as much as it is naturalized by its formative local environment or *Umwelt*.

The contingency of this subjectivity is reinforced when Dickinson's speaker distances herself from the robin as an absolute "Criterion" by arguing that, were she "Cuckoo born," she would "swear by him."[20] At this point, her imagery of habituation and familiarity becomes complicated by the fact that the cuckoo, too, is contingent. Therefore, the cuckoo fails to function as the kind of transcendental reference point required for her ability to "swear by him." Given the cuckoo's contingency, any oath sworn on him fails to carry substantive meaning. If swearing is a verbal construct that derives its claim to authority from an appeal to a transcendent signified, the cuckoo's position as such a signified makes swearing itself an act of absurdity. Then again, swearing by the contingent cuckoo is not absurd if such a move reconceptualizes meaning itself as a form of biopoetics; that is, as deriving its meaning not from transcendent but from environmental relations – the interplay, in Uexküll's terms, "between organisms and their environments, among organisms . . . across species."

The subject-forming power of the local risks positing the environment as deterministic, except that Dickinson's poem cannily guards against the pitfalls of what would amount to biological (or at least environmental) essentialism. Even as the cuckoo reinforces the relationship between environment and subjectivity, it also disrupts any essentialist connection between the two. As an engaged ornithologist, Dickinson would have known that the European variety of cuckoos, which her focus on Britain invokes, is a so-called brood parasite: the cuckoo lays eggs in other birds' nests and has those other birds hatch the cuckoo chicks. Once hatched, the cuckoo chick displaces the other birds, pushing them out of the nest. The (involuntary) adoptive parents then spend all their efforts nurturing the intruding cuckoo. In Dickinson's poem, the intruding cuckoo reinforces the relationship between subjectivity and environment but disrupts their connection to essentialism; if anything, the cuckoo establishes a sense of relativism even as it explains environmental subject formation. What begins as a trope of local authenticity thus becomes a trope of a locale that authenticates itself via its disavowed relations. In stanza one, "were I Cuckoo born" (line 3) finds an echo in "were I Britain born" (line 8). If we ignore the image of the cuckoo, the poem reads as if it sets up a dichotomy between Dickinson's locally produced experience, and the way that experience differs from being born in Britain – and this is indeed how the poem is usually read. But the image of the cuckoo explodes that difference, making the larger world central to the production of the local environment. In wanting to "swear by" the cuckoo, Dickinson suggests that allegiance is always environmental, but that the experience of environments is a worldwide phenomenon. Instead of gesturing to the environment as the site of indigenous poetic production and authenticity (that she would "swear" by), Dickinson sees the environment as *Umwelt*, as produced by the broader global context in which *Umwelt* also functions as world.

Dickinson drives the point home by linking the cuckoo to the "ode familiar." "Familiar" is a pun here, connecting biopoetics with biological family of origin yet using the cuckoo, who is remote from his own family and destructive of other families, to indicate that it is his poetry – his "ode" – that produces the "familiar" which is a point of arrival not a place of origin. The ode's "familiarity" arises from a cross-species encounter between the cuckoo's singing and the speaker's listening. The transformation of that singing into an "ode" can occur only in that cross-species environmental encounter. That encounter – or "circulation of mutuality," as Dickinson called it in her early letter – has two effects: first, the construction of subjectivity which itself is no longer discernibly human but has become posthuman; and second, the acknowledgment that subjectivity emerges in environmental contexts, where the *Umwelt* that is the environment itself produces a sense of itself as the *Welt* or world.

The notion that subjectivity does not just stem broadly from the environment but from a selective relationship to that environment is crucial to Uexküll's work. In theorizing this kind of subjective environmental perspective, Uexküll draws on the example of a meadow to explain what he calls the perception world, defined by "all the features accessible to the subject," which are not the same as all accessible features per se but reflect the particularities by which subjects perceive their environments: for each subject, "many qualities of the colorful meadow vanish completely, others lose their coherence with another, and new connections are created. A new world arises in each bubble."[21] By drawing our attention to the way in which perception selects from a broader spectrum of possibilities, Dickinson makes it possible for being "poor in world" to function as a kind of "world-forming."

"As a bird her nest": Posthuman Sisters

We see Dickinson play with these selective subject-forming processes in one of her earliest extant poems, "One Sister have I in the house," where she conceptualizes home as selective world-building:

> [. . .] One came the road that I came –
> And wore my last year's gown –
> The other, as a bird her nest
> Builded our hearts among.
>
> She did not sing as we did –
> It was a different tune –
> Herself to her a music
> As Bumble bee of June [. . .]   (F5)

Modulating between the house and the hedge in the second stanza, Dickinson describes Sue's arrival in ways that foreground many of the environmental relations we have seen: "The other, as a bird her nest / Builded our hearts among." Arguing that she sang a "different tune" and likening her to a "Bumble bee of June," Dickinson imagines traversing "the hills" with Sue, whose "hum ... deceives the Butterfly." Sue's ability not only to traverse nature but to mimic it to a point of deception indicates that the poem's guiding image not only makes animate nature a metaphor for Sue but vice versa, that Sue is a metaphor for animate nature (much like Carlo and/as the greatest work of art). While readings of the poem tend to emphasize the "thrill of sympathy" that marks Dickinson's early relationship with Sue, the poem also stages for us Dickinson's insight into a "circulation of mutuality" that is environmentally situated and constitutive of the subjectivities that enter into the encounter. In the act of reorienting her "childhood" at the far reaches of geographical "miles," Dickinson ends on a note of worlding that expands from the surrounding house and hedge to a world beyond the hills and years to the "dew" and morn of a "single star" chosen from "out the wide night's numbers." On the one hand, the poem engages in an act of home- and world-building that maps Sue as well as the poem's speaker onto a cosmic scale. On the other hand, the engagement with the larger world for Dickinson becomes an act of singular selection: "I chose this single star // From out the wide night's numbers." This selection reflects a crucial act of environmental subject formation: it demonstrates how making poor in world and making rich in world go hand in hand.

If world-making defines Heidegger's notion of human subjectivity, then this reorientation toward making poor in world brings us back to the possibility I raised early in this essay, namely that we need to evaluate Dickinson's poetry for its experimentations with posthuman subjectivity. "One Sister" seems an unlikely place to locate such posthumanism, in that the poem is usually read as highlighting the intimacy between the speaker and "Sue." However, the poem sustains a posthumanist reading when it insistently intertwines human and nonhuman beings in a vast tangle of relationships: the alliterative bird, bumble bee, and butterfly as well as the house, hedge, hearts, and hills verbally highlight being and (or we may say, being in) *Umwelt*. Moreover, we do not have to rely on later theorizations of *Umwelt* but can establish these posthuman dimensions via widely disseminated environmental writing contemporary with Dickinson. Her 1858 poem might very well have been reworking discussions of nonhuman subjectivity circulated in the popular press and brought to their fullest fruition some years later in Charles Darwin's *The Expression of the Emotions in Man and Animals* (1872). In 1856, *Putnam's Monthly Magazine of American Literature, Science, and Art* published an article on the question "Have Animals Souls?" Starting from the religious claim that the second covenant binds animals and men to "our Maker," the article laments the insufficiency of vocabulary for naming animals and discusses the difficulties of distinguishing among rocks and plants and animals.[22]

Although the article insists that men and animals differ, it assesses "man" as a "macrocosm, uniting in himself all the various bodily and psychical parts of animals, and superadding to them qualities peculiarly his own."[23] This idea of man as a macrocosm relies on cross-species aggregation, of "uniting" different species' bodily and psychological parts and making man a hybrid – the kind we might get when Dickinson's speaker decides she will "just wear [her] Wings" in "Some keep the Sabbath." The article imagines that hybridity as both physical and environmental in thinking about the body within – and the body itself as – an environment, or macrocosm. That environment takes on the function of creating a home in the world, along the lines of Dickinson imagining that "One Sister" can build a home in both the hearts and the stars. The article's writer points out that "Animals discern their domiciles, even with the lowest capacities," asking in the case of the tortoise whether "home-sickness carried the slow, heartless creature four thousand miles back through 'the ocean, where there is no track and no high-road?' It must be more than a mere dull submission to habit, that attaches even animals to their childhood's home."[24] In a radical reinvention of domesticity, the article departs from the gendering of a private domestic sphere and instead envisions the home as a form of creaturely cognition. Qualifying this capacity to "choose their dwellings," the article argues that "to distinguish food, home, and enemies are lowest gifts; but to distinguish, in love or in hatred, others of the same kind as such, shows already a certain self-consciousness – an individual existence."[25] Individual existence is relational – that is, it manifests in domestic and (cross-) species discernment. "One Sister have I in the house" serves as an exegesis of these propositions, for it envisions a reconstruction of home via a process of affective selection that defines the subject in natural contexts without essentializing either one.

Life, the Great Equalizer

The radical equality among living creatures that this statement implies is one that Dickinson explores repeatedly. Uexküll insists that "[a]ll animal subjects, from the simplest to the most complex, are inserted into their environments to the same degree of perfection"[26] – or, as Dickinson succinctly claims, "the Gnat's supremacy is large as Thine." The poem bearing this aphoristic line inquires into the parameters and meanings of such equivalence:

> A Toad, can die of Light –
> Death is the Common Right
> Of Toads and Men –
> Of Earl and Midge
> The privilege –
> Why swagger, then?
> The Gnat's supremacy is large as Thine –   (F419)

The poem's first stanza picks up on the commonplace that death is the great equalizer. It imagines that the commonly shared fact of death applies to "Toads and Men" alike, and it crosses hierarchies to a point of emptying out the very notion of "privilege." The logic to her claim is that death equalizes subjectivity. But the more pressing question then becomes whether that kind of radical egalitarianism can apply in life. In the second stanza, she addresses that question: "Life – is a different Thing –." There are two ways of reading her response. One is to see her claim that life is different as indicating that the differences erased by death still pertain in life. However, the image of wine that follows this claim (So measure Wine – / Naked of Flask – Naked of Cask – / Bare Rhine –)" and the stanza's concluding question ("Which Ruby's mine?") align the second stanza with the first in establishing life as a posthuman relationship to *Umwelt*. Using wine as a metaphor and attempting to "measure" life, Dickinson upends the notion that life is measurable. The speaker strips wine (literally making it "Naked" and "Bare") of its measures (that is, its "Flask" or "Cask"). The "Measure" for Wine then becomes "Bare Rhine." This phrase creates a pun in that "Rhine" is another word for "Wine." By that logic, life becomes its own measure. But the phrase "Rhine" also reinstates the process by which Life becomes differentiated or, in the poet's lines, "a different Thing." "Rhine" functions as a synonym for "Wine" because the region along the river Rhine in Germany produces some of the best vintages. "Rhine" is then not just a synonym for wine but also refers to the environment in which wine comes into being. "Rhine" is also the *Umwelt* that forms the wine – which is, in Dickinson's stanza, life, to which it becomes analogous. The concluding question, "Which Ruby's mine?" becomes absurd: it is impossible to ascribe greater value – a "Ruby" – to any part of the "Rhine." Life is as great an equalizer as death.

But what then happens to a sense of life as individuated – as "mine"? The short answer is that Dickinson makes biopoetics' environmental relations the condition for articulating a sense of posthuman subjectivity. As Sarah Blackwood has argued, Dickinson became invested in "the ramifications of self-disidentity" and "explored the possibility that a dialectical relationship exists between the self and the world."[27] That sense of dialectical relationship between self and world emerges in the more immersive form of biopoetics in Dickinson's famous first letter to Higginson: "Are you too deeply occupied to say if my Verse is alive? The Mind is so near itself – it cannot see, distinctly – and I have none to ask – Should you think it breathed – and had you the leisure to tell me, I should feel quick gratitude" (L260). Dickinson imagines an immersion that goes "too deeply" – but attaches that to herself. Arguing that the "mind is so near itself," she indicates that she is immersed in an environment. That environment dissolves and constitutes the self, at once objectifying the "mind ... itself" yet positing an "I." The paradox of an environmental immersion that veers toward solipsism becomes the middle ground between object and subject worlds: she wants to know if her verse "breathed" but then ties the animation (and animality) of breath back to herself, echoing the language of birth's quickening by saying "I should feel *quick* gratitude" (emphasis added). The quickening is animate and environmental, premised on Higginson taking the slow-time (leisure) of nature to "tell" her that her verse "breathed."[28] It is in that image that Dickinson invents her poetry itself as an environment, a subject-forming world that finds expression in and beyond human language in biopoetics.

Although Higginson was not always her most astute reader, in his later writing about their relationship, he insightfully picks up on Dickinson's posthuman framing of her poetry when he describes her handwriting as "so peculiar that it seemed as if the writer might have taken her first lessons by studying the famous fossil bird-tracks in the museum of that college town," Amherst.[29] Dismissive as this observation may seem at first glance, his comment gestures toward his recognition of her biopoetics and marks her influence on him. Higginson himself had published observations on the "Life of Birds" in 1862 and had seen the fossilized bird-tracks in Amherst during his visit to Dickinson in 1870. Enthusiastically praising the fossils, he wrote to his wife in a letter dated August 17, 1870, that "the collection of bird tracks of extinct birds in stone is very wonderful & unique & other good things" (L342b). The image of a fossilized bird-track is both animal and environmental. It connects the human viewer to animals that produce material traces. Analogizing Dickinson's writing, then, to the "famous fossil bird-tracks in the museum" amounts to a compliment and an interpretation of Dickinson's work. She is able to create a similar cross-species encounter by producing material tracks that function as a biopoetics in that they become interpretable across species lines and generate their own environments of signification. Whereas we might differentiate dog from doggerel, Dickinson is able to sustain both in her poems; in the process of making meaning out of seeming antitheses, she is able to bring the material and figurative in connection with one another and to reshape poetic subjectivity in the process.

Higginson gives fullest expression to this interpretation when he describes his first encounter with Dickinson: "[A]n instinct told me that the slightest attempt at direct cross-examination would make her withdraw into her shell; I could only sit still and watch, as one does in the woods;

I must name my bird without a gun, as recommended by Emerson."[30] Higginson falls back on "instinct" in encountering Dickinson and abandons the mode of verbal interrogation for one of observation. He imagines Dickinson as a creature who has two environments, that of the world she encounters and that of "her shell" – that is, a protective environment within the larger ecology. Like her two sisters, Dickinson inhabits the world of the house and the world of the hedge. It is this environment that Higginson himself inhabits, taking the position of sitting "still" and watching, "as one does in the woods." While we have often been suspicious of Higginson's depictions of Dickinson, we might instead see that he pays tribute to the entanglements of species and world-making that Dickinson produces in her work.

Conclusion

If Uexküll was the "forerunner of biosemiotics," then Dickinson might be a forerunner of this forerunner.[31] Reading her as a practitioner and theorist of biosemiotics shapes our understanding of Dickinson as a poet whose selective environment in Amherst was not simply a given but was a deliberate and radical act of interpretation. Her poetry repeatedly *creates* this selective environment and casts it as an impoverishment of world that opens up expansive subjectivities that stretch beyond the human. This posthumanism places her in dialogue with some of the preeminent theorists of environmental subjectivity. Dickinson already anticipates such dialogue in her seemingly reclusive work; after all, the "Soul *selects* her own Society" before she shuts the door (F409, emphasis added), and perhaps it is even fair to say that selecting her own society enables the subjectivity implied by "Soul" to take shape in the first place. Taking the "thrill of sympathy" to its far reaches, where subjectivities become environmental, Dickinson's poems nevertheless make positions of posthuman subjectivity legible by their own biopoetics. Engaging in the "circulation of mutuality," these works open up senses of being to the sensory environment and make being poor in world a form of intensified subjectivity. Whether it is Carlo's literal bite within the metaphors of a Valentine, the Sabbath that she attends wearing her wings, Sue being like a "bird" in her domestic estrangements, or the gnat and toad being equal to Earl and Midge, Dickinson engages with the environment as a source of perspectival subject-making that pushes beyond the limitations of the merely human and opens up a realm of posthuman poesis. In the end, the Robin may very well be a criterion for tune, but we might as well swear on the cuckoo.

Notes

1. See page 3 of this volume.
2. See for instance Jacques Derrida, "The Animal That Therefore I am (More to Follow)," *Critical Inquiry* 28.2 (2002): 369–418.
3. For a thorough exploration of Dickinson and philosophy, see the essays in *Emily Dickinson and Philosophy*, Jed Deppman, Marianne Noble, and Gary Lee Stonum (eds.) (Cambridge: Cambridge University Press, 2013), and particularly Deppman's essay on "Being" in Dickinson and Heidegger, "Astonished Thinking: Dickinson and Heidegger," 227–249.
4. For a fuller discussion of Dickinson's poetic engagement with Carlo, see Colleen Glenney Boggs, *Animalia Americana: Animal Representations and Biopolitical Subjectivity* (New York: Columbia University Press), 143–155. On Dickinson's engagement with animals and anthropomorphism, see Aaron Shackelford, "Dickinson's Animals and Anthropomorphism," *EDJ* 19.2 (2010): 47–66.
5. N. Katherine Hayles, *How We Became Posthuman: Virtual Bodies in Cybernetics, Literature, and Informatics* (Chicago and London: University of Chicago Press, 1999). See also Neil Badmington, *Posthumanism* (New York: Palgrave, 2000); "Theorizing Posthumanism," *Cultural Critique* 53 (2003): 10–27.
6. Cary Wolfe, *What Is Posthumanism?* (Minneapolis and London: University of Minnesota Press, 2010), 127.
7. Donna Haraway, "Encounters with Companion Species: Entangling Dogs, Baboons, Philosophers and Biologists," *Configurations* 14 (2006): 99, 105. For her work on posthumanism in relation to technology, see "A Manifesto for Cyborgs: Science, Technology and Socialist Feminism in the 1980s," in *Identities: Race, Class, Gender, and Nationality*, Linda Martin Alcoff and Eduardo Mendieta (eds.) (Oxford: Blackwell Publishing, 2003), 369–391.
8. Theo Davis, *Ornamental Aesthetics: The Poetry of Attending in Thoreau, Dickinson, and Whitman* (New York: Oxford University Press, 2016), 1.
9. Ibid., 3.
10. Martin Heidegger, "The Animal Is Poor in World," in *Animal Philosophy: Essential Readings in Continental Thought*, Matthew Calarco and Peter Atterton (eds.) (London and New York: Continuum, 2004), 17.
11. Ibid.
12. Sandra M. Gilbert and Susan Gubar, *The Madwoman in the Attic: The Woman Writer and the Nineteenth-Century Literary Imagination* (Boston: Yale University Press, 1979), 591; Wendy Martin, *An American*

Triptych: Anne Bradstreet, Emily Dickinson, Adrienne Rich (Chapel Hill: UNC Press Books, 1984), 80.
13. Joseph D. O'Neil, "Translator's Introduction," in *Jakob Von Uexküll, a Foray into the Worlds of Animals and Humans, with a Theory of Meaning* (Minneapolis and London: University of Minnesota Press, 2010), 35.
14. Ibid.
15. Dorion Sagan, "Introduction," ibid., 2.
16. Ibid., 6.
17. For such a transatlantic reading that is attentive to environment, see Paul Gilroy, *Antipodean America: Australasia and the Constitution of U.S. Literature* (Oxford: Oxford University Press, 2014), esp. 196–200.
18. See Juliana Chow, "'Because I see – New Englandly –': Seeing Species in the Nineteenth-Century and Emily Dickinson's Regional Specificity," *ESQ: A Journal of the American Renaissance* 60.3 (2014): 413–449.
19. In one of her earliest poems (1854), Dickinson portrays the Robin's migration and the transience of his tune: "I have a Bird in spring / Which for myself doth sing. – / The spring decoys. / And as the summer nears – / And as the Rose appears, / Robin is gone" (F4). In fact, the Robin goes elsewhere to learn tunes to introduce to the poet: "Yet do I not repine / Knowing that Bird of mine / Though flown – / Learneth beyond the sea / Melody new for me / And will return."
20. Christine Gerhardt has described this view as "bioregional" (a term coined by Peter Berg and Raymond F. Dasmann to argue for a relation between geographical terrain and terrain of consciousness); see Christine Gerhardt, "'Often Seen – but Seldom Felt': Emily Dickinson's Reluctant Ecology of Place," *EDJ* 15.2 (2006): 69. For her more recent assessment of Dickinson and environment, see the article that appeared as part of a special issue on "Dickinson's Environments": Christine Gerhardt, "Emily Dickinson Now: Environments, Ecologies, Politics: Commentary," *ESQ: A Journal of Nineteenth-Century American Literature and Culture* 63.2 (2017): 329–355.
21. Jakob von Uexküll, *A Foray into the Worlds of Animals and Humans, with a Theory of Meaning* (Minneapolis and London: University of Minnesota Press, 2010), 43.
22. "Have Animals Souls?," *Putnam's Monthly Magazine of American Literature, Science, and Art*, April 1856, 361–362.
23. Ibid., 363.
24. Ibid., 366.
25. Ibid., 366–367.
26. Uexküll, *A Foray into the Worlds of Animals and Humans, with a Theory of Meaning*, 50.
27. Sarah Blackwood, "'The Inner Brand': Emily Dickinson, Portraiture, and the Narrative of Liberal Interiority," *EDJ* 14.2 (2005): 55, 56.

28. Midori Asahina reads the relationship between Dickinson and Higginson in regard to their roles as naturalists; see Midori Asahina, "'Fascination' Is Absolute of Clime': Reading Emily Dickinson's Correspondence with Higginson as Naturalist," *EDJ* 14.2 (2005): 103–119. For Dickinson's interest in science, see Nina Baym, *American Women of Letters* (New Brunswick, NJ: Rutgers University Press, 2002), especially 133–151.
29. Thomas Wentworth Higginson, "Emily Dickinson's Letters," *Atlantic Monthly*, October 1891, 444.
30. Ibid., 453.
31. Sagan, "Introduction," 4.

CHAPTER 8

Dickinson and Historical Ecopoetics

Gillian Kidd Osborne

In some ways, a historical ecopoetics of Dickinson has already been accomplished. Christine Gerhardt has shown Dickinson's work to be "proto-ecological," a reflection of the incipient environmental movements of the mid to late nineteenth century.[1] Other critics have found in Dickinson's work effects of the nineteenth century's great theory of nature, Darwin's natural selection, and a bleaker imagination of nature than Romanticism's most important poet of nature, Wordsworth.[2] Such readings extend decades of historical and cultural criticism of the poet by situating Dickinson within the history of science and within environmental literary history.[3] Another feature of a historical environmental reassessment of Dickinson has been the extension of critical exploration of Dickinson's manuscripts into a broader understanding of Dickinson's investment in materials and materiality. Dickinson cared not only about paper but also for the once-living plants, animals, and insects she documents materially (those floral posies she sent with letter-poems) and descriptively (all those robins, flitting in and out of poems).[4]

Environmental readings of Dickinson have also found evidence of a particularly subtle environmental intelligence in the complexities of this poet's formal practices. Juliana Chow, Scott Knickerbocker, and others have joined Gerhardt in showing how Dickinson's rigorous aesthetics resist the flat celebrations of what Timothy Morton has critiqued as "eco-mimesis," the dream of directly translating nature into language.[5] Chow qualifies Dickinson's attention to the natural world as "poetic-empiric," a mode of acknowledgment that is about being with rather than cataloguing or governing, while Knickerbocker similarly sees in the artifice of her verse a resistance to exerting control over a wilderness Dickinson honored even in her own backyard.[6] These scholars effectively reactivate what has otherwise become an outlying formalism in Dickinson criticism to assess the ways Dickinson complicates description of the natural world, turning her poems into ethical meditations on the difficulty of coming to see or know nonhuman others at all. Theo Davis's recent theorization of the instability of "attention" in Dickinson's poetics, though it does not align itself specifically with an ecocritical frame, sheds particular light on this Dickinson, whose poems are characterized fundamentally by the powerful epistemological experiences they produce.[7]

In this essay, I build on these studies, but my aim is more "slant" (F1263). Moving beyond the extension of history from the cultural to the ecological, human to nonhuman, I suggest that the most saliently environmental features of Dickinson's poetics come into focus when we approach her poetry not as documentation of the past or of materials but as transitive, relational, a kind of dial that quivers and diverges in response to the basic motility of time. More directly, this is an argument that what makes Dickinson's poems, or any poem, meaningfully environmental has almost nothing to do with poetic content – what is in a poem – but with poetic context – how we receive it. By combining historical poetics and ecopoetics, I draw together two very different understandings of the proper interpretive context of a poem before offering a third alternative: a reading practice that is interpenetrated and interrupted, neither here nor there, now nor then.

First, I explain the structural commonalities and divergences among historical poetics, ecopoetics, and my method of combining the two. Then, I demonstrate some features of this method through a reading of several Dickinson poems, ones in which a bobolink, a "Bird of Birds," appears and disappears.

Historical poetics and ecopoetics have very different understandings of what comprises the relevant interpretive context of a poem. In brief, historical poetics focuses on the compositional context of a poem – where, when, and how it was made – while ecopoetics has been mainly concerned with the reception of poems – what a poem can do in response to evolving conditions of environmental degradation. Historical poetics has been particularly important for nineteenth-century American literary studies in resurrecting knowledge of the centrality of poetry as a cultural form in nineteenth-century life and revealing the diversity of poetry's generic forms prior to Modernism, New Criticism, and the entrenchment of the lyric.[8] Although ecopoetics has proved a useful hermeneutic for some critics in their reappraisal of poetic traditions from Romanticism through contemporary experimentalism, it has been more widely embraced by poets to justify poetic practice as a critical, and ethical, activity in itself.[9]

Despite these differences, however, both historical poetics and ecopoetics respond to critical practices from New Criticism to Structuralism to

New Formalism that elide context in order to grant meaningful agency to the internal workings of a poem. Historical poetics represents New Historicism finally catching up with poems after decades of scholarship on prose, while ecopoetics has been a relatively underexplored "tributary of ecocriticism," a rivulet the river has mainly ignored.[10] While New Historicism and ecocriticism arose in response to a period of high theory that some critics understood as placing too much emphasis on texts, these two approaches turned to different contexts in compensation: the human and the nonhuman. Historical poetics extends the project of New Historicism with readings of underrepresented populations of poets while expanding historical cultural knowledge of a particular historical period and place, mainly at the national level. Meanwhile, despite its relative marginality, ecopoetics has similarly shared many of the same concerns of ecocritical readings of prose: a critique of anthropocentrism, the cultivation of an ethical stance to the Earth, and an evaluation of literary works in terms of what forms of attention, imagination, or activism they might elicit.

For the purposes of this essay, what interests me most in both historical poetics and ecopoetics is their mutual emphasis on context, on approaching poetry from the outside in. Both ground what really matters about a poem somewhere outside the poem itself. In historical poetics, this produces a crisis of reading, in which, as Michael Cohen wittily examines, objects of inquiry can seem to recede beyond a critic's faculties of basic reception: the nineteenth-century archive is filled with poems, so why is it so hard to actually read them? In contrast, ecopoetics grapples with a crisis of relevance: how can a cultural form as relatively impotent in the present as poetry stand up to species loss, motivate for environmental justice, or make cities greener? Cohen considers why it is so hard to read nineteenth-century poems, while John Felstiner earnestly wonders in the title of a volume that returns to this question throughout: *Can Poetry Save the Earth?*[11]

The relation of humans as writers and readers to human history and to the Earth's history is quite different, however. We see this in the fact that most environmental histories follow a narrative of declension, while human histories are more easily spun as progressive.[12] The relation between scale and narrative structure is key. Historical criticism remains defined by times and places that only make sense in relation to human life-scales: the nation, the century. When we read a poem in relation to its historical and cultural context, we learn something about the poem and about the human society that produced it. Meanwhile, despite calls for a planetary intelligence or imaginations of deep history or deep future as part of ecological thinking, the central feature of this scale of environmental thinking is that it supercedes the human: environmental thought at the scale of the planet or a millennia can only be thought relationally, as an abstraction in relation to the present and its materials.[13] This means that when we read environmentally, we're confronted by multiple levels of illegibility: how little we likely know of an environmental context other than our own, or, additionally, how little we know of the environmental context in which we currently live, read, and write. Even within a relatively limited scope – a state, say, or a bioregion – we're confronted by how unstable even the most proximate of environmental contexts is.

If we investigate Massachusetts further, for example, with the help of science and environmental history – reviewing lists of plants and animals, geological maps, weather diaries – as the particulars of a time and place come into focus we are confronted by both loss and recovery. These spring flowers are no longer there, yet the white-tailed deer, almost regionally extinct in the 1840s, is now pervasive, almost invasive, shitting on fields, responsible for some of those missing wildflowers.[14]

One of the ways of combining historical poetics and ecopoetics is by shifting focus from the nation, or the planet, to the bioregion: a non-human specification of space that nevertheless has relevance to human scales of life and cultural production. This would entail reading Dickinson not in relation to other nineteenth-century American poets appearing in print culture or circulating in manuscript among neighbors and friends but rather in relation to those writing under the duress of mid-winter at this particular latitude or in proximity to the Connecticut River and its floodplain and in view of Amherst's low-lying hills. Although, this need not mean only reading poems emerging from Amherst and its environs or its winters. Comparatively, we could read river-system poems springing up around the Connecticut in relation to the poems of other river systems: the rich aesthetic traditions surrounding China's Three Gorges, for instance (and trans-temporally, through the construction of dams that have affected both bioregions and the human cultures each sustains).[15]

Reading Dickinson in this vein offers a new account of her relation to the Deerfield poet Frederick Goddard Tuckerman. Tuckerman published a single book of poems in 1860, but he continued to compose poetry until his death in 1873. Though Tuckerman has been more or less forgotten, his late work, the sonnets, and his long poem "The Cricket" have at different times attracted some critical attention.[16] Some of that appraisal has already linked him to Dickinson. Most notably, Yvor Winters saw in Dickinson and Tuckerman's treatment of natural particulars a kind of

American Symbolism, a demonstration of "sensory perception" so "acute" that it becomes unstable, raising imagery into "the force of abstract statement."[17] In a bioregional reading, however, Tuckerman and Dickinson are connected to each other not through style or the content of their descriptions but by their mutual attention to the place where they lived and wrote. Dickinson and Tuckerman likely never read one another's poems and never met, though biography obliquely binds them. Tuckerman's brother, the Amherst professor and lichenologist Edward Tuckerman, was an acquaintance of the Dickinson family, particularly of Austin and Sue next door; Dickinson sent several letters to Edward Tuckerman's wife, Sarah, and even one to the wife of Frederick Goddard Tuckerman's son, Frederick, who came to stay with his Amherst relatives after his father's death.[18] These lines of indirection – biography told "slant" – are instructive when we expand from the human sphere to the biological and geological conditions surrounding these two poets.

When Thomas Wentworth Higginson visited Amherst, he described the "Hills everywhere, hardly mountains," that form a bedrock for both Dickinson and Tuckerman's poems (L342a). Hills are one of Dickinson's many keywords – at once a limit to her visible world and a horizon to something grander, the undulating lip along which Amherst could become "Eden" (or Eden, Amherst) (L354). Think of the many Dickinson poems in which these geological foundations become the basic ground on which all other relations, human and nonhuman, build: in "Alter! When the Hills do –," for example, a lover stakes her commitment on the endurance of these not quite mountains (F755). In the vicinity of Amherst, and viewed from the span of a human life, hills are the constant to an otherwise perennial flux. As such, Dickinson's hills help us to see nature as a whole as unfixed, evolving. In another poem, Dickinson unravels a vision of "Nature" by flitting through a catalogue that begins with what seems most stable, "The Hill," before catapulting, noun to noun, dash to dash, into the more evanescent – "Squirrel – Eclipse" – and culminating with another of Dickinson's keywords, the ever-fleeing "Bumble bee" (F721). Indeed, the hills, in their deep geologic endurance, have an inhuman perspective that negates human capacities for sight and intelligence on a shorter scale: "The Hills erect their Purple Heads / The Rivers lean to see / Yet man has not of all the Throng / A Curiosity" (F1728). Hills, and particularly the vantage over landscape they provide, the expansion of an otherwise geographically and historically limited human view, are so central to Tuckerman's poetry that one of the domed peaks over Deerfield has been named for him: "The Poet's Seat." In both Dickinson's and Tuckerman's poetry, the

Dickinson and Historical Ecopoetics 141

underlying fact of hills and rivers stands adjacent to the agitations of the seasons, plants and animals, human hearts. In "The Stranger," Tuckerman names the place where he writes ("westland Massachusetts") "a natural water-shed." And in "Sidney," the low "mountains and the summer sky" above and the "Dark-channelled Deerfield" River below define the boundaries of a world composed of "accidents and adjuncts," of relations between and among the geological, the biological, and the biographical – between the outsides and insides of poems.[19]

The accidents and adjuncts of bioregional life inform my understanding of what a historical ecopoetics might accomplish as well. While comparative readings of Tuckerman's and Dickinson's hill poems are one way to expand these indirect connections between the environmental conditions outside of poems, and the lives that play out inside of writing and reading, I want to turn from such comparisons to emphasize how much these two poets understand writing and reading as permeable, open to externals. For Dickinson, we need look no further than "I dwell in Possibility," her iconic ars poetica with its chambered stanzas "numerous of Windows," "Cedars," and "Sky" (F466). While Dickinson's poem creates a vision of writing as visited by, available to, what lives outside of language, one of Tuckerman's sonnets gives a complementary account of reading as interrupted by light and birds. This sonnet is from Tuckerman's third sequence and begins with his poetic speaker in a customary state of being neither here nor there:

> Once on a day, alone but not elate,
> I sat perusing a forgotten sage
> And turning hopelessly a dim old page
> Of history, long disused and out of date,
> Reading "his Method" till I lost my own.
> When suddenly there fell a gold presage
> Of sunset sunshine on the letters thrown.
> The day had been one cloud, but now a bird
> Shot into song. I left my hermitage
> With happy heart; but ere I reached the gate
> The sun was gone, the bird, and bleak and drear,
> All but an icy breath the balsams stirred:
> I turned again and, entering with a groan,
> Sat darkly down to Dagoraus Whear.[20]

Tuckerman's poem meditates on what it means to read history in relation to present context. As the poem begins, time and experience are contained, a single occasion, "Once" and "on a day." But this containment is dissolved by the absorption of reading: "Reading 'his Method' till I lost my own." The book that this reader sinks into here is Degory Wheare's *Of the Reason and Method of Reading Histories*, but we don't know that yet; rather, we learn that, though the historian is forgotten, his work has a presence so consuming in the present that it can lose a reader. In the next four lines, the speaker begins to give us a sense of the "Method" that Wheare's has temporarily replaced, as his experience of the text is interrupted by light and music. Although Tuckerman sets up seeming contrasts between before and after – dark and light, dullness and song – he actually muddles these conditions. The "sunlight" that falls on his book is from a "sunset"; a cloud is transposed not into light but into "a bird" and "song." And before the reader can access the world that interrupted his reading, another shift occurs, turning around a bird: "but ere I reached the gate / The sun was gone, the bird, and bleak and drear, / All but an icy breath the balsams stirred." The first half of this sentence describes what isn't there; the second, what is. The bird could be either here or gone. The speaker only has access to the bird's song while reading, as much as he longs for a more immediate connection. At the end of the poem, it's back to the book, in hopes of further interruption.

Tuckerman's poem accurately describes reading as itself environmental, imbricated in the context and conditions of reception, and suggests the transhistorical nature of how we experience literary history. In this regard, Tuckerman's poem usefully enacts what I understand to be a method of historical ecopoetics, a practice of reading that is also, in terms described by Rita Felski, "postcritical," attuned to the "transtemporal liveliness of texts."[21] To see how such a reading practice affects how we understand what makes a poem environmental in particular, let's consider a particular type of bird in particular poems by Dickinson.

A historical ecopoetics of Dickinson can begin by expanding the context of her poems from the historical and cultural to a nature–culture matrix that includes the effects humans have on environments. Dickinson's most productive period as a poet, for example, fell within the decade of peak deforestation in Massachusetts.[22] In the 1860s, after a century of steady clearing to make way for agriculture and pasturage, forests in the state had shrunk to around 30 percent of their previous size. By the final decades of Dickinson's writing life, however, that trend had already begun to reverse, as farmers abandoned their fields for more productive land in the Midwest. Massachusetts's forests began to remake themselves, first in stands of white pine, then in harder wood. Today, the state is among the most forested in the country, and the many stone walls ambling through its woodlands remain as visible signs that what is now damp and shaded, leaf-littered, was once a field. Some of the plant and animal species that Dickinson writes of have been affected by this environmental history. Bobolinks, meadow-dwellers, who appear in several of Dickinson's poems, were more common in the mid-nineteenth century than they are today, despite recent efforts at habitat management. There are simply fewer fence posts for them and fewer grasses in which to nest.[23]

It is possible to trace some of this transformation from open land to forest, and its effect on meadow birds, in the way Dickinson writes of bobolinks from the 1860s onward. In earlier poems like "No Bobolink – reverse His Singing" (F766) and "Some – keep the Sabbath – going to church" (F236B), Dickinson is a "regenerate lyricist" at her most exuberant, worshiping with "a Bobolink – for a Chorister" and an agrarian "Orchard – for a dome," modeling her music on the common transport of the "Brave Bobolink['s]" song.[24] In the first of these, the bobolink's singing is an "Anodyne" to transformations of the landscape, particularly the removal of "the only Tree / Ever He minded occupying." In these early poems, context – the environmental context of deforestation and the cultural-historical context of evangelical Christianity – turn the poem inward, toward itself. Each is a meditation, mediated by a bobolink, on "Singing" as an experience that redefines and remakes context: poetry as a context of its own.

By the 1870s and 1880s, the context outside of poems had changed, as some of the open spaces preferred by bobolinks began to cede to saplings. In poems of those decades, such as "The Way to know the Bobolink" (F1348) and "The Bobolink is gone" (F1620), these birds have become less common, more difficult to see, to know, or to mimic musically. In the two poems from the 1860s, poetry compensates for an absence exterior to the poem: the speaker stays home from church in order to worship otherwise, while the bobolink replaces his missing tree – his "Best Horizon – gone" – with song. But in these later poems, Dickinson shifts absence from context to the poems' central figure: now, it is not trees that are missing but "The Bird of Birds" who "is gone."

A historical ecopoetics of Dickinson can start here – with an expansion of human historical context to a bioregional context, one in which poetry registers ecological transformation, catastrophic or ameliorative, the destruction or preservation of habitat, the presence or absence of particular species within a particular bioregional space, in or across time. Ecopoetics has been formatively shaped by similar readings. In *The Song of the Earth*, for instance, Jonathan Bate reads Byron's "Darkness" and Keats's "Ode to

Autumn" as poems whose bleak anxieties and autumnal relief reflect the seasonal disorders produced by volcanic explosions in Indonesia and the resulting fluctuations in global temperature and weather.[25] But Dickinson's poems also direct us away from such equations between their contexts and their content, not least of all through Dickinson's skepticism about the efficacy of names.

While nature writing is often valued for the accuracy of its attentions – the ability of an author to correctly identify, and thereby bring into view, a rare animal or a plant in all its minute particularity – Dickinson noticeably resists the talismanic mimesis so often attributed to scientific names. She playfully tropes such resistance in poems like "'Arcturus' is his other name / I'd rather call him Star," in which the speaker pulls "a flower from the woods" only to have "A monster with a glass" calculate "stamens" and contain the flower neatly "in a 'Class'!" (F117). For Dickinson, a name does not deliver a thing. And a poem, especially, provides only an experience of coming to know. This is one of the reasons – the other being that her culture approved of such practices – why Dickinson sent flowers so often along with poems in letters. These floral-literary bundles are performances that poems transmit: partial transmissions, a clamor after correspondence. The poems are not the posies. They are what happens between flower and word. This is also why even though, as an adolescent student of botany and later a skilled gardener, Dickinson was familiar with many species of plants, she almost exclusively names only the most common, or "poetical," of flowers in her poems: rose, lily, clover, daisy.[26] Even the most seemingly easy to identify flower should, if approached through poetry, become exotic.

Dickinson's approach to naming plants differs markedly from Tuckerman's, and the difference between them can help us to think about how poems engage with environmental context more generally. Readers have long interpreted Tuckerman's and Dickinson's transcriptions of the same region differently. Tuckerman has been praised as a poet who, as various critics have put it, attends to the "minute and faithful and tender rendering" of "natural detail."[27] This appreciation of Tuckerman's care for the particular begins with Emerson, to whom Tuckerman sent a copy of his book *Poems* in 1860. In response, Emerson admired the poet's "love of native flowers, and the skill to name them."[28] Tuckerman's penchant for the particular, Dickinson's preference for the generic: these differences can make Tuckerman seem, as Stephanie Burt has called him, a more convincing poet of "the inhuman biosphere."[29] But Dickinson's attraction to the generic, and her resistance to more particular names, produce a participatory poetics that involves a reader even more directly, valuing the context of reading over the content of a poem.

In contrast to loco-descriptive verse, I call Dickinson's penchant to complicate naming *bio-descriptive*. Whereas loco-description seeks to orient a reader in time and place, Dickinson's bio-descriptive poetry can seem to disorient a reader, riddling. In "Pink – small – and punctual" (F1357), Dickinson withholds the name of the flower she describes in order to foreground physiological characteristics ("Pink," "small," "Aromatic," "low"), seasonal appearance ("Covert in April," "Candid in May"), or habitat (alongside "Moss" or on a "Knoll"). Combining these factual qualities of the plant with the fanciful effects it might produce in an observer – "Next to the Robin / In every human Soul" – Dickinson invites a reader to participate in the process of identification. A bio-descriptive poem engages or activates reading, converting poetic description into poetic experience, bringing a poem about life to life.

This effect depends upon where and when a poem appears. Dickinson sent one copy of "Pink – small – and punctual" to Higginson, signing the poem "Arbutus." In this version, the poem's answer comes at its end, and a reader must still traverse the space of the poem before arriving there. Later, Higginson and Mabel Loomis Todd printed the poem in the second series of Dickinson's verse, under the heading "Poems of Nature," titling it "Mayflower."[30] Giving the poem a title takes away its participatory challenge: you already know what you're looking for before the poem begins. This is an example, then, of how decades of manuscript criticism can help us to understand not only Dickinson's involvement with the materials of composition – paper, envelopes, chocolate wrappers, and string – but also how her poems direct us as readers toward meditation on materials outside paper or poetry. "Pink – small – and punctual" can include us in an early springtime hunt for trailing arbutus, if we follow its bio-descriptive trail.

In another of Dickinson's bio-descriptive poems, "You'll know Her – by Her Foot," this appeal to a reader is formalized through direct address (F604). Across stanzas, a bird begins to appear in all her finery: "Boot," "Vest," "Jacket," "Cap." But these are "Velvet" trimmings and not the thing itself. And "as she closer stands," the poem's, and the reader's, ability to distinguish appearance from being, content from context, breaks down, resulting in a headache that splits one bird in two: "the Robin in your Brain" and "the other."[31] "You'll know Her – by Her Foot" offers a useful comparison to one of Dickinson's later poems in which a bobolink appears: "The Way to know the Bobolink."

While "You'll know Her – by Her Foot" provides another example of Dickinson's skepticism of naming as a means of knowing that we explored earlier, "The Way to know the Bobolink" quickly names the object of its attention before moving on to other complications. Here, what is complicated about the bobolink is not identifying the bird but understanding its experience as relational, comprising both interiority and exteriority, an experience proper to an individual and to the role that individual plays within a broader environmental context. In the first stanza, for example, we come to know the bobolink not as a singular creature but through relation:

> The Way to know the Bobolink
> From every other Bird
> Precisely as the Joy of him –
> Obliged to be inferred.

Not only is the bobolink set in relation to other birds but it is also set in relation to the viewer, or reader, who can only learn of it through "infer-[ence]." This stanza hinges on the imprecision of "precisely." Swinging forward and back, this precision could open onto knowledge (the reader's), "Joy" (a bird's), or the weird action of the reader, an obligation toward inference, which, by stanza's end, stands in for knowledge. In "You'll know Her – by Her Foot," it's a bird you can't know. Here, it's something even more difficult to know than a body: the interiority of another being, an emotion belonging to a bird. In the next two stanzas, Dickinson suggests that this emotion might be intuited through the bird's exterior appearance and behaviors: the bobolink's gaudy black and yellow coloring when mating, his "impudent Habiliment / Attired to defy." Following this quick brush stroke of the bird's appearance, however, we're back to "Sentiments" again: the bobolink is "seditious," an "Apostac[tic]" "Puck."

The poem looks around in search of an appropriate context, a set of conditions through which to understand the bird's behavior: a court of "Majesty," perhaps, or Shakespeare's stage. But the move from description to indirect reporting on behavior suggests that neither content nor context will adequately help us "know" this bird. Rather, this bobolink is "Extrinsic to Attention":

> Extrinsic to Attention
> Too intimate with Joy –
> He compliments Existence
> Until allured away

> By Seasons or his Children –
> Adult and urgent grown –
> Or, unforeseen Aggrandizement
> Or, happily, Renown –
>
> By Contrast certifying
> The Bird of Birds is gone –
> How nullified the Meadow –
> Her Sorcerer withdrawn! (F1348)

We can't know the bobolink both because its interior experience is too wholly its own, "Too intimate" to be "inferred," and because we can't quite imagine the fullness of its environmental context. What lures it out of its self and into singular relation between "Joy" and what Dickinson calls elsewhere the "General Nature" are more particular contexts, necessities of relation[32] – "By Seasons or his Children – / Adult and urgent grown" – or feats of avian achievement a poet can't quite imagine but can nevertheless acknowledge: "Or, unforeseen Aggrandizement / Or, happily, Renown." In the final stanza of this poem, all that's left of the bird is the negative relation between its being and the environmental context it occupied: "How nullified the Meadow – / Her Sorcerer withdrawn!" It's only when the bird disappears that we see the "Meadow" for what it was: a meaningless context but for the lives, relations, it supports, not only its birds but its grasses, its flowers; the seasons that direct it; the rains that water it or sap it dry; its fences; possibly, its readers.

The reforestation of Massachusetts "nullified" many of the pastures that previously made up that state, leaving its stone fences to wind through woods, over a hundred years later, covered in moss. A historical ecopoetics of Dickinson, however, helps us to think not only about these changes in the landscape through time and the ways such changes may or may not be registered in poems. It also reminds us of how poetry is, like a bobolink, like anyone or anything, comprised of relation, how its own nullifications, absences, holes can guide us to read both through and with a text, toward both the time and place in which it appeared and into the time and place where it is received.

Historical poetics often posits history as a counter to abstraction. When claims are made for Poetry with a capital P, "poetry in the general sense," history counters with the specifics of poetry in its time and place – with a genre, or a publication practice, something bounded that can be more tangibly described.[33] Similarly, ecopoetics abjures the abstractions of effusing over the natural world out of deference to who and what is harmed by an ongoing endangerment and destruction: it is not enough to accurately describe "the beautiful bird," as Juliana Spahr puts it; what of "the bulldozer" annihilating "the bird's habitat"?[34] A historical ecopoetics is neither abstract nor about accurate identification of the full complexities of environmental conditions, past or present. It is a practice of reading in relation, here to there, then to now. Dickinson's poems model this dynamic interplay between the particular and the evolving, actively troubling the notion that a poem's purpose is to document any creature or its context, in favor of poetry that responds and relates. A poem may come into being through the poet's prolonged, and formalized, consideration of a bird, a bird that represents both an individual and a species, a past life and a present. As Darwin showed, species exist in relation to time and place; evolution is driven by fluctuations in environment and the response of individuals through time. A poem is similar: it comes into being once; it carries on, through context, cataclysm, or daily life, into a new context. Reading is itself an environmental act, setting the environmental conditions of composition, and the environmental conditions of reception, in relation.

Notes

1. Christine Gerhardt, *A Place for Humility: Whitman, Dickinson, and the Natural World* (Iowa City: University of Iowa Press, 2014), 7; Christine Gerhardt, "'Often Seen – but Seldom Felt': Emily Dickinson's Reluctant Ecology of Place," *EDJ* 15.1 (2006): 57, 59.
2. Joan Kirby, "'[W]e thought Darwin had thrown "the Redeemeer" away': Darwinizing with Emily Dickinson," *EDJ* 19.1 (2010): 18; Li-hsin Hsu, "'The light that never was on sea or land': William Wordsworth in America and Emily Dickinson's 'Frostier Style,'" *EDJ* 25.2 (2016): 34–35.
3. Much of the richest criticism on Dickinson of the past four decades could be footnoted here. The following provides only an overview of the variety of what context might mean in regards to Dickinson's work: Eliza Richards, ed., *Emily Dickinson in Context* (New York: Cambridge University Press, 2013). For more on Dickinson in relation to the nineteenth century, see especially: Barton St. Armand, *Emily Dickinson and Her Culture: The Soul's Society* (New York: Cambridge University Press, 1984); Cristanne Miller, *Reading in Time: Emily Dickinson in the NineteenthCentury* (Amherst: University of Massachusetts Press, 2012).
4. For more on Dickinson and her manuscripts, see especially Sharon Cameron, *Choosing Not Choosing* (Chicago: University of Chicago Press, 1992), and Alexandra Socarides, *Dickinson Unbound: Paper, Process, Poetics* (New York:

Oxford University Press, 2012). On Dickinson and new materialism, see Monique Allewaert, "Toward a Materialist Figuration: A Slight Manifesto," *English Language Notes* 51.2 (Fall/Winter 2013): 61–77.

5. Timothy Morton, *Ecology without Nature: Rethinking Environmental Aesthetics* (Cambridge: Harvard University Press, 2007), passim; Robert Kern addresses poetic alternatives to ecomimesis here: "'Birds of a Feather': Emily Dickinson, Alberto Manguel, and the Nature Poet's Dilemma," *ISLE* 16.2 (March 1, 2009): 327.

6. Juliana Chow, "'Because I see – New Englandly –': Seeing Species in the Nineteenth-Century and Emily Dickinson's Regional Specificity," *ESQ: A Journal of the American Renaissance* 60.3 (2014): 416; Scott Knickerbocker, "Emily Dickinson's Ethical Artifice," *ISLE* 15.2 (July 2008): 185–197.

7. Theo Davis, "Dickinson's Ornamental Form," in *Ornamental Aesthetics: The Poetry of Attending in Thoreau, Dickinson, and Whitman* (New York: Oxford University Press, 2016), 90–140.

8. For an articulation of historical poetics and its stakes, see: Virginia Jackson, *Dickinson's Misery: A Theory of Lyric Reading* (Princeton: Princeton University Press, 2005), especially 31–38; Yopie Prins, "Dysprosody, Historical Poetics, and *The Science of English Verse*," *PMLA* 123.1 (January 2008): 229–233.

9. For an overview of ecopoetics, see especially: Jonathan Bate, *The Song of the Earth* (Cambridge: Harvard University Press, 2000); J. Scott Bryson, ed., *Ecopoetry: A Critical Introduction* (Salt Lake City: University of Utah Press, 2002); Jed Rasula, *This Compost: Ecological Imperatives in American Poetry* (Athens: University of Georgia Press, 2002); Margaret Ronda, "Anthropogenic Poetics," *Minnesota Review* 83 (2014): 102–111; Jonathan Skinner, "Editor's Statement," *Ecopoetics* 1 (2001–2002): 5–8.

10. M. Jimmie Killingsworth, *Walt Whitman and the Earth: A Study of Ecopoetics* (Iowa City: Iowa University Press, 2006), 6. For an overview of this history, see Angela Hume and Gillian Osborne, "Introduction: Ecopoetics as Expanded Critical Practice," in *Ecopoetics: Essays in the Field* (Iowa City: University of Iowa Press, 2018), 1–16.

11. Michael C. Cohen, *The Social Lives of Poems in Nineteenth-Century America* (Philadelphia: University of Pennsylvania Press, 2015), 1–15; John Felstiner, *Can Poetry Save the Earth? A Field Guide to Nature Poems* (New Haven: Yale University Press, 2009).

12. Whether environmental history necessarily tends toward declension is a topic of ongoing debate for environmental historians. For an overview of that debate, see J. Donald Hughes, *What Is Environmental History? (What Is History?)* (Malden, MA: Polity Press, 2015), 106–108.

13. On planetary intelligence, see Ursula Heise, *Sense of Place, Sense of Planet: The Environmental Imagination of the Global* (Oxford: Oxford University Press, 2008); the experience of deep histories and futures within the present is a feature of what Timothy Morton calls "the ecological thought": *The Ecological Thought* (Cambridge, Harvard University Press, 2010),

passim; for more on the implications of this attitude for literary studies, see *Anthropocene Reading: Literary History in Geologic Times*, Tobias Menely and Jesse Oak Taylor (eds.) (University Park: Penn State Press, 2017).
14. Richard B. Primack's study of the area around Concord, Massachusetts, using Thoreau's phenological records and contemporary field studies is exemplary: *Walden Warming: Climate Change Comes to Thoreau's Woods* (Chicago: University of Chicago Press, 2014).
15. Corey Byrnes, *Fixing Landscape* (New York: Columbia University Press, forthcoming).
16. Witter Bynner, "Introduction," in *The Sonnets of Frederick Goddard Tuckerman* (New York: Alfred Knopf, 1931), 3–36; N. Scott Momaday, "The Heretical Cricket," *The Southern Review* 3.1 (January 1, 1967): 43–50; Stephanie Burt, "Introduction," in *Selected Poems of Frederick Goddard Tuckerman* (Cambridge: Belknap Press, 2010).
17. Yvor Winters, "Foreward," in *The Complete Poems of Frederick Goddard Tuckerman*, N. Scott Momaday (ed.) (New York: Oxford University Press, 1965), ix.
18. See *The Letters of Emily Dickinson*, Thomas H. Johnson (ed.) (Cambridge: Harvard University Press, 1958), L528, L565, L673, L725, L739, L904, L1035.
19. Frederick Goddard Tuckerman, *The Complete Poems of Frederick Goddard Tuckerman*, Scott N. Momaday (ed.) (New York: Oxford University Press, 1965), 117, 157–158.
20. Ibid., 41.
21. Rita Felski, *The Limits of Critique* (Chicago: University of Chicago Press, 2015), 154.
22. Gerhardt and Chow both discuss deforestation in their studies of Dickinson, though not in relation to her productivity: Gerhardt, "Often Seen – but Seldom Felt," 58; Chow, 438.
23. John F. O'Keefe and David R. Foster, "An Ecological History of Massachusetts Forests," in *Stepping Back to Look Forward: A History of the Massachusetts Forest* (Cambridge: Harvard University Press, 1998), 32–43, 53–54.
24. On Dickinson and the "regenerate lyric," see Elisa New, "Beyond Circumference: Dickinson," in *The Regenerate Lyric: Theology and Innovation in American Poetry* (New York: Cambridge University Press, 1993), 151–182.
25. Bate, 94–118.
26. On the "poetical" associations of plant study, see Dickinson, L315; on Dickinson as gardener and student of botany, see Judith Farr, *The Gardens of Emily Dickinson* (Cambridge: Harvard University Press, 2005), and Richard B. Sewall, "Science and the Poet: Emily Dickinson's Herbarium and 'The Clue Divine,'" in *Emily Dickinson's Herbarium: A Facsimile Edition* (Cambridge: Belknap Press, 2006), 19–33.
27. Walter Prichard Eaton, "A Forgotten American Poet," *Forum* Vol. XLI (January 1909): 64; Yvor Winters, x.

28. Ralph Waldo Emerson, "Letter to Frederick Goddard Tuckerman, March 28, 1861," qtd. Winters, xx; Eaton, 62–70; *The Complete Poems of Frederick Goddard Tuckerman*, N. Scott Momaday (ed.) (New York: Oxford University Press, 1965); Stephanie Burt, "Introduction," in *Selected Poems of Frederick Goddard Tuckerman*, Ben Masur (ed.) (Cambridge: Harvard University Press, 2010), xiii; for further appraisal of Tuckerman's appreciation for accurate naming of natural forms, see Burt, xxii–xxiii.
29. Burt, xiii.
30. F1357C & D; Dickinson, "Mayflower," in *Poems of Emily Dickinson*, first series, Mabel Loomis Todd and Thomas Wentworth Higginson (eds.) (Boston: Roberts Brothers, 1890), 70.
31. I offer a more extended reading of this poem in "Dickinson's Lyric Materialism," *EDJ* 21.1 (2012): 57–78.
32. F778.
33. On poetry in the general sense, and for a discussion of the ways in which this attitude is not, in itself, ahistorical, see Percy Bysshe Shelley, *Selected Poetry & Prose* (New York: Norton, 2002), 511; and Oren Izenberg, *Being Numerous: Poetry and the Ground of Social Life* (Princeton: Princeton University Press, 2011), 16–17, 32–33.
34. Juliana Spahr, *Well Then There Now* (Jaffrey, NH: A Black Sparrow Book, 2011), 69.

PART III

Nineteenth-Century Histories

CHAPTER 9

Dickinson's Physics
Cody Marrs

Force abounds in Dickinson's writing. In countless letters, fascicles, and fragments, force both halts and propels, providing her various "Firmaments" with a sense of form and motion: "The Lassitudes of Contemplation / Beget a force" (F1613); "Crisis is a Hair / Toward which forces / creep" (F1067); "The Truth is stirless, other force may be presumed to move" (F882). Even happiness, it seems, is a force – as is frost, best conceived by the "force of its result" (F911). It is one of those keywords in Dickinson's writings – much like *circumference* or *melody* – that crystallizes her poetry and philosophy alike, condensing her worldview into a single, charged, multivalent word.

But what exactly does force entail for Dickinson? Like almost everything else in her writings, it plurisignifies: it is a figure for pressure; a numerical concept; a synonym for agent, or consequence. But I would like to suggest that it is also a vital part of Dickinson's poetics of nature. When force materializes in her works, it discloses the successive transformations through which the natural world takes form. If, as Alphonso Wood claims in his book on botany (which Dickinson almost certainly read), natural science is "divided into three departments" – the animal, mineral, and vegetable kingdoms – force is what connects these realms, harmonizing nature through a physics of transformation.[1] Many nineteenth-century scientists made precisely this point, demonstrating in experiment after experiment that energy, as Michael Faraday put it, is but a vibrant web of connected "lines of force."[2] Dickinson's poems simultaneously extend and reroute these scientific ideas by drawing attention to the causal link between power and change and to the interrelation of seemingly separate states.

In other words, there is a physics to Dickinson's poems: a system of related motions and pressures that reveal force to be both the sign and vehicle of nature's ceaseless change. Dickinson's poetic inquiries into energy and matter, I shall argue, not only provide a new framework through which her poems can be reread; they also offer a novel way of understanding Dickinson's connections to nineteenth-century science more generally. The field is currently at a crossroads in this regard. For a while now – certainly for the past two decades – a great deal of critical attention has been paid to the situated, discursive circumstances of literary texts. Scholars have contextualized Dickinson's writings vis-à-vis numerous intellectual, literary, and political cultures and recovered the historical particulars of the Dickinson household, as well as nineteenth-century Amherst and the United States more broadly – in short, the conditions of possibility that marked and defined Dickinson's lived world. Yet those fine-grained contextualizations tend to posit a relatively stable and continuous authorial self: the very subject roundly contested in recent scholarship in historical poetics, new materialism, and posthumanist criticism. Posthumanist inquiry tends to decenter the subject and foreground other networks or formations – e.g., the genealogies of poetic genres, the contiguity of human and nonhuman life – that exceed the individual author and her mind.

Rather than resolving this critical tension (something far beyond the purview of this essay), I would like to take a cue from Dickinson and try to dwell in mutual possibility. By "choosing not choosing,"[3] as it were, I wish to articulate these approaches through one another and, by doing so, throw into sharper relief their critical advantages, investments, and limitations. Such a hermeneutic is merited, and perhaps altogether obligated by Dickinson's own writings, which tend to position her (and us) somewhere between humanism and posthumanism. Dickinson's physics repeatedly merge the human into a motley range of nonhuman forces, not so as to utterly blur any distinction between them but to find the poetry in their mutual entanglement. To better understand that entanglement, I will turn first to Dickinson's scientific and intellectual contexts, then consider the types of perception and subjectivity that are conjured up by her poems about nature.

Dickinson lived and wrote through a golden age in physics. When she was a child, Michael Faraday discovered electromagnetic induction (that is, the extraction of electricity from magnetic forces) and Leon Foucault constructed his famous pendulum, providing physical verification for the earth's rotation. By the time she was composing her final poems, scientists had verified the wave theory of light, discovered the Doppler Effect, shored up the kinetic theory of gases, laid the foundations for modern thermodynamics, and were close to discovering both photoelectricity and radio waves. The guiding thread in this scientific work, the through-line for nineteenth-century physics, was the continuous transformation of energy: its ceaseless permutation into allied forms. What in the eighteenth century was called the universal fluid, or fire, was in the nineteenth century found to be a multiform process of change in energy's modes and appearances. Light and heat, for instance, are types of electromagnetic waves, and those in turn can generate electricity. From Rudolf Clausius's expanded set of molecular motions (articulated in his 1857 treatise "The Nature of the Motion which we call Heat"[4]) to Joseph Henry's discovery of mutual induction, the underlying insight verified by these theories and experiments is that there is no such thing as cessation. There is only transference, and force is its vehicle. That insight became the first law of thermodynamics, as stated by William Thompson in the 1850s: "[E]nergy can neither be created nor destroyed; rather, it transforms from one form to another."

These scientific ideas and discoveries circulated widely across the Dickinsons' periodicals. The magazines to which they subscribed – *Harper's*, *Atlantic Monthly*, and, later, *Scribner's* – reviewed books on physics, chemistry, and the inductive sciences. They featured articles on "Animal Mechanics," "Kepler," and "The Progress of the Electric Telegraph," as well as essays that discussed the technological, therapeutic, and artistic consequences of these recent theories and experiments.[5] One 1860 essay hailed the era's scientists for revealing nature's innate "similitude[s]" and asked: "May we not hope to see the principle of these beautiful natural contrivances applied to a variety of useful purposes in art?"[6] Another article, printed in the *Atlantic Monthly* in 1864, recapitulated John Tyndall's account of thermometric and radiant heat, proclaiming that the "old view of the forces, which regarded them as [disparate] material entities, may now be ... abandoned." "Light, Heat, Electricity, Magnetism, etc.," the article continues, are "kindred and convertible forms of motion in matter itself," an insight encapsulated

> by the terms "Conservation and Correlation of Forces." The first term implies that force is indestructible, that an impulse of power can no more be annihilated than a particle of matter, and that the total amount of energy in the universe remains forever the same ... [while the] phrase "Correlation of Forces" is employed ... to express their mutual convertability, or change from one to another. Thus, heat excites electricity, and through that force, magnetism, chemical action, and light ... Or we can begin with [magnetism or] chemical action and obtain the same train of effects.[7]

Faraday's theory of force's universal exchangeability – the extraction of electricity from magnetic forces – spread far and wide. It was of particular interest to the Transcendentalists, who saw this "mutual convertability" as a model and a metaphor for nature's insatiable appetite for change. Emerson, who met Faraday and read his work, posited that the world is "nothing but a bundle of forces": "What agencies of electricity, gravity, light, affinity combine to make every plant what it is, and in a manner so quiet that the presence of these tremendous powers is not ordinarily suspected." To explain this combining and recombining of forces, which discloses nature's one universal law ("There is no loss, only transference"), Emerson quotes directly from Faraday's essay "On the Conservation of Force" (1857): "A grain of water is known to have electric relations equivalent to a very powerful flash of lightning."[8] Thoreau similarly assesses and celebrates that universal law in *Walden*. For Thoreau, nature's endless transitions point toward a broader cycle between life and death that ensures "nothing [is] inorganic" and there is never any "decay of the vital forces." The Earth's "living poetry" takes shape through a perpetual transmutation of matter, symbolized above all by Walden Pond itself, whose "sky water" evaporates, crystallizes, freezes, and thaws but remains gloriously undefiled.[9]

There are several compelling reasons for reading Dickinson vis-à-vis these appropriations of nineteenth-century physics. Not only do her poems traffic in these same terms and concepts ("Chemical conviction / That nought be lost," "I cannot make the Force / Nor mould it into word," etc.); her poems also tend to enlist them in ways that evince nature's movements and permutations (F1070, F1725). Moreover, almost everything we have learned about Dickinson's mind testifies to its sublative, boundary-crossing nature. This is someone who saw poetry, botany, and philosophy as contiguous endeavors, and who – as Jed Deppman notes – often referred to her poems not as poems but as specimens of "thought."[10] Michael Kerns points out that "the mental science most prominent during the years when Dickinson was in school and until around 1860 gestured significantly toward the methods of natural science and made extensive use of metaphors drawn from physics and biology."[11] Approaching Dickinson anew with a view toward her physics also extends two of the major trends in recent Dickinson studies: efforts to reconstruct her intellectual and discursive contexts, which have revealed just how intense and multifaceted Dickinson's interest in nature really was, and reassessments of her relation to the era's genre system, which have shown her poems to be highly mediated through various generic conventions, formats, and patterns. Some of those contexts and conventions, I am arguing, derive from nineteenth-century theories of force.

Although Dickinson sometimes registers skepticism toward science – indeed a kind of skepticism toward skepticism itself ("now do you doubt that your bird was true?" [F905]) – her poems also inquire into the origins of transformation, often by evoking, even experimenting, with the elements through words and lines. Here, for instance, is Dickinson writing sometime in 1864 (i.e., the year the *Atlantic* published its article on Faraday):

> Banish Air from Air –
> Divide Light if you dare –
> They'll meet
> While Cubes in a Drop
> Or Pellets of Shape
> Fit –
>
> Films cannot annul
> Odors return whole
> Force flame
> And with a Blonde push
> Over your impotence
> Flits Steam.   (F963)

The poem works on several levels. It is partly about the inadequacy of language: it begins by describing the impossible – banishing air from air, dividing light itself – and, as such, is one of Dickinson's many poems about the gap between nature and our linguistic resources for apprehending and describing it. Judith Farr draws attention to the sly "placement of the word 'Fit,'" which "describes the union of two streams of air [meeting] in one word."[12] But it is also important to take seriously the way that the poem positions itself, both verbally and conceptually, in natural science. Its claim, or germ of suggestion, is that any separation of the elements is destined to fail; everything inevitably returns, pushing or "flitting" into an altered form. This is, to draw out the concluding metaphor, how steam is generated: heated water becomes air – energy converted and elementally transfigured. And that change is both lodged and announced in the word "force," curiously poised here between "whole" and "flame," functioning simultaneously as a figure for nature's fundamental unity and as the vehicle for this fiery push. That connection is also forged in the meter. The lines "Force flame" and "Flits Steam" extend the hymnal melody, but they can also be read as spondees that mirror each other, rhythmically articulating the principle of unity out of division, showing how poetic energy can be drawn from the engine of language, or air from air.

In other poems, conversion takes a different form:

> The Chemical conviction
> That Nought be lost
> Enable in Disaster
> My fractured Trust –
>
> The Faces of the Atoms
> If I shall see
> How more the Finished Creatures
> Departed Me! (F1070)

Critics have tended to read the poem as a kind of dialogue with Edward Hitchcock, the Amherst-based scientist whose books lined the Dickinsons' shelves.[13] The poem's dialogic quality is underscored by the opening lines: if the conservation of energy is a "conviction," then it is allied – as Hitchcock repeatedly argued – with faith. In *The Religion of Geology* (1851), Hitchcock explains this conviction: "[C]hemistry informs us, that no case of combustion ... annihilates the least particle of matter"; fire merely "changes the form of substances," and "there is no reason whatever to suppose that one particle of matter has been annihilated since the world began."[14] Yet the realization that "Nought be lost" is merely the poem's starting point. Across its lines, the poem plays with the idea that both material and immaterial forces – both energy and emotions – convert into allied forms. Hence the rescuing of "Trust" even in "Disaster." The second stanza pivots toward a very different branch of physics: atomic theory. Instead of Hitchcock's "particles" we find "Atoms," the basic unit of all known matter theorized by ancient philosophers such as Democritus and Lucretius then rediscovered in the nineteenth century by scientists such as John Dalton, who showed how atoms determine proportional reactions, and J. J. Thomson, who used cathode rays to demonstrate the existence of electrons.[15] This burgeoning interest in atomism, Mark Noble has argued, was at once scientific and literary, and it influenced several of Dickinson's contemporaries, from Melville ("Not the smallest atom stirs or lives in matter," says Ahab, "but has its cunning duplicate in the mind") to Emerson ("every atom in nature draws to every other atom"). This atomist poetry, according to Noble, tends to "rethink the composition of the human in material terms," and that rethinking certainly occurs in Dickinson's poem.[16] If atoms have faces and trust adheres to the same laws as chemical matter, then we must reconsider, perhaps radically, what distinguishes the human from the nonhuman.

In that regard Dickinson anticipates many of our contemporary ecological concerns. Indeed, it is very tempting to view Dickinson through a twenty-first-century lens and read her poems as bearing witness to the beginning of the "end of nature," the tragic consequences of which now unfold before us on a daily basis.[17] As the glaciers melt, species disappear, soils deplete, shores erode, and storms intensify beyond any previous measure, one wants nothing more than to see in Dickinson a version of ourselves reflected back. Some of her poems even seem to answer that wish, evoking atoms, chemicals, birds, rays of light, and waves of sound that seem, from our perspective on the razor's edge of the Anthropocene, to depict nature in utterly recognizable ways, fleshing out the co-imbrication of all organic and inorganic life. Dickinson's poems, in short, seem to either leap forward into our own ecological era or record the moment of its birth.

Nonetheless, a balance must be struck between reading anachronistically and reading historically. Despite the myriad ways in which Dickinson's poems seem to limn the Anthropocene and pitch themselves as posthumanist reflections, Dickinson's view of nature and the human was different from ours in certain crucial respects. To the degree that posthumanism is predicated, as Pramod Nayar puts it, on a "radical decentering of the traditional sovereign, coherent, and autonomous human," it is a project that Dickinson herself does not advance, largely because it was not yet conceptually available or cognitively possible.[18] In Dickinson's poems, we are part of the environment, but we are never entirely reducible to it. Even her most nature-centric poems tend to foreground nature's indecipherability in ways that separate and divide us from the natural world. In fact, the overwhelming suggestion of many of her poems is not that nature and humanity are the *same* but that the human mind cannot adequately *comprehend* nature's motions and aesthetics. Thus, the designless life recorded in "Four trees – opon a solitary Acre –" (F778) merely exists, Dickinson says, without "Order or Apparent Action." "What deed," she asks

> is Their's unto the General
> Nature –
> What Plan
> They severally – retard – or further –
> Unknown –

These lines hint at a troubling possibility: nature might not, in fact, be entirely knowable. Its order – its laws and exchanges – can certainly be felt, but part of it always remains unavailable to human comprehension. Hence the decidedly humanist emphasis on "conviction" in F1070, as well as the "Me" that lingers, cogently and powerfully, at the end of that poem: "How more the Finished Creatures / Departed Me!"

This doesn't mean the mind should not attempt such comprehension, however. And the mind gets *closest* – approximating if not fully grasping nature's vibrancy – through physics, poetry, and other permutations of natural philosophy. Dickinson's poems may not collapse the boundary between the human and the nonhuman, but they certainly show what passes *through* that boundary. Our ideas and emotions, in particular, seem to obey the same laws as nature's elements, exchanging form after form in response to various forces, both internal and external. Dickinson's interest in transference animates F568:

> It knew no lapse, nor Diminution –
> But large – serene –
> Burned on – until through Dissolution –
> It failed from Men –
>
> I could not deem these Planetary forces
> Annulled –
> But suffered an Exchange of Territory –
> Or World –

This enduring force could be friendship, art, or the sun itself (a possibility underscored by Dickinson's planetary language). Whatever "It" may be, it "burns" slowly but surely, continually producing warmth of one form or another. The end point that it finally reaches ("until through Dissolution – / It failed from Men –") is not an end point at all: dissolution is a term from chemistry that refers to the dissolving of a compound's elements – an "exchange" of states. That exchange, which involves transference rather than lapsing or diminishing, echoes what nineteenth-century physicists discovered about entropy. One of the insights of Clausius and Maxwell was that, in any closed system, energy remains constant: it can be converted but not expunged. Although the poem is hardly a meditation on energy, it *is* a meditation on the continuation of forces both human and nonhuman. That which gives us life and heat, it would seem, persists even in unfamiliar states or territories far afield.

The prospect that such poems are bound up, both rhetorically and philosophically, with nineteenth-century physics accords with recent work by Eliza Richards, Alexandra Socarides, and others on Dickinson's mediated poetics.[19] If "Dickinson's work registers the circulation of a broad range of nineteenth-century ideas and practices, both elite and popular"[20] – from newspaper poetry to hymn revision and epistolary writing, all of which enmesh Dickinson in various "information networks" – one of those networks, establishing vectors and relays for Dickinson's corpus, is physics, both in the broadest sense of theories and experiments on natural science, and more specifically, the work on thermodynamics that unfolded across her career, revealing the interrelations between energy in all of its phases. Yet this is not simply a matter of historical context or homology. Dickinson not only taps into a vast web of theories and discoveries of natural succession; she also plays with such relational change in her practices of composition, which tend to involve sets of poems that flow into and out of one another, converting a certain theme, impression, or idea into allied forms. "Banish Air from Air," for example, is not merely a poem *about* the impossibility of division; it partakes in a sequence of poems that enact and test out that very idea. Fascicle 27, in which the poem first appears, concerns the permanence of suffering. It features surgeons who "do not blanch at pain" (F552); death dressing each house "in crape" (F556); and tunneling through the "Rock" of the "Universe" only to find "Cobwebs" wove "in Adamant" and "Battlements" of "Straw" (F554). The entire fascicle is about the enduring force of pain and grief, which, instead of terminating, tend to "suffer an Exchange," ceaselessly transferring themselves into other states or moods.

In other words: Dickinson's poems, like the natural world they evoke, depend on transference. It "knew no lapse" moves between affirmation and negation, converting the former into the latter across its lines. The intransitive verbs ("annulled," "failed," "burned"), qualifying prepositions ("But," "nor," "or"), and short, staccato-like statements test out the poem's idea – in short, that endings are not really endings – verbally and syntactically, through a network of sense and sound. In this respect, "It knew no lapse" evinces Helen Vendler's claim that Dickinson tends to think, first and foremost, in terms of sequencing: she is chiefly interested in how experience gets divided up and reordered (hence her ardent and repeated use of syntactic extensions and "inactive verbs of state"[21]). While Vendler almost certainly overstates Dickinson's investment in sequential harmony, her underlying suggestion is clarifying. If Dickinson's poems are marked by their peculiar motion, it helps us see how Dickinson's engagements with the physics of force are not merely thematic: they also shape the poems themselves, as lines convert into other lines, words get remade and reused, and letters become poems (and vice versa).

"It knew no lapse" is a case in point. A version of the second stanza also appears in an 1863 letter to Thomas Wentworth Higginson, recently sent south to command the First South Carolina Volunteers. "Dear friend," she writes, "I did not deem that planetary forces annulled, but suffered an exchange of territory, or world. I should have liked to see you before you became improbable. War feels to me an oblique place. Should there be other summers, would you perhaps come?" (L280). Scholarly attention has tended to focus on her geometric figure – the war's obliqueness, its indirect or off-center relation to her, back in Amherst – but she is also clearly thinking with, and through, physics. Her statement concerns the fate of forces: whether they convert (or "suffer an exchange") or disappear. True entropy is impossible in a closed system – or in a friendship. Higginson, she fears, might be gone, but physics provides comfort: he cannot be "annulled" any more than the planets themselves, which revolve in perpetuity around the burning sun. The impossibility of annulment is further reinforced by Dickinson's recycled language: she turns a letter into a poem into a fascicle, approaching the act of writing as a series of allied exchanges.

If, as I've argued elsewhere,[22] Dickinson conceived of the war as a vast annulment – as an upheaval defined by undoing and erasure – then her engagements with physics are vital to her Civil War poetics. For Dickinson the terror provoked by the war was as metaphysical as it was physical. This is why so many of her Civil War poems are shot through with moments of erasure: to Dickinson, death and absence seemed to be the struggle's defining features. Yet everything she learned from science indicated that cessation was invariably a moment of transference. Whether she combined this scientific insight with a lapsed Calvinism, entertaining the possibility that souls too "suffer an Exchange" of forms, or simply held fast to the inexorability of matter, physics seems to have provided her what was otherwise untenable in the war's theodic rupture: faith by other means; a sense of peace secured in the midst of untold suffering.

In this respect "It knew no lapse" resembles a wide range of wartime poems that Dickinson wrote about the origins and modalities of change. Here is poem F616, likely composed in 1863, the bloodiest year of the struggle:

> If any sink, assure that this, now standing –
> Failed like Themselves – and conscious that it rose –
> Grew by the Fact, and not the Understanding
> How Weakness passed – or Force – arose –

> Tell that the Worst, is easy in a Moment –
> Dread, but the Whizzing, before the Ball –
> When the Ball enters, enters Silence –
> Dying – annuls the power to kill –

Death, as Whitman put it, turns out to be very "different from what any one supposed."[23] It is a type of sinking, a fall occasioned by gravity and the bullet, two "Forces" that exceed our ability to understand them. Once more, Dickinson's ambiguous pronouns – "assure that this," "conscious that it rose" – both invite and perplex, pushing us toward some reckoning with death, now reaping a bloody harvest. Nonetheless, if true annulment is impossible, "the power to kill" is only temporarily rescinded – or, more accurately, it gets transferred from one soldier to another. And if the crux of that transference lies in the mystery of "Force," we learn that physics is not simply a branch of science. It is a wide-ranging inquiry conducted through poems and proofs – experiments whether in word or deed – into the very conditions of our existence. It is an inquiry into nature's flux and into the changes that ceaselessly reconstitute us, thereby making us who, and what, we are.

Dickinson's entanglements in physics thus bear on a variety of questions in the field: issues of secular versus postsecular interpretation; debates about the materiality of Dickinson's poems. Yet, in keeping with the tenor and spirit of *The New Emily Dickinson Studies*, I want to conclude with one final remark about Dickinson and posthumanist reading. Nineteenth-century literary studies is currently being transformed by materialisms and ecologies that decenter, scatter, and subvert the human subject around which almost everything in Dickinson's world, from nature to history, revolved. As I have suggested in the preceding pages, this posthumanist reframing helps disclose Dickinson's interest in and uses of nineteenth-century physics, which she approached not merely as a set of ideas but as a kind of model for writing itself. Nonetheless, Dickinson also obliges us to ask what, exactly, the "post" in posthumanism entails. Is it a version of "anti," more politely lodged? Or might it be something like a revisionary extension, an afterglow of humanism in the Age of the Anthropocene? If it's the latter, then Dickinson's poems may indeed provide nineteenth-century anticipations, as critics turn not *against* humanism but *after* it, in keeping with the term's etymology ("post" as in *later*, or *subsequent to*). In that respect Dickinson offers neither a posthumanism *avant la lettre* nor an old humanism that is now hopelessly outmoded but something else altogether: a humanism that, in its very account of nature's forces and exchanges, gestures toward its own sublation.

Notes

1. Alphonso Wood, *A Class-Book of Botany* (New Hampshire, 1846), 14
2. The phrase is omnipresent in Faraday's essays and reports. See, for instance, *On the Physical Character of the Lines of Magnetic Force* (1852) and *On the Various Forces in Nature* (London: Chatto and Windus, 1873). In *The Electric Life of Michael Faraday* (New York: Walker & Co., 2006), Alan Hirshfield describes the idea, hatched after Faraday's experiments with magnetism, this way: "[L]ines of force are, in most cases, actually curves ... And if lines of force exist for magnetism, then why not for electric charges? Or even for gravity? ... Faraday began to suspect that force arises, not when some impulse shoots instantaneously from a seat of power to a remote object ... but when the object encounters the lines of force that inevitably surround all magnetic, electrical, and gravitating bodies" (130).
3. I am referring to Sharon Cameron's account of Dickinson's predilection for drawing multiple, overlapping connections: between words and meanings; ideas and feelings; even versions of individual poems. See Cameron, *Choosing Not Choosing* (Chicago: University of Chicago Press, 1992).
4. Clausius, "The Nature of the Motion Which We Call Heat," *Philosophical Magazine* 14 (1857): 108–27.
5. See, for instance, "Animal Mechanics," *Harper's New Monthly Magazine* 5.28 (September 1852): 524–526; "Kepler," *Atlantic Monthly* 5.30 (April 1860): 457–468; "The Progress of the Electric Telegraph," *Atlantic Monthly* 5.29 (March 1860): 290–298.
6. "Animal Mechanics," 526.
7. Review of Tyndall's *Heat Considered as a Mode of Motion*, in "Reviews and Literary Notices," *Atlantic Monthly* 13.78 (April 1864): 513.
8. Emerson, "Perpetual Forces," in *The Later Lectures of Ralph Waldo Emerson*, Vol. 2: 1855–1871, Ronald A. Bosco and Joel Myerson (eds.) (Athens, GA: University of Georgia Press, 2001), 300.
9. Thoreau, *Walden; or, Life in the Woods* (Boston and New York: Houghton Mifflin and Co., 1906), 340, 69, 341, 209. On Dickinson's relation to Transcendentalism, see Michelle Kohler, *Miles of Stare: Transcendentalism and the Problem of Vision in Nineteenth-Century America* (Tuscaloosa: University of Alabama Press, 2014), 105–136.
10. Deppman, introduction, in *Trying to Think with Emily Dickinson* (Amherst: University of Massachusetts Press, 2008).
11. Kerns, "Emily Dickinson: Anatomist of the Mind," in *Emily Dickinson and Philosophy*, Jed Deppman, Marianne Noble, and Gary Lee Stonum (eds.) (New York: Cambridge University Press, 2013), 20.

12. Farr, *The Passion of Emily Dickinson* (Cambridge, MA: Harvard University Press, 1992), 328.
13. See Hiroko Uno, "'Chemical Conviction': Dickinson, Hitchcock, and the Poetry of Science," *EDJ* 7.2 (1998): 95–111; Richard Sewall, *The Life of Emily Dickinson* (Cambridge, MA: Harvard University Press, 1994), 343–363; and Helen Vendler, *Dickinson: Selected Poems and Commentaries* (Cambridge, MA: Harvard University Press, 2010), 400–403.
14. Hitchcock, *The Religion of Geology and Its Connected Sciences* (Boston: Phillips, Samson, and Co., 1851), 22.
15. For an overview of the development of atomic theory, see Bernard Pullman, *The Atom in the History of Human Thought*, trans. Axel Reisinger (Oxford: Oxford University Press, 1998).
16. Noble, *American Poetic Materialism from Whitman to Stevens* (New York: Cambridge University Press, 2014), 6; Melville, *Moby-Dick*, Hershel Parker and Harrison Hayford (eds.) (New York: Norton, 2002), 250; Emerson, "Education," in *Lectures and Biographical Sketches* (Boston: Houghton Mifflin and Co., 1884), 130.
17. The phrase comes from Bill McKibben, *The End of Nature* (New York: Random House, 2006).
18. Nayar, *Posthumanism* (Cambridge and Malden: Polity, 2013), 2.
19. See, for example, Faith Barrett, *To Fight Aloud Is Very Brave: American Poetry and the Civil War* (Amherst: University of Massachusetts Press, 2012), 130–186; Virginia Jackson, *Dickinson's Misery: A Theory of Lyric Reading* (Princeton: Princeton University Press, 2006); Michelle Kohler, "Dickinson and the Poetics of Revolution," *EDJ* 19.2 (2010): 20–46; Eliza Richards, "'How News Must Feel When Traveling': Dickinson and Civil War Media," in *Companion to Emily Dickinson*, Martha Nell Smith and Mary Loeffelholz (eds.) (London: Blackwell, 2006), 157–180; Alexandra Socarides, *Dickinson Unbound: Paper, Process, Poetics* (New York: Oxford University Press, 2012). See also Part 1 of this volume, "Poetics and the Imagination," as well as the essays in "Networking Dickinson" (2015), a special issue of *EDJ* edited by Eliza Richards and Alexandra Socarides.
20. Richards and Socarides, "Editorial Note," *EDJ* 23.1 (2014): vi.
21. Vendler, *Poets Thinking: Pope, Whitman, Dickinson, Yeats* (Cambridge, MA: Harvard University Press, 2004), 64–91, 67.
22. See Cody Marrs, *Nineteenth-Century American Literature and the Long Civil War* (New York: Cambridge University Press, 2015), 122–152.
23. Whitman, *Leaves of Grass* (Brooklyn, 1855), 17.

CHAPTER 10

Dickinson's Geographic Poetics
Grant Rosson

Emily Dickinson's geography books might very well have offered the famously reclusive poet an abundance of information about places in the world that she would never see for herself. Scholars have shown with clarity and specificity that Dickinson did indeed learn a great deal about the world outside her native Amherst, Massachusetts, from a variety of print resources, including local newspapers, national magazines, and books of all types from the United States and abroad.[1] But the special influence she drew from her geography textbooks has been largely overlooked. Such an oversight perhaps stems from the fact that when Dickinson is most explicit about her engagement with her geographies she does not use them in the ways we might expect. Instead of mining her geography books for metaphors, imagery, or even general information about places distant from Amherst,[2] Dickinson more fundamentally emulates their basic function: describing the nature of the world's varied places for the benefit of readers elsewhere, who might never see or experience such places firsthand. Dickinson emulates her geography books in order to disclose (or not, as we'll see) two domains of special significance to her, each outside of any prospective reader's direct experience: the first, that part of the world to which she had unique access – her home and yard in Amherst; and the second, the world to which no one has access – the realm of heaven. This essay, then, is less about Dickinson as a consumer of geography than it is about the ways she produces geography, folding geographic functions into her poems, not because she is elsewhere but because her readers are.

By integrating some of geography's basic functions into her poems, Dickinson experiments with using poetry as a vehicle for communicating positive knowledge about the present state of the external world. Instead of using her poems to stage the disclosure of personal interiority, as lyric poems often do, Dickinson turns the focus of her poetry outward, toward the project of disclosing the interiors of places necessarily unfamiliar to her readers: her home and heaven.[3] What interests Dickinson in this turn outward – and what geographic discourse helps her organize – is the radical interiority of these places, their closed-off-ness and their resistance to disclosure. This chapter argues, then, that Dickinson draws on nineteenth-century geographic discourse in order to develop a way to grapple with the disclosure of the internal natures of places that are all but inaccessible to those outside them. If we have thought of lyric poetry as a vehicle for the disclosure of personal interiority, Dickinson's engagement with geographic discourse demonstrates that she conceived of her poems as vehicles for the disclosure of other kinds of inaccessible interiors as well.[4]

In what follows, I first offer an account of mid-nineteenth-century geography as Dickinson would have encountered it, and then I turn to two sets of poems, each of which is organized around one of the two instances of the term "Geography" that occur in Dickinson's nearly eighteen-hundred poems. In the first set, we see Dickinson borrowing the figure of a volcano from her geography books to characterize not herself, as we have so often supposed, but her home and yard in Amherst. By invoking the figure of a volcano as it was presented in her geography books, Dickinson conveys not only the tumultuous nature of her home but also the difficulty of rendering such a mutable and multiform space legible to those outside of it. More significant than the use of her geography's volcano as a figure for a dynamic home environment, however, is Dickinson's adoption of geography's general precept regarding the value of developing and collating knowledge of all the world's places, including her own. Dickinson's volcano poems exhibit, first, her interest in producing an account of her personal domain and, second, her sense of lyric poetry as a powerful tool with which to accomplish geography's distinct aims. We then see Dickinson enlist this powerful tool in a second, more experimental set of poems, in which she tests the proposal that the simple instructional forms that geographical primers used to teach children about this world could also help her and her readers conceptualize the nature of heaven, even where the methods of science, philosophy, and theology could not.

The geography books Dickinson had access to at home and at school would have given her an overview of the various approaches to geography that were current in mid-nineteenth-century America. From the "Peter Parley" series, which Dickinson likely read at her primary school, the Amherst Academy, she would have received an education in the basic elements of world geography, including names, locations, and descriptions of distinguishing features of places around the world. She would have received a more detailed education from secondary-school texts like

Jedidiah Morse's *American Universal Geography*, a text held in the Dickinson family library, and Emma Hart Willard and William Channing Woodbridge's *Universal Geography*, a book listed on the curriculum at Mount Holyoke Female Seminary, which Dickinson attended at age sixteen.[5] These more advanced geographies were encyclopedic, often multi-volume books that aimed to characterize and provide key facts about any and all parts of the known world. Unlike works of travel writing, which would typically guide a reader through one person's experience of a place or series of places, books of geography resisted prioritizing one person's experience or one set of places over another. That is, while travel writings, like those of Dickinson's own friends Samuel Bowles and Helen Hunt Jackson, often aimed to be narrow and intimate, geographies strove to be both comprehensive and impersonal. Morse's *American Universal Geography* comprised two volumes and several thousand individual entries on all areas of the globe, largely gathered from unattributed source materials. The similarly encyclopedic Willard-Woodbridge *Universal Geography* comprised nearly thirteen hundred individual entries, including descriptions, statistics, and firsthand accounts of the world's cities, states, countries, continents, and landforms. Such expansive works served largely as reference material for secondary and college students, as well as a general readership. Morse described his *American Universal Geography*, for example, as an efficient and inexpensive way for US citizens to become informed about both their own country and what he referred to collectively as "the other parts of the world":

> Every citizen of the United States ought to be thoroughly acquainted with the Geography of his own country, and to have some idea, at least, of the other parts of the world; but as many of them cannot afford the time and expense necessary to acquire a complete knowledge of the several parts of the Globe, this book offers them such information as their situation in life may require.[6]

In contrast, *Peter Parley's Geography for Beginners* was designed for primary-school children and adopted the catechistic form typical of primers, beginning with a series of questions and answers, which students would memorize and recite for their instructors, followed by a series of short narrative chapters. Despite its comparatively elementary form, *Parley's Geography* was still global in scope, providing its school-aged readers with an overview of landforms, accounts of each state in the Union, descriptions of distant countries and continents, as well as etchings depicting people, plants, animals, and significant structures from around the world. The aim of *Parley's*, as stated in its preface, even resembles that of Morse's *Geography*: "In studying a book of geography, I wish you to get that knowledge which you would acquire by travelling over the different parts of the world."[7]

Despite the prevalence and variety of geography texts in the nineteenth century, scholars of geography[8] have largely regarded such books as trivial and inconsequential to the development of geographic thought, based on the fact that they were produced before geography's establishment as a systematized professional and academic discipline. That is, at the same time that the study of earth sciences like geology and natural history were being conducted under the aegis of academic institutions in America – notably at Amherst College, just down the road from Dickinson's home, under the direction of Professor Edward Hitchcock – the field of geography operated outside of structured institutional frameworks until roughly the 1870s, when the first university geography departments were established.[9] As a result, the field of geography was uniquely open to those who would have been excluded from participating in other more established fields of inquiry. This meant that the representative texts of American geography were, by necessity, written by nonspecialists from a variety of backgrounds: Morse was a Congregational minister; the "Peter Parley" series was created by the Boston book publisher Samuel Griswold Goodrich; and Emma Hart Willard and William Channing Woodbridge were prominent educational reformers. Throughout the century, enterprising figures like these produced a steady stream of geography books to market to schools and libraries, each new volume touting a novel "system of geography" based on one educational or ideological rationale or another, and each new edition purporting to incorporate all the latest available knowledge (whether it did or not). Although geography scholars have largely dismissed nineteenth-century geography books as inconsequential to geography's later, more systematic and technically rigorous developments, their accessibility allowed many to engage with and contribute to what was, in fact, an expansive and rich discourse. Such a vital and comparatively open market for geography books in America even provided employment to a number of now-famous literary writers, including Charles Brockden Brown, Nathaniel Hawthorne, and Harriet Beecher Stowe.[10] That Dickinson should also have engaged, in her own way, in the practice of geography speaks not only to the inclusiveness of that discourse but also to the wide compass of her intellectual undertakings and the extensive reach of her poetry's functionality, as we can begin to see in her "volcano" poems.

Scholars have typically read instances of volcanoes in Dickinson's poems within a conventional lyric framework, regarding them as figures for the poet herself. Perhaps most famously, Adrienne Rich, in her influential essay "Vesuvius at Home: The Power of Emily Dickinson," argues that Dickinson's volcanoes illustrate the explosive power of a woman living "under pressure of concealment" – namely, in the repressive environment of a home in patriarchal Victorian New England.[11] Rich argues that under such conditions Dickinson "feels herself to be Vesuvius at home" to such an extent that she eventually "explodes into poetry." Elizabeth Petrino even extends this reading by putting it into a literary-historical context by calling attention to other nineteenth-century American women writers who invoke volcanoes as well as "extreme climates and distant locales" in order to "depict their alienation in the home."[12] But Dickinson's volcano poems are not exclusively concerned with characterizing the poet herself. The poem from which Rich derives her essay's title, for example, challenges the dominant lyric reading of Dickinson's volcanoes by clearly distinguishing between the speaker and the volcano: the poem's speaker reports climbing a "Lava step" up to a "Crater" to contemplate a "Volcano nearer here," the titular "Vesuvius at Home." The "Volcano," then, is not a figure for a human subject but a description of a physical environment. The poem thereby forgoes the more typical lyric function of communicating human interiority in favor of taking on a geographic function: communicating the nature of a place. In this and other poems, we can see Dickinson borrowing the figure of a volcano from her geography books – especially the Willard and Woodbridge *Universal Geography*, described above – not just to characterize her home as volatile and unpredictable but also to test out geography's distinct modes of communicating about space.

Dickinson in fact begins her "Vesuvius at Home" (F1691) poem by explicitly aligning it with contemporary geographic discourse. In its opening lines, the poem calls attention to a gap in her geography book, which accounts for volcanoes all across the world but fails to note the existence of a certain "Volcano nearer here":

> Volcanoes be in Sicily
> And South America
> I judge from my Geography
> Volcano nearer here
> A Lava step at any time
> Am I inclined to climb
> A Crater I may contemplate
> Vesuvius at Home

Dickinson's Geographic Poetics 173

In its second quatrain, this brief eight-line poem introduces the as-yet unknown "Volcano" by noting some of its features – its "Lava step" and its "Crater." The final line then locates the "Volcano" more precisely than simply "nearer here," referring to it as "Vesuvius at Home," a phrase that identifies the "Volcano" as a feature of a domestic space. In this light, we can note that the poem's account of climbing up a "Lava step" and peering down into a "Crater" neatly maps onto the architecture of the Dickinson home itself, in which a central staircase winds up three stories such that leaning over the bannister on any floor provides an overhead view of the home's first-floor entryway, a crater-like, quasi-public space for family and visitors, whom Dickinson, in her reclusive later years, might have hoped to avoid. By describing the "Home" and the "Volcano" in the context of geographic discourse ("my Geography"), the poem does not conflate the two. Rather, it simply identifies the location of the "Volcano" ("at Home") and makes a claim for its inclusion, with all the world's other volcanoes, in a general body of geographic knowledge.

Although the poem presents the "Volcano" as a feature of the "Home," it is nonetheless difficult to discern what precise characteristics the "Volcano" is intended to embody. If the poem means to portray a precarious place, always on the verge of explosion, that idea is contradicted by the speaker's apparent freedom of movement, as indicated by the couplet "A Lava step at any time / Am I inclined to climb." Her autonomy in the midst of the volcano is even stressed by that couplet's enjambment and inverted syntax. The first line, "A Lava step at any time," implies the danger and unpredictability of the volcano by suggesting that the speaker could "step" into its "Lava" at "any time." But her apparent vulnerability is then overturned by the second line, "Am I inclined to climb," which gives the speaker agency and transforms the "Lava step" from a perilous action (stepping into a surprise lava puddle) into a physical step that she can use to climb the "Volcano" whenever she is "inclined." The poem therefore equivocates regarding the degree, or even the existence, of the volcano's threat. In short, the poem does not presume anything about the volcano's interior. Rather, in the manner of a geography, it restrains its description, offering only an account of the volcano's exterior.

The poem's resistance to presuming the nature of the volcano's interior is most apparent in its penultimate line: "A Crater I may contemplate." In this line, the poem resists disclosing – or imagining – two interiors simultaneously: that of the speaker's mind and that of the volcanic "Crater." If lyrics are thought to comprise a poet's contemplations, this particular instance only introduces the *possibility* of contemplation without offering the *substance* of any contemplation, even on a site as ripe for sublime reflection as a volcanic crater. In fact, the only instance in which the poem refers to any interior at all – either of the "Volcano," the "Home," or the lyric "I" – is in the word "inclined," which indicates the speaker's compulsion, her desire to climb the volcano. But even this slight indication of the speaker's interiority is dissembling: the word "inclined" is a pun that merges the speaker's internal mentality, her inclination, with the volcano's external physicality, its incline. The word "inclined" would describe the speaker's physical posture when climbing as much as it would describe her frame of mind – in both ways, she is "inclined to climb." The poem adopts the mode of geography in two ways, then: first, by forgoing assumptions about the nature of the physical world; and second, by de-emphasizing, or relinquishing altogether, any intimation of the speaker's particular interiority.

By indicating only the exterior of the "Volcano nearer here" and, additionally, by resisting the disclosure of any personal interiority, Dickinson follows the mode of description modeled by her "Geography" – specifically, the volcano section of the Willard and Woodbridge *Universal Geography*, the textbook listed on the curriculum of Dickinson's secondary school, Mount Holyoke Female Seminary.[13] The first entries in the book's volcano section include all the basic terms in the poem, including definitions of "lava" and "crater" and mentions of volcanoes located "near Sicily" and "at Terra del Fuego [sic]" in South America. More than simply offering a compendium of key terms, however, this geography offers a characterization of volcanoes that resonates with Dickinson's volcano poems more generally, as a phenomenon that is internally dynamic and outwardly inconspicuous. Rather than exhaustively detailing the internal mechanics of active volcanoes, as a geology book would,[14] the geography describes volcanoes more broadly, in comparison to other landforms. According to the Willard-Woodbridge geography, volcanoes are distinguished by their mutable physicality, on account of their "internal fire." On the basis of outward appearance alone, however, it notes that volcanoes are virtually indistinguishable from their innocuous counterpart, the mountain:

> Volcanoes have not the same *permanency of character* as other features of the globe. They are in fact, only mountains which are subject to the action of

internal fire, and their number and character are liable to continual change from its effects.[15]

Such a description marks volcanoes as a distinctly difficult phenomenon to identify, given the disparity between their interiors and their exteriors. As a result, the geographical record of the world's volcanoes is undoubtedly incomplete, a fact that licenses Dickinson's account of the "Volcano" that she has identified. Her account is further justified by volcanoes' distinct potential to "burst forth" – to suddenly come into existence – especially in America and perhaps even in Dickinson's seemingly tranquil Amherst:

> Some *ancient volcanoes* have become extinct or dormant, and *new ones* have burst forth, within the memory of man [...] More than 200 *volcanoes* are *known* to exist in the world, one half of which are in America; but many of them have never been described, and have scarcely received a name in works of geography.[16]

By describing and giving a name – "Vesuvius at Home" – to the as-yet unknown "Volcano," Dickinson constructs her poem as a contribution to geographic knowledge, in accordance with both the conception of volcanoes and the mode of description modeled by her geography book.

In a poem that reads like an extension of the "Vesuvius at Home" poem, however, Dickinson is confronted by another fundamental aspect of geographic discourse and of discourse in general: the matter of communicating knowledge to an outside readership. Though she is able to adopt geography's descriptive aspects in writing alone, as the "Vesuvius at Home" poem demonstrates, in the poem that begins "On my volcano grows the Grass" (F1743) she recognizes that fulfilling geography's discursive aspects, by publicizing the nature of her world, could have singularly disruptive consequences. This poem therefore registers a shift in Dickinson's regard for geography, from appreciation for its power as a mode of communicating the nature of a place to reservation about the prospect of fully discharging that power.

In its first stanza, the poem describes a "volcano" as something markedly inconspicuous, even undetectable, a description reminiscent of her geography book's account of a volcano:

> On my volcano grows the Grass
> A meditative spot
> An acre for a Bird to choose
> Would be the general Thought

Though this "volcano" is evident to the speaker, its true nature would not be obvious to any outside observer, since by all accounts ("the general Thought") the "acre" would look like any other. To the speaker, though, the volcano is not only apparent but also normalized, as indicated by the inversion of the typical structure of metaphor: rather than comparing something common (a yard) to something uncommon (a volcano), the poem does the opposite, describing the "volcano" in terms of a typical grass-covered yard. From a position of privileged knowledge, then, the speaker begins to reveal the volcano's internal nature in the poem's second and final stanza:

> How red the Fire rocks below
> How insecure the sod
> Did I disclose
> Would populate with awe my solitude.

This stanza does, in one sense, "disclose" the "Fire rocks below," by noting their existence in its own text. But it also registers the potential for another kind of disclosure, a disclosure that would have the effect of fundamentally undoing the place it described – not by destroying it with "Fire rocks" but by undermining the "solitude" it offered through an influx of people in "awe" at the existence of a volcano hidden in their midst. With this poem, Dickinson recognizes the power of fully participating in geographic discourse, by pointing out the disruptive – if not destructive – consequences of disclosing the nature of her own domain. Her final engagement with geographic discourse in this poem, then, is her acknowledgement that she need not engage in it fully: the poem forestalls the disclosure it imagines by expressing it as a conditional statement, positing it as a possibility rather than a certainty. As a result, she demonstrates, if only to herself, her dominion over her own place in the world.

In light of the disruptive consequences arrived at in this poem's final line, it is conceivable that Dickinson would have withheld the knowledge of her "volcano" entirely. At the very least, it appears that she tightly controlled its disclosure, as the two poems examined here are extant only in the form of transcriptions made by Dickinson's sister-in-law, Susan. These poems therefore show that Dickinson appreciated the power of geographic discourse to such an extent that she was compelled to exercise discretion about fully implementing it, resisting the prospect of circulating the nature of her home as broadly as her geographies circulated the nature of the world outside it, or even as broadly as she circulated certain other poems.

As a point of comparison to the preceding poems, we can see how Dickinson goes through with disclosing the internal nature of her home in a letter she sent to a friend, Joseph Lyman. Though this letter also invokes a volcano – the volcanic island of Juan Fernandez – it does not depict the Dickinson home as a tempestuous place. Rather, it illustrates a quiet equilibrium between the home's inhabitants, each of whom is said to occupy his or her own geographic locale, despite living together in the same house. In this letter, Dickinson adopts the mantle of the geographer more fully than she does in her volcano poems, not only by preparing it specifically for circulation but also by assembling it from perspectives other than her own. Producing a more equitable account, however, also entails revealing less about each domain, especially those of others, thereby demonstrating the advantages of depth and specificity that accompany the risks she associates with her geographic poems.

Dickinson begins the letter by relaying her father's account of his life in geographic terms, wherein the isle of Juan Fernandez serves as a representation of his remoteness:

> Father says in fugitive moments when he forgets the barrister and lapses into the man, says that his life has been passed in a wilderness or on an island – of late he says on an island. And so it is, for in the morning I hear his voice and methinks it comes from afar & has a sea tone & there is a hum of hoarseness about & a suggestion of remoteness as far as the isle of Juan Fernandez.[17]

Expanding on her father's account of his life, she conceives of the home as a space simultaneously containing both close intimacies (a father who "lapses into the man" in order to make a personal confession) and extreme distances (his remoteness otherwise). As a result, she also recognizes that the same house can be experienced and understood in a radically different way by each person who inhabits it. This insight leads her to draw a conclusion about the relationship between physical spaces and the individual selves that occupy them – namely, that the two are not necessarily related:

> So I conclude that space & time are things of the body & have little or nothing to do with our selves. My Country is Truth. Vinnie lives much of the time in the State of Regret. I like Truth – it is a free Democracy.

Though Dickinson, Vinnie, and their father occupy the house together, in the same "space & time," she notes that each of their "selves" resides in its own distinct domain. She might have gone on to elaborate on the nature of "[her] Country" and its features, as she does in the "On my volcano" poem, but in this context, in a letter intended to circulate as a general report on the state of her home, she follows the example of a "universal" geography, understood as "a view of the present state of all empires, kingdoms, states, and republics in the known world," as Morse's *American Universal Geography* promises on its title page. That is, she endeavors to account for the several individual domains in the home, to the extent that she can know them in their "present state": an "island" for her father, a "State" for her sister Vinnie, and a "Country" for herself. Where this letter shows Dickinson producing and disclosing a more inclusive account of her world, though, it also demonstrates by comparison the distinct power of her geographic poems to reveal the nature of a place with precision and nuance.

Having recognized its distinct – and potentially disruptive – power, Dickinson resists adopting a geographic poetics for the purposes of disclosing the nature of her own place in the world. However, she readily applies that same powerful poetics toward the problem of conceiving and articulating the nature of heaven, a place – if we can call it that – of enduring interest to Dickinson throughout her life, as attested by the many poems she wrote on various aspects of the subject. Where she evidently finds geography about places in the world to be fraught with problems related to the necessary subjectivity of any representation – despite the claims of so-called "universal" geographies – such issues would not apply to a geography of a truly universal realm such as heaven. She therefore endeavors to conceive of a heavenly geography, without any of the reluctance that one might expect would attend such a task.

Nina Baym has explored Dickinson's interest in the nature of heaven in the context of contemporary scientific inquiry, particularly the work of Amherst College faculty, especially the geologist Edward Hitchcock. By cataloging references to scientific discourse in Dickinson's poetry, Baym determines that "Dickinson's overriding intellectual poetic projects where science is concerned are to query the existence of 'heaven.'"[18] Ultimately, Baym finds that Dickinson, by writing poetry, is able to "do theological work that scientists never pretend to do, and theologians only pretend to do" – that is, to "write, with excruciating exactness, of how it feels to live in a world where the answers to the most important questions are by their nature unknowable."[19] According to this account, the value that Dickinson added to contemporary inquiries into the existence of heaven derives from the capacity of poetry to articulate feeling. However, because Baym's study, like many, does not consider geography to be within the purview of nineteenth-century science, it fails to recognize not only the significance of geography textbooks to Dickinson's attempts to articulate the nature of heaven but also the fundamental influence they had on her conception of poetry as a mode not only of feeling but of instruction, especially on topics that evaded ready comprehension.

On the one hand, geography books offered Dickinson a model for describing heaven as a place analogous to Earth, as in the poems that begin "I went to Heaven – / 'Twas a small town" (F577) and "I know where Wells grow – Droughtless Wells" (F695). Such poems list attributes that might be conceived of as heavenly, if only by comparison to their earthly counterparts: "Lit with a Ruby," "Stiller than the fields / At the full dew," "Where Mosses go no more away." But geographies were also at the foundation of Dickinson's attempts to develop a more innovative approach to the problem of conceiving heaven. In a series of poems that explicitly invoke educational primers, like those in the "Peter Parley" series, Dickinson builds on geographies' methods of educating students about parts of the world beyond their own experience in order to propose that a similar approach, folded into her own poetic forms, might establish, or at least help facilitate a conception of, the nature of heaven.

In a poem she sent to Susan Dickinson, in April 1860 (F164), Dickinson proclaims that the beauty of an April day is so great that it is beyond her ability to express it. She imagines, however, that such a task would be little more than simple schoolwork for "Saints" in heaven:

> I cant tell you – but you feel it
> Nor can you tell me
> Saints, with ravished slate and pencil
> Solve our April Day!

By invoking "slate and pencil," school supplies typical of nineteenth-century classrooms, Dickinson suggests that the work of solving (in the sense of explaining, according to her 1844 Webster) an "April Day" would be a rote, repetitive exercise for "Saints" – done with such regularity that their "slate and pencil" become "ravished." The poem elaborates on both components of this conceit in its final stanzas. The penultimate stanza reiterates that the speaker and her interlocutor – the poem's "you" and "me" – are not equipped to express the day's beauty in language:

> Not for me – to prate about it!
> Not for you – to say
> To some fashionable Lady
> "Charming April Day"!

The final stanza, then, elaborates on the schoolwork of the "Saints," suggesting that they acquired their descriptive skills by studying primers written by "Heaven's 'Peter Parley'," an imagined counterpart to Earth's "Peter Parley," the pseudonymous author known for publishing geography schoolbooks for children, including *Peter Parley's Geography for Beginners* and *Peter Parley's Universal History on the Basis of Geography*:

> Rather – Heaven's "Peter Parley"!
> By which children slow
> To sublimer Recitation
> Are prepared to go!

Such a primer would, presumably, introduce its readers to features of heaven and prepare them to describe it in "sublimer Recitation." If such a primer were available to Dickinson, it could potentially solve her problem of describing Earth's beauty by providing her more sufficient terms than simply "'Charming April Day'!" She might even confirm the descriptions of heaven she attempted in her other poems. Ultimately, though, this poem shows Dickinson proposing that the methods employed by nineteenth-century schoolbooks – namely, "slow" methodical learning through rote memorization and recitation – could inculcate "sublimer" abilities, such as the ability to describe places otherwise indescribable, whether heaven-on-earth or heaven itself. Forgoing the methods of more advanced sciences, then, Dickinson proposes that the methods devised for facilitating children's understandings of "this World" might also be useful for understanding the next.

Dickinson puts this proposed strategy into practice in another poem, which begins by questioning the act of speculating about the nature of heaven and ends by describing – or attempting to describe – in three carefully chosen terms heaven's "Geography" (F476). The poem begins "We pray – to Heaven – / We prate – of Heaven," reusing the term "prate" from the "April Day" poem ("Not for me – to prate about it!") to dismiss the notion of presuming to know enough to speak about heaven. (The term has a similar meaning to the more common "prattle," meaning to talk idly or foolishly.) Its recurrence here suggests that Dickinson considered geography as a means of organizing what would otherwise be senseless chatter. To that end, the poem immediately elevates its critique in a series of questions regarding the applicability of earthly logic and physics to inquiries into the nature of heaven:

> We pray – to Heaven –
> We prate – of Heaven –
> Relate – when Neighbors die –
> At what o'clock to heaven – they fled –
> Who saw them – Wherefore fly?

The poem speculates that structures like time ("what o'clock") and movement through space ("Wherefore fly?") may not necessarily apply in heaven. The poem thereby raises doubt about the possibility of even formulating appropriate questions about a supernal realm from an earthly standpoint.

Yet the poem proceeds, in the next stanza, to ask questions of that exact kind, using a three-term structure as the basis of its inquiry – "Is Heaven a Place – a Sky – a Tree?" – followed by a pronouncement on certain distinctions between Earth and heaven:

> Is Heaven a Place – a Sky – a Tree?
> Location's narrow way is for Ourselves –
> Unto the Dead
> There's no Geography –
>
> But State – Endowal – Focus –
> Where – Omnipresence – fly?

The first line's simple structure (A, B, C), simple terms ("Place," "Sky," "Tree"), and simple question would not be out of place in the catechism of a geographical primer like "Peter Parley's." (In fact, in a poem dated the same year, 1862, Dickinson expressly refers to her "Primer" as "just my A – B – C.") The lines that follow continue the work of the first stanza, declaring that the concept of location is not applicable to heaven. It then begins to claim that heaven has "no Geography" at all – it has neither a geography book nor space itself. However, that thought continues in the next line, where the qualifier "But" shifts the claim from negative to positive, from flatly denying heaven's "Geography" to attempting to describe it. That is, rather than declaring that there is "no Geography" at all in heaven, the poem asserts that there is "no Geography – / *But*" – that is, no geography except – "State – Endowal – Focus." With this three-termed description, Dickinson attempts to circumvent earthly structures in order to describe the unknown, unseen, unseeable, and potentially unknowable, by describing heaven's geography as a list of nouns ungoverned by the specifics of space and time invoked in the poem's first stanza: "State," a condition of being; "Endowal," a condition of having been given; and "Focus," a one-dimensional point. She imagines that certain conditions persist in heaven even if others – like space and time – do not. For Dickinson, then, the geographic primer offers a basic form in which to organize and communicate a concept that does not adhere to earthly structures that typically govern concepts of place – namely, space and time.

By answering the initial three-termed question about the nature of heaven ("Is Heaven a Place – a Sky – a Tree?") with a three-termed response ("State – Endowal – Focus") the poem takes the form of a catechism and fulfills the promise of the imagined heavenly primer, "Heaven's 'Peter Parley,'" in the "April Day" poem, moving from simple terms to "sublimer Recitation." The poem guides its reader, step by step, over the seemingly insurmountable separation between Earth and heaven – a separation manifested, we should note, by the break between stanzas – through a recitation of the very heavenly "Geography" it proposes: "State – Endowal – Focus." Then, rather than ending with its answer about heaven, the poem continues to follow a catechistic form by concluding with a question about the nature of God: "Where – Omnipresence – fly?" Though up to this point the poem has guided the recitation, supplying both question and answer, it leaves this final question open, inviting the reader to participate more fully in the exercise it leads, perhaps expecting a three-termed response to this three-termed question.

The fundamental difficulty of this poem's lesson, the "sublimer Recitation" that it puts forward, is affirmed by the fact that its two-line final stanza ("But State – Endowal – Focus – / Where – Omnipresence – fly?") was excluded from early print versions of the poem.[20] The stanza break that precedes these lines, also present in the manuscript, even encourages such a clean excision, following the grammatical end of the previous clause. The problem with removing these lines, however, is that it leaves the reader mouthing a claim – "Unto the Dead / There's no Geography" – that is fundamentally at odds with the conception of "Geography" that this chapter shows Dickinson harbored. Dickinson conceived of geography, just as nineteenth-century geographers did, as a discourse in need of constant updating, of new additions, information, and representations, in order to keep pace with the ever-evolving "present state" of the known world. Even if it were true, as this poem begins to suggest, that "There [is] no Geography" of heaven, in the present, that would only hold, following this concept of geography, until one was created. In keeping with this concept, Dickinson effects such a creation in the very next line. And, given her sense that the structures of space and time do not govern in heaven as they do on Earth, that creation, that heavenly geography, would presumably endure, without need of further emendation, as apposite in that moment as any. For her reader, then, Dickinson offers a truly universal geography of heaven.

Like the geographies that she emulates and borrows from, Dickinson's geographic writings on her home and heaven are fundamentally poetic: not in the sense that they have meter and rhyme, but in the sense that they are creative, that they endeavor to bring something – or in this case, some place – formerly unknown or unrecognized into existence, even if only in the mind of a reader. In that case, what Dickinson wrote of heaven in an 1862 poem also applies to her understanding of her home, when rendered geographically: that it is "so far of the Mind" and therefore "'Tis vast – as our Capacity" (F413). In writing her geographies of home and heaven, then, Dickinson aims to increase her prospective reader's "Capacity" for understanding the two places that most occupied *her* mind, not just noting their existence or their location but bringing them into concrete relation with the rest of the known world, a feat she accomplishes by rendering them both in the terms and structures of the discourse that proclaimed most earnestly to document it. That same poem's closing line then also pertains to both the heaven that she imagined and the home that she endeavored to account for each time she wrote about it: "No further 'tis, than Here," where "Here" points to both the place that she occupied and the words on the page. In doing so, she puts a world directly before her readers, if not to invite them in then at least to give them a sense of the place, however separated from it, in time and distance, they may be.

Notes

1. For an overview of Dickinson's reading, see Jane Eberwein, "Dickinson's Local, Global, and Cosmic Perspectives," in *The Emily Dickinson Handbook*, Gudrun Grabher, Roland Hagenbüchle, and Cristanne Miller (eds.) (Amherst: University of Massachusetts Press, 2004). See also Cristanne Miller, *Reading in Time: Emily Dickinson in the Nineteenth Century* (Amherst: University of Massachusetts Press, 2012); Jack Capps, *Emily Dickinson's Reading* (Cambridge, MA: Harvard University Press, 1966); and Barton Levi St. Armand, *Emily Dickinson and Her Culture: The Soul's Society* (Cambridge: Cambridge University Press, 1984).
2. For studies of geographic terms in Dickinson's writing, see Robin Peel, *Emily Dickinson and the Hill of Science* (Madison, NJ: Fairleigh Dickinson University Press, 2010), 188–235, and Rebecca Patterson, *Emily Dickinson's Imagery* (Amherst: University of Amherst Press, 1979), 140–179. See also Carlton Lowenberg, *Emily Dickinson's Textbooks*, Territa A. Lowenberg and Carla L. Brown (eds.) (Lafayette, CA: C. Lowenberg, 1986).

3. The question of whether or not Dickinson's poems are *lyric* poems, precisely, has been the subject of recent critical debates, voiced most notably in Virginia Jackson, *Dickinson's Misery: A Theory of Lyric Reading* (Princeton: Princeton University Press, 2005). Rather than attempting to resolve what Dickinson's poems *are*, this essay is more concerned with observing what they attempt to *do*, following a model offered by Jed Deppman, whose book contends that Dickinson used her poetry as a means of thinking, or "trying to think," through "difficult projects of thought" (57). See Jed Deppman, *Trying to Think with Emily Dickinson* (Amherst: University of Massachusetts Press, 2008).
4. Dickinson follows a mode of accounting for the world distinct from the mode she adopts in many of her poems on the subject of nature and the environment. Compared to those poems that can be read productively through the lens of ecocriticism, for example, Dickinson's geographic poems are not necessarily or primarily concerned with addressing moral, ethical, or political questions regarding current (or future) interactions between human and nonhuman nature. Following the example of her geography books, Dickinson's geographic poems instead prioritize epistemological and ontological concerns, particularly regarding questions of what it is possible to know, learn, and communicate about the world and its physical features. For extended ecocritical readings of Dickinson, see Christine Gerhardt, *A Place for Humility: Whitman, Dickinson, and the Natural World* (Iowa City: University Of Iowa Press, 2014). Based on the specificity of their concerns, then, Dickinson's geographic poems should also be distinguished from instances in which she appeals to other natural sciences – especially geology, as we will see in this chapter's analysis of Dickinson's volcano poems. Given that geography was a nonprofessional and nonacademic practice through much of the nineteenth century, the province of amateurs and nonspecialists, Dickinson could engage in, and even contribute to, the discourse itself rather than only borrow its metaphors for the purpose of illustrating aspects of her personal experience or thought, as she did with terms and concepts from more specialized – and therefore more restricted – disciplines, such as astronomy or geology. For Dickinson's uses of astronomical language, see Brad Ricca, "Emily Dickinson: Learn'd Astronomer," *EDJ* 9.2 (2000): 96–108. For an extended study of Dickinson's engagements with nineteenth-century scientific discourses, see Robin Peel, *The Hill of Science*. Additionally, studies of Dickinson's inquiries into epistemological problems have not taken her engagement with nineteenth-century geography textbooks into consideration, opting to focus instead on her invocations of more advanced thought, in the form of scientific, philosophical, and theological discourses. See Nina Baym, *American Women of Letters and the Nineteenth-Century Sciences: Styles of Affiliation* (New Brunswick, NJ: Rutgers University Press, 2002), 133–151; Richard E. Brantley, *Emily Dickinson's Rich Conversation: Poetry, Philosophy, Science* (New York: Palgrave Macmillan, 2013); and Michelle Kohler, *Miles of Stare:*

Transcendentalism and the Problem of Literary Vision in Nineteenth-Century America (Tuscaloosa: University of Alabama Press, 2014), 105–136.
5. Richard Sewall, *The Life of Emily Dickinson* (Cambridge, MA: Harvard University Press, 1994), 362.
6. Jedidiah Morse, *American Universal Geography*, 6th ed (Boston: Thomas & Andrews, 1812), v.
7. Samuel Griswold Goodrich, *Peter Parley's Geography for Beginners* (New York: Huntington and Savage, 1847), 10.
8. See, for example, Margarita Bowen, *Empiricism and Geographical Thought: From Francis Bacon to Alexander von Humboldt* (Cambridge: Cambridge University Press, 1981), 171; Anne Godlewska, *Geography Unbound: French Geographic Science from Cassini to Humboldt* (Chicago: University of Chicago Press, 1999). More inclusive histories of geographic thought include David N. Livingstone, *The Geographical Tradition: Episodes in the History of a Contested Enterprise* (Oxford, UK, and Cambridge, MA: Blackwell, 1993); Geoffrey J. Martin, *All Possible Worlds: A History of Geographical Ideas*, 4th ed (New York: Oxford University Press, 2005); and Geoffrey J. Martin, *American Geography and Geographers: Toward Geographical Science* (Oxford and New York: Oxford University Press, 2015).
9. See Susan Schulten, *The Geographical Imagination in America, 1880–1950* (Chicago: University of Chicago Press, 2001), 70; Helena Michie and Ronald R. Thomas, eds., *Nineteenth-Century Geographies: The Transformation of Space from the Victorian Age to the American Century* (New Brunswick, NJ: Rutgers University Press, 2003), 11; Godlewska, *Geography Unbound*, 4–5.
10. For studies of geography and American literature, see especially Martin Brückner, *The Geographic Revolution in Early America: Maps, Literary, and National Identity* (Chapel Hill: University of North Carolina Press, 2006); Hsuan L. Hsu, *Geography and the Production of Space in Nineteenth-Century American Literature* (Cambridge and New York: Cambridge University Press, 2010); Martin Brückner and Hsuan Hsu, eds., *American Literary Geographies: Spatial Practice and Cultural Production, 1500–1900* (Newark: University of Delaware Press, 2007); Martha Schoolman, *Abolitionist Geographies* (Minneapolis: University of Minnesota Press, 2014).
11. Adrienne Rich, "Vesuvius at Home: The Power of Emily Dickinson," *Parnassus* 5.1 (1976).
12. Elizabeth A. Petrino, *Emily Dickinson and Her Contemporaries: Women's Verse in America, 1820–1885* (Hanover: University Press of New England, 1998), 194–200.
13. For the list of textbooks assigned at Mount Holyoke, see Sewall, *The Life of Emily Dickinson*, 367. For an extensive list of possible literary sources for Dickinson's volcano imagery, see Patterson, *Emily Dickinson's Imagery*, 171–174.

14. See Edward Hitchcock's *Elementary Geology* (1842) and its section on volcanoes, titled "Operation of Igneous Agencies in Producing Geological Changes."
15. Emma Hart Willard and William Channing Woodbridge, *Universal Geography*, 7th ed (Hartford: John Beach, 1836), 42.
16. Ibid., 42–43.
17. Richard Sewall, *The Lyman Letters: New Light on Emily Dickinson and Her Family* (Amherst: University of Amherst Press, 1965), 70–71.
18. Baym, 147.
19. Ibid., 151.
20. See Franklin's note to this poem (F476).

CHAPTER 11

Global Dickinson

Páraic Finnerty

For much of the last century, making a case for a global Dickinson would have seemed a daunting task. To place the American poet famous for shutting herself away from the world within an international context would seem paradoxical for, and even impertinent to, a writer who so carefully guarded her privacy and refused to publish her work. Although one of her most famous poems begins by addressing a far-flung audience – "This is my letter to the World / That never wrote to Me" – it ends with the speaker asking *only* her "Sweet countrymen" to "Judge tenderly" of her (F519). Following the import of this poem, which was used as a preface for the first edition of Dickinson's posthumously published poetry (1890), the early reception of Dickinson's work located it firmly within her nation's interpretative boundaries and presented her as a quintessentially American or New England poet, whose retiring life and decision to preserve her manuscript poems against the onslaught of publication harked back to an earlier, more innocent time.[1] For many twentieth- and twenty-first-century readers, Dickinson's focus on that which is interior and local has meant that her poetry has functioned as the last bastion of the personal and unmediated in a publicity-driven international public sphere.

The transnational turn in American studies, however, has unsettled just such interpretative paradigms, deriving as they do from the discipline's long-standing emphasis on what is geographically, politically, culturally, and historically unique about the United States. Twenty-first-century scholars have questioned narratives of US exceptionalism that confine analysis and research to the boundaries of US history and geography. The production and reception of US literature are now increasingly positioned within a global context, and the inextricably transnational nature of this nation and its culture are being explored.[2] Pointing to the "channels, kinship networks, routes of transit, and forms of attachment" that "[bind] America to the rest of the world," Wai Chee Dimock argues for American writing's indebtedness to "a crisscrossing set of pathways, open-ended and ever multiplying, weaving in and out of other geographies, other languages and cultures."[3] Calling attention to the relatively short history of the United States, Dimock demonstrates the ways its literature's intercontinental connections go backward and forward in "deep time" and cross vast distances of space. The ideal of a global civil society, for her, stems from just such transnational connections between disparate communities that literary culture and acts of reading facilitate. Paul Giles's work has also moved the discussion of American literature away from nationalist narratives of independence to ones of global interdependence, foregrounding the international dimensions of US literature that accentuate "relations between the United States and the rest of the world in terms of more complex, analogical processes of convergence and divergence."[4] He argues that "the nationalist phase of American literature and culture extended from 1865 until about 1981 and that the current transnational phase actually has more in common with writing from the periods on either side of the War of Independence, when national boundaries were much more inchoate and unsettled."[5] Dimock's and Giles's respective scholarship has thrown new light on the manner in which nineteenth-century writers such as Henry David Thoreau, Ralph Waldo Emerson, Margaret Fuller, Henry Wadsworth Longfellow, Herman Melville, and Nathaniel Hawthorne – even when they argued strongly for the establishment of a distinctive, national literature – were shaped by and engaged with the cosmopolitan leanings and global exchanges of their culture.

In line with these trajectories, twenty-first-century Dickinson scholarship has internationalized the poet. Recent publications, such as the essay collection *The International Reception of Emily Dickinson* (2009), offer an indication of the interpretative nuances given to Dickinson's work by readers, translators, and scholars from Germany, Austria, Switzerland, Ukraine, Japan, Israel, Brazil, Portugal, Sweden, Norway, the Low Countries, francophone Europe and North America, Britain, Ireland, and Australia.[6] Not only have Dickinson's writings reached the world beyond her "countrymen," but scholars have drawn attention to the ways in which the complexities of nineteenth-century globalization are reflected in what Giles calls her poetry's "antithetical play of alternating forces and perspectives" of local and foreign that decenters any given perspective and points to the relativity and provinciality of discernment, whether that of a New Englander or a British monarch (F256).[7] Building on such work, this essay offers a new way of approaching the fact that, although her writings gesture toward the uniqueness of her specific environment and the importance of seeing, as one poem puts it, "New Englandly" (F256), there is also a proclivity in her work to link the familiar to that which is alluringly "other" or exotic. Through cataloguing, in turn, her European, Latin American, Asian, and African imagery, we see her charting her country's multiple entanglements with other nations and cultures, but what newly emerges is her penchant for using the compressed space of her poems to move effortlessly from one part of the world to another, as well as across the span of world history. Her accounts of globalization are paired with her compact style, which, as I will argue, intensifies her depiction of international interdependence, combining notions of expansiveness with formal contractedness. These poems that include multiple global references and involve condensations of transgeographical and transhistorical global connectedness greatly internationalize Dickinson's signature interiorized speakers, indicating her sense that subjectivity in her era had become constituted by and mapped through a complexity of global coordinates. Her poems' sparse, dense, telegraph-like form, furthermore, evokes the rapidity and shifting nature of transnational connectedness though the era's proliferation of technologies that increasingly facilitated and sped up exchange and communication between individuals across the globe.

While Dickinson's writings evoke her native land, its history, its natural qualities, and associative artifacts, the majority of her geographic references are to countries, regions, cities, towns, mountains, volcanoes, seas, and rivers associated with Europe, South America, Asia, Africa, and Australia and to people, animals, edifices, or objects connected with these locations.[8] Her writings' global features seem to stem from her belief in the "Entice[ment]" of connecting things, ideas, and moments that are "Opposites" (F612) and from her determination to "dwell" in a "Possibility" that imaginatively defies national, geographical, and historical boundaries (F466). Typically, she uses such foreign imagery, as Cristanne Miller argues, to "express complex desires, critique the world she knew, and describe things she loved" but also to symbolize the poet's role as a "potential or psychological traveler" into "the previously unimagined or unknown."[9] The almost routine nature of her reaching outside her nation's boundaries suggests, however, the ways in which in her era globalization had become normalized.

Dickinson, despite her home-loving nature, was conditioned by her education and reading to have an international focus. Dickinson's study of Geography at Amherst Academy and Mount Holyoke, for example, meant that she was predisposed to interrelate a place's history, human and nonhuman inhabitants, geological features, religion, and culture and to view comparatively the various locations that mark what in one poem she calls the "Divisions of the Earth" (F1152). Such ideals were reinforced by her reading of foreign news in *The Springfield Republican* as well as by pieces on travel, exploration, and adventure in the periodicals to which the Dickinson family subscribed, including *Harper's New Monthly*, *The Atlantic Monthly*, and *Scribner's Monthly*. What we know of Dickinson's reading and the extant Dickinson family library confirm the vogue for travel writing, both fictional and nonfictional, and the availability of historical and contemporary accounts of colonialism. Print culture ensured that Dickinson's quotidian reality and personal identity were shaped by the ubiquity of narratives of transcultural interactions. Dickinson's transnational poetry, then, reflects the fact that the "unfamiliar and strange" and the "unknowable and inaccessible" were inherent elements of a worldview that was continually complicated by ongoing discoveries, whether scientific, geographical, geological, or astronomical, and by concurrent reports of encounters with racial, ethnic, and national difference.[10]

Nineteenth-century migration and technological developments also internationalized many facets of life – travel, communication, commerce, media, and politics – and lessened the psychological and practical distance between that which was once geographically far. For example, the laying of the Atlantic telegraph cable, according to the *Springfield Republican* on August 7, 1858, turned "the world into a nutshell" and transformed it into a "vast community."[11] While presenting the reading of literature as frugally facilitating a "Human Soul['s]" "Travel" to "Lands away," her poem "There is no Frigate like a Book" (F1286) also connotes a new ease of movement from one part of the world to another. Dickinson's imaginative journeys through reading were supplemented by accounts given by those within Dickinson's circle of family, friends, and neighbors who travelled to Europe and beyond, whom she sometimes asked to function as her proxies. She wrote the following to Thomas Wentworth Higginson: "To have seen Stratford on Avon – and the Dresden Madonna, must be almost Peace – And perhaps you have spoken with George Eliot. Will you 'tell me about it?'" (L553). She asks Samuel Bowles, "[I]f you touch [Elizabeth Barrett Browning's] Grave, put one hand on the Head, for me – her unmentioned Mourner" (L266), and she instructs Mabel Loomis Todd to "Touch Shakespeare for me" (L1004). Her poetic connections of the domestic and the exotic also reflect the increasing multiculturalism of her society, owing to immigration to the United States, which affected her through her relationships with her family's Irish servants. Journeying consecutively through her appropriation and complication of stereotypes and commonplace ideas about Europe, South America, Africa, and Asia, we see the ways in which her foreign references signpost a world of alternatives to and within any nation-based construction of gender, race, and identity, variations that her compressed style combines.

Underlining her culture's transatlantic connections, the majority of her global references relate to Europe. Dickinson associates Europe with the fine manufactured goods of Brussels and Kidderminster (F510), Sevres (F706), and Geneva (F259); great achievements in literature, music, and the arts (F327, F378, F523); high fashion (F96, F254); and social hierarchy (F575, F602). Typically, places in Europe, such as Vevay, Paris, Venice, and Exeter in "Pigmy Seraphs – gone astray –" (F96), are positioned in comparative relations with presumably New England settings – in this poem, a garden of bumblebees and flowers. Although such geographical analogies sometimes lead to a preference or validation of one location over another, the priority is to join the familiar and unfamiliar to approximate most accurately the transnational elements of everyday experiences or events. In other poems, Dickinson's speakers travel to Charlotte Brontë's grave in Haworth (F146) and Elizabeth Barrett Browning's home in Florence (F637), or present recognition as suddenly being identified as a "Bourbon" queen summoned to "Exeter" (F575). Her European references, however, are also about traversing the continent's national and regional borders. A poem such as "I think the Hemlock likes to stand" (F400) seems to evoke racial ideologies in 1850s and 1860s New England when members of Dickinson's class sought to align themselves with the races of Northern Europe whose colder climate was associated "with purity and excellence," "the mind in control of the senses and the sensual," intellect, austerity, severity, and "the subtle and not the spectacular."[12] The Hemlock's ability to thrive and be sustained by coldness, "Austerity," snow, "the Gnash of Northern winds," and "Lapland's – nescessity" and to create the "best Norwegian Wines" is contrasted with those "satin Races," the playful "children on the Don," and "Dnieper Wrestlers" from Eastern and Southeastern Europe whose lives are associated with vivacity and spontaneity:

> The Hemlock's nature thrives – on cold –
> The Gnash of Northern winds
> Is sweetest nutriment – to him –
> His best Norwegian Wines –
>
> To satin Races – he is nought –
> But children on the Don,
> Beneath his Tabernacles, play,
> And Dnieper Wrestlers, run. (F400)

While she is trafficking in nineteenth-century stereotypes, there is no explicit maligning of those from Southern Europe, associated with heat and passionate excess. Rather Dickinson, as she so often does, juxtaposes binaries to highlight the interdependence of opposites, such as pleasure and restraint, or desire and duty, and refuses to validate one or the other. She presents a transnational perspective involving the possibility of dual or shifting allegiances between northern rigidity and southern fluidity. The poem's global scope rests not merely on the relations established between two European regions, that are intensified by the poem's form, but also on the constitution of the speaker's New World identity as observer and inheritor of these Old World antipathies. While Dickinson's speaker conceptualizes the influence of European regions on their inhabitants, the poem reveals that identities, including the speaker's own, are invested in and constituted by larger global relations.

A comparable externalizing of American self-division is also evident in "Our lives are Swiss" (F129), which describes one afternoon when the Alps "neglect their curtains" and the "Swiss," associated with a life of conformity and restrictive morality, look longingly at Italy:

> Our lives are Swiss –
> So still – so cool –
> Till some odd afternoon
> The Alps neglect their curtains
> And we look further on.
> *Italy* stands the other side.
> While like a guard between –
> The solemn Alps –
> The siren Alps
> Forever intervene –   (F129)

Connecting local with global, Dickinson associates New England restraint with cool Switzerland's regularity and then implies that Italy exemplifies the possibility of living otherwise, with vivacity and impulsiveness. The poem's structure, like the Alps themselves, links rather than separates the country from where American dogmatic Calvinism originated and a land associated with Catholicism, great art, and sensory excess. Such poems corroborate Alison Byerly's argument that nineteenth-century realist fiction and travel writing offered readers a form of virtuality that caused and came to symbolize the experience of personal fragmentation and dissonance. Tapping into these ideas, Dickinson's references to other geographical locations confirm that travel becomes, as Byerly argues, "a metaphor for the imaginative displacement of the self," which gives "a sense of being in two places at once, constantly negotiating the space between them."[13] Creating complex global crossings, underlined by the poem's brevity, Dickinson's Swiss-identifying and Scandinavian-admiring New England speakers are haunted by a glimpse at or imagined journeys to a different, Southern way of life, the notion of an alternative selfhood, and experiences deferred or forbidden. Although not absolved of the racialized underpinnings of this North and South binary, in these poems Dickinson resists the idea that her native land and its citizens are integrated and unified entities, preferring to present their complexity in and through their openness to a range of global influences.

In other poems, while Dickinson relates European locations and geographical features to aspects of American life, she places these connections in an explicitly international frame. She connotes powerful forces within local or domestic individuals using Italy's volcanoes Vesuvius and Etna (F165, F517, F1161, F1691). Her volcanic poems present hidden rage or desire, as well as warn against complacency about volcanoes closer to home that sometimes "bask" and "purr" but never actually erupt and let their "pleasure through" (F1161, 1869; F764, 1863). Her most famous depiction of repressed or reserved potentiality, however, has recourse to transnationally interconnected volcanoes "in Sicily" and those in "South America," with a "Volcano nearer here," "Vesuvius at Home" (F1619). In "More Life – went out – when He went" (F415) the profound loss of just such a powerful individual requires the latitude of global imagery: she connotes his vitality by interrelating the South American volcano "Popocatapel" and "Etna's Scarlets" and his extinction as "reduc[ing] / The Ethiop within" (F415). Whether distinguishing between volcanic depths and calm surfaces or a "finer" individual and the "Ordinary" masses, Dickinson draws on a multicontinental range of imagery to capture complex subjectivities but also subjectivity's extranational basis and reach. In a similar manner, Dickinson presents commanding, unmoving structures such as Tenerife (F752), the Alps (F108, F129, F977), and the Apennines (F191, F203) within the dynamics of worldwide relations. In "We see – Comparatively –" (F580), Dickinson uses a spectacular intercontinental crossing to formulate the way in which the subjective experience of presence and absence, possession and loss are now globally measured:

> This Morning's finer Verdict –
> Makes scarcely worth the toil –
> A furrow – Our Cordillera –
> Our Appenine – a knoll –

This, the poem's second stanza, formally and spatially links the European Apennines and the cordillera associated with South American mountain ranges to underline the power of poetry to bind opposites and incongruities and to reflect broader global relationships. Her poetics help chart an interiority of cosmopolitan range and a diversity and plurality of perspectives and experiences. Similarly, in "They leave us with the Infinite" (F352), the speaker attempting to describe the "Infinite" imagines the global scope of his incredible powers:

> And whom he foundeth, with his Arm
> As Himmaleh, shall stand –
> Gibraltar's everlasting Shoe
> Poised lightly on his Hand

The Infinite, in a manner analogous to Dickinson's poem, is geographically far-reaching, crossing climatic zones to link an Asian mountain range with the geological gateway to the Mediterranean Sea, which divides Europe from Africa. Despite her poetry's strong transatlantic affiliations, Dickinson also specializes in capturing globalization's effect on subjective and intersubjective experience through interrelating regions, nations, and continents and underlining their associations through her poetic concision.

Dickinson's references to Latin America counter any attempt to contain her or her work within a nation-based conception of temporal and spatial reach. Rebecca Patterson argues that in Dickinson's writing "all South America, the Caribbean, Mexico, and Central America" are "embedded in this matrix of symbols signifying incalculable wealth or unobtainable desire," suggesting that Dickinson "may have been drawn to her Latin American images by a kind of hemispheric patriotism."[14] Recent scholarship by Anna Brickhouse and Kirsten Silva Gruesz offers a new context for Patterson's claim, identifying a nineteenth-century transamerican literary network of multi-directional relations among the United States, Latin America, and the Caribbean.[15] Dickinson's Latin American references suggest that she, like Washington Irving, Hawthorne, James Fenimore Cooper, Walt Whitman, William Cullen Bryant, John Greenleaf Whittier, and Longfellow, saw herself as part of a literary culture extending across the Americas that facilitated cross-continental sensibilities and exchanges. Showing the influence of these hemispheric affinities, her poetry evokes the bounteousness and beauty of Bolivia (F118, F1162), Mexico (F1505), Brazil (F288, F661, F944), Buenos Ayre (F418), and the imposing

Chimborazo (F452), Andes (F897), and Cordillera (F281, F580, F1041) as well as the colors purple, cochineal, and emerald associated with this region. She domesticates such imagery to delineate interior and exterior experiences relating to the natural world and interpersonal relations. For instance, connoting the gold of Peru (F266, F418, F1462), the diamonds of Brazil (F687), the emeralds of Mexico/Vera Cruz (F726), the diamonds of Bolivia (F565), silver mines of Potosi (F118, F1162), and cargoes of goods from Balize (F1127), San Domingo (F95, F726, F1064, F1488), and the Bahamas (F726), Dickinson's speakers map uneven relations of power or desire between individuals within the context of this region's links with international trade and colonization.

Conveying some of these ideas about Latin America, "I could bring You Jewels – had I a mind to –" presents a speaker-trader who deals in the precious gemstones of this region and could provide these treasures "had [she] a mind to"; however, the already-rich addressee is instead offered exotic colors and odors from St Domingo, Vera Cruz, and the Bahamas:

> I could bring You Jewels – had I a mind to –
> But You have enough – of those –
> I could bring You Odors from St Domingo –
> Colors – from Vera Cruz –
>
> Berries of the Bahamas – have I –
> But this little Blaze
> Flickering to itself – in the meadow –
> Suits Me – more than those –
>
> Never a Fellow matched this Topaz –
> And his Emerald Swing –
> Dower itself – for Bobadilo –
> Better – Could I bring? (F726)

Again, as in her European poems, this poem charts transcontinental movement: from St Domingo to Mexico to the Bahamas. Tapping into the speed of international markets and communications, the presumably US-based speaker is not describing journeys or specific locations but rather displaying the assurance of her economic kudos and symbolic trading power. In its evoking of global trade, the poem recalls "Your Riches – taught me – Poverty" (F418) with its interconnection of the riches of Argentina and Peru with the wealth of India and Golconda, as well as "What would I give to see his face?" (F266) whose speaker crosses the globe, going from Zanzibar, Peru, and Venice, to find something to please a reclusive addressee. Although the speaker's own location is less important than her position as a center for the exchange of foreign and exotic goods, she still claims the superior value of a hidden local "little Blaze / Flickering to itself – in the meadow." Her reference to "Bobadilo" places these erotic and commercial relations in the context of European imperialism. Dickinson may be evoking Francisco de Bobadilla, the Spanish governor of Santo Domingo who ordered the arrest of Christopher Columbus and sent him back to Spain in chains, before seizing the treasures Columbus had taken from the island's inhabitants.[16] More provocatively, she may connote Isabel de Bobadilla, who was the wife of Hernando de Soto and became, in her husband's absence, the first governor of Cuba, suggesting the poem's addressee could be a powerful male or female figure.[17] Here, as in her other Latin American allusions to the journeys of goods and people and discoveries of European explorers/colonizers such as Francisco Pizarro González (F136, F368), Christopher Columbus (F2, F561), and Hernando de Soto (F814), she renders global and political that which is subjective and private. In this, although Dickinson's texts foreground the international scale of European exploitation, they participate in practices of objectification and exoticization, and they abstract colonialism's horrors.

Dickinson's use of the word "Domingo" is particularly thought-provoking, as she is choosing a culturally charged term that was shorthand for the Haitian Revolution (1791–1804), a bloody insurrection of slaves against their European oppressors which led to the foundation of the first Black Republic in 1804.[18] Throughout the antebellum period, "Domingo" was a watchword for what might happen in the United States, particularly in the slave-owning southern states. Dickinson's "Domingo" (F95, F726, F1064, F1488) encodes, as Erica Fretwell notes, "lawless violence in the taste for personhood," "[her imagining of] what freedom might taste like for African Americans," and her "domestic[ation of] the racially exotic."[19] By positioning "Odors from St Domingo" within a commercial and erotic marketplace, this 1863 poem foregrounds the slave trade, its materialistic roots, and the personhood and type of interpersonal relations denied to slaves. Dickinson's phrase connotes the intrinsic value of liberty, whether that enjoyed by Haitian slaves who revolted or that sought by African Americans whose status as commodities was being fought over in the Civil War. But her poem elides the realities of colonialism, revolution, and war, and exoticizes the racial other, to acknowledge phenomena and persons of inestimable worth that transcend marketplaces and symbolize freedom from forces of restraint, whether internal or external. The poem's transnational and transhistorical scope and interconnection of European imperialism, slavery, and global trade are finally subordinate to the speaker's depiction of an exclusive, private relationship and domestic drama.[20]

Dickinson's references to Asia, like those to Latin America, depict it as a remote, mysterious region of "fabulous wealth and luxury"; her Asiatic imagery primarily relates to "the Bible land, India and the Indies, and an intermediate region consisting of Arabia, Turkey, Persia, and the Caspian Sea."[21] She refers to the exoticism, treasures, and color of India (F228, F388, F418, F606, F1509), Golconda (F418), Cashmere (F98, F111, F162, F176, F749), Burma (F1488), and Malaysia (F417, F451), appropriating and disrupting these popular associations by incorporating them into her more localized explorations of natural phenomena, subjective states, and interpersonal relations. Scholars such as Cristanne Miller and Li-hsin Hsu have demonstrated the influence of pervasive ideas about the "Orient" in New England print culture, at a time of increased actual interactions between Americans and Asians on US soil. These realities shape Dickinson's representation of Asia, its human and nonhuman inhabitants, geography, and artifacts.[22] As with her South American imaginary, we see Dickinson's representations of Asia connoting desire, natural beauty, and luxury but also raising the specter of European exploitation. Again, Dickinson's globalism creates points of sympathetic identification with those exploited. For example, the poem "Civilization – spurns – the Leopard" (F276) is structured to imply that the speaker does, and the reader should, feel affinity with the Asiatic "other" against the spurning, rebuking, and frowning European "Signor":

> Civilization – spurns – the Leopard!
> Was the Leopard – bold?
> Deserts – never rebuked her Satin –
> Ethiop – her Gold –
> Tawny – her Customs –
> She was Conscious –
> Spotted – her Dun Gown –
> This was the Leopard's nature – Signor –
> Need – a keeper – frown?
>
> Pity – the Pard – that left her Asia!
> Memories – of Palm –
> Cannot be stifled – with Narcotic –
> Nor suppressed – with Balm – (F276)

As Leslie McAbee notes, if the "speaker's assumed intimacy with the cat allows the reader to travel imaginatively through the Leopard's memories to a land 'of Palm,'" the "glancing reference to the global opium trade further contributes to the Leopard's status as an exoticized Oriental commodity."[23] Again, as in "I could bring You Jewels – had I a mind to –," Dickinson's text highlights European civilization's historical and contemporary exploitation of the rest of the world but also reenacts colonialism's naturalization of the exchange and display of the exotic other. Dickinson exhibits this transnational leopard, a native of both Asia and Africa, that can traverse humanity's categories and borders; however, the leopard's global range ends in confinement as she has been tempted away from her beloved "Deserts" by "Signor." The speaker symbolically appropriates the leopard's memories of her native habitat and old customs that cannot be lessened with either narcotics or balm.

Patterson describes Dickinson's African imagery as a kaleidoscope of color, shape, and exuberance, often associated with spectacular events that bring the exotic to small New England towns.[24] To a large extent Dickinson's allusions to Egypt (F584), Tunis (F1489), Ethiopia (F276, F415, F1678), Timbuctoo (F801), Tripoli (F806, F1562, F1563, F1650), the Red Sea (F1681), Numidian (F1395), Sahara (F1262, F1708), Zanzibar (F266), and Libya (F862) follow the same pattern of deployment and complication discussed so far. A poem that refers to Tunis, however, offers the best example of what this essay is newly identifying as Dickinson's predilection for global crisscrossing within the compact space of an individual poem. Dickinson's most-distributed poem, "A Route of Evanescence" (F1489), hyperbolically connotes speed and compression through reference to effortless topographical movements from one location to another. The poem rapidly connects a New England garden with South American color and then both of these with Africa through a complex allusion to a play by the epitome of European literary culture, William Shakespeare:

> A Route of Evanescence
> With a delusive wheel
> A Resonance of Emerald
> A Rush of Cochineal
> And every Blossom on the Bush
> Adjusts it's tumbled Head –
> The Mail from Tunis – probably –
> An easy morning's ride –

The flashes of the bird's colors as it disappears into the distance are "Emerald" and "cochineal," associated with Latin America, while "The

Mail from Tunis" connects its magical journey into invisibility with Ariel from Shakespeare's *The Tempest*. The Shakespearean allusion evokes the moment in the play when Prospero's brother Antonio suggests to Sebastian that he kill his sleeping brother, Alonso, the king of Naples. The murder would allow Sebastian to assume the Neapolitan throne now, as Alonso's son, Ferdinand, is presumed dead and his daughter, Claribel, is incommunicado in Tunis. To prevent this conspiracy, Ariel transforms into a hummingbird to waken the nobleman Gonzalo, functioning in Dickinson's clipped phrase as the sudden postal intervention of Claribel. This telegram-like poem reflects her era's internationalization of communications, trade, and travel that disrupts the strictures of nation. The hummingbird's swiftness underscores her poetry's resistance to being bound in any spatial location or by any one perspective. Dickinson's terse poem contains and contracts the globalization and exoticization it maps, relating her local hummingbird's "easy morning ride" to Shakespeare's play about European journeys, treachery, and colonization and to the exotic colors and treasures associated in the nineteenth century with South American trade and exploitation.

The references to European colonization and Shakespeare point to the fact that some of Dickinson's global poems not only cross geographical boundaries but also temporal ones.[25] Dickinson's allusions to that which is geographically and historically distant correspond to what Dimock calls the "deep time" of the planet Earth that highlights its "multitudinous life," "binding continents and millennia into many loops of relations" and "loosening up the chronology and geography of the nation."[26] While many poems use brief allusions to historical events or figures, "A precious – mouldering pleasure – 'tis –"(F569) comes closest to Dimock's claim for American literature's participation in world literature and for the artist and artwork as transcending national, geographical, and historical boundaries. Her poem celebrates literature as a means of bringing nations together and reading as a cosmopolitan practice that forges a planetary community through the sharing of the world's cultural treasures. The venerability of "Antique Book[s]" is connected with the historical knowledge they provide:

> His quaint opinions – to inspect –
> His thought to ascertain
> On Themes concern our mutual mind –
> The Literature of Man –

> What interested Scholars – most –
> What Competitions ran –
> When Plato – was a Certainty –
> And Sophocles – a Man –
>
> When Sappho – was a living Girl –
> And Beatrice wore
> The Gown that Dante – deified –
> Facts Centuries before
> . . .

Although in previously discussed poems, Dickinson associates European civilization with exploitation and bloodshed, here Europe is connected with classical and Renaissance writers whose works facilitate shared imagined journeys back in time, through the centuries, to alternative perspectives as well as to the origins of Western culture. Other Dickinson poems evoke Greek (F391, F524, F1023, F1606) and Etruscan (F300, F1574) civilization as a means of giving private, seemingly unique events a larger historical scope. Dickinson's multiple global references that involve temporal as well as territorial crossings underline her vision of a planetary subjectivity and of poetry's unique ability to capture such worldwide connectedness.

Further evidence can also be put forward for the inclusion of Dickinson in Dimock's list of "American poet[s] recklessly embracing the aesthetic heritage of the world" and commingling American experiences with world history.[27] Her poetry interlinks the world's continents and cultures but also highlights the Earth's temporal expanse. For example, in poem F124E, "Safe in their Alabaster Chambers," Dickinson offers a bleak account of the dead, excluded from the world of the living and waiting in safety for the promised "Resurrection." Yet through a brief reference to the powerful Doges of Venice, the poem unites the living and the dead as insignificant within a planetary and historical span:

> Grand go the Years – in the Crescent – above them –
> Worlds scoop their Arcs –
> And Firmaments – row –
> Diadems – drop – and Doges – surrender –
> Soundless as dots – on a Disc of snow –

Temporal, astronomical, political, and meteorological activity, the poem suggests, has always taken place "above" the dead, who, of course, are not safe from the processes of decay so central to geological "deep time." Similarly, in "We dream – it is good we are dreaming –" (F584) and "It is an honorable Thought" (F1115), Dickinson extends their geographical and historical breadth through references to Egyptian civilization. In the first poem, it is better to fantasize about one's metaphysical possibilities than to face the fact that, as has happened previously in history, each human life and death will be reduced to "Shafts of Granite" "With just an age – and name – / And perhaps a phrase in Egyptian." The second poem more positively imagines an "immortal Place" for humanity, presumably in heaven, "Though Pyramids decay / And Kingdoms, like the Orchard/ Flit Russetly away." Dickinson's poetic movements between near and far, and past and present, correspond to what Dimock describes as a "shuttl[ing] back and forth between two scales, two lengths of temporal measurement" in American literature when repositioned in its global relations. As Dimock puts it, "scale enlargement here undoes human singularity and preserves it through that undoing."[28] Providing global and planetary scope, Dickinson's references render individual experiences trivial, singular, private, local, commonplace, and inconsequential but also give them an objective part within the world's history.

Drawing on the energies of globalization, Dickinson's compressed style brings together that which is historically and geographically separated, maximizing reach within a minimized space. She delights in poetry's power to traverse the globe, to go, as she puts it in one poem, "From Amherst to Cashmere" (F176), and in globalization's challenge to fixed personal and national identities which she locates within an international traffic that encourages fluidity, otherness, and intertextuality. Dickinson's practice, however, can be read as containing that which is different or distant, of controlling space and interaction through strategies of careful separation and selection within progressively crowded systems of worldwide exchange. Although her poems gesture toward the notion of an international community and a shared human history, the "very brevity" of her global references signals her "readiness to trade on" biased assumptions about race and nationality.[29] Further explication of a global Dickinson, as this essay shows, requires scrutiny of her writing's deployment of problematic stereotypes and ideologies and a return to discussions of Dickinson and race.

Notes

1. Jane Donahue Eberwein, Stephanie Farrar, and Cristanne Miller, eds., *Dickinson in Her Own Time: A Biographical Chronicle of Her Life* (University of Iowa Press, 2015), xxi–xxiv.

2. See Yogita Goyal, ed., *The Cambridge Companion to Transnational American Literature* (Cambridge: Cambridge University Press, 2017).
3. Wai Chee Dimock, *Through Other Continents: American Literature Across Deep Time* (Princeton: Princeton University Press, 2006), 3.
4. Paul Giles, *The Global Remapping of American Literature* (Princeton: Princeton University Press, 2011), 23.
5. Giles, *Global Remapping*, 21.
6. Domhnall Mitchell and Maria Stuart, eds., *The International Reception of Emily Dickinson* (London: Continuum, 2009).
7. Paul Giles, "'The Earth reversed her Hemispheres': Dickinson's Global Antipodality," *EDJ* 20.1 (2011): 14.
8. "Of the 162 placenames in Dickinson's poems, 70 refer to places in Europe, 17 to the Middle East, 12 each refer to Africa and North America, 11 each to Central America and Eurasia, 10 each to Asia and South America, and 1 reference each to Austronesia and the North Pole." Cynthia L. Hallen and Malina M. Nielson, "Emily Dickinson's Placenames," *Names: A Journal of Onomastics* 54.1 (March 2006): 6.
9. Cristanne Miller, *Reading in Time: Emily Dickinson in the Nineteenth Century* (Amherst: University of Massachusetts Press, 2012), 118, 143.
10. Robin Peel, *Emily Dickinson and the Hill of Science* (Madison and Teaneck: Fairleigh Dickinson University Press, 2010), 192.
11. Quoted in Miller, *Reading in Time*, 122.
12. Domhnall Mitchell, "Northern Lights: Class, Color, Culture, and Emily Dickinson," *EDJ* 9.2 (2000): 75, 79.
13. Alison Byerly, *Are We There Yet: Virtual Travel and Victorian Realism* (Ann Arbor: Michigan University Press, 2013), 2, 204.
14. Rebecca Patterson, *Emily Dickinson's Imagery* (Amherst: University of Massachusetts Press, 1979), 143, 148.
15. Anna Brickhouse, *Transamerican Literary Relations and the Nineteenth-Century Public Sphere* (Cambridge: Cambridge University Press, 2004), 29, 126; Kirsten Silva Gruesz, *Ambassadors of Culture: The Transamerican Origins of Latino Writing* (Princeton: Princeton University Press, 2002), 6, 37.
16. The Emily Dickinson Lexicon: http://edl.byu.edu/lexicon/term/585406.
17. Peel, *Emily Dickinson*, 222.
18. See Ed Folsom and Kenneth M. Price, "Dickinson, Slavery, and the San Domingo Moment." The Classroom Electric, 2001. http://whitmanarchive.org/resources/teaching/dickinson/index.html.
19. Erica Fretwell, "Emily Dickinson in Domingo," *J19: The Journal of Nineteenth-Century Americanists* 1.1 (2013): 72, 74, 76.
20. See Kirsten Silva Gruesz, "The Geographical Imagination in Whitman and Dickinson," The Classroom Electric, 2001. www.classroomelectric.org/volume1/gruesz/index.htm; Stephanie Browner, "Love and Conquest: The Erotics of Colonial Discourse in Emily Dickinson's Poems and Letters," The Classroom Electric, 2001. www.classroomelectric.org/volume1/browner2/
21. Paterson, *Emily Dickinson's Imagery*, 157, 156.

22. See Miller, *Reading in Time*, 118–146; Li-hsin Hsu, "Emily Dickinson's Asian Consumption," *EDJ* 22.2 (2013): 1–25.
23. Leslie McAbee, "Through the Tiger's Eye: Constructing Animal Exoticism in Emily Dickinson's 'Big Cat' Poems," *EDJ* 26.1 (2017): 9, 10.
24. Patterson, *Emily Dickinson's Imagery*, 148–156.
25. Páraic Finnerty, *Emily Dickinson's Shakespeare* (Amherst: University of Massachusetts Press, 2006).
26. Dimock, *Through Other Continents*, 3, 4.
27. Ibid., 108.
28. Ibid., 87–88.
29. Paula Bernat Bennett, "'The Negro never knew': Emily Dickinson and Racial Typology in the Nineteenth Century," *Legacy* 19.1 (2002): 56.

CHAPTER 12

Dickinson and George Moses Horton
Faith Barrett

In *Playing in the Dark*, Toni Morrison urges scholars to consider how texts by white canonical authors respond to the presence of people of African descent on American soil from the time of the nation's founding.[1] Morrison contends that the "Americanness" of canonical white writers is fundamentally shaped by their ambivalent responses to racial ideologies. With the historical turn in Dickinson studies, scholars have now read her poems with attention to their racially inflected imagery.[2] Scholars have also read Dickinson in relation to non-canonical white women writers.[3] Few, however, have offered comparative readings that position Dickinson's project in relation to the work of African American poets.[4] What do we lose by failing to pursue such comparative readings? What are the rewards of pursuing them? And what are the potential risks or limits of such readings? These are some of the questions this essay will explore through a comparative analysis of Dickinson and the enslaved poet George Moses Horton. While scholars who have analyzed race in Dickinson's work have often focused on poems that explicitly address racial hierarchies, this essay will instead attend to a set of conventions and themes that these two writers share in spite of their very different life circumstances.

In their poems, Horton and Dickinson juxtapose images of freedom of movement with images of physical immobility, an immobility that presents embodiment as a kind of captivity.[5] In Horton's poetics as in Dickinson's, this dialectic of stasis and movement is a defining feature. This essay then will examine a pair of poems that foreground this tension between immobility and movement, considering how each writer uses poetic conventions to represent and contest the conditions of his or her confinement. At the same time, however, my essay will also grapple with the problems of this comparison. As I will go on to suggest, Horton's enslaved condition certainly shapes the tension between immobility and movement in his pieces; Dickinson's reclusiveness and her experience of gender expectations for white middle-class women shape the analogous tension in her poems. The circumstances of these two writers' lives are of course incommensurable: Horton's enslavement cannot be likened to Dickinson's oppression as a white middle-class woman. Dickinson's poems, however, sometimes pursue such comparisons themselves. Working for the cause of women's rights in the antebellum era, white women writers appropriated the experience of enslaved women of color to represent the oppression of women more broadly, and Dickinson draws on this discourse.[6] Critical race theory reminds white scholars to be ever attentive to the ways that the lenses of white privilege both appropriate and exclude the experience of people of color. Surely one reason Dickinson has rarely been read in relation to African American poets is that such a comparison obliges us to reckon with her white privilege in ways that are potentially uncomfortable for white scholars. It is of course inherently problematic to liken her representation of confinement – shaped by gender roles for white middle-class women and also her probable agoraphobia – with the representation of slavery in works by writers of color. Yet if we neglect Dickinson's own use of such imagery, we risk pursuing "race-free" readings that both perpetuate and obscure Dickinson's white privilege.

To put this idea in other words, we will fail to resituate Dickinson fully in her nineteenth-century context if we do not read her poems in relation to the work of her African American contemporaries; and work by African American poets can and should be read in relation to the work of canonical white poets, including Dickinson. We need to pursue these comparative readings both because they will advance scholarship about Dickinson and because they will allow us to resituate African American poets in the multiple discursive contexts in which they lived and wrote. At the same time, we need to pursue these readings with careful attention to the differences of race and class and experience that separate writers of color from canonical white figures. Before turning to two specific poems, then, I want to reflect further on the similarities and differences in these two writers' thematic commitments; I will also consider how their radically different life circumstances shape those commitments.

In Dickinson's poems, the tension between images of free movement and images of confinement is certainly shaped by her experience of traditional gender roles. While Emerson argues that each individual must establish his own relationship to nature, Dickinson's poems often reflect on the limits of this model for middle-class women. Though women in mid-nineteenth-century New England could and did take solitary walks in rural settings, such behavior was limited not only by domestic duties but also by a moral code that did not yet wholly accord genteel women such liberties. In his late essay "Walking," Thoreau laments this confinement: "How womankind, who are confined to the house still more than men, stand it I do not know."[7] He goes on to conjecture that "most of them do not *stand* it at all," suggesting that women are anesthetized to the point of daytime slumber. Calling for layers of corsets and crinolines, dress codes for genteel women also conspired to limit their movements.[8] Little wonder then that Dickinson's poems offer us speakers who are either entrapped in interior spaces – hemmed in perhaps by household duties and societal expectations – or who roam the woods and fields, imaginatively freed from these constraints.

The tension between entrapment and mobility in Horton's work is a direct response to his enslaved condition.[9] Writing in his home state of North Carolina, Horton uses images of free movement to protest implicitly the control that slave masters exercised over every aspect of a slave's existence, from the rationing of food and clothing to the hours of labor to the granting of written passes for travel. Born into slavery at the end of the eighteenth century, Horton began as a young man to make weekly walks on Sundays from his master's farm to the university campus at Chapel Hill. There he sold fruit, ran errands, and worked as a jack-of-all-trades for the young white male students. He also began composing made-to-order love poems for the young white women the students were pursuing. So successful was he at this latter activity that he eventually persuaded his master to let him hire his own time. From the 1820s until the outbreak of the Civil War, Horton lived in Chapel Hill supporting himself by writing love poems for paying clients. During that time he also published two collections of poetry, *The Hope of Liberty* (1829) and his *Poetical Works* (1845). While he had used his first collection to plead for his emancipation, by the time he completed his *Poetical Works* in 1845, the Nat Turner rebellion (1831) had resulted in a tightening of Southern laws controlling free and enslaved African Americans. Because Horton can no longer protest his enslavement explicitly, he turns instead to indirect means. Horton's *Poetical Works* is arguably the most multilayered and ambivalent of his three known collections because of the ways it offers oblique resistance to slavery.

Horton's and Dickinson's life experiences were radically different; there are nonetheless some striking similarities in their writing practices. Both were known in their respective communities as poets; both lived in towns that were strongly shaped by universities, providing access to editors, readers, books, and magazines; both developed poet personae, writing poems about poetic inspiration. Moreover, both circulated their poems in manuscript form, and both built their reputations as poets on this practice. Dickinson sent many poems to friends and family members, and Horton's made-to-order poems clearly also circulated among the family members of their intended addressees. Although Horton, unlike Dickinson, also chose to publish his work in book form, his ability to see those collections into print was certainly shaped by the fact that he had built a reputation as a poet-for-hire. Through circulation of their handwritten poems, Horton and Dickinson achieve a kind of freedom of movement that corresponds to the freedom of movement displayed by some of their poet-speakers.

I am excited by the idea that manuscript circulation enables both writers to achieve an imaginative mobility, but ultimately this comparison emphasizes the very different circumstances that shaped that circulation in each writer's case. Every writerly decision Horton makes during the antebellum years is necessarily shaped by his relationship with the white Southern readers on whom his income and his identity as a poet depend; as Leon Jackson argues, Horton's writing was embedded in a patronage economy that was shaped by white paternalist racism.[10] By contrast, situated in her white middle-class family home, Dickinson chooses not to publish and thereby absents herself from the pressures of the print marketplace. Her freedom from financial pressures enables her to experiment, both formally and thematically. The arguments that her poems offer about racial hierarchies are a case in point. "Color – Caste – Denomination," for example, contends that racial difference is a human construct, one that an all-knowing God will not recognize in the afterlife (F836).[11] But in reading "Publication – is the Auction," we find a poet-speaker who figures participation in the print literary marketplace as a dirty undertaking, one that would soil the superior Whiteness of the poet but for the fact that she retreats to her "Garret" where she can write for herself alone (F788).[12] Still more problematically, this poem appropriates the slave auction as a metaphor for the white elite writer's decision about whether or not to publish, to auction off her "Mind." As these examples make clear, Dickinson's decision not to seek print publication frees her not only from the obligation to be politically consistent but also from the obligation to write poems that endorse the beliefs of her readers. She chooses which poems to send to friends and relatives and, to the best of our knowledge, she chooses *not to send* the majority of her poems to anyone, thereby preserving a discursive space in which she can experiment with different personae and arguments.[13] Dickinson's polyvalent and contradictory poems, with few specific historical references, thus become a screen onto which scholars can project precisely those political arguments they hope to find.

With each of his decisions potentially having an impact on his ability to gain white supporters, Horton has starkly different reasons for avoiding specific historical references. Though *Poetical Works* includes a few pieces that focus on particular events, Horton situates the majority of them in a seemingly timeless romantic world. Many of the poems work with the literary conventions of courtly love, representing the society of the white elite Southerners who were Horton's paying clients. Poems in this collection typically present speakers whose race – and sometimes also gender – remains indeterminate. Accustomed to ventriloquizing the perspectives of white Southerners, Horton invents, in his *Poetical Works*, speakers who inhabit a realm of leisured privacy. Musical gatherings with friends; walks in the countryside; reflections on friendship, on Christianity, and on mortality: these are the activities and questions pursued by many of Horton's speakers. While he represents these pursuits as genteel and appropriate pastimes for the white readers this collection addresses, it is clear from our own vantage point that Horton's decision to write these kinds of poems in the first person works as a form of resistance to his enslavement. Horton's poems thus offer us a shifting array of possibilities for the identities of their speakers. While he has very different reasons from Dickinson for writing a poetry that refuses to identify speakers and contexts, some of the methods we have applied so productively to reading Dickinson's ambiguities can strengthen our approaches to Horton's ambiguities as well.

I want to turn now to readings of two specific poems, considering them as test cases for this process of comparative reading. Both of these poems foreground the relationship between stasis and movement that I noted earlier; both also rely on gothic conventions to represent human vulnerability; and finally both only obliquely identify their speakers and contexts. As I will go on to suggest, reading the two poets together can enrich our understanding of the ways they use literary convention to protest the circumstances of their respective forms of confinement. Finally, however, I will also consider how significant differences between the two pieces limit the possibilities of this comparison – a limitation that also productively clarifies the politics and poetics of each poet.

Horton's "The Fearful Traveller in the Haunted Castle" offers a prime example of the tension in his poems between staying put and moving freely. A mash-up of a gothic tale about night terrors and an animal fable about a nimble rat, the poem also exemplifies the ways Horton uses literary conventions to protest implicitly the brutality of slavery. Read in relation to its historical context, the poem seems to respond to the violent aftermath of the Nat Turner rebellion. The poem opens with its speaker lying in bed, hearing the nighttime sounds of a "haunted" dwelling:

> Oft do I hear those windows ope
> And shut with dread surprise,
> And spirits murmur as they grope,
> But break not on the eyes.
>
> Still fancy spies the winding sheet,
> The phantom and the shroud,
> And bids the pulse of horror beat
> Throughout my ears aloud.
>
> Some unknown finger thumps the door,
> From one of faltering voice,
> Till some one seems to walk the floor
> With an alarming noise.
>
> The drum of horror holds her sound,
> Which will not let me sleep,
> When ghastly breezes float around,
> And hidden goblins creep.
>
> Methinks I hear some constant groan,
> The din of all the dead,
> While trembling thus I lie alone,
> Upon this restless bed.[14]

As in the majority of the poems in *Poetical Works*, Horton does not explicitly identify the speaker's race. Because Horton's speakers often ventriloquize the perspectives of his white readers, "The Fearful Traveller" can be read as representing the night terrors of a white traveler, far from home, who fears for his life. Furthermore, given the frequency with which Horton imagines the perspectives of white elite women in *Poetical Works* and given the conventions of the gothic, which place the white female body in jeopardy, it is also possible to read the poem's speaker as a white woman.

Yet while the poem can certainly be read as expressing the fears of a white traveler, it also points toward the experience of enslaved African Americans. Indeed "The Fearful Traveller" evokes the night terrors of both blacks and whites in the aftermath of the Turner rebellion: blacks fear the violence of the nighttime raids that followed this and every slave uprising, while whites fear a reprise of the nighttime killings perpetrated by Turner and his followers. Beyond the immediate context of slave rebellions, however, these stanzas also suggest how often nights might be filled with terror for enslaved African Americans, who might hear the sounds of nighttime rapes or punishments as they lay in their beds. When the speaker describes "the din of all the dead," the phrase evokes generations of enslaved men and women who have died violent deaths at the hands of whites.[15] What haunts the speaker then is this long lineage of suffering.

As if to defuse the threat of possible political readings, however, what began as a tale of haunting abruptly becomes a comic animal fable in the poem's second half. In the turn from the gothic to the comic, Horton demonstrates his dexterity at working with different kinds of literary conventions; he may also be demonstrating his interest in live performance. In order to build clientele, he may well have performed his poems for student audiences, and the quick turn from gothic to comic in "The Fearful Traveller" could certainly have been played for laughs. In the last five stanzas, when daylight arrives, the speaker realizes that the nighttime noises he heard resulted from a battle of wits between cats and rats:

> At length the blaze of morning broke
> On my impatient view,
> And truth or fancy told the joke
> And bade the night adieu.
>
> 'Twas but the noise of prowling rats,
> Which ran with all their speed,
> Pursued in haste by hungry cats,
> Which on the vermin feed.
>
> The cat growl'd as she held her prey
> Which shrieked with all its might,
> And drove the balm of sleep away
> Throughout the live-long night.
>
> Those creatures crumbling off the cheese
> Which on the table lay;
> Some cats, too quick the rogues to seize,
> With rumbling lost their prey.
>
> Thus man is often his own elf,
> Who makes the night his ghost,
> And shrinks with horror from himself,
> Which is to fear the most.[16]

The intense focus on the speaker's immobility in stanzas one through five contrasts strongly with the speed of the animals' chase in stanzas seven through nine.

Yet if the poem ends with the exhortation to dismiss one's own night terrors ("Thus man is often his own elf, / Who makes the night his ghost"), the stanzas that come before that conclusion leave a stronger impression than the poem's closing moral. The lively tale of the "prowling rats" who escape the "hungry cats" implicitly celebrates the rats' ingenuity while it mocks the cats' pride: "Some cats, too quick rogues to seize, / With rumbling lost their prey." This stanza too points toward the violent house raids perpetrated by whites against blacks in the aftermath of the Turner rebellion; simultaneously, the stanza also points toward Turner's ingenuity in evading capture for several weeks. The rats' triumph at escaping strongly suggests that the speaker's allegiances lie with the prey animals. The poem thus aligns its nimble rats with African American trickster figures like those whom Williams Wells Brown and Harriet Jacobs, among other writers, present in their slave narratives.[17] In foregrounding the rats' resourcefulness, Horton's text, like Brown's and Jacobs', suggests that African Americans have strategies for resisting white power.

Like Horton's "Fearful Traveller," Dickinson's "The Soul has Bandaged moments –" (F360) contrasts an opening gothic scene of terrified immobility with a later scene of frenzied movement. As I will go on to suggest, reading the Dickinson poem in relation to Horton's brings the imagery of bondage in the Dickinson poem into sharper focus. Moreover, reading the two poems in relation to one another foregrounds the ways that both represent human embodiment as a form of captivity. The paragraphs that follow will develop a reading of the Dickinson poem on its own terms before taking up the task of thinking about the two poems in relation to one another.

Dickinson's poem opens with an omniscient narrator describing the terror experienced by a woman threatened with sexual assault:

> The Soul has Bandaged moments –
> When too appalled to stir –
> She feels some ghastly Fright come up
> And stop to look at her –
>
> Salute her, with long fingers –
> Caress her freezing hair –
> Sip, Goblin, from the very lips

> The Lover – hovered – o'er
> Unworthy that a thought so mean
> Accost a Theme – so – fair –

Though it is the woman's "Soul" that is frozen with fear, her body is the recipient of the unwanted gaze and caress. The poem's insistence on figuring the "Soul" in embodied terms underlines the perilous inseparability of affective and embodied experience for the female figure. By calling the woman "fair," the poem both points toward her beauty and suggests that her "fair" skin or hair is what makes her beautiful.

In stanza three, the poem represents the Soul's "escape" as a dance, an intensely pleasurable and embodied form of movement:

> The soul has moments of escape –
> When bursting all the doors –
> She dances like a Bomb, abroad,
> And swings opon the Hours,
>
> As do the Bee – delirious borne –
> Long dungeoned from his Rose –
> Touch Liberty – then know no more –
> But Noon, and Paradise

In these stanzas, the poem pivots from interior images of a woman immobilized by terror to exterior images of giddy animal movement. The line "Long dungeoned from his Rose" implies that the bee has been kept from the desired contact with the flower, a contact that "Liberty" now enables him to make. But that contact may annihilate consciousness and perhaps also life itself, as the Bee then "know[s] no more" than "Noon, and Paradise," as if it were transported to an empty but Edenic afterlife. Touching "Liberty" thus suggests both the Bee's emancipation and also its demise. While the fourth stanza identifies the Bee as masculine, the poem has altered the actual sex of the pollinating insect, thereby establishing gender opposition between the Bee and the Rose, while also aligning free movement with the masculine.

In the poem's final stanzas, the female figure falls back into a confining embodiment, even as the poem's central metaphor falls back into the feminine gender:

> The Soul's retaken moments –
> When, Felon led along,
> With shackles on the plumed feet,
> And staples, in the song,

> The Horror welcomes her, again,
> These, are not brayed of Tongue –

The Soul has been "retaken" by embodiment. Her movement is now limited by "shackles," and her "song," by "staples." The poem concludes by likening the possibility of the Soul speaking of its suffering to *braying*, the harsh sound made by the donkey. While the poem's middle stanzas figure insect embodiment as liberatory, donkey embodiment here represents the inarticulate and burdensome weight of the female human body.

In spite of the striking similarities in the imagery of the Horton and Dickinson poems, I have unfolded my readings of them along parallel but separate tracks. This separation results partly from the fact that the Horton poem can be read so productively in relation to the immediate historical context of the Turner rebellion; the Dickinson poem, by contrast, expresses a more generalized fear about (white) women's sexual vulnerability and does not seem to point toward any specific historic event. Another reason the two readings tend to pull apart is the very different tonal arc each poem traverses. While Horton uses a tonal shift to defuse the risks of his poem, Dickinson's becomes only angrier and more despairing as it progresses. To the best of our knowledge, Dickinson did not send "The Soul has Bandaged moments –" to any recipient. Thus, while Horton's every choice is shaped by his need to reach white Southern readers, Dickinson apparently sought no readers for this poem, preserving for herself a private space for discursive exploration.

Having unfolded these two discrete readings, however, I now want to consider the rewards and the limits of the comparison. One result of reading the two poems together is that we are reminded of the changing of gender identities that shapes the narrative of each. If we read the speaker of the first half of Horton's poem as a white woman – the conventional gothic damsel in distress – then it is possible to imagine that the tonal change in the second half of the poem coincides with a change in the gender of its speaker. When the poem's final stanza argues that "man is often his own elf," it implicitly mocks the narcissism of the white male psyche: the terrified speaker imagines that every nighttime noise he hears represents a threat to himself. At the same time, Horton's penultimate stanza also emphasizes the aggressive animal nature that lies at the heart of the human psyche: the pursuit and conflict of the cats and rats is instinctual. Neither humans nor animals, the poem suggests, can escape the drive to dominate; this is why man "shrinks with horror from himself." The poem thus likens the violence that upholds white supremacy in the

South with the prey drive in the animal kingdom. With this image of inexorable violence, the Horton poem does in fact match the despairing finish of the Dickinson poem; that despair is partially masked, however, by self-deprecating comedy.

Like Horton's poem, Dickinson's too emphasizes the inescapability of threats to the body. In "The Soul has Bandaged moments –," the turn from human to animal figures is a turn toward an exhilarating and masculine freedom of movement: by making the pollinating bee masculine, the poem aligns the freedom of movement in stanzas three and four with male embodiment. But that freedom, of course, proves only temporary. Unlike Horton's speaker who wakes – possibly in a male body – to find his night terrors have a seemingly harmless cause, Dickinson's female figure wakes back up into the "Horror" of a threatened sexual assault and the prison of the female body. When the Soul falls back into the feminine gender, her body gets figured as a braying donkey's: the female body is a beast of burden. The Soul is "retaken" by the "shackles" and "staples," the constraints of femininity that bind her steps.

Yet by representing female embodiment as walking with "shackles," the poem also clearly invokes enslavement. Is the reference to "shackles" subordinated to a larger argument about the confining limits of embodied *white* female experience? Probably, given that the figure is identified as "fair" and given also the ways that Dickinson's poems frequently assume, without stating, the whiteness of their female characters. Nonetheless because it draws its shackle imagery from the abolition movement, the poem points toward the vulnerability of female bodies, both black and white, to sexual assault by men.[18] Indeed if we read the poem again, keeping its closing image of "shackles" in mind, we note that its female figure, like an enslaved African American woman on the auction block, is inspected and prodded by a man. The liberating dance that she performs – "She dances like a Bomb, abroad" – offers an imagined, and precarious, escape from the auction's degradation. But this freedom is only a temporary reprieve: she "Touch[es] Liberty – then know[s] no more." The "retaken" enslaved woman is led away in "shackles" at the auction's end.

In a widely disseminated image of the antebellum era, a female slave in chains kneels before a white woman, who holds in her left hand the scales of justice as she extends her right hand toward the kneeling figure. The legend above the image reads: "Am I not a woman and a sister?" Below the image is a Bible verse: "Remember them that are in bonds as bound with them" (Hebrews, 13:3).[19] Can we read the final stanza of "The Soul has Bandaged moments –" as responding, if only obliquely, to this image? Can we read the "shackles" in Dickinson's poem as those of the enslaved woman, or must we read them as the constraints of traditional gender roles for white middle-class women? To put this another way, if I can argue that Horton's poem is potentially ventriloquizing both the perspective of a white elite woman and that of an enslaved African American, can I argue that Dickinson's poem too potentially represents the sexual vulnerability of both white and enslaved African American women? If the Horton poem allows for multiple possible readings, does the Dickinson poem as well?

While the Dickinson poem certainly makes this reading *tenable*, the use of the adjective "fair" strongly suggests the whiteness of the woman; that decision effectively pushes the suffering of enslaved African American women into the background, making this reading only a secondary possibility. While Horton *cannot* make the racial identities of his human figures explicit, Dickinson has the freedom of choice. This is another way in which the two writer's circumstances – and therefore also their choices – are incommensurable. What Dickinson's poem puts squarely in the foreground is the idea that the *fair* female body is always vulnerable to male inspection and assault, a circumstance that places her in metaphorical shackles. The white reader's expectation that the person in peril in a gothic text is a white woman further works to support the figure's implied whiteness. Only as a secondary possibility does the poem point toward the peril faced by enslaved African American women.[20] The tension built into the Dickinson poem is thus the tension that led many white middle-class women to choose the cause of white women's rights over the cause of African American rights during the ratification of the Fifteenth Amendment in the spring of 1869. Like Elizabeth Cady Stanton, Dickinson's poem prioritizes white women's rights over those of African Americans.[21]

Reading these two poems together yields significant insights that can deepen our understanding of both Horton and Dickinson. My experience suggests that the methods we have applied to the study of Dickinson – including, among others, analysis of the circulation of her pieces and of their pronoun ambiguities – can be productively applied to Horton's work. Reading Horton comparatively with Dickinson can also teach us to attend with greater care to his strategic and inventive use of poetic conventions to protest his enslavement, sharpening our awareness, for example, of the angrier undercurrents in "The Fearful Traveller"; beneath the comic surfaces of the poem's second half lies a much darker argument about the inevitability of human aggression.

Clearly the developing critical conversation about Horton's poems can also enrich our approaches to race in Dickinson's work. Because Horton must in his *Poetical Works* represent race only obliquely, reading Dickinson's poetry in relation to Horton's brings her oblique and often fleeting references to racial difference into sharper relief and can help us understand what is at stake in these references. When Dickinson uses the enslaved African American or the rhetoric of abolition as metaphors for the experience of the white middle-class woman, we must consider how those choices map "whiteness" and "blackness" in relation to nineteenth-century racial ideologies. As Toni Morrison reminds us, the long-standing meditation on freedom in American writing is always shaped by the presence of enslaved people of African descent within the nation's borders.[22] She goes on to argue, "Even, and especially, when American texts are not 'about' Africanist presences [...], the shadow hovers in implication."[23] To borrow Morrison's phrase, we have not yet fully reckoned with the ways Dickinson "romances the shadow."

Notes

I would like to thank Michelle Kohler, Kathy Glass, and Desirée Henderson for their invaluable responses to earlier drafts of this essay.

1. See Morrison, *Playing in the Dark: Whiteness and the Literary Imagination* (New York: Random House, 1992), especially chapter 1.
2. For essays that attend to Dickinson's appropriation of abolitionist rhetoric, see Benjamin Friedlander, "Auctions of the Mind: Emily Dickinson and Abolition," *Arizona Quarterly* 54.1 (1998): 1–26; and Daneen Wardrop, "'That Minute Domingo': Dickinson's Cooptation of Abolitionist Diction and Franklin's Variorum Edition," *EDJ* 8.2 (1999): 72–86. For essays that attend to Dickinson's ambivalent representations of whiteness, see Vivian Pollak, "Dickinson and the Poetics of Whiteness," *EDJ* 9.2 (Fall 2000): 84–95; and Domnhall Mitchell, "Northern Lights: Class, Color, Culture, and Emily Dickinson," *EDJ* 9.2 (2000): 75–83. For an essay that examines racism in Dickinson's poems and letters, see Paula Bernat Bennett, "'The Negro Never Knew': Emily Dickinson and Racial Typology in the Nineteenth Century," *Legacy* 19.1 (2002): 53–61. Páraic Finnerty examines her responses to racial difference in "'We Think of Others Possessing You with the Throes of Othello': Dickinson Playing Othello, Race and Tommaso Salvini," *EDJ* 11.1 (2002): 81–90. More recently, Erica Fretwell examines Dickinson's responses to the successful slave rebellion in Haiti by reading images of taste, sweetness, and lawlessness in her poems: "Emily Dickinson in Domingo," *J19* 1.1 (Spring 2013):

71–96. In addition, Ed Folsom and Kenneth M. Price's "Dickinson, Slavery, and the San Domingo Moment" (https://whitmanarchive.org/resources/teaching/dickinson/index.html) influenced many of these essays and opened up important new avenues for theorizing race in Dickinson's work. In *Touching Liberty: Abolition, Feminism and the Politics of the Body* (Berkeley: University of California, 1993), Karen Sánchez-Eppler reads Dickinson's arguments about embodiment in relation to the rhetoric of abolition and women's rights. She argues that, in Dickinson's work, "the project of affirming freedom and identity has been internalized and so appears disjoined from any political or social program" (11). She goes on to note, however, that "this relocation ought not to be understood as a complete disjunction from antebellum activism" since abolitionists were often the first to argue that reform must begin within the self (11). My reading of Dickinson in this essay is indebted to Sánchez-Eppler's.

3. See, for example, Cheryl Walker, *The Nightingale's Burden: Women Poets and American Culture before 1900* (Indiana University Press, 1983); and Elizabeth Petrino, *Emily Dickinson and Her Contemporaries: Women's Verse in America, 1820–1885* (Lebanon, NH: University Press of New England, 1998).

4. A noteworthy exception to some of the critical tendencies in Dickinson studies that I have mentioned above is Janet Gray, *Race and Time: American Women's Poetry from Antislavery to Racial Modernity* (Iowa City: University of Iowa Press, 2004). Gray reads Dickinson in relation to non-canonical women poets, both white and black, and she also analyzes Dickinson's representation of racial difference. I note too that Erica Fretwell reads Dickinson very productively in relation to freewoman Malinda Russell's *Domestic Cookbook* (1866).

5. Joan Sherman did groundbreaking work to recover Horton's poetry, editing the first twentieth-century edition of his poems: *George Moses Horton: The Black Bard of North Carolina* (University of North Carolina Press, 1997). Leon Jackson analyzes Horton's position as a poet-for-hire in relation to the economics of authorship in the antebellum era in "The Black Bard and the Black Market," in *The Business of Letters: Authorial Economies in Antebellum America* (Stanford University Press, 2008). Other critical studies of Horton include my own essays about him: "Romantic Visions and Southern Stances," in *To Fight Aloud Is Very Brave: American Poetry and the Civil War* (University of Massachusetts Press, 2012), 225–250; "'Naked Genius': The Civil War Poems of George Moses Horton," in *The Literary Cultures of the American Civil War*, Timothy Sweet (ed.) (Athens: University of Georgia Press, 2016), 77–96; and "Great and Noble Lines: Dave the Potter, George Moses Horton, and the Possibilities of Poetry," in *Where Is All My Relation? The Poetics of Dave the Potter*, Michael Chaney (ed.) (Oxford University Press, 2018), 26–50.

6. For a recent study of the abolition movement that attends to the relationship between abolition and the struggle for women's rights, see Manisha Sinha, *The Slave's Cause: A History of Abolition* (New Haven: Yale University Press, 2017). For a collection that examines the relationship between abolition and women's rights from multiple perspectives, see Kathryn Kish Sklar and James

Brewer Stewart, eds., *Women's Rights and Transatlantic Slavery in the Era of Emancipation* (New Haven: Yale University Press, 2007).
7. Henry David Thoreau, "Walking," in *Essays*, Jeffrey S. Cramer (ed.) (New Haven: Yale University Press, 2013), 246.
8. While dress reform for women was proposed as early as the 1850s, middle-class women were nonetheless expected to wear corsets and crinolines for social occasions, and walking dresses too were worn with corsets. See, for example, Catherine Beecher's call for clothing that allows women to move freely in *Physiology and Calisthenics for Schools and Families* (Harper and Brothers, 1856), 186.
9. For an essay on Horton's life and his cultural context, see Sherman's "Introduction" to *The Black Bard of North Carolina*.
10. Jackson, 57–59.
11. For a fuller version of this reading, see my *To Fight Aloud Is Very Brave*, 181–185. By reading Dickinson as a poet who revels in the association of sweetness and lawlessness with blackness, Fretwell too offers a reading that makes Dickinson's politics seem admirable.
12. For a reading that foregrounds this poem's problematic association of whiteness with purity, see Gray, 54. For a reading that considers what this poem suggests about Dickinson's view of the Civil War, see Friedlander, especially 14–18.
13. Franklin notes that Dickinson sent hundreds of poems to as many as forty recipients, with the majority of these going to just a few persons. The recipients who received the most were Susan Gilbert Dickinson (about 250), Thomas Wentworth Higginson (about 100), and her cousins Louise and Frances Norcross (71). See Franklin's variorum vol. III, 1547.
14. Horton, *Poetical Works* (D. Heartt, 1845), 27–28.
15. I am grateful to Kathy Glass for proposing this reading of this stanza.
16. Horton, 28–29.
17. In chapter 21, Jacobs describes how she bores a hole in the wall of her hiding place, allowing her to observe activity in the street below. In chapter 25, she describes the letters she wrote and had mailed from New York, tricking her master into believing that she had escaped to that city. See *Incidents in the Life of a Slave Girl* (Harvard University Press, 1987). In chapter 6, Brown describes how he deceives his master into thinking he has been whipped by the jailer, when Brown has in fact sent another man in his stead. See *Narrative of William W. Brown* (Boston: Antislavery Society, 1847), 54–57.
18. As Saidiya Hartman points out, however, "the actual or attempted rape of an enslaved woman was an offense neither recognized nor punished by law" (79). Hartman goes on to argue that a discourse of seduction obscures the relationship between "consent and coercion" and "intimacy and domination" in Southern slave codes (81). See Saidiya Hartman, *Scenes of Subjection: Terror, Slavery, and Self-Making in Nineteenth-Century America* (Oxford: Oxford University Press, 1997).

19. The engraved image appears on the title page of the enlarged second edition of Lydia Maria Child's *Authentic Anecdotes of American Slavery* (Newburyport, MA: Charles Whipple, 1838), available on Google Books.
20. In her reading of this poem, Sánchez-Eppler argues that "Dickinson does not attribute bondage and sexual vulnerability to any particular object of oppression (slaves or women) [. . .]; rather these politically resonant terms characterize the predicament of all who own a body and soul" (128). In my reading, however, this poem takes as its central concern the vulnerability of the white female body.
21. At the 1869 meeting of the American Equal Rights Association, Stanton argued that white women ought to be admitted to the vote before black men.
22. Morrison, 37.
23. Ibid., 46–47.

CHAPTER 13

Dickinson and the Diary

Desirée Henderson

In 1851, Emily Dickinson wrote a letter to her brother Austin, who was teaching in Boston, in which she mischievously accuses him of murdering his pupils. She begs for the gruesome details of his reign of terror because she "[likes] to get such facts to set down in my journal," adding, in the same mock-gothic vein, "I dont [sic] think deaths or murders can ever come amiss in a young woman's journal" (L43). Four months later, in another letter to Austin, Dickinson prefaces a detailed description of an ordinary day with the statement that "'Keeping a diary' is not familiar to me as to your sister Vinnie, but her own bright example is quite a comfort to me, so I'll try" (L60). In the first instance, Dickinson not only claims to write a diary but also indicates an awareness of the gendered conventions of diary writing. Dickinson transforms the domesticated diary into a blood-soaked record to extend, and to bring home, the image she has spun of a topsy-turvy universe in which teachers murder students. In the second instance, Dickinson denies writing a diary and displaces the practice onto her younger sister Lavinia; she describes diary writing as a method of representation she recognizes as having value but one she does not elect to practice – except, apparently, when she does. "I'll try" to write diaristically, she states, and the letter that follows mimics a diarist's close observation of the quotidian.[1]

These references to diaries raise tantalizing archival questions. Did Dickinson keep a diary? If so, what happened to it? The archival record provides no evidence of such a diary, which, had it existed, almost certainly would have been destroyed along with Dickinson's other personal papers after she died.[2] Rather than presenting a research dead end, however, Dickinson's epistolary statements raise an equally intriguing interpretative question: to what extent was Dickinson responding in her poetry to the culture of diary writing that flourished in the nineteenth century and was widely practiced by those around her, including her family members? In this essay I argue that Dickinson's poems demonstrate that she thought about and positioned her writing against the prevailing conventions of the diary, including the genre's association with memory. Dickinson's depiction of memory and its material forms challenges the idea that a diary could function as a textual receptacle for recording and preserving an individual's memories. At the same time, in her skepticism about the diary's functionality, Dickinson proves herself to be an insightful critic of the genre, mapping out key questions about the diary's appeal and its limitations that may guide diary readers even today.

To propose parallels between Dickinson's poetry and the diary genre should not be surprising; after all, she composed deeply interior poems and preserved them in small handwritten booklets that she kept hidden from friends and family members. Yet, even though Dickinson's manuscript poetry shares recognizable formal and content-level characteristics with the diary, it is a comparison that has not gained traction within Dickinson scholarship. This is particularly notable given the effort that has been expended in recent years to situate Dickinson within other nineteenth-century manuscript traditions. Dickinson is now understood to have been influenced by a cluster of manuscript practices generally classified as women's writing: portfolios, commonplace books, scrapbooks, autograph albums, cookbooks, herbariums, and so forth. Comparatively reading Dickinson's fascicles against such material texts has facilitated a new appreciation of Dickinson's embeddedness within, and resistance to, the forms of expression considered appropriate for young women of her age. At the same time, Dickinson's relationship to epistolarity has gained increased attention, and she is now seen as a writer deeply invested in the letter as a form of creative writing and as a mechanism for circulating her poems. This work has opened up innovative ways of exploring manuscript materials that have been historically devalued. Indeed, the field of Dickinson studies can arguably be credited with establishing many of the theories and methodologies that today define the study of manuscripts in nineteenth-century America.

So why not the diary? Scholarship on the diary genre offers a plausible explanation: the persistent negative perception of the diary as a literary form. The diary's status within literary culture remains ambiguous, and many still hesitate to rank a diary as equal in merit to conventional literary genres or even to newly recovered manuscript ones. Critics frequently treat the diary as a special case, segregated from other similar genres by virtue of its purported privacy, self-referentiality, and lack of artistry. Philippe Lejeune lists the common accusations levied against the genre: "unwholesome, hypocritical, cowardly, worthless, artificial, sterile, shriveling, and feminine."[3] Writing specifically of women's diaries, Jennifer Sinor states, "The diary, as a form of writing, has so long been delegitimated, unseen, feminized, and privatized that the fact that there are any women's diaries left from the past to read is astonishing."[4] The term "feminine" is perhaps the most damning: the long-standing perception of the diary as woman's writing has all but guaranteed its marginal status in canonical literary histories.[5] Even within a field like Dickinson studies, which is invested in revaluing feminized literary forms, the dubious status of the diary casts a long shadow. To place Dickinson's poems in conversation with the diary may appear to reassert the gendered characterizations that were deployed in the past to minimize her work and its significance. This approach may also appear to affirm the idea that Dickinson's poems are autobiographical texts, comparable to self-disclosing diary entries – a line of analysis almost wholly rejected by scholars who take seriously Dickinson's admonition that her poems represent not her but a fictional persona.[6]

My analysis begins with the premise that diaries are complex works of literature whose historical marginalization is the result of gendered value systems that deserve to be dismantled. As a consequence, locating Dickinson within diary culture neither minimizes her work nor limits its expressive possibilities. Instead, this context provides a new framework for understanding the ways in which Dickinson responded to the prevalent literary practices of her day. In this essay, I introduce two communities of diary writers in which Dickinson was embedded: the schoolgirl diarists at Mount Holyoke Female Academy and Dickinson's family and social circle in Amherst. Whether or not she wrote a diary herself, Dickinson would have been exposed to diary writing through these communities and would certainly have been aware of the conventions of the genre. While, as I show, there are formal characteristics that link Dickinson's fascicles with the diaries written by her friends and family members, my focus is less on material form and more on the diary's impact on Dickinson's thinking about and representation of autobiographical memory.

Diaries serve many purposes, but among them is the function of the *aide-mémoire*: a record of past events that makes the memory of those events available for retrospective consideration. Despite the wide variety of diary forms and practices undertaken throughout the nineteenth century, the perception of the diary as a textual record that preserves experience for later recollection runs throughout most diaries and establishes one of the defining characteristics of the genre. I suggest that while Dickinson recognizes the diary's purpose as a memory receptacle, she maintains a skeptical attitude regarding the genre's ability to accomplish this goal. Instead, in poems that explore the textual and spatial qualities of memory, Dickinson focuses on the failures inherent to memory preservation. Although my analysis is centered on how these themes put Dickinson in conversation with the diary, I conclude by proposing that a full account of Dickinson's response to the literary and manuscript practices of her era remains to be written. What other genres and forms have yet to be considered as influences or contexts? In what ways do the generic hierarchies that structure modern literary criticism continue to limit our appreciation of the heterogeneous cultural traditions within which Dickinson wrote?

Dickinson's Diary Communities

One of the communities of diary writers that Dickinson would have been familiar with was at the Mount Holyoke Female Seminary that she attended in 1846–1848. Keeping a diary was a common practice of students at boarding schools and, in some instances, was actively encouraged by educational institutions. Whether prescribed or not, the diaries in the Mount Holyoke archive indicate that school attendance and diary writing were understood to be concurrent activities, as most are aligned with the academic calendar. Another striking characteristic of the Mount Holyoke diaries is that most were made of folded sheets of paper, hand-stitched along the margin. The physical parallels between such diaries and Dickinson's fascicles are significant. In both cases, young women writers elected to employ a bookmaking technique that was no longer strictly necessary, given the widespread availability of pre-printed notebooks and diaries.[7] Melanie Hubbard argues that Dickinson likely learned her technique of hand-making booklets at Mount Holyoke: "Obviously the girls were well acquainted with the idea of writing down, sewing up, and circulating items of interest in what was a vibrant manuscript culture both in and out of the curriculum."[8] Yet, Dickinson's fascicles differ from the manuscript diaries constructed by her fellow students in a significant way: Dickinson stacked sheets of paper before stitching the fascicle bindings, while the diaries are for the most part composed of nested sheets of paper. As Alexandra Socarides has demonstrated, Dickinson's use of stacked rather than nested sheets is a defining characteristic of her material poetics.[9] It may also be one of the first clues regarding Dickinson's discontent with what she saw of diary writing practices at Mount Holyoke, where the memory-keeping function of the genre was explicitly aligned with spiritual self-scrutiny and relationship-building.

The diary's role as an *aide-mémoire* was employed in many Mount Holyoke diaries for the specific purpose of helping the diarist look back over her actions and evaluate their compliance to religious codes of behavior. Jane Hunter argues that many nineteenth-century girls' diaries display such self-disciplining moves, as societal norms of "denial and repression" were internalized through the practice of self-narration.[10] For instance, Mount Holyoke student Elizabeth Welch describes reviewing her past misdeeds, "the remembrance of which makes me sad," as an activity that motivates her to "guard myself more . . . [and] to weigh my conduct."[11] This use of the memory record for the objective of spiritual correction or repentance was conjoined in other diaries with a social function, as the Mount Holyoke diaries were often circulated, shared, and commented upon by others. The communal aspect of the diary was common in this era, as many diaries were shared with small circles of friends or family members, but it was intensified by the boarding school setting, where sharing diaries was a way of cementing the intimate friendships that formed between schoolgirls as well as creating a material record of these relationships for the inevitable time when the girls would be separated. When Harriet Wells invites her roommate, Hattie Crane, to write in her diary, she solicits the entry with the words "Write something in my journal that I may have it to think of you by," and Hattie replies, on the same page, that "thoughts of Holyoke will ever bring with them pleasing remembrances of thee."[12] In entries like these, we see how the diary provided a space in which the author could record her own memories and also ensure that she remembers, and is remembered by, others.

From this brief introduction to the Mount Holyoke diaries, I turn to the other diary writing community with which Dickinson would have been familiar: her immediate family and Amherst social circle. The fact that many members of Dickinson's family and community were diarists is one well known to literary critics as these texts are frequently referenced in Dickinson biographies, yet they have generally not been considered as possible influences upon Dickinson's poetry, as I argue here. The diary written by Dickinson's sister Lavinia provides a point of entrance into this topic, not least because Dickinson's epistolary comment, "'Keeping a diary' is not familiar to me as to your sister Vinnie," was made to Austin in 1851, and Lavinia's diary from that same year remains extant (L60). It is impossible to know whether other volumes were written and lost or whether Lavinia's diary writing was a short-lived practice. The surviving volume differs from the handmade objects in the Mount Holyoke archive: it is a pre-bound and pre-formatted pocket diary, possessing a black leather cover and tuck closure and measuring 10 inches high. Like most pocket diaries, each page provides room for three dated entries which, given the restricted space, results in a schematic picture of each day that relies heavily upon the diarist's recollection to fill in the gaps in the record. Although Lavinia presumably found this format sufficient to her needs, Dickinson does not: in her letter to Austin on October 30, 1851, Dickinson writes that she will try to follow Lavinia's "bright example" and proceeds to fill several pages in a detailed account of the Dickinson family home life (L60). Lavinia's diary entry from the same day reads in full: "Martha Kingman dead. Rainy day. Cut out work, all day."[13] (See Figure 13.1.) In other words, although she cites Lavinia's pocket diary as her inspiration, Dickinson's choices as a letter writer implicitly point to what she saw as the inability of the pocket diary form to record or convey the fullness of experience.

Dickinson's brother Austin also kept a diary, of which eight volumes from the late 1880s survive. Austin favored a popular pre-printed pocket diary known as the Standard Edition, the "leader in commercial diary brands."[14] Austin's diary entries are for the most part brief, formulaic, and non-reflective; he records the weather and his work activities through the repeated phrase "I in office." However, even his dry recital of events partakes of the *aide-mémoire* function when Austin demarcates significant moments with both verbal and visual codes, with the clear intention of highlighting these experiences for future reference. One of the most remarked-upon of such moments in his diaries is the inscription of the word "Rubicon" on September 11, 1882; it was the word Austin and Mabel Loomis Todd used to refer to the day they embarked upon their affair (the phrase appears in Todd's diary on that day as well).[15] Practices like these turn the diary into a cryptic record, the meaning of which is available exclusively to the diarist who alone is able to translate the coded reference into the memory it commemorates.

Within Dickinson's social circle, it is Mabel Loomis Todd who stands out as an exemplar of nineteenth-century diary writing. Although Dickinson and Todd never met face-to-face, Todd remains important to my analysis because her sixty-two volumes of diaries, journals, and commonplace books illustrate the kind of diary writing that was common among educated and literary women of the era. Todd's was a lifelong practice, not a schoolgirl activity, and one that crossed multiple formats: she often kept a pocket diary and a more expressive journal simultaneously. Like other diarists, Todd recorded her experiences for her own recollection, but her role in promoting Dickinson's literary reputation gave her

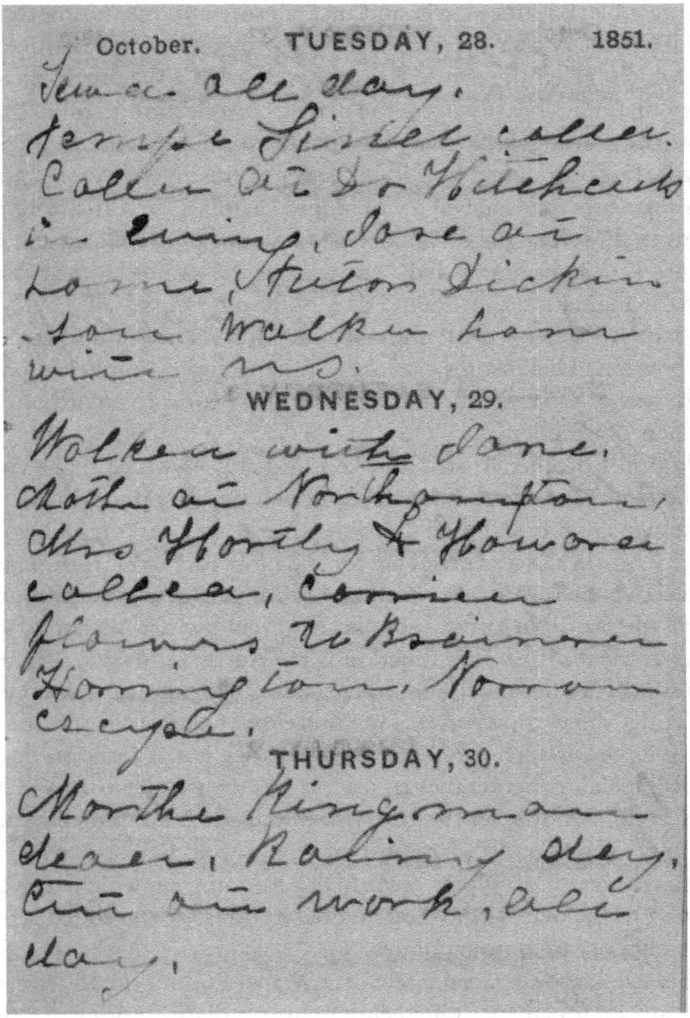
October. TUESDAY, 28. 1851.

Sewed all day. Temple Fisher called. Called at Dr Hitchcocks in evening. Jane at home, Sexton Dickinson walked home with us.

WEDNESDAY, 29.

Walked with Jane. Mother at Northampton. Mrs Hartly & Howard called, Carried flowers to Brainard Harrington, Norman escaped.

THURSDAY, 30.

Martha Kingman dead. Raining day. Cut out work, all day.

Figure 13.1 Lavinia Dickinson, Diary, 1851. Dickinson family papers, 1757–1934. MS Am 1118.95 (226). Houghton Library, Harvard University, October 30, 1851.

a unique insight into the value that personal writing can accrue posthumously. Todd carefully labeled and preserved both her own and Austin's diaries within her impressive archive of Dickinsoniana with the expectation that they would be valued by posterity. In an entry in one of her last diaries, written in 1930, Todd describes reading back through her journals to reconstruct details about Dickinson's life, showing how individual memories could become invested with historical or literary significance.[16]

The diaries kept by the schoolgirls at Mount Holyoke and by Lavinia Dickinson, Austin Dickinson, and Mabel Loomis Todd speak to the prevalence of diary writing in the nineteenth century. Emily Dickinson was surrounded by people – many close intimates and people she admired – who were regularly recording their experiences in diaries, suggesting that the motivations behind and conventions of diary writing would have been well known to her. This collection of diaries also demonstrates the diversity of diary writing practices at the time: utilizing an assortment of material formats, written during various periods of life, and displaying different attitudes toward actual or potential readers. They also convey the multiple uses to which the *aide-mémoire* function of the diary could be put: for spiritual self-scrutiny; for sustaining and documenting intimate relationships; for recording both ordinary and extraordinary life experiences; and for preserving an individual life for oneself and for history. In the section that follows, I consider what this context reveals about Dickinson's own conception of memory. Dickinson did not, as far as we know, undertake to write a diary, but I argue that she did think about the diary as a genre and that her poems exhibit that this thinking centered on what genres like the diary could and could not do to preserve memory.

Dickinson's Memory Receptacles

In her poetry, Dickinson often expressed skepticism about the act of recollection, noting the unrecoverable gap between original experience and the memory of it. For instance, in one poem Dickinson's speaker describes the process by which memory forms as losing a precious object and being left only with the memory of it. She "held a Jewel in my fingers – / And went to sleep –," telling herself, "'Twill keep" (F261). Instead,

> I woke – and chid my honest fingers,
> The Gem was gone –
> And now, an Amethyst remembrance
> Is all I own –

The shift of language from the unspecific "Jewel" or "Gem" to the specific "Amethyst" is the key to Dickinson's critique. Although it might seem that an amethyst is superior to a generic jewel, the poem reverses these values by suggesting that the comprehensive language of genus (jewel, gem) allowed for a range of colors, textures, and forms. By contrast, the amethyst memory is a singular thing, no longer possessing such broad possibilities. The poem's attitude toward this transaction is hard to pin down, but, whether authentically or ironically mournful ("all I own"), these lines testify to the inadequacy of memory to reproduce the fullness of experience.

However skeptical Dickinson may have been about the function of memory, her poems are often sympathetic toward the impulse to try to preserve memories, particularly of deceased or absent loved ones. She writes frequently of the role of objects as reminders of absent individuals: keepsakes, souvenirs, tokens, and *memento mori*. Dickinson's location within a culture that privileged such objects is documented by scholars such as Barton Levi St. Armand, who notes that mementos of the dead took on the status of "sacred relic[s]" in the nineteenth century.[17] Dickinson describes memorial objects in poems like "In Ebon Box, when years have flown" and "Death sets a Thing significant," showing how ordinary things come to act as prompts to the living to recall the memory of the dead. Nor are keepsakes for mourners only; material tokens are for lovers as well: "'Tis Customary as we part / A Trinket – to confer – / It helps to stimulate the faith / When Lovers be afar –" (F628). In these poems, Dickinson acknowledges the legitimacy of the cultural practice of employing commemorative objects, recognizing that they may be necessary to assist the imperfect ability of the human mind to remember or the human heart to sustain affection despite death or distance.

Dickinson is less confident that an individual's memories of *herself* can be preserved in or through material objects. She remains sympathetic toward the human impulse to record memories and cognizant of the important role that an external object can play in serving as a memory prompt. Yet, her thinking about what form that receptacle might take ultimately leads her to question textual forms like the diary. The poem "I cautious, scanned my little life" (F175) presents some of Dickinson's most extended thoughts on autobiographical memory and its preservation. The first three stanzas read,

> I cautious, scanned my little life –
> I winnowed what would fade
> From what w'd last till Heads like mine
> Should be a'dreaming laid.

> I put the latter in a Barn –
> The former, blew away.
> I went one winter morning
> And lo, my priceless Hay
>
> Was not opon the "Scaffold" –
> Was not opon the "Beam" –
> And from a thriving Farmer –
> A Cynic, I became.

The opening stanza describes self-narration as a process of selection and valuation: identifying what is worth recording and what can be allowed to "[blow] away." This process is posed against the certainty of forgetting; without this effort to preserve some aspects of the life, they will inevitably be lost. (The poem echoes the imagery of "I held a Jewel in my fingers" in its parallel between sleeping and forgetting: the memory will be lost when the speaker even momentarily allows her attention to falter, as she must inevitably do.) Yet, once the speaker has identified "what would fade," she is content to allow the other parts of life to blow away. By implication, the poem suggests that while the great majority of life's experiences are insignificant, the winnowing process of self-narration enables the speaker to identify and save what is most important.

The speaker's effort at preservation takes the form of placing "what would fade" in a barn. The barn functions in the poem as a material memory receptacle: a container for the poet's curated life stories. The extended metaphor at the poem's core – in which the speaker's memories are akin to hay stored in a barn – draws upon a set of agricultural references to characterize the process of memory. Hay is the cut, dried, and preserved version of grass; having lost the green freshness of grass, hay gains durability and longevity and, as a result, greater value for farmers as fodder for their animals. In another poem, Dickinson imagines the experience of grass, which dies when it is cut but then spends its afterlife "in Sovreign [sic] Barns," where it "dream[s] the Days away" – a bucolic image that causes the speaker to conclude, "I wish I were a Hay" (F379). In "I cautious, scanned my little life," Dickinson revisits this imagery by imagining hay as the dried, preserved version of a green or living memory. Unlike "I held a Jewel in my fingers," in which Dickinson portrays the transformation of an original experience into its "Amethyst remembrance" as a kind of loss, here she appears to consider the process of preserving memories (making hay from grass) to be both sufficient and necessary to the work of recollection.

What fails in "I cautious, scanned my little life" is not the practice of autobiographical self-narration but the container the speaker has chosen: the barn. When the speaker returns to her memories, they are gone, though the cause remains uncertain. The three potential culprits cover a range of actors: human ("Thief"); natural ("wind"); and divine ("deity") (F175). The poem's focus is on the impact of this loss upon the speaker: "from a thriving Farmer / A Cynic, I became." The speaker is transformed from an individual with a clear and productive role as the harvester of a sustaining food source to a person whose path is uncertain. The use of anaphoric repetition in stanzas three and four conveys the speaker's futile and seemingly unfocused search as she flails about in pursuit of the unknown cause. As the final stanza tells us, her "business" now is to "ransack," a verb that directly contrasts with the farmer's work of planting and harvesting and instead evokes the destructive act of pillaging someone else's crops. To reconstruct her lost memories is a violent and potentially destructive enterprise that opposes the cautious, evaluative role the speaker inhabited in the opening lines.

But the poem concludes with three lines that exhibit a significant tonal and linguistic shift: "How is it Hearts, with Thee? / Are thou within the little Barn / Love provided Thee?"[18] Despite the speaker's claim to be a cynic, the use of strong active words like "business," "find," and especially "ransack," and the proliferation of exclamation marks, the poem ends on a wistful and poignant note. The speaker is not out ransacking the world in search of her lost memories. Instead, she is posing a tender question, using intimate language regarding the deep-hearted matter of the poem: Can any memory survive? Is there any method, mechanism, or genre that will keep precious memories safe?

When read through the context of nineteenth-century diary culture, "I cautious, scanned my little life" take on new resonance. The barn is a diary-like object, a container for memories that deserve to be recorded. It is called upon to do what diaries do in the sense of holding, for future reference, a preserved version of the original. Yet, insofar as "I cautious, scanned my little life" represents Dickinson thinking about the diary as a form, she appears to have concluded that it is a flawed receptacle for keeping memories safe. The flaw in the barn is its openness to a third party who steals the speaker's memories. The intervention of this individual can be understood to dramatize the unsettling prospect of an unsanctioned reader gaining access to a diarist's intimate thoughts. Although sharing diaries was common in the nineteenth century, evident both at Mount Holyoke and among Dickinson's family members, not all diarists embraced this practice, and many would have shared the poem's sense of violation. It may also be the case that the unsanctioned reader in "I cautious, scanned my little life" references Dickinson's own anxiety about readers gaining access to her fascicles or poems without her approval, as other scholars have argued.[19] In Dickinson's imagined scenario, the unwanted reader blocks the speaker's own access to her memories: they no longer belong to her, a transformation of ownership that conveys the inadequacy of the barn as a protected space.

In employing the barn to evoke a diary-like textual function, it is notable that Dickinson does not employ textual imagery but instead defaults to an architectural image. This rhetorical move may initially appear designed to sidestep the gendered associations of the diary. The unfeminine if not outright masculine agricultural identities and spaces cited in the poem insulate the speaker's autobiographical acts from the minimizing judgments often lodged against diary writing. Dickinson voiced just such judgments in her letters to Austin, conveying her awareness of the domesticated limits imposed upon young women's journals, and we have seen that such attitudes persist to the present day. However, the conclusion of the poem complicates this gendered critique as it introduces the possibility of another, perhaps more intimate, textual form: "the little Barn." How does the little barn compare to the barn initially referenced in the poem? The language of scale is one clue, as are the two contrasting modes of composition: caution versus love. In distinguishing between these two affective registers, Dickinson imagines an alternative text that succeeds where the initial barn fails precisely because the little barn fulfills the gendered expectations of the diary: the small size and emotional language used to characterize the little barn confirms its status as a feminized form. Perhaps the crisis of loss portrayed in "I cautious, scanned my little life" is actually the result of the speaker's failure to keep a diary, a genre that admits the all-too-often disregarded dimensions of women's interior lives. In other words, what initially appears to be an outright rejection of the diary as a memory-preserving textual space ends up as an unfulfilled wish for a different, more effective, and perhaps more feminine diary.

In another poem, Dickinson revisits the scene of memory-making but arrives at a contrasting conclusion regarding the value of recorded memory. She continues to use a material place as a metaphor for memory, but, in this instance, her intention is to warn readers about the dangers that memories may present if they are successfully preserved.

> That sacred Closet when you sweep –
> Entitled "Memory" –
> Select a reverential Broom –
> And do it silently –
>
> 'Twill be a Labor of surprise –
> Besides Identity
> Of other Interlocutors
> A probability –
>
> August the Dust of that Domain –
> Unchallenged – let it lie –
> You cannot supersede itself –
> But it can silence you. (F1385)

Once again, memory is formed through cleaning up – though sweeping implies a less selective process than scanning. Once again, memories are stored within a specific material container – here, a closet. In this poem Dickinson replaces the space of nature, animals, and men (the barn) with an interior space (the closet) that appears both domestic and feminine given the presence of a broom-wielding laborer. In a sense, this poem realizes the wish that concludes the poem above for a female-gendered space to hold memory for the purpose of future recollection.

However, the difference in the two poems' spatial imagery is accompanied by a distinct judgment regarding the efficacy of the container. If the speaker in "I cautious, scanned my little life" longed to return to her stored memories and find them safely stored in the barn, the speaker in "That sacred Closet when you sweep" describes the fulfillment of that longing as presenting unforeseen dangers. Insofar as the "sacred Closet" references texts like diaries that record memory, in this poem the container is not flawed but works all too well. The memories stored in the closet are not dry, inert objects but lively, talkative agents who surprise the main character with their account of the past. Her memories have been preserved, but they have also been rendered "other": alienated from their originator and offering up counter-narratives that disrupt her static conception of the past. Dickinson's concern in this poem is not the viability of the container but the fraught experience of entering the closet to reencounter what was stored there – what might be understood in this context as rereading one's diary. She warns against it: what you will find will surprise you, including the probability of encountering perspectives or forgotten memories that challenge your preferred version of events. Better to let the dust lie upon those stored memories, or to let the memories themselves fall into dust.

As a commentary on memory receptacles like diaries, "That sacred Closet when you sweep" reaches the emphatic conclusion that they are dangerous, as the permanence of the written record renders the diarist herself mute.

Dickinson's exploration of the materiality of human memory in these two poems stands out in greater relief when placed against the culture of diary writing that flourished in her lifetime and that was a central mode of self-expression for many of her closest and most beloved friends and family members. She was well aware that one of the most commonly practiced methods for recording memory in the nineteenth century was diary keeping, but she appears dubious about the efficacy of diaristic texts, as she is about remembrance more generally. In these poems she questions whether a written record is adequate to the task of preserving memory and what the consequences might be if it is. She considers but ultimately rejects both the possibility and the desirability of capturing individual memory in textual form. Without explicit reference to the diary, Dickinson nevertheless participates in the culture of diary writing by exploring the *aide-mémoire* function of the genre. In fact, her critical examination of the materiality, durability, and efficacy of texts like diaries provides a useful framework for exploring the historical role of life writing, both as practiced and as imagined.

Dickinson's Outer Archives

Despite remarkable efforts by Dickinson scholars to explore the diversity of literary forms, including manuscript materials, that circulated within her social circle, there is still more work to be done to fully appreciate the heterogeneity of her influences. We are called upon to question entrenched generic hierarchies and other structures of thought that prevent us from seeing surprising points of connection between Dickinson's poetry and other written or unwritten forms of expression. In this essay, I proposed that the long-standing marginalization of the diary genre has prevented critics from considering how it may have exercised influence over Dickinson's thinking, particularly about the concept of memory. Although I have focused on poems that display this thought process through metaphor and imagery, the literary context invites further exploration of material composition practices, such as the parallels between handmade diaries and Dickinson's fascicles. This context may even necessitate a reconsideration of the unpopular notion that Dickinson's poems have something in common with diary entries.

However, my analysis proposes that an alternate trajectory is in order. It is not simply that new archives will enable new readings of Dickinson's poems, although that remains both true and essential. It is also the case that Dickinson's poems can teach us to read the materials within the nineteenth-century archive. It should come as no surprise that Dickinson was an astute reader of texts, alert to their declared goals as well as to their inherent limitations. As I have shown, Dickinson's commentary opens up the diary to new analysis, presenting conceptually rich and challenging insights about the relationship between genre conventions and individual experience. Although the diaries kept by Dickinson's friends and family members have been scoured for information about the poet, they have not been explored as literary texts. Dickinson's own poems prompt us to reevaluate this entrenched methodology. Although I have suggested that Dickinson was critical of the diary, she was dismissive of neither the genre nor its practitioners, and we should learn from her example. By reversing our critical gaze, we have the opportunity to consider what Dickinson has to teach us about the genres, forms, and voices that constitute her literary culture, even those that reside along the margins of the archive.

Notes

Thanks to Michelle Kohler, Timothy Morris, Alexandra Socarides, and especially Faith Barrett for suggestions and advice. The archival research for this project was supported by a grant from the University of Texas Arlington.

1. In this essay, I favor the term "diary" but, as is clear from Dickinson's letters, diary and journal were interchangeable terms in the nineteenth century, as they continue to be today.
2. See Millicent Todd Bingham, *Ancestors' Brocades: The Literary Debut of Emily Dickinson* (New York: Harper & Brothers, 1945), 17–18.
3. Philippe Lejeune, *On Diary*, Jeremy D. Popkin and Julie Rak (eds.), trans. Katherine Durnin (Honolulu: University of Hawaii Press, 2009), 147.
4. Jennifer Sinor, *The Extraordinary Work of Ordinary Writing: Annie Ray's Diary* (Iowa City: University Iowa Press, 2002), 27.
5. Many feminist scholars have, by contrast, reclaimed and celebrated the association between the diary and female experience. See, for instance, Suzanne L. Bunkers and Cynthia A. Huff, eds., *Inscribing the Daily: Critical Essays on Women's Diaries* (Amherst: University of Massachusetts Press, 1996).
6. See Dickinson's famous statement regarding her poetic persona in Dickinson, *Letters*, L268. There are a few notable exceptions to the critical blind spot regarding Dickinson and the diary to which I am indebted, including

Richard Sewell, *The Life of Emily Dickinson* (New York: Farrar, Straus, & Giroux, 1974, 1980); Paul Crumbley, *Inflections of the Pen: Dash and Voice in Emily Dickinson* (Lexington: University Press of Kentucky, 1997); Connie Ann Kirk, "Climates of the Creative Process: Dickinson's Epistolary Journal," in *A Companion to Emily Dickinson*, Martha Nell Smith and Mary Loeffelholz (eds.) (Malden, MA: Blackwell, 2008), 334–347; and Alexandra Socarides, *Dickinson Unbound: Paper, Process, Poetics* (New York: Oxford University Press, 2012).

7. On the mass production of pre-printed diaries, see Molly McCarthy, *The Accidental Diarist: A History of the Daily Planner in America* (Chicago: University Chicago Press, 2013).
8. Melanie Hubbard, "The Word Made Flesh: Dickinson's Variants and the Life of Language," in *Dickinson's Fascicles: A Spectrum of Possibilities*, Paul Crumbley and Eleanor Heginbotham (eds.) (Columbus: Ohio State University Press, 2016), 39.
9. Socarides, *Dickinson Unbound*, 32.
10. Jane H. Hunter, "Inscribing the Self in the Heart of the Family: Diaries and Girlhood in Late-Victorian America," *American Quarterly* 44.1 (1992): 63.
11. Elizabeth Mary Bell Welch, Diary, 1846–48. Welch Papers (MS 0775). Mount Holyoke College Archives and Special Collections, February 20 and June 5, 1846.
12. Harriet A. Wells Royce, Journals, 1845–49 (MS 0581). Mount Holyoke College Archives and Special Collections, March 9, 1845.
13. Lavinia Dickinson, Diary, 1851. Dickinson family papers, 1757–1934. MS Am 1118.95 (226). Houghton Library, Harvard University, http://nrs.harvard.edu/urn-3:FHCL.HOUGH:11350672, October 30, 1851.
14. McCarthy, *Accidental Diarist*, 153.
15. The "Rubicon" diary entries figure significantly in Lyndall Gordon's *Lives Like Loaded Guns: Emily Dickinson and Her Family's Feuds* (New York: Penguin, 2010). Both Austin Dickinson's and Mabel Loomis Todd's diaries are in the Mabel Loomis Todd Papers (MS 496C), Sterling Memorial Library, Yale University.
16. See the entry in Todd's Journal XIII on November 1, 1930.
17. Barton Levi St. Armand, *Emily Dickinson and Her Culture: The Soul's Society* (Cambridge: Cambridge University Press, 1984), 60.
18. For a fascicle reading of this final stanza, see Eleanor Elson Heginbotham, "Magical Transformations: 'Necromancy Sweet,' Texts and Identity in Fascicle 8," in *Dickinson's Fascicles: A Spectrum of Possibilities*, Paul Crumbley and Eleanor Elson Heginbotham (eds.) (Columbus: Ohio State University Press, 2016), 82–83.
19. See Eleanor Elson Heginbotham, *Reading the Fascicles of Emily Dickinson: Dwelling in Possibilities* (Columbus: Ohio State University Press, 2003), 67–68.

PART IV

Receptions, Archives, Readerships

CHAPTER 14

Textures Newly Visible: Seeing and Feeling the Online Dickinson Archives

Seth Perlow

Emily Dickinson's admirers endeavored to make her handwriting visible from the very start. As early as 1891, a manuscript image appeared as the frontispiece to *Poems: Second Series*.[1] Since then, an array of manuscript images have appeared in a variety of contexts: in edited collections, scholarly journals, museum displays, academic monographs, coffee-table books, and even on quilts. A culmination came in 2013, when Amherst College and Harvard University launched the two largest online archives of Dickinson manuscript images.[2] These archives represent a new phase in the publication of Dickinson manuscripts: they are more comprehensive than earlier online collections and visually richer than their book-bound counterparts. They enable anyone with Internet access to view Dickinson's manuscripts and to explore the complex textual apparatus that editors have developed. Ironically, even as these online archives support new ways to study Dickinson, they also perpetuate familiar assumptions about the value of seeing her handwriting, encouraging us to invest Dickinson's script with gnomic powers. The manuscript images do not necessarily make her poems easier to read. Instead, they endow her papers with an almost magical allure, holding out the promise of a close encounter with the poet's own lyrical passions.

The most rigorous studies of Dickinson's manuscripts usually avoid such mystifications. Nevertheless, three common traits of the most influential manuscript-oriented scholarship make it possible to anticipate the strengths and limitations of these new digital archives. First, close readings of the manuscripts gained traction contemporaneously with the development of new technologies to reproduce holograph images, starting in the 1980s. Even when scholars directly consult the manuscripts, rather than facsimiles, they respond to the development of new technologies for reproducing Dickinson's handwriting. For example, when a scholar publishes holograph images alongside her criticism, she may need to consider what details the images will or will not make visible – a technological issue – and to adjust her argumentation accordingly. The online archives intensify this feedback between reading equipment and interpretive habits. Second, although we learn a lot from the manuscripts about the wording of Dickinson's poems, the most influential studies of the manuscripts emphasize factors other than the verbal text. Scholars discuss how Dickinson folds and binds her papers, for instance, or they describe the small objects (a pencil, a dried flower, a dead cricket) that she encloses with her letters.[3] Attention to details other than wording validates the impulse to find something more than textual information in Dickinson's manuscripts. Third, even when critics do glean new textual facts from the manuscripts, they often find a degree of complexity that makes the reader feel, strangely, that she *knows less* about the text than before. The ambiguity of a line break or the matrix of variant words at the bottom of a page, for instance, renders the text of the poem less determinate. As Alexandra Socarides writes, "the more time I spent with Dickinson's materials, the more they challenged my understanding of what Dickinson was doing and the identity of what she was writing."[4] Equivalent statements about disrupted knowledge appear in manuscript-oriented criticism by Susan Howe, Martha Nell Smith, Virginia Jackson, and others. Thus we should not assume that the online archives will primarily clarify our understanding of Dickinson's texts. They also support other, less informational ways of responding to the poems. For many readers, the value of seeing Dickinson's manuscripts, and indeed the value of her poems in general, rests on the idea that they do not simply give us information, that they enjoy a poetic exemption from the rationalist's cut and dried facts.

The scholars mentioned above and many others have paid close attention to the materials Dickinson used to write, but less has been said about the equipment we use to read her work.[5] The online Dickinson archives do indeed offer new ways to interface with her writing. As our technologies for reading Dickinson continue to develop, they not only improve our historical understanding of her but also reorganize her continuing influence upon poets and readers today. My exploration of the online archives therefore extends the historical-constructivist critique of "lyric reading" into the present and the future of Dickinson's reception.[6] Whereas influential scholars like Jackson and Socarides address the manuscripts as *historical* objects that can help us to track the differences between Dickinson's understanding of poetic genres and our own, this chapter addresses the online collections as artifacts of the *present*, interfaces that reshape how we relate to the poems and their author. The Dickinson of the online archives is new, then, not only because the Internet has made her handwriting more widely visible but also because these collections open new questions about how today's technologies reshape Emily Dickinson, and our ways of reading her, for the future.

The online archives are part of a broad technological system for reading Dickinson's poetry, a system with its own complex histories. To understand the archives' place within this system, and their influence upon literary interpretation, requires attention not just to individual poems but to the physical and conceptual equipment that enables reading. My goal is to describe how the online archives build upon a history of reading habits that have made Dickinson's holograph images particularly intensive sites of intellectual contestation and affective response. Although the online archives give a clearer view of Dickinson's manuscripts, ironically these new collections also entrench old attitudes about images of her handwriting. I link such reading habits with the commodification of Dickinson manuscript images, which continues to limit scholarship. My structural analysis of the online archives will indicate how they invite conventional ways of reading and forestall more innovative possibilities. To conclude, this chapter suggests that if the online archives bring something new to the reading of Emily Dickinson, they do so by emphasizing the textural and gestural dimensions of her manuscripts. This tactile register, however, is as old as it is new, for it further entrenches the affective investments that have long attended the encounter with Dickinson's handwriting.

"Something" in the Handwriting

The online archives make it dramatically easier to see Dickinson's manuscripts. The sites' accessibility and visual richness make them excellent teaching aids. Although they offer detailed views of the poems as Dickinson wrote them, the online archives also join a long tradition of Dickinson facsimiles that promise something more than new information about the texts per se. Readers describe this "something more" in different ways, often preferring mystified imprecision over critical incisiveness. Since the 1890s, many have claimed that Dickinson's manuscript images provide an affectively intense experience of contact with the poet. Our eyes trace the pen-strokes that registered Dickinson's own emotions as she lived. The holograph images are intellectually instructive as well, but the affective intensities around them indicate an attraction to manuscript images that has long informed how Dickinson gets read. The manuscript image often stands in place of the absent poet with whom readers hope to feel more intimate. If the poet's inner life remains enigmatic after we read her poems, the visual encounter with her handwriting might compensate, providing a closer brush with the personal Dickinson. This section offers a history of such substitutive claims that manuscript images offer something more than textual information; it then assesses the influence of this rhetoric upon the online archives.

From the first publication of a Dickinson holograph image, as the frontispiece to *Poems: Second Series* (1891), readers have found that these facsimiles do something other than clarify our knowledge about Dickinson's texts. Mabel Loomis Todd, in her preface to that volume, describes the "perplexing footnotes" in Dickinson's manuscripts, which provide alternate wordings that leave her editors less sure how a poem should read.[7] Such perplexity remains among the most common effects of manuscript images today. The meanings Todd does find in the handwriting refer to Dickinson's personhood rather than her texts. Todd compares the early script to "the delicate, running Italian hand of our elder gentlewomen," situating the poet within a social epoch and class.[8] When the later handwriting becomes "bolder and more abrupt," Todd believes this indicates "breadth of thought," and she describes its "effect" as "exceedingly quaint and strong."[9] The visual encounter with Dickinson's script carries a powerful affective charge. For Todd and many after her, manuscript images indicate Dickinson's personal qualities more than they clarify the text of her poems.

Todd also acknowledges one important kind of textual information that editors do find in Dickinson's handwriting: her changing script "makes it possible to arrange the poems with general chronologic accuracy."[10] Even here, though, Dickinson's handwriting does not provide very reliable information. Theodora Ward offers the most extensive comments on the handwriting's chronology in a note that appears in the front of Thomas Johnson's 1955 variorum edition. Ward makes questionably subtle distinctions between handwriting from one year and the next. For instance, she distinguishes between manuscripts from 1880 and 1879 by noting a lowercase *y* that is "straight, except as an initial letter" and observing a "new form of *V*," which "was formerly rounded at base, now pointed."[11] One's handwriting does change over time, but from day to day and year to year I think my own handwriting is not consistent enough to be dated on the basis of such fine details – nor, in most cases, is Dickinson's.[12] The pursuit of chronological facts in Dickinson's handwriting does not yield certainty but again lands the reader in a thicket of complexities. Indeed, Ward also describes the handwriting in qualitative terms that, like Todd's comments, indicate more about the poet than about the text. Ward sees the script of 1853 as "freer, less cramped" than before, and she views the handwriting from 1862 as "less agitated" than in the previous year.[13] Ward thereby suggests that seeing a Dickinson manuscript can disclose not only chronological information but also traces of the poet's emotional state.

In the last wave of commentary about holograph images before the online archives began to appear, critics continued to describe such images as sources of something more than textual information. Scholars differ on what the manuscripts do provide, but many agree they do not primarily improve our knowledge about the texts. Susan Howe's *My Emily Dickinson* (1985), which responds in part to R. W. Franklin's facsimile edition, *The Manuscript Books of Emily Dickinson* (1981), emphasizes the affective intensity of seeing Dickinson's handwriting. Howe avers that the manuscripts, "through shock and through subtraction of the ordinary," disrupt our understanding of Dickinson.[14] In 1993, Howe extends her arguments in an essay where she claims that the manuscripts should be viewed as "artistic structures" in their own right and not, as Franklin believes, as drafts for conventionally typeset poems.[15] The notion of manuscripts as "artistic structures" puts a finer point on the claim that manuscript images offer something more than textual information. As Walter Benn Michaels notes, in an otherwise unconvincing critique of Howe, "the poems, becoming 'drawing,' cease to be text."[16] I have located no instance where Howe equates the manuscripts with "drawing," but Michaels's vocabulary clarifies the debate. When a holograph image gets addressed as a visual field, rather than a verbal text, we can expect viewers to see it as something more than a series of words in a certain order.

In 1994, Martha Nell Smith launched the first online archive, the *Dickinson Electronic Archives*. By making it easier to see Dickinson's manuscripts, such archives open new possibilities for teaching and researching her work. They also perpetuate the belief that manuscript images offer something more than textual information. The *Dickinson Electronic Archives* includes manuscript images and transcriptions of writing by Emily Dickinson and others; teaching resources; articles about editing Dickinson for the web; and other materials. I will focus on one section of the archive, a digital article by Smith and Lara Vetter called "Emily Dickinson Writing a Poem," which presents a series of facsimile images related to "Safe in their Alabaster Chambers" (F124). These documents include a correspondence between Emily and Susan Dickinson in which the latter expresses dissatisfaction with an early version of the poem's second stanza. The first version of the poem displayed in "Dickinson Writing" is its printing in the *Springfield Daily Republican*, March 1, 1862, where it is titled "The Sleeping":

> Safe in their alabaster chambers,
> Untouched by morning.
>   And untouched by noon,
> Sleep the meek members of the Resurrection,
>   Rafter of satin, and roof of stone.
>
> Light laughs the breeze
> In her castle above them,
>   Babbles the bee in a stolid ear,
> Pipe the sweet birds in ignorant cadences:
>   Ah! what sagacity perished here![17]

In a letter, Susan objects to this second stanza because its warmth and light contradict the cold of the sepulcher described in the first. Such a clear rationale for Dickinson's revisions to this poem would not be available without considering Susan's letters. "Dickinson Writing" includes a note from Emily to Susan, in which the former asks, "Perhaps this verse would please you better – Sue." The note contains this entirely new version of the second stanza:

> Grand go the Years – in the
> Crescent – above them –
> Worlds scoop their Arcs –
> And Firmaments – row –
> Diadems – drop – and Doges –
> Surrender –
> Soundless as dots – on a
> Disc of Snow –[18]

This stanza redoubles the chill of the first, instead of contradicting it, but the correspondence reveals that Susan remained unsatisfied, leading Emily to make further attempts. The materials in "Dickinson Writing" shed light on the textual history of this poem and underscore the role Susan Dickinson played in her sister-in-law's compositional process. The correspondence between Emily and Susan offers information beyond the scope of Dickinson's particular texts, enabling us to imagine more vividly her personal relationships.

The details of this correspondence, however, are also available in Franklin's variorum edition. To see the handwritten letters lends visual pleasure to a story whose facts can be learned without manuscript images. "Dickinson Writing" also reframes the complexities of the manuscripts as intellectually generative, especially for students. Smith's commentary includes questions that raise uncertainties about the identity of the poem at hand: "Is it a two-stanza poem with four different second stanzas . . . ? Is it a three-stanza poem, as rendered in its 1890 posthumous printing? Or is it in fact five one-stanza poems?" Like other facsimile technologies, the first online archive takes manuscript images as windows onto the personal life behind Dickinson's poems, and it frames these images as productively unsettling our knowledge of the texts. These facsimiles may not give readers information they could not get from a typeset edition, but such images illustrate the complexity of Dickinson's poems and of their production.

Similar attitudes influence the rhetorical presentation of the larger archives that appeared in 2013. In a publicity video for *Emily Dickinson Archive*, the Harvard project, general editor Leslie A. Morris does not mention that the archive will help those concerned with the finer points of Dickinson's forms and variants. Instead she avows, "There's something about the handwriting and the energy that I think conveys to people some of the passion that she felt."[19] Here again, to see the poet's handwriting provides "something" ineffable, something affective, rather than anything informational. Instead of claiming that the archive will improve users' knowledge about particular poems, this statement finds a benefit in seeing the handwriting in general, regardless of the specific words on the page. Readers often believe that poems describe the poet's emotional experiences, but, in the context of the online Dickinson archives, some consider her handwriting, rather than her words, as the most powerful reflection of Dickinson's emotional life. The online archives continue a long tradition of theorizing the visual encounter with Dickinson holograph images as "perplexing" and affectively intense – as enabling us to experience the same passions Dickinson felt. These images stand in for the affective energies of a living person who is now deceased; they hold out the promise of personal intimacy with her.

Not all online literary archives privilege manuscript images as the Dickinson archives do. For example, *The Walt Whitman Archive* includes numerous manuscript images, but it gives equal billing to Whitman's published work, teaching aids, and other resources.[20] Even after entering the manuscript section and clicking a title, the user first encounters a transcription, together with icons to access each image. The archive thus presents Whitman's works first as verbal texts and second as holograph images; it emphasizes the wording of a page over its appearance. The same is true of other single-author archives – such as Jerome McGann's seminal *Rossetti Archive*, which makes transcriptions as easy to see as manuscript images – and of larger archives in other subfields, such as *Early English Books Online*, where transcriptions are as easy to see as page images.[21] None of the three emphasizes visual access to high-definition manuscript images.

Unlike comparable sites, the online Dickinson archives seem more like collections of images than of literary texts. Both the Harvard and Amherst archives direct visitors toward manuscript images first and predominantly. Some will note that, unlike Dickinson, Whitman supervised publication of his work, making it reasonable to emphasize typeset versions of his writing and not hers. But Whitman's corpus is arguably as complex as Dickinson's. Textual scholars continue to learn from his manuscripts. Indeed, the short novel *Jack Engle*, not attributed to Whitman until 2017, was recovered through close study of his notebooks.[22] Despite the continuing importance of Whitman's manuscripts for scholars and editors, the manuscripts do not become the sole focus of the archive. Hence, differences between the Dickinson archives and others have less to do with publication history and more to do with present-day reading habits and design choices. The Amherst archive displays a grid of manuscript thumbnails along with a search bar at the top and a sidebar for filtering the collection. Clicking a thumbnail loads a page dedicated to that manuscript; its central feature is an image of the manuscript, with catalog data below. The page also offers buttons to enlarge the image or to download a higher-resolution version. Notably, the Amherst archive does not provide transcriptions. The Harvard archive does provide transcriptions but subordinates these to the images. The default window for each poem displays the manuscript image, and only by clicking a small, inconspicuous tab can users view transcriptions. Both major Dickinson archives privilege the visual encounter with manuscript images. Their design choices implicitly ratify Howe's suggestion to view the manuscripts not as texts but as images, visual creations irreducible to type.

Those curating online Dickinson archives rarely undertake the new textual research common among print editors. The Harvard project in particular serves not only as a scholarly tool but also as a companion to existing Harvard editions. The creators of the Harvard archive aver that it "is not a new edition of Dickinson's poems."[23] Rather, the first and as yet only phase of the site "focuses on gathering images of those poems included in *The Poems of Emily Dickinson: Variorum Edition*, edited by

R. W. Franklin (Cambridge: Belknap Press of the Harvard University Press, 1998)."[24] Some therefore view the Harvard archive as a marketing appendage to the three-volume Franklin edition. Harvard, by this account, promotes their (expensive) edition of Dickinson by using it to organize a collection of manuscript images that might otherwise unsettle the regularizing influence of such typeset editions.[25] An online archive, especially one prioritizing images, could have loosened the constraints that editors have historically placed upon Dickinson's texts, but that opportunity is lost here. The *Emily Dickinson Archive* instead entrenches the Franklin edition, asserting its authority over even the source manuscripts themselves. The images in this archive come to seem like window dressing for a preexisting book. As the Franklin edition's privilege within the Harvard archive suggests, and as the next section of this essay demonstrates, the development of online Dickinson archives has less to do with new technological possibilities than with the ongoing commodification of Dickinson's manuscript images. Facsimiles of her handwriting have become increasingly subject to possessive strategies that express their value as property.

Possession and Control of the Poems

Long-standing disputes about who owns Dickinson's poetry continue to influence and constrain the online archives by framing the manuscript images as commodities to be bought, sold, licensed, and restricted. Shortly after the poet's death, her manuscripts became divided between the Dickinson family and her first posthumous editor, Mabel Loomis Todd, a division that persists to this day. Todd received the manuscripts not as gifts but as loans to aid the publication effort; when a lawsuit estranged her from the Dickinsons, she refused to return the manuscripts. The two families maintained their separate collections until the 1950s, when the Dickinsons' manuscripts were sold to Harvard and the Todds' donated to Amherst.[26] If the manuscripts had remained together, we might have seen a complete edition sooner, but the poems instead appeared piecemeal over the decades. Even Thomas Johnson's 1955 variorum suffers, according to R. W. Franklin, because Johnson had limited access to Todd's collection.[27] The division of the manuscripts similarly hindered those developing the first online archives in the 1990s. Early online collections such as Smith's *Dickinson Electronic Archives* and Marta Werner's *Radical Scatters* (1999) adopted more focused, less comprehensive strategies because they could not straightforwardly secure images and permissions from the multiple institutions holding Dickinson manuscripts.[28] A comprehensive online archive became feasible only when the largest such institutions, Amherst and Harvard, became directly involved. Since the late 1990s, when Internet connections became fast enough for images, a reasonably comprehensive online archive of Dickinson manuscripts has been possible technologically, just not logistically.

Harvard's claims of ownership have presented substantial impediments to new online archives. Harvard possesses a bit more than half of the manuscripts, but it claims rights to the entirety of Emily Dickinson's poetry, letters, and other writings.[29] Harvard University Press does grant permission to (and collect fees from) scholars wishing to reproduce images of manuscripts the university holds or to cite Dickinson's writings, but the press does not offer a schedule of fees. It sets fees on a case-by-case basis and with sufficient flexibility that one scholar, who wished to remain anonymous, suggested I feign a dearth of funding when I request permissions. Amherst College, by contrast, permits the reproduction of all Dickinson manuscript images in their collection, without fee or restriction, and makes no claims to own the texts of Dickinson's work. Ironically, the manuscripts that Mabel Loomis Todd refused to return to the Dickinson family now constitute the more open archive, while those sold to Harvard by the heirs of Emily Dickinson have become restricted, hindering the publication and study of her poetry.[30]

This possessive climate led those building the first online archives to narrow their focus. The *Dickinson Electronic Archives* aimed "to edit and encode all of Dickinson's corpus," but it started with more modest efforts to display the poet's correspondence with Susan Dickinson.[31] It also developed "samplers" or "digital articles," small collections of manuscript images with transcriptions and commentary. These are precursors to what today's *Dickinson Electronic Archives* calls "exhibitions," a hybrid genre that mixes critical interpretation, digital curation, textual editing, and online pedagogy. Second to the increased visibility of Dickinson's manuscripts, the most interesting outcome of the online Dickinson archives has been this new, specifically Web-based genre of scholarship. "Emily Dickinson Writing a Poem," the above-mentioned exhibition about "Safe in their Alabaster Chambers," was the first such digital article in the *Dickinson Electronic Archives*. It not only enables new interpretations of "Safe" but also works well as a teaching aid. Martha Nell Smith recalls that its narrow scope made it easier to get permissions from Harvard, which initially wanted to control access to the article by requiring a password.[32] Other digital articles address Dickinson's comedic writing,

Textures Newly Visible 249

the manuscripts that have been mutilated since her death, and other subsets of her work.[33] These exhibitions provide frameworks for critical commentary within sufficiently narrow portions of the corpus that no one mistakes them for comprehensive archives or editions.

Because they could not strive for comprehensiveness, the early online archives tended to highlight their own principles of selection, unpacking the insights these selections made available. For example, Marta Werner's *Radical Scatters* identifies differences between the poet's early and late work. The modern copyright environment did not produce these differences, but it did encourage the kind of focused digital collection through which Werner makes her case. Her emphasis on late fragments conveniently prioritizes the unrestricted Amherst collection rather than the tightly controlled Harvard holdings.[34] Like other archives that appeared before 2013, *Radical Scatters* can be treated as a finished scholarly work or as an open archive. The partialness of such collections suggests readers view them as focused critical analyses, but they also provide flexible platforms for users to explore, potentially resulting in new insights and interpretations. The ambivalence between these two effects helps to indicate the possessive constraints in spite of which Werner, Smith, and others developed the first generation of online Dickinson archives.

Radical Scatters offers several curatorial innovations, some of which later intensified the commodification of Dickinson's work. In addition to conventional transcriptions, the site provides XML transcriptions, manuscript images, and another form of transcription that Werner calls "diplomatic transcriptions."[35] The latter are type transcriptions set upon an outline of the original page shape, with the type scaled and arranged to match the manuscript. By offering detailed metadata and multiple kinds of transcription, *Radical Scatters* avoids fixating upon the appearance of Dickinson's handwriting. Werner's innovations nonetheless enable the further commodification of manuscript images. In 2013, Werner and Jen Bervin released a coedited volume, *The Gorgeous Nothings: Emily Dickinson's Envelope Poems*, which follows *Radical Scatters* in collecting poems written on scraps and envelopes. *The Gorgeous Nothings* is a beautiful coffee-table book that presents full-color, full-scale photos of Dickinson's manuscripts and, on facing pages, diplomatic transcriptions of the kind Werner offers in *Radical Scatters*. The book's generous proportions and glossy images frame the paper codex as a visually alluring commodity; its unwieldiness and partial coverage make it less useful for research than for decoration. In the same year that it became possible to view most of Dickinson's manuscripts for free online, *The Gorgeous Nothings* reemphasized the visual value of the poet's manuscripts. By framing manuscript images as beautiful objects for sale, *The Gorgeous Nothings* extends the long tradition of commodifying Dickinson's handwriting – an auction of the mind, so to speak, that has even influenced the design of the free online archives.

Werner and Smith have made valuable contributions to Dickinson's online presence despite Harvard's efforts to restrict the circulation of her poems and manuscript images. Harvard controls Dickinson's work by intimidation rather than litigation; the mere threat of a legal dispute with such an institution suffices to keep its claims untested.[36] The online archives have thus developed under significant constraints, and new print editions, when not suppressed, have appeared with Harvard's consent and often under its colophon.[37] Harvard University Press asks to review "all applications to quote or reprint Emily Dickinson material," no matter the source, and states that "we will let you know which selections are public domain."[38] Not all authors and presses comply with this request. When I did, Harvard kindly charged me no fee to cite Dickinson in an academic monograph, but even if Harvard waived fees in every case, the permissions process would still have a chilling effect. As arbiter of its own rights, Harvard coerces editors and scholars to participate in the commodification of Dickinson's work. Willingly or not, those who ask Harvard's permission to cite or edit Dickinson help to frame her work as private property, owned and controlled, and thereby hinder free inquiry into how we can preserve and disseminate her writing.

Texture and Gesture in the New Archives

Amherst's online *Emily Dickinson Collection* and the collaborative *Emily Dickinson Archive* led by Harvard, both of which appeared in 2013, influence how future readers will interact with Dickinson's work. Their user interfaces both encourage and impede specific ways of reading Dickinson. Surprisingly, they do little to facilitate the forms of computer-aided analysis that have burgeoned in other literary fields. Rather, in addition to intensifying the fixation on seeing the poet's handwriting, these archives construct more tactile, gestural modes of contact with it, thereby opening new ways to feel close to Emily Dickinson.

The Amherst and Harvard archives make Dickinson more accessible to human readers but not necessarily to computerized analysis. Computers enable scholars to examine more objects than a single person could otherwise address – say, thousands of paintings or novels. Comparable analyses of Dickinson's work might look at the macro-scale development of her

Textures Newly Visible 251

lexicon, stationeries, poetic forms, or other factors that direct human attention cannot readily address. As Mary Loeffelholz recognizes, such macro-analyses "would wire Dickinson's writings into the larger network of nineteenth-century letters and beyond," but they "have not yet been much attempted in Dickinson studies."[39] Why not? The most common types of computerized literary analysis rely upon large bodies of e-text, words legible to computers. The Harvard archive provides the only complete, reliable e-text of Dickinson's poems, but these transcripts can be accessed only one poem at a time. Before a computer could analyze the full Dickinson corpus, a human would have to find a way (or do the manual work) of downloading, cataloging, and combining every poem. *The Internet Archive* and other sites contain larger e-texts of Dickinson's work, but these are full of errors and poorly cataloged, partly because they encroach upon Harvard's copyright claims. One reason Dickinson scholars have not undertaken the computerized analysis Loeffelholz imagines, then, is that Harvard does not provide an open and complete e-text usable for such analysis and prevents other online archives from doing so.[40]

Because the Amherst and Harvard archives treat the manuscripts primarily as images, one might think they instead encourage visual methods of computerized analysis. Digitally inclined scholars have used software to analyze various dimensions of visual culture – as, for instance, when Lev Manovich and Jeremy Douglas graph the color saturation of 4,535 *Time* magazine covers published since 1923.[41] Perhaps similar techniques could offer new perspectives on the Dickinson manuscripts. But the archives' usefulness is limited in this case as well. Neither major archive offers a means to download manuscript images in bulk. To analyze the full collection, one would first have to navigate manually to each item and download it – or else write a script to step through the URLs for each file. The structure of Amherst's archive makes automated collection easier, but even here it proves challenging for those not comfortable writing code, especially given the difficulty of associating each image with the correct metadata. Worse, when users download an image from the Harvard archive, they get a lower-resolution image than the site itself displays. Images download at 72 pixels per inch, rather than the 600 pixels per inch at which they were scanned.[42] (By comparison, printers often source images for publication at 300 pixels per inch or better.) When users view an image directly on the Harvard site instead of downloading it, the site draws on a database of smaller images that each cover part of the manuscript, like tiles. As users scroll and zoom, the archive stitches together the necessary tiles on the fly. In theory this method saves network bandwidth, but, given the file sizes involved, it seems like a solution in search of a problem – or else a way to restrict access to high-definition manuscript images. Someone using the *Emily Dickinson Archive* can zoom closely enough to see the very grain of Dickinson's pencil strokes, but someone downloading the same image will find it pixelates far sooner. The Amherst archive again performs better: its download button serves a single jpeg image at 600 pixels per inch, the site's maximum resolution. Images download from Amherst with filenames that match their record numbers in the digital collection. Those downloaded from Harvard come compressed inside appropriately named folders, but the images are all named "image.jpg," making the arrangement of metadata for bulk analysis even trickier. Hence, both archives discourage computerized analysis of Dickinson's work. Instead the online archives privilege the close encounter with one manuscript image at a time.

Indeed, the latest online archives offer images so vivid that the experience of seeing them exceeds the visual register and invokes the material textures of the manuscripts. Although no website conveys the aura of the manuscripts as powerfully as the physical archives, these new online archives come close. They enable users to view manuscripts in astounding detail, for the images do not blur or pixelate even when displayed at several times their original size. The effect is not only visual but also tactile. Earlier facsimiles show the stroke of the poet's pen, tracing her gestures as she wrote. The recent images, however, develop a textural aesthetic that subtends this gestural tracing. The facsimiles of 1891 or 1981 disclose the shape of Dickinson's handwriting, but those of 2013 make visible the tiny veins within a crease of paper, the warp and woof of the stationery, the little frays around a pinhole, and the uneven pattern of lead within a pencil stroke, which throws the paper's texture into relief. The artist's term for this last effect is *frottage*, rubbing. Even as these textural effects seem distinct from the gestures of the poet's writing, the erotic connotations of frottage associate such effects with a long allegorical tradition whereby the visible tactility of the poet's manuscripts stands in for the erotic physicality of her body. These almost-microscopic textural details convey the objecthood of the manuscripts, visually dramatizing their materiality.

While this textural dimension allows a feeling of extremely close encounter with the poet and her work, such gratuitously detailed views rarely provide useful information. For example, when users view "The way Hope builds his House" (F1512) on the Harvard site, they will notice that it is written on an unfolded envelope whose pentagonal shape resembles the outline of a house. This detail tells us something about Dickinson's relation to her compositional equipment, but a lower-quality facsimile would still show the shape of the page. The online archives reveal much more. They make it possible to see that Dickinson's pencil was dull when she wrote this poem, that the envelope tore slightly on its left edge, that the ribbed embossing is deeper in some places than others. Those few scholars who can learn something from such minute details, from the position of a pinhole or the texture of a stationery, will likely continue to study the manuscripts in person, rather than rely upon images that cannot even be downloaded. These new textural effects inaugurate a new phase in the history of Dickinson facsimiles, as they make visible not only her handwriting but also the manuscripts' physical textures. These visible textures resemble earlier effects, however, insomuch as they lead us to focus on something *other* than the wording of Dickinson's poems when we look at her manuscripts. They perpetuate the idea that manuscript images do not simply give textual information but bring us closer to the actual materials of the poet's life.

The *Emily Dickinson Archive* also emphasizes gesture in the scene of reading. The site privileges the reader's embodied gestures as a way to interface with Dickinson's work. This online archive supports the multi-touch interface mechanics first popularized on the iPhone. It employs the "pinch to zoom" metaphor: users can enlarge an image by spreading two fingertips apart on a touchscreen or touchpad, and pinching fingers together shrinks the image. This metaphor frames the reader's interaction with manuscript images as tactile, gestural. The images literally respond to our touch. The archive also employs a "page turn" effect borrowed from e-reading platforms such as iBooks. Users can flip to the next manuscript image by swiping one finger laterally from the edge of the image, as though turning a paper page; a visual effect tracks the finger, showing the triangular curl of the virtual page being turned. Both of these gestural tropes seek to naturalize the interface with digital images by making it more intuitive and intimate, less arbitrary and distanced. Such hopes for gestural interfacing shape how critics imagine future scholarship. For example, when Mary Loeffelholz writes that "I would love to slide a button from 1850 to 1865 to 1886 and watch the cumulative history of Dickinson's correspondences burgeoning before my eyes," she couches the promise of digital scholarship in terms of the pleasures of gestural interfacing, of the button we "love" to slide back and forth.[43] The skeuomorphic page-turning animation in the *Emily Dickinson Archive* goes even further. It invokes gestures and visual effects specifically associated with paper, the technology these archives simultaneously put on display and make obsolete. In Harvard's publicity video for the archive, a man demonstrates both the page-turn and pinch-to-zoom gestures on an iPad.[44] The video makes a complex series of promises about the archive. Its images offer such rich detail that one almost feels able to touch the manuscript itself, feel its texture; indeed, the gestural controls invite us to touch the manuscript images, if not the originals. For many users, to see these manuscripts will also prove touching in the emotional sense, for they give us vivid new impressions of Dickinson's writing. The archive joins a long history of facsimile technologies that support emotionally stirring encounters with Dickinson through images of her manuscripts.

The gestural interface of *Emily Dickinson Archive* reflects a broader tension between paper and electronic platforms for poetry. On one hand, the online Dickinson archives sustain a lyrical mode of response that prioritizes the textures and gestures associated with paper, from the author's pen-strokes to the reader's page-turning. On the other hand, even as they focus on the touch of paper, these archives help to make it obsolete: one finds fewer reasons to buy paper facsimiles of the manuscripts or, perhaps, to consult the originals in Massachusetts. The tropes of texture and gesture thus encapsulate the challenges these technological developments set forth for traditional ways of valuing poems, including Dickinson's. By making it easier to view Emily Dickinson's manuscripts, these archives provide vivid new perspectives on her work, and they also open new avenues of affective contact with the poet, helping to fulfill a desire for intimacy with her that reaches back to the earliest facsimile images. At the same time, by reauthorizing and making more explicit certain long-standing attitudes about her manuscripts, today's online archives clarify the old logics of poetic value that inform her reception today. In the future, one hopes that other kinds of digital archives might facilitate less conventional ways of interfacing with Dickinson's work.

Notes

1. Emily Dickinson, *Poems: Second Series*, Mabel Loomis Todd and T. W. Higginson (eds.) (Boston: Roberts Brothers, 1891).
2. The archive I call Harvard's, *Emily Dickinson Archive*, contains manuscripts from several institutions, including Harvard, Amherst, and the Boston Public Library. Members of its advisory board have complained of Harvard's unwillingness, as project leader, to take advice, so many now see it as a Harvard project rather than a collaboration. It can be found at www.edickinson.org. Amherst's *Emily Dickinson Collection* can be found at https://acdc.amherst.edu/browse/collection/collection:ed.

3. Cf. Alexandra Socarides, *Dickinson Unbound: Paper, Process, Poetics* (New York: Oxford University Press, 2012), 20–48, 78–104; and Virginia Jackson, *Dickinson's Misery: A Theory of Lyric Reading* (Princeton: Princeton University Press, 2005), 82–92, 133–137.
4. Socarides, 15.
5. A notable exception is Lori Emerson, *Reading Writing Interfaces: From the Digital to the Bookbound* (Minneapolis: University of Minnesota Press, 2014), which discusses computer interfaces with a "digital Dickinson."
6. The foundational account of lyric reading comes from Jackson, *Dickinson's Misery*. Among others, Socarides's work with the manuscripts in *Dickinson Unbound* draws out the implications of Jackson's critique.
7. Mabel Loomis Todd, "Preface," in Emily Dickinson, *Poems: Second Series*, 5.
8. Ibid., 5–6.
9. Ibid., 6.
10. Ibid.
11. Theodora Ward, "Characteristics of the Handwriting," in *The Poems of Emily Dickinson*, Thomas Johnson (ed.) (Cambridge: Harvard University Press, 1955), lviii.
12. In the introduction to his variorum, R. W. Franklin expresses polite skepticism about the accuracy of Ward's handwriting chronology. As Franklin puts it in his earlier book, "what with Emily Dickinson was a habit of handwriting was not a consistent one." R. W. Franklin, *The Editing of Emily Dickinson: A Reconsideration* (Madison: University of Wisconsin Press, 1967), 120. See also R. W. Franklin, "Introduction," in *The Poems of Emily Dickinson: Variorum Edition*, R. W. Franklin (ed.) (Cambridge: Harvard University Press, 1998), 37–39.
13. Theodora Ward, "Characteristics," lii, liv.
14. Susan Howe, *My Emily Dickinson* (New York: New Directions, 1985), 51.
15. Susan Howe, *The Birth-mark: Unsettling the Wilderness of American Literary History* (Middletown: Wesleyan University Press, 1993), 142.
16. Walter Benn Michaels, *The Shape of the Signifier: 1967 to the End of History* (Princeton: Princeton University Press, 2004), 3. The weakness of Michaels's critique lies in conflating the manuscript's visibility with its material objecthood, a confusion Howe does not share. Understood as a visual rather than a textual field, a manuscript remains open to facsimile reproduction; as a singular physical object, it does not.
17. Martha Nell Smith and Lara Vetter, "Emily Dickinson Writing a Poem," 1998, *Dickinson Electronic Archives*, http://archive.emilydickinson.org/safe.
18. Ibid.
19. Leslie A. Morris, "Emily Dickinson Archive," YouTube video, 1:53, posted by Harvard University Press, September 18, 2013, www.youtu.be/97YjkıtAGoo.
20. Cf. www.whitmanarchive.org.
21. Cf. www.rossettiarchive.org and https://eebo.chadwyck.com/home.
22. Cf. Zachary Turpin, "Introduction to Walt Whitman's 'Life and Adventures of Jack Engle,'" *Walt Whitman Quarterly Review* 34.3 (2017): 225–261.

23. "About," *Emily Dickinson Archive*, www.edickinson.org/about.
24. Ibid.
25. For an account of the controversy that accompanied the launch of the Harvard archive, see Sarah Schweitzer, "Trove of Emily Dickinson manuscripts to appear online," *Boston Globe*, October 20, 2013, web.
26. The best account of the custody of Dickinson's manuscripts and early publication efforts appears in R. W. Franklin, "Introduction," 1–7.
27. Ibid., 6.
28. In addition to Amherst and Harvard, numerous other institutions hold smaller collections of Dickinson manuscripts – the Boston Public Library, the Library of Congress, Yale University, and others.
29. Cf. www.hup.harvard.edu/rights/permissions-frequently-asked-questions .html.
30. In 1994, for example, Harvard denied Philip Stambovsky permission to publish a new edition of Dickinson poems then under development at the University of North Carolina Press. Rather than enable Dickinson scholars to assess Stambovsky's edition, Harvard unilaterally decided it was "not in the best interest of preserving or presenting the integrity of the Dickinson work." Domhnall Mitchell, *Measures of Possibility: Emily Dickinson's Manuscripts* (Amherst, MA: University of Massachusetts Press, 2005), 19–20.
31. "About the Archives," *Dickinson Electronic Archives*, http://archive.emilydickin son.org/about_the_site.html.
32. Martha Nell Smith, conversation with the author, April 7, 2017, Washington, DC.
33. Cf. http://archive.emilydickinson.org/DAintro.html.
34. Marta L. Werner, *Radical Scatters: Emily Dickinson's Late Fragments and Related Texts, 1870–1886*, University of Nebraska-Lincoln, 1999, http://radi calscatters.unl.edu/index.html. Only 12 items in the archive come from Harvard, with 109 from Amherst and 11 from six other institutions.
35. On diplomatic transcription, see Gregory A. Pass, *Descriptive Cataloging of Ancient, Medieval, Renaissance, and Early Modern Manuscripts*, Bibliographic Standards Committee, Rare Books and Manuscripts Section, Association of College and Research Libraries (Chicago: American Library Association, 2003). What Werner calls diplomatic transcriptions might more accurately be considered type facsimiles, since they do not employ "a system of editorial signs," as Pass puts it, to represent characteristics of the source manuscript but instead directly render the source's structure in type (144–145). Werner employs the same transcription style in her book *Emily Dickinson's Open Folios: Scenes of Reading, Surfaces of Writing* (Ann Arbor: University of Michigan Press, 1996). XML is a document markup language that is both human- and computer-readable. It includes detailed formatting tags and other elements that describe a text's wording and structure. Cf. www.tei-c .org.
36. Experts suggest Harvard's broadest claims of ownership might not hold up. The author in question has been dead since 1886 – long enough, perhaps, that

her work should be public domain. More importantly, before the sale to Harvard, Dickinson's heirs did not vigorously defend their supposed rights; Todd and her heirs had already published Dickinson without legal challenge, weakening any future assertion of these rights. Cf. Elizabeth Horan, "Technically Outside the Law: Who Permits, Who Profits, and Why," *The Emily Dickinson Journal* 10.1 (2001): 42.

37. In addition to the suppressed Stambovsky edition mentioned above, one wonders how Cristanne Miller's recent edition, *Emily Dickinson's Poems: As She Preserved Them* (Cambridge: Harvard University Press, 2016), might have developed differently if the project had more autonomy from Harvard.
38. Cf. www.hup.harvard.edu/rights/permissions-frequently-asked-questions.html.
39. Mary Loeffelholz, "Networking Dickinson: Some Thought Experiments in Digital Humanities," *EDJ* 23.1 (2014): 108.
40. Ironically, Dickinson's poems were the basis for one of the first computer-generated literary concordances, S. P. Rosenbaum's *A Concordance to the Poems of Emily Dickinson* (Ithaca: Cornell University Press, 1964). Although Dickinson has occasioned little computer-aided analysis, the *Emily Dickinson Lexicon* and the Victorian Literary Studies *Hyper-Concordance* do provide valuable research capabilities. Cf. http://edl.byu.edu and http://victorian-studies.net/concordance/dickinson.
41. Cf. Jeremy Douglass and Lev Manovich, "Time covers," Software Studies Initiative, 2009, http://lab.softwarestudies.com/p/research_14.html.
42. Leslie A. Morris, "Emily Dickinson archive query," email to the author, February 13, 2015.
43. Mary Loeffelholz, "Networking Dickinson," 112.
44. "Emily Dickinson Archive," YouTube video, 1:53, posted by Harvard University Press, September 18, 2013, www.youtu.be/97YjkItAGoo.

CHAPTER 15

Coloring Dickinson: Race, Influence, and Lyric Dis-reading

Evie Shockley

*how sound comes into a word, coloured
by who pays what for speaking.*

Audre Lorde, "Coal"

We choose our influences. But as with all choices, some are more meaningful – more profoundly self-motivated, less constrained – than others. The current discourse on American poetics, as composed by scholars and poets alike, regularly cites Emily Dickinson and Walt Whitman as its two indispensable forebears, one or both of whom influence American poets almost by default. They appear, for instance, as the first two figures – and the only ones wholly of the nineteenth century – in the canonizing pages of the *Norton Anthology of Modern and Contemporary Poetry*.[1] Poets representing a wide swath of aesthetic territory gesture toward this once-unlikely pair, who somehow signify both what is quintessentially American and what is quintessentially innovative (that is, what defines the national poetry and what betokens the possible alternatives to the norm) at the same time. As Mary Jo Bang has put it, "much, if not most, of contemporary poetry is, at least tangentially, descended from [Dickinson, who], alongside Whitman, created what now appears as a break with a new beginning that others have since added to by torquing, torturing, or in whatever way, hammer-slamming poetry into its present zeitgeist."[2] In particular, because of her unique placement as a woman in the tradition – chronologically early (having written, if not widely published, well prior to modernism) *and* critically acknowledged as a genius – Dickinson is often figured as the progenitor of feminist or women's poetry in the United States. Indeed, as Zofia Burr writes, Dickinson's "canonization ... as the exemplary American woman poet" has meant that "[t]he critical reception of her poetry has served as a crucial site for constructing the terms for the reception of poetry by American women in general."[3] Thus, for many

Coloring Dickinson: Race, Influence, and Lyric Dis-reading 259

twentieth- and even twenty-first-century women poets, Dickinson looms as a powerful influence – less a matter of choice than an inevitability to be embraced or gotten around.

It must be said, however, that the "long shadow" of Dickinson's work tends to bring white women poets more frequently into view.[4] The scholarship on her influence has most often featured Marianne Moore and H. D., among the modernists; Sylvia Plath and Elizabeth Bishop, at midcentury; and in the (increasingly unwieldy) contemporary period, Adrienne Rich, Susan Howe, Kathy Acker, and Alice Fulton.[5] Women poets of color, however, seldom come up for sustained attention in Dickinson scholarship, and the few who have are exclusively African American.[6] Presumably because of her particularly high esteem in American poetry, Gwendolyn Brooks receives the most consideration, with a chapter in each of two monographs. Burr studies Brooks's strategies of lyric address, along with those of Josephine Miles, Audre Lorde, and Maya Angelou, in light of Dickinson's. She argues that the later poets must all confront and negotiate the expectation, created by Dickinson's reception, that women's poetry will "focus inward" rather than casting its address into the public realm.[7] Lesley Wheeler also works on Brooks, productively analyzing how women poets – beginning with Dickinson and also including Moore, H. D., Bishop, and Rita Dove – have figured the lyric poem as an "enclosure": part shelter, part prison.[8] Lorde, Angelou, and Dove, as most readers will have recognized, are the additional black poets to figure in any substantive way in the Dickinson scholarship. Other African American women and, emphatically, women of color belonging to other racial and ethnic groups, from Joy Harjo and Sandra Cisneros to Julia Alvarez and Meena Alexander, also cite Dickinson's work as important to their formation as artists or their poetics, but the scholarship has yet to account for these engagements.

While this notable blind spot is interesting in itself, my aim in this essay is not to uncover its extent by illuminating the number of African American, Latina, Native American, and Asian American women whose poetry is admittedly or arguably (or inevitably) indebted to Dickinson's work. Instead, I want to reckon with *how* women of color negotiate their Dickinsonian inheritance. In pursuing this line of inquiry, I am asking us to think about agency and choice. Dickinson's singularity as a canonical nineteenth-century woman poet and her enshrinement as a foremother of American women's poetry have of course given women of color strong incentives to engage with her compelling work. But – in addition to the problems any woman might have with Dickinson's oeuvre (which can seem to some too idiosyncratic and strange, to others too tepid and conventional) or with the socially privileged gender stereotypes comprising her "reclusive Belle of Amherst" mythos – an obstacle of particular significance to women of color emerges in Dickinson's minimal or, worse, offensive treatment of race and racially inflected issues. Must women of color poets betray their own racial politics or "set aside" part of their identity to embrace Dickinson? What kind of choice is that, particularly for writers whose early exposure to poetry was shaped by a much more limited canon than young poets encounter today? On what other terms do (or might) these women negotiate the Dickinsonian legacy?

This essay investigates these questions. In the first section, I give a brief overview of the shape race takes in Dickinson's poetry. In the process, I point to some of the most interesting recent scholarship, but without rehearsing the literature in depth, because my concern is not with proving or disproving Dickinson's attitudes on race. As the second section demonstrates, I am interested in outlining how women of color may be engaging with Dickinson – in a process that neither excuses the racism (or silence on race) in her poems *nor* sidelines these readers' racial subjectivity. Building on the work of José Esteban Muñoz, I call this process *lyric dis-reading* and argue that it enables women of color poets to choose Dickinson as an influence in a meaningful way, on their own terms. Finally, having developed these ideas in the first two sections through examinations of the work of Toi Derricotte, I offer in the third section further examples of what lyric dis-reading of Dickinson might look like by working speculatively on the engagement of two poets, one African American (Brooks, in a new take) and one Asian American (Marilyn Chin), with Dickinson as an influence. Ultimately, the essay argues that by variously "coloring" (or implicitly racializing) the meaning of Dickinson's poetry, women of color create the conditions for their own artistic development. This labor is a type of work that poets who write from marginalized identities routinely have to do, to write themselves into the literatures of white supremacist nations.

Derricotte Among Dickinson's "Daughters"

In April 1986, Toi Derricotte participated in a two-day "Celebration of Emily Dickinson and American Women's Poetry" held at Seton Hall University to mark the centennial of Dickinson's death.[9] Among the works she read was a poem written for the occasion – indeed, *on* the occasion – ultimately entitled "Sitting with Myself in the Seton Hall Deli at 12 O'clock Thursday Before I Read with the Great Poets at the

Emily Dickinson Poetry Festival."[10] The final stanza of the poem, as it was later published, includes these lines:

> "Tell all the truth, but tell it slant."
> We don't have time to slant. ...
> ...
> We are her daughters.
> But could she accept us?
> Was her white
> a put-down of the black?
> Is she ready for
> all these various voices? (23)

The "we" of Derricotte's familial claim on Dickinson not only references the other women poets on the program, who were predominantly white, but also contemplates the women (poets or not) in the festival audience and, arguably, the poem's subsequent women readers as well.[11] Derricotte's remarks emphasized that she has "loved Emily Dickinson for many, many years, for many reasons," despite the straightforward, un-*slant*-ed questions she has about how Dickinson felt ("*Was* her white" a supremacist white?) and might now feel ("*Is* she ready" to hear different ideas?) about an interracial or multiracial sisterhood.[12]

Whether we receive a Dickinson who is lovelorn and isolated or, instead, explosive and self-aware, the poet typically comes to us characterized as notably under-engaged or exasperatingly subtle with regard to matters of race and the sociopolitical phenomena associated with it in her day, such as slavery, the Civil War, and American imperialism. Although Whitman's legacy has become more complicated as information emerges about his personal views on race, his poetry nonetheless championed democratic ideals that explicitly encompassed the enslaved African; as a result, his work has appealed to twentieth-century black poets from Langston Hughes to June Jordan.[13] By contrast, Dickinson's poetic legacy is entangled with a subjectivity and mythos of white womanhood that excludes, estranges, or eludes women of color. While there are certainly poems invoking or suggesting race in her oeuvre (such as "The Malay – took the Pearl –" or "A solemn thing – it was – I said –" [F451, F307]), they tend to trade in stereotypes or instrumentalize raced figures and issues. Where Whitman explicitly repudiates the logic of the slave auction ("Gentlemen look on this wonder. / Whatever the bids of the bidders they cannot be high enough for it"),[14] Dickinson seemingly relegates it to the subtext of her poetry. She would have us reject "Publication," metaphorically deemed "the Auction / Of the Mind" – but in order to preserve our ability to "go / White – unto the White Creator" (F788). Though she would "reduce no Human Spirit / To Disgrace of Price," Dickinson makes no comment on the disgraceful practice of putting a price on human bodies and lives.[15] Such scholars as Pollak, Cristanne Miller, Faith Barrett, Erica Fretwell, and Benjamin Friedlander, among others, have argued (or conceded) that Dickinson's politics appear to be pro-slavery, despite her stance as an anti-war supporter of the Union[16]; that her racial ideology is bound up in the symbolism Christianity attaches to whiteness and blackness; and that her references to people of color and related places abroad participate in "romantic racialism," exoticism, and orientalism.[17]

Only the 1864 poem "Color – Caste – Denomination –" seems to argue against the significance of race; the poem contends that "the Brand" of racial and religious difference will ultimately be "Rub[bed] away" by "Death's large – Democratic fingers," creating from "Chrysalis of Blonde – or Umber – / Equal Butterfly –" (F836).[18] But even here, although constructing *death* as unconcerned with the distinctions that structure her society before and after the Civil War, the poem seems quite complacent and uncurious about the people *living* and suffering under the very un-"Equal" conditions those distinctions underwrite. Moreover, her use of the word "Brand" as a metaphor for the differences that death will "Obscur[e]" is *so* apt an echo of "Hue," given the practice of literally branding enslaved people's bodies, that its application to religious "Tenets" in the same breath comes off as gross insensitivity. This unsettling metaphorical reference to brands stands oddly alongside an orientalist racial gesture, as Miller notes: "Curiously, ... in this 1864 poem about 'Color,' the only race mentioned is the Circassian." Miller explains that the Circassians of Turkey were figured in American popular culture in the 1850s and early 1860s "as a racial borderland" between a "tribal Muslim" brownness ("Umber") and a white beauty associated with their origins in Caucasus (and the women's enslavement in Turkish harems).[19] The juxtaposition of these images leaves us with a Dickinson whose otherwise seemingly boundless imagination falls short at the very moments the woman of color, reading her, comes most nearly into view.

Thus, Derricotte stutter-steps between asserting her status as Dickinson's "daughter" and wondering if her foremother is prepared to acknowledge the relationship. When she asks "Was her white / a put-down of the black?" she may have in mind such Dickinson lines as "Mine – by the Right of the White Election!" or these:

> A solemn thing – it was – I said –
> A Woman – white – to be –
> And wear – if God should count me fit –
> Her blameless mystery – (F307)[20]

Such scholars as Mitchell, Pollak, and Wesley King have gamely tackled the question of whether Dickinson's affirmations of whiteness could be extracted from the racialized white/black dichotomy that permeated nineteenth-century US culture.[21] But my focus here is ultimately not on the proper parsing of Dickinson's racism. I have wanted merely to establish the challenges that women of color would meet with in reading Dickinson as a model or entry-point for their own poetry. I am interested in *how* Derricotte maintains her claim on Dickinson as "our mother," even with such questions still weighing on her as her poem about the celebration of Dickinson's centennial draws to a close. What facilitates the connection of Dickinson's unlooked-for daughters to their reluctant mother? Or, put differently, what reading strategies make possible, for twentieth- and twenty-first-century women of color poets, these familiar and familial gestures toward Dickinson?

Dis-reading Dickinson

To answer these questions, I begin by returning to Derricotte's reading at Seton Hall, which is available as audio and transcription in the *Dickinson Electronic Archives*. Just before reading her freshly drafted poem, Derricotte shares a short, two-stanza poem of Dickinson's that reveals, she argues, that the poet "experienced a little self-doubt":[22]

> I took my Power in my Hand –
> And went against the World –
> 'Twas not so much as David – had –
> But I – was twice as bold –
>
> I aimed my Pebble – but Myself
> Was all the one that fell –
> Was it Goliath – was too large –
> Or was myself – too small? (F660)

As a lead-in to Derricotte's own poem – which begins, "When I read with them, when I hear them, / I will know / I'm inferior" – the Dickinson poem is significant and telling.[23] By preceding her piece with Dickinson's meditation on the "Power" an individual might attempt to wield "against the World –," and specifically an attempt that *fails*, Derricotte brilliantly brings her audience into a more sympathetic frame of mind, creating a context in which her poem can better be heard. She knows in 1986 – as the transcript reveals – that her listeners have no commonly shared view about the relationship of politics and poetry; and she knows that her poem, which analyzes power, is going to close with gestures toward the racism in Dickinson's language and the "various voices" that will join Derricotte's to write poems that question power and decry white supremacism.[24] Considering the resistance to "political poetry," ongoing a full decade after the height of the Black Arts Movement, Derricotte is shrewd to cite Dickinson's concession that even being "twice as bold" is not always enough to enable the "Pebble" of oneself to instantly change "the World."

Equally important, for our purposes, is the way Dickinson's poem sounds notes that ring profoundly in African American culture. The identification of African Americans with the Christian Bible's underdogs is a recurring thread in African American culture, beginning from its earliest years.[25] Indeed, Phillis Wheatley retells the story of David's battle with Goliath in heroic couplets, in her 1773 collection of poems. This story, like that in which the children of Israel are freed from Egyptian slavery and led to the promised land, has often signified for African Americans their long struggle for freedom and against white racism. What happens if we imagine Derricotte here to be quietly revealing, drawing on, and implicitly inviting her audience to consider the racial subtext that, I will say, "colors" her reading of Dickinson's poem?

I propose that women of color do – some of us, some of the time – "color" our readings of Dickinson's work. My thinking about the process by which such readings are produced builds upon the generative work of José Muñoz. In *Disidentifications: Queers of Color and the Performance of Politics*, Muñoz theorizes the strategy a "minority subject" uses "to resist and confound socially prescriptive patterns of identification."[26] In deriving his theory, he focuses on the predicament of queers of color, who must form their sense of self in a society that offers them limited opportunities to form identification on the basis of race/ethnicity *and* sexuality without encountering "phobic charges in both fields."[27] The value of his work for my inquiry here lies in its investigation of a process by which the subject does not simply *identify* with the locus or discourse offered by the dominant ideology, which would require an erasure of its unacceptable aspects; nor, on the other hand, does she *counteridentify*, which would require an outright rejection of a locus or discourse that may have elements within it that she needs. The subject instead *disidentifies*, which is to say she "scrambles and reconstructs the encoded message of a cultural text in a fashion that both exposes the encoded message's universalizing and exclusionary machinations and recircuits its workings to account for, include, and empower minority identities and identifications."[28] Disidentification is, in the first instance perhaps, a matter of the subject's development or her very survival, but the performance of disidentification also works to open up possibilities within the dominant culture that have wider effect.

I want to draw a line from Muñoz's compelling work on how disidentification operates with regard to performance and spectatorship (in film, performance art, television, and other modes) to our question at hand about how women of color might forge a beneficial relationship with Dickinson as a poetic influence. This question is not primarily about whether or how such poets identify with Dickinson *herself*, though that inquiry is not altogether unrelated to what we are concerned with. However, ours is a question of how women of color poets read her *poetry*, so as to make it more habitable for them as women poets writing in the long shadow of her work. Let us call this process *lyric dis-reading*. It is "dis-" rather than "mis-"reading, because what takes place is not based in misapprehension, a lack of knowledge, or a lack of skill. What we find instead is a poet/reader engaging with a text "that is not culturally coded to 'connect' with" her and choosing to invest it with meaning that makes the poem resonant for her,[29] *without* overlooking the fact that the reading of the poem thus produced would not be entirely consonant with the kinds of readings (e.g., strictly text-based, historicized, biographical, or based in authorial intent) that we are taught to generate.

I would argue that there is something particular – not unique or even rare, but, at the same time, distinguishing – about Dickinson's poetry that makes it open to this process I am describing. That "something" is invoked in my calling the process "lyric" dis-reading. Of course, it is not lost on me that Dickinson's work has been at the center of recent debates about the genre or history of the lyric. Virginia Jackson and Yopie Prins argue that, while the lyric is not a genre of ancient pedigree in the way that most poetry critics of the last hundred years say it is, our saying it is and our insistence on reading poems as though it were have made it a genre of a different sort with a much more recent provenance (in a feat of criticism-as-Austinian-performative-language). Their discussion of the lyric is useful here in that it reminds us that New Criticism's close reading hermeneutic "focus[ed] on making poetry available to all kinds of readers."[30] While it is disputable whether "all" the kinds of readers the New Critics had in mind included Latinas and women of Native American, Asian American, and African

American heritage, we might consider the ways in which such women could find it perversely empowering to be able to approach a poem on New Critical terms.[31] Imagining that "the poet [has] turn[ed] his back on his listeners," in a figurative sense, creates the context in which women of color can, in turn, ignore the poet and infuse the poem's first-person speaker with qualities the poet herself might not be considered to have.[32] Dickinson's "lyric I" – to revise a formulation of Jackson and Prins' – can speak *as* no one in particular and thus to all of us.[33]

But there is still a leap – a mighty conceptual effort – to be made, in the context of US poetry, before we can get from a speaker who is "no one in particular" to a speaker who is or might be black or brown. What Dorothy Wang has observed with regard to Asian American poetry is true for the work of people of color generally: "[I]n a racially diverse (and riven) nation such as the United States, ... a reader is not likely to automatically identify (with) the speaker of a poem written by a Chinese American female poet as a 'universal' subject, 'readily identified with anyone.'"[34] Moreover, in this national tradition, poetry about race or the cultural formations of people of color has long been conflated with "protest poetry," and there is, one gathers, nothing less lyric than protest poetry – notwithstanding the lyric's alleged voraciousness as a genre.[35] To speak of lyric dis-reading, then, is to recognize women of color authorizing themselves to determine when and how a poem may be read as lyric. This self-authorizing gesture disrupts exclusionary patterns in the ways the poetic tradition replicates itself and makes sociocultural meaning. The woman of color poet engaging in lyric dis-reading "colors" a Dickinson poem: this practice reconstitutes the poem for her and, in so doing, both leaves open *and* puts into relief the problem that Dickinson's poems were not written with women of color readers in mind. Importantly, because the point of lyric dis-reading is not to foreclose that critique,[36] we would *not* expect anyone to perform lyric dis-reading of those few Dickinson poems that actually invoke matters of race thematically or traffic in racial(ized) imagery. Lyric dis-reading does not seek to un-write Dickinson's troubling views on race; rather, it works to make Dickinson's oeuvre provide something useful to a poetic heir she never imagined having, without depriving that heir of the ability to critique racism and orientalism where she encounters it. In arguing that women poets of color may find it possible to embrace Dickinson's influence and legacy by racializing, or "coloring," the meaning of some of her poems, I intend to call attention to the kinds of creative labor that

Coloring Dickinson: Race, Influence, and Lyric Dis-reading   267

poets of color must regularly perform in making a space for themselves within literary traditions grounded in white supremacist cultures.[37]

Lyric dis-reading is an effort in furtherance of agency: it can facilitate a woman of color poet's decision to *choose* Dickinson's influence. The emergence of each such unlooked-for heir makes it easier for others subsequently to join her – and this is true not only in terms of setting a precedent but in the way such choices may, in turn, impact the scholarship. For example, Dickinson scholarship might look much whiter still today had Gwendolyn Brooks not signaled her engagement with the earlier poet's work. The final section of this essay enlarges on the discussion of Derricotte's 1986 remarks and poem above, by offering speculative sketches of how Brooks and Asian American poet Marilyn Chin similarly embrace Dickinson's influence through lyric dis-reading.

Imagining Brooks's and Chin's Lyrics Dis-readings

Brooks has been exceptionally useful as a sign of what Vivian Pollak calls "these appealing multicultural connections between Dickinson and African American women poets," enabling claims about Dickinson as progenitor of American women's poetry to appear inclusive, while maintaining white women's poetry and concerns as the norm.[38] In addition to appearing in both of the monographs that treat women of color as heirs to Dickinson, Brooks was among the participants in the Seton Hall celebration of Dickinson in 1986. On that occasion, she explained that she had encountered Dickinson first in school textbooks, without being drawn to the work, but, upon discovering a collection of previously unpublished Dickinson poems in her junior college library, she "was absolutely enchanted" by Dickinson's "way of putting common words together so they made new magic."[39] One of the ways that magic is arguably made is through the use of slant rhyme, which technique is certainly a mark of Dickinson's influence on Brooks. A Dickinson poem about the mercilessness of spring in the aftermath of bereavement ("I dreaded that first Robin, so"), rhymes "now" with "though," "by" with "me," "gown" with "own," and "Plumes" with "Drums," as it catalogs the seasonal signs of rebirth (the robin, daffodils, growing grass, and bees) that will not redeem her permanent loss (F347).[40] It is easy to see how Brooks's ear might be tuned to hear such glancing sonic echoes as appropriate for the "off-rhyme situation" confronted by the African American soldiers of World War II.[41] We should not be surprised to find the ghost of Dickinson in the rhymes Brooks employs, for instance, in "mentors," a poem from her sonnet series about those soldiers, depicting the emotional tension between memories of slain comrades and scenes of post-war celebration: "dead"/"overglad," "frosts"/ "ghosts," "whisper"/"unclasp her," and "banquet"/"quit."[42]

Yet Brooks suggests that her aesthetic affiliation with Dickinson's work is deeply complicated by the dissimilarity of their circumstances and their subject matter. The poems Brooks shares at the celebration – including "To Black Women," "the mother," "the children of the poor," "The Near-Johannesburg Boy," and "We Real Cool" – are representative of her oeuvre's emphasis on the voices and experiences of black people. Early in her reading, she notes: "Thinking about Emily Dickinson, as I made up my little list of poems to offer, I said 'You know, this is almost hopeless, because Emily and I are absolutely different in the details of our lives.'"[43] She juxtaposes Dickinson's formal influence on her work with the social circumstances and experiences that constituted her (black) identity, wondering:

> [W]hat would Emily have made out of the late sixties? In which I found such help, lots of mistakes and clumsinesses, but a lot of help, too. That help helped form what I am today. So I just said I will just come there and offer them what I have to give. And if it is not Emilian, well, that's unfortunate or fortunate.[44]

We hear in her question two senses of the phrase "made out of."[45] She wonders what Dickinson would have *thought about* the Black Power and Black Arts Movements, to which Brooks implicitly refers; but she also contemplates what Dickinson would have *created from* this material, this explosive – volcanic – social moment of black self-determination and black aesthetics (among other revolutionary ideas). This period "helped form" Brooks as a poet who understands precisely how – and for whom – it is "fortunate" that her work is "Gwendolynian" rather than "Emilian."[46] Ironically, even as she emphasizes the distance between their formative experiences and, thus, their poetics, Brooks's use of this intimate and playful form of naming – modeled on her own self-identificatory terminology – forges a link between Dickinson and herself.

How does she sustain this balance? Arguably, through lyric dis-reading. The courageous Brooks who broke with literary and social convention in the late 1960s, by – among other things – leaving the publishing giant Harper & Row for Dudley Randall's fledgling Broadside Press, may well have returned in that moment to a poem that countenances just such rebelliousness:

Coloring Dickinson: Race, Influence, and Lyric Dis-reading 269

> The Soul selects her own Society –
> Then – shuts the Door –
> To her divine Majority –
> Present no more –
>
> Unmoved – she notes the Chariots – pausing –
> At her low Gate –
> Unmoved – an Emperor be kneeling
> Opon her mat – (F409)[47]

Here Brooks would encounter the voice of a woman whose determinations about whom to admit into her inner circle are not to be questioned. Brooks's decision to cast her lot with the Black Arts Movement poets and independent black publishers, turning "her attention" away from the powerful (imperial) primarily white literary establishment, was in this vein. That Dickinson's poem uses the word "Soul" – a "mascon," in Stephen Henderson's theoretical parlance – would only have encouraged Brooks's lyric dis-reading.[48] For Brooks, "Soul" would have recalled W. E. B. Du Bois's indispensable volume *The Souls of Black Folk*, as well as late-twentieth-century black popular culture usages.

We might imagine Brooks thinking bemusedly about this poem's "Emilian" analysis of power as she posed for a photograph in Amherst, Massachusetts, pleasant but unsmiling beside the bronze plaque identifying the Dickinson Homestead as a Registered National Historic Landmark.[49] The caption she provides for the image (included in her first autobiography) speaks to her affinity for Dickinson, while remembering – and reminding us – that Brooks would not have been an invited guest at Dickinson's home: "I think Emily, after the first shock at my intrusion, would have approved of my natural."[50] This statement collapses a century's time, allowing Dickinson's nineteenth-century "shock" at the appearance of a black woman at the Homestead – as a fellow poet, rather than as a laundress[51] – to coexist with her anticipated "approval" of Brooks's twentieth-century embrace of an overt black aesthetic. Brooks's caption, an act of disidentification, underwrites the lyric dis-reading of Dickinson's poem that I have proposed. Here, Brooks does not ignore Dickinson's attitude toward race but invokes it even as she reworks Dickinson's rebellion against nineteenth-century (white) gender and aesthetic norms into an endorsement of Brooks's rebellion against the gender and aesthetic norms of (black) "respectability" a century later. Brooks's lyric dis-reading empowers her to select Dickinson as a "Soul" sister.

Marilyn Chin has selected both Brooks and Dickinson as aesthetic beacons for her work. Both poets' names appear frequently in Chin's interviews when she is asked about her influences – and both figures figure more than once in her prize-winning 2014 poetry collection, *Hard Love Province*. But Dickinson recurs in discussions of Chin's poetics perhaps more than any other American poet. Notably, it is as an *American* poet that Dickinson figures in Chin's aesthetic lineage. Chin was born in Hong Kong but raised in Oregon; her education in poetry began early with her grandmother's recitations from memory of 300 Tang dynasty poems and later included the American canon she was introduced to in high school.[52] Building on this foundation, she studied Chinese poetry as an undergraduate, then American poetry in the Iowa Writers' Workshop for an MFA, where she also served as a translator-editor for the International Writing Program. Chin centers her "bi-cultural and bi-lingual," "Pacific-rim" identity in her poetics and emphatically works to "merge" or "meld[]" Chinese culture with American culture, and Chinese poetry with American poetry, even at the risk of seeming to "cater[] to Orientalism."[53] One of the ways she affects this merger – and avoids the concomitant risk – is by locating the "bi-cultural" encounter in experiments with poetic form. In *Hard Love Province*, a book of elegies and homages, she invents and "trie[s] to exhaust the 'Chinese American' quatrain, a happy hybrid of the Chinese *jue-ju* cut-verse form and the English song quatrain."[54] In an interview with Nissa Parmar, Chin lists the "female mentors" she honors in the poems and, subsequently, the poets she is "sampling" from the "rich global history" of the quatrain.[55] Dickinson, along with Plath, appears in *both* catalogues. Formally, Chin was interested in Dickinson's "tight, vivid quatrains in the Western tradition," which she sought to meld with the normally "self-contained" eastern quatrain (the *jue-ju*) as the "form the elegy would take" in her work.[56] But her engagement with Dickinson is thematic as well; Chin's elegies specifically invoke the metaphysical Dickinson, the Dickinson who looks death in the face and describes what she sees. Indeed, it is Dickinson's elegies, I imagine, that facilitate her lyric dis-readings of Dickinson.

To my knowledge, Chin has not questioned or made note of Dickinson's views or silences on race in the ways Derricotte and Brooks did. But we know that matters of race and the political are central to Chin's poetics from statements like this one: "I believe that I am an activist and that I write socially conscious poetry, but with all the pyrotechnics of masterful art."[57] So there is some irony in that the same interview in which she articulates a great debt "to American women poets," including

Dickinson and "the Feminist movement" broadly, for giving her the "courage to speak" has her specifying "race" as the "'urgent material' that [she was] currently trying to uncover" in her work.[58] Dickinson's poetry may have inspired Chin's feminism, but it rarely spoke on race, as we have seen, and – when it did – not in an activist vein. Chin asserts that her enthusiasm for unbounded cultural fusion, which fuels her "Chinese [American] quatrains," must be placed alongside her desire "to talk back to Pound and the modernists" (an aesthetic category in which she includes Dickinson, interestingly), on the subject of Chinese poetry and how it is to be understood in the West.[59] By the same token, I would suggest that her critique of Dickinson's silence on race may be embedded in the poems Chin designates as homage.

Consider the stanzas about Dickinson and Plath in the poem "From a Notebook of an Ex-Revolutionary." Linked by the subtitle "*(DUELING QUATRAINS),*" they read:

> *Sylvia*
> You baked me a cake   and it's not even my birthday
> I ate a slice politely   though it's wormy and stale
> How thin you are   dear Sylvia   how terribly thin
> You must be suffering from poetry
>
> *Emily*
> Eternity suits you   Emily   new rouge on your cheeks
> *Entertainment Today*   wants to interview you
> How Mr. So and So Higginson   spurned your love
> How Mr. So and So Johnson   mended your bones[60]

The tone of these lines is laced with irony, and determining precisely how that irony is directed is no easy task. Even the subtitle is ambiguous. Are the pair of quatrains dueling each other? Are they the word-weapons with which Chin duels with two poets whose work she feels drawn to and inspired by, despite the racism one encounters there? Or both? Dorothy Wang has called Chin "a master at deploying irony as a tool and weapon, one that is often clever and multilayered – and disguised."[61] Irony's usefulness derives from its ability to "carry ... various semantic and emotional registers at once."[62] Wang explains that, for Chin and other "minority" poets, irony facilitates the expression of critiques of racism, along with other subjects considered "taboo," in part because such irony can be so easily misread that its sharpest digs may pass by some readers unnoticed.[63] Here, the second quatrain seems to compliment Dickinson – especially when compared to the unsparing pronouncement that Plath's cake is "wormy and stale." But it's not the differences between the quatrains that matter most here; it's the similarities that are telling. Indeed, the speaker in the first quatrain is *telling* us that she speaks and acts politely about things that are repellant to her. Yes, the "*Emily*" quatrain seems to speak appreciatively about Dickinson's posthumous popularity ("Eternity suits you"). But there is surely a measure of backhanded compliment in the suggestion that our interest in Dickinson "*Today*" lies not in her work but in the "*Entertainment*" value of her social life. That backhand catches not only Dickinson but contemporary readers and critics as well. What does it say about us that our attention, from Chin's perspective, is trained more on the unmemorable ("So and So"), mediocre ("So[-]So"?) men in her life than on Dickinson herself?

We might also think about irony in the second half of the first line of this quatrain: the Dickinson we encounter now has "new rouge on [her] cheeks." Does Chin simply wish us to think of a rosy blush as a symbol of life (through art) after death? Read ironically, the "rouge" might also gesture toward the replacement of the virginal, "little-girl" image of Dickinson disseminated early on, by her heirs, with that of the "Vesuvian" and passionate (if possibly "spurned") woman we find in some feminist accounts of more recent origin.[64] In either case, the image also implicitly calls attention to the whiteness of the cheeks before the "new rouge" is applied.

This connection Chin draws between color and Dickinson's long poetic afterlife is apt, insofar as it suggests to me one way in which Chin may be quietly constructing her lyric dis-reading of Dickinson: by "coloring," or racializing, Dickinson's fascination with the hereafter. Discussing her use of repetition, Chin notes that the focus of Chinese poems is on "loss and ... perishing, becoming nothing. Cold cold mountains and long long valleys – the Chinese are obsessed with eternity ... How does one translate that feeling of grief that is 'grief grief,' that is 'deep deep'?"[65] Chin apparently sees Dickinson as sharing this "Chinese" obsession with the "inexhaustible" nature of death and grief, imagining the consoling idea "that art is 'immortal'" as being "in the forefront of Emily Dickinson's mind as she carefully prepared her packets of poems to leave in her dresser for eternity."[66] The formal characteristics of Dickinson's work would only reinforce this connection. Speaking about her recent work, Chin tells an interviewer:

> I'm working with space, silences. When one reads those Chinese poems, one can contemplate the spaces as well as the characters. To grieve is one thing,

but the silences between the harsh words, the weeping, the inner self-condemnation, and the rages and wailing and the abstract pings and phonemes – to me, the silences are just as important. The silence, the breath, is where we hold both grief and forgiveness.[67]

The spaces and silences created by Dickinson's enjambed lines and dashes, apportioning her striking images and relentless "explor[ation of] states of psychic extremity," bring her writing both formally and thematically into the orbit of Chin's interest in Chinese poetry.

There is evidence of Chin working through this connection in her poem "Nocturnes," whose final stanza reads:

> A deathblow is life blow to some
>   Tell them   Emily   those woolly ministers
>
> Chopin's fingers play soft   soft soft
>   Comforting   the beasts   and   flowers[68]

Made up of thirteen sections, mostly comprising quatrains that visually resemble this one, "Nocturnes" is a dark (and, at times, darkly humorous) meditation on our literal and figurative nights. Dickinson contributes to the quatrain not only her name but also its first line, which is also the first line of a poem of Dickinson's own, which reads in its entirety:

> A Death blow is a Life blow, to Some,
> Who till they died, did not alive become
> Who had they lived had died, but when
> They died, Vitality begun.   (F966B)

In the context of Chin's work, Dickinson's poem – already curious and "unorthodox," from a Christian perspective – takes on the quality of a koan. "Nocturnes" is filled with similar paradoxes and inscrutable observations that complicate our ideas about death, life, and eternity. The second line of Chin's quatrain suggests that the understanding represented in Dickinson's poem shows, dare I say, greater enlightenment than the vague, "woolly" notions of the (Christian) "ministers." Arguably, the purpose to which Chin puts Dickinson's line indicates that she is reading her predecessor's quatrain as something more or other than a conventional rearticulation of the Christian doctrine of everlasting life. In the final section of "Nocturnes," following a disconcerting mix of poignant images and ironic gestures that all point to life's injustice (including depictions of divinities too "detached," self-indulgent, or self-loathing to be concerned about us), Chin's borrowed line proposes a lyric dis-reading that renders

Dickinson's poem more resonant with the attitude toward grief that she associates with the Chinese. If indeed, as Chin writes earlier in her poem, there is "No eternity in the land you love / Only eternal ... suffering," Dickinson's poem might suggest that *this* life is the only one that concerns us, and we only *really* begin to live after we have confronted our own death through the death of some beloved other.

In the penultimate poem of *Hard Love Province*, "Goodbye," Chin imagines a scene of parting with the "beautiful boyfriend" whose unexpected death from an aneurysm was one of the key inspirations of the collection.[69] The poem concludes:

> I waved at the road until his bumper vanished
> The traffic flowed toward eternity as my eyes teared up
> Better stop crying he'll call me a sissy

Those familiar with Chin's work will recognize as characteristic her quick tonal shift, which saves the line from the sentimentality it dares to approach.[70] But only those of her readers who are also readers of Dickinson will appreciate her transformation of Dickinson's "Carriage," containing "Death" and "Immortality," into a car that drives Chin's beloved to his rest. How large is the overlap between the readers and scholars of Dickinson and those of Chin? Not large enough, it is safe to say. This essay, I hope, will have demonstrated something of how impoverished our understanding of Dickinson's legacy is and will be until it can more fully account for whether and how women of color poets have tangled (and been entangled) with it. My epigraph, drawn from Audre Lorde's poem "Coal," reminds us that the sound of a poem's words is "coloured / by who pays what for speaking."[71] We must learn to listen, literally and metaphorically, to women of color poets, for how Dickinson's words might sound when such women (dis-)read and (re-)write them. A quick, informal survey of some women of color poets in my circle of acquaintance alone revealed that a multi-generational, multi-racial, and aesthetically diverse group of poets are producing brilliant work with a range of potentially disparate and complicated relationships to Dickinson's poetry. Collectively, whether they see her as a "major" influence, an "anti-influence," or something else altogether, these poets – including Marilyn Nelson, Ada Limón, Sharan Strange, Monica Youn, Kiki Petrosino, Camille Dungy, Ruth Ellen Kocher, Amber Flora Thomas, Brenda Shaughnessy, Tonya Foster, Raina Léon, l. francine harris, and Yesenia Montilla – find in her work a set of fascinating possibilities for structure, language, or subject matter. Yet they also cite tensions between the interest of her poetry, on one hand, and the facts and mythology of Dickinson's life and persona, on the

Coloring Dickinson: Race, Influence, and Lyric Dis-reading 275

other. It is our job to study what they make of the poetry Dickinson made and how their acts of making reconstitute part of the tradition to meet their own needs as writers. What will we apprehend – about their work, about Dickinson's, about influence, race, gender, and America – when the colors of these poets' "various voices" are truly heard? An incredible amount of challenging and rewarding research awaits us.

Notes

1. *The Norton Anthology of Modern and Contemporary Poetry*, Jahan Ramazani, Richard Ellmann, et al. (eds.), 3rd ed. (New York: Norton, 2003). See also Farnoosh Fathi, "'Tell all the truth but tell it slant –': Dickinson's Poetics of Indirection in Contemporary Poetry," *EDJ* 17.2 (2008): 77–99.
2. Mary Jo Bang, "I.E., On Emily & Influence," *EDJ* 15.2 (2006): 67.
3. Zofia Burr, *Of Women, Poetry, and Power: Strategies of Address in Dickinson, Miles, Brooks, Lorde, and Angelou* (Urbana: University of Illinois Press, 2002), 1–2.
4. I draw this phrase from the title of Albert Gelpi's essay "Emily Dickinson's Long Shadow: Susan Howe & Fanny Howe," *EDJ* 17.2 (2008): 100–112.
5. See, e.g., Vivian Pollak, *Our Emily Dickinsons: American Women Poets and the Intimacies of Difference* (Philadelphia: University of Pennsylvania Press, 2017); Thomas Gardner, "Dickinson's Influence," in *Emily Dickinson in Context*, Eliza Richards (ed.) (New York: Cambridge University Press, 2013): 332–342; Thomas Gardner, *A Door Ajar: Contemporary Writers and Emily Dickinson* (New York: Oxford University Press, 2006); Gelpi, "Emily Dickinson's Long Shadow"; Burr, *Of Women, Poetry, and Power: Strategies of Address in Dickinson, Miles, Brooks, Lorde, and Angelou* (Urbana: University of Illinois Press, 2002); and Lesley Wheeler, *The Poetics of Enclosure: American Women Poets from Dickinson to Dove* (Knoxville: University of Tennessee Press, 2002).
6. Not precisely about Dickinson's influence, Karen Jackson Ford's *Gender and the Poetics of Excess* nonetheless leads off with Dickinson, follows with Gertrude Stein and Plath, and concludes with a chapter discussing nine Black Arts Movement poets (interestingly, both men and women) who have also deployed "poetic excess" to amplify their voices from the aesthetic – and, in this case, political – margins. *Gender and the Poetics of Excess: Moments of Brocade* (Jackson: University of Mississippi Press, 1997).
7. Burr, 2. All the poets in Burr's study, as she notes, write from positions of less privilege and differently inflected gender than Dickinson, in terms of race, class, sexuality, and/or physical ability.
8. Lesley Wheeler, *The Poetics of Enclosure: American Women Poets from Dickinson to Dove* (Knoxville: University of Tennessee Press, 2002), 6.
9. Shirley Horner, "Emily Dickinson Tribute," *New York Times* (Nat'l Ed.), April 6, 1986, NJ11.

10. The draft version of the poem, as initially read by Derricotte at the celebration, appears in "Folio One" of the *Dickinson Electronic Archives*. A revised version was published in *Visiting Emily: Poems Inspired by the Life & Work of Emily Dickinson*, Sheila Coghill and Thom Tammaro (eds.) (Iowa City: University of Iowa Press, 2000), 21–23.
11. Gwendolyn Brooks, Audre Lorde, and Michelle Cliff were the other African American poets scheduled to appear, according to the *New York Times* announcement, though only Brooks and Derricotte seem to have actually read. No women of color from other ethnicities were formally included in this event.
12. Toi Derricotte, "We Ain't Seen Nothing Yet!", Folio One, *Dickinson Electronic Archives*.
13. See, e.g., George Hutchinson and David Drews, "Racial Attitudes," The Walt Whitman Archive. Langston Hughes's "I, Too" alludes to Whitman's "I Hear America Singing"; June Jordan writes about the morality and accessibility of Whitman's poetry in her essay "For the Sake of a People's Poetry: Walt Whitman and the Rest of Us." The Hughes, Whitman, and Jordan texts are available on the Poetry Foundation website.
14. Walt Whitman, "I Sing the Body Electric," *The Poetry Foundation*.
15. Benjamin Friedlander, "Auctions of the Mind: Emily Dickinson and Abolition," *Arizona Quarterly* 54.1 (1998): 1–26, offers a thorough-going investigation of Dickinson's poem (including a brief discussion of the Whitman lines that I came to through Jordan) and, ultimately, a complicated argument for reading it as a poem against abolition (though not a defense of slavery), as opposed to treating "Publication" in the straightforward way that I do. The essay is deeply researched and well worth wrangling with on its own terms. However, my more conventional reading of the poem – much more likely an interpretation for most readers – is more to the point here, where we are concerned with how poets (*qua* poets) would navigate this poem.
16. I mean here to suggest that Dickinson's mindset, which is entirely compatible with the abolitionist views of her father and her friend Thomas Higginson, constitutes an example of what Douglas Jones has described as the "proslavery imagination." Douglas A. Jones, *The Captive Stage: Performance and the Proslavery Imagination of the Antebellum North* (Ann Arbor: University of Michigan Press, 2014).
17. For "romantic racialism," see Vivian R. Pollak, "Dickinson and the Poetics of Whiteness," *EDJ* 9.2 (2000): 86; for orientalism, see chapter five, "Becoming a Poet in 'turbaned seas,'" in Cristanne Miller, *Reading in Time: Emily Dickinson in the Nineteenth Century* (Amherst: University of Massachusetts Press, 2012), 118–146; for exoticism, see Erica Fretwell, "Emily Dickinson in Domingo," *J19* 1.1 (2013): 77–81.
18. In writing this essay, I used the versions of poems printed in Cristanne Miller, ed., *Emily Dickinson's Poems: As She Preserved Them* (Cambridge, MA: Harvard University Press, 2016), although I rely on Franklin's numbering to identify them.
19. Miller, 124–128.

20. While I intend to suggest here that the language cuts against Dickinson, at the very least trading in the biblical white/black dichotomy that undergirds racial binaries in white supremacist discourse, see Pollak's argument that the poem should be read as constructing this gendered whiteness as both burdensome and contested ("Dickinson" 86, 88).
21. Wesley King, "The White Symbolic of Emily Dickinson," *EDJ* 18.1 (2009): 44–68.
22. Derricotte, Folio One.
23. Derricotte, "Sitting with Myself," 21.
24. Derricotte, Folio One. Just before reading the quoted Dickinson poem, Derricotte refers to "a little debate" about the role of politics among the attendees, adding: "I wish we could go into a separate room and break into groups and everybody talk about politics and poetry, because obviously there's a lot here to be said from various people."
25. See, e.g., Erica Edwards, *Charisma and the Fictions of Black Leadership* (Minneapolis: University of Minnesota Press, 2012), 81–86, for a discussion of "the mythologized exodus out of Egypt" as a story connected to black American nationalism and freedom struggles (here, with a focus on and critique of the use of the Moses figure to underwrite charismatic black male leadership).
26. José Esteban Muñoz, *Disidentifications: Queers of Color and the Performance of Politics* (Minneapolis: University of Minnesota Press, 1999), 28.
27. Ibid., 11.
28. Ibid., 11, 31.
29. Ibid., 12.
30. *Lyric Theory Reader*, 5.
31. For an argument that it might not be perverse, but fitting, to link African American critics and writers to the development of New Criticism, see Sonya Posmentier, "Blueprints for Negro Reading: Sterling Brown's Study Guides," in *A Companion to the Harlem Renaissance*, Cherene Sherrard-Johnson (ed.) (New York: Wiley, 2015), 119–135.
32. *Lyric Theory Reader*, quoting Northrup Frye, 4.
33. Jackson and Prins' original observation is about the audience of the lyric: "[T]he first-person speaker of the lyric," they write, "could speak to no one in particular and thus to all of us." *Lyric Theory Reader*, 5.
34. Dorothy Wang, *Thinking Its Presence: Form, Race, and Subjectivity in Contemporary Asian American Poetry* (Stanford, CA: Stanford University Press, 2014), 156.
35. For instance, John Stuart Mill's influential discussion of the lyric explicitly excludes a popular poem of his day from that category, on the ground that it "directly addressed its readers for political purposes." *Lyric Theory Reader*, 3.
36. Cf., Muñoz, 31.
37. Muñoz discusses a similar point about disidentification as an act of agency, in a gloss of Michele Wallace's essay on "Race, Gender, and Psychoanalysis in Forties Film." Her analysis (of the way black women insistently identified

Joan Crawford and other stars as "looking black") leads him to write: "Black female viewers are not merely passive subjects who are possessed by the well-worn paradigms of identification that the classical narrative produces; rather, they are active participant spectators who can mutate and restructure stale patterns within dominant media." Muñoz, 29.
38. Pollak, *Our Emily Dickinsons*, 20.
39. Gwendolyn Brooks, "Emily & I Are Absolutely Different in the Details of Our Lives," Folio One, *Dickinson Electronic Archives*. Brooks says she was nineteen at the time, which means it was likely *Unpublished Poems of Emily Dickinson* (Boston: Little Brown & Co, 1935) that presented a new, more compelling Dickinson to Brooks.
40. I selected this poem from among those included in the Untermeyer double-volume that Brooks read from frequently in the years when she would have been writing her first two books. *Modern American Poetry; Modern British Poetry: A Critical Anthology*, comb. ed., ed. Louis Untermeyer (New York: Harcourt, Brace, 1942), 88–89. See Kevin Bezner, "A Life Distilled: An Interview with Gwendolyn Brooks," in *Conversations with Gwendolyn Brooks*, Gloria Wade Gayles (ed.) (Jackson, MS: University Press of Mississippi, 2003), 119.
41. Brooks, qtd. in Elizabeth Alexander, "Introduction," *The Essential Gwendolyn Brooks*, Elizabeth Alexander (ed.) (The Library of America, 2005), xviii.
42. Brooks, *Essential Gwendolyn Brooks*, 25.
43. Brooks, Folio One.
44. The transcription of Brooks's remarks renders "Emilian" as "a million" – an understandable substitution for a transcriber unfamiliar with Brooks's neologisms. The audio recording, available on the same page, allowed me to catch and correct this mistake.
45. Audio accessible at www.emilydickinson.org/titanic-operas/folio-one/gwendolyn-brooks.
46. Brooks, Folio One. Brooks refers to her life as "Gwendolynian" in her autobiography. Brooks, *Report from Part One* (Detroit: Broadside Press, 1972), 46.
47. Again, a version of this poem appears in the Untermeyer anthology that Brooks read from during her early career.
48. As Lorrie Smith writes: "[I]t is important to recognize that "tradition," "spirit," "soul," and "roots" are what [literary critic Stephen] Henderson describes as "mascon" ideas in black literary culture – symbols grounded in a "massive concentration of Black experiential energy" (353). Lorrie Smith, "Black Arts to Def Jam: Performing Black 'Spirit Work' across Generations," in *New Thoughts on the Black Arts Movement*, Lisa Gail Collins and Margo Natalie Crawford (eds.) (New Brunswick, NJ: Rutgers University Press, 2006), 349–367.
49. For the photo, see Brooks, *Report*, 107. For instances of scholars using the photo and its inclusion in her autobiography as evidence of Brooks's connection to Dickinson, see Burr, 1; Wheeler, 92; and Pollak, *Our Emily*, 20.
50. Brooks, *Report*, 107.
51. Aífe Murray confirms that Dickinson had hired help from an African American woman on at least one occasion. The poet writes in an April 1853

Coloring Dickinson: Race, Influence, and Lyric Dis-reading 279

letter to her brother, Austin, that "Mrs. Scott is ironing here today"; Murray identifies this as a reference to "Sally Ann Brown Scott, an African American woman who worked as a housekeeper in Amherst" in this period (76–77). Aífe Murray, *Maid as Muse: How Servants Changed Emily Dickinson's Life and Language* (Durham, NH: University of New Hampshire Press, 2009).

52. Patricia Kirkpatrick and Rita Moe, "An Interview with Marilyn Chin," recorded at Hamline University, March 19, 2002; Pilar Graham, "All Immigrant Ears: An Interview with Poet Marilyn Chin," *The California Journal of Women Writers*, January 27, 2014 (conducted in February 2005).
53. Kirkpatrick and Moe; Brigitte Wallinger-Schorn, *"So There It Is": An Exploration of Cultural Hybridity in Contemporary Asian American Poetry* (New York: Rodopi, 2011), 204; King-Kok Cheung, "Slanted Allusions: Transnational Poetics and Politics of Marilyn Chin and Russell Leong," *Positions: East Asia Cultures Critique* 22.1 (2014): 237.
54. Nissa Parmar, "'Double Happiness': An Interview with Marilyn Chin," *Contemporary Women's Writing* 8.3 (2014): 260. Wallinger-Schorn explains that the *jue-ju* is "a quatrain consisting of five or seven Chinese characters per line" that employs "a rigid tonal pattern and a structure of grammatical and semantic parallelism," among other features. *"So There It Is,"* 196.
55. Parmar, 260.
56. Irene Hsiao, "Elegies, Allergies, and Other Elusions: Marilyn Chin Talks Hard Love," *Los Angeles Review of Books*, April 3, 2015. See also Parmar, 253, for Chin's interest in "Dickinsonian hymn verse."
57. Graham.
58. Ibid.
59. Parmar, 253, 260.
60. Marilyn Chin, *Hard Love Province* (New York: Norton, 2014), 46.
61. Wang, 107.
62. Ibid., 108.
63. Ibid., 108, 111–112.
64. Adrienne Rich, "Vesuvius at Home," *Parnassus: Poetry in Review* 5.1 (1976).
65. Hsiao.
66. Marilyn Chin, "Q&A: Marilyn Chin," Poetry Foundation, December 4, 2012.
67. Hsiao.
68. Chin, *Hard Love*, 24.
69. Chin, "Q&A"; Chin, *Hard Love*, 77.
70. See Wang, 116.
71. Audre Lorde, *The Collected Poems of Audre Lorde* (New York: Norton, 1997), 163.

CHAPTER 16

Dickinson, Disability, and a Crip Editorial Practice

Clare Mullaney

This poem contains twenty-four lines and is written in ink on a standard bifolium stationery sheet, cream-colored with lightly ruled lines. Stab marks are visible on the right and left sides of both sheets (each about a third of the way down and up from the page), which indicates that the poem was once part of a fascicle. The poem contains six diagonal cross-outs (positioned from right to left) in its first line over the word "down," which is replaced with "up." The handwriting is somewhat irregular and difficult to read. Dickinson's letters are generally not spaced apart, but there are significant spaces between words, measuring roughly one fingertip between them. Some of the crosses on her "t" and "T" are particularly long and detached from the word itself, especially in "stitches" (first stanza), "Tucks" (third stanza,) and "stitches," "Straight," and "stitch" (second page). Her dashes are smaller than in later drafts, and they measure roughly two millimeters in length. The bottom half of the second page begins a new poem, which starts with the line: "So well that I can live."

Above is a description I've written of the manuscript of Emily Dickinson's poem "Dont put up my Thread + Needle," which was written in 1863. The passage might strike us as both familiar and unfamiliar. It resembles what we find in R. W. Franklin's 1981 facsimile edition of Dickinson's manuscript poems where he offers brief descriptions of her individual fascicles. Describing Fascicle 32, which contains "Dont put up my Thread + Needle" (F681A), Franklin writes: "The stationery, embossed with a capital within a plain horizontal oval, is laid, cream, and lightly ruled."[1] Description is a common methodology in bibliographic or textual studies. Rather than mere afterthoughts, such descriptions are integral to the edition's presentation of her manuscripts – just as important, and just as thoughtfully produced, as her facsimiles. But description is also a crucial practice within disability studies, and this practice is what may register as unfamiliar: I offer a script for an audio description of Dickinson's poem, one based on the assumption that not all readers of Dickinson are able to see the facsimile of her manuscript. Intended for the purpose of accessibility, audio descriptions aid blind or visually impaired people who cannot access visual media in traditional formats. As disability studies scholar Georgina Kleege notes, audio descriptions first began in the 1980s at theater performances and are now more common for television and movie screenings.[2] It is impossible to offer a purely objective description of Dickinson's manuscript, but here, in an effort to make textual presentation accessible, I describe – at length – her poem's bibliographic features: the size of the page, whether she was writing in ink or pencil, her handwriting (or how she forms her letters), cross-outs, the number of lines in the poem, and the length of her dashes. Even for readers who can see Dickinson's poem, a rearticulation of these bibliographic features in a narrative format (which could be made available in both audio file and print, so deaf readers can also access them) is useful, especially for readers unfamiliar with Dickinson's compositional techniques. Explaining what Dickinson's manuscripts look like helps all readers understand how a text is made – and how Dickinson, in particular, designed her poems on the page. More broadly, my description takes a key feature of bibliography and yokes it specifically to an accessible practice, attending to the material engagements of both writer and reader.

Two principles of current editorial theory have a shared investment with disability studies: (1) an emphasis on presenting texts in multiple formats, or an understanding of how the material form in which a text is presented changes its meaning (resulting in editorial intervention); and (2) the privileging of a text's individual idiosyncrasies (resulting in editorial restraint). To reflect on how disability reorients these editorial principles, it is useful to both enlist and reframe Jerome McGann's influential work on what he terms the "textual condition": he casts textuality, in particular the writing and production of texts, as a material and social phenomenon.[3] In this essay, I consider how the definition of the "textual condition" might change when *condition*, or the author's writerly circumstance (what McGann calls "a scene of writing"), is understood through the lens of disability as a poor or so-called abnormal state of health. What I call a crip editorial practice emphasizes how disability influences the material conditions of textual production and how, in turn, the material conditions of reading might enable or disable their readers.[4] As such, Dickinson's "textual conditions" become most evident when we confront the clash between those editorial practices aimed at preserving Dickinson's writing and those attentive to the needs of disabled readers.

My description of "Dont put up my Thread + Needle" shows how an editorial ethics framed by disability must consider how bodies engage in reading and how reading formats impinge on readerly access. As a result, I will be concerned with how readers' bodies might influence editorial decisions. But first I ask how we might edit Dickinson's poems with *her* body in mind. Since her death, critics have labeled Dickinson with a long list of medical conditions, including agoraphobia, lupus, Bright's disease, tuberculosis, epilepsy, and even psychosis. To avoid pathologizing Dickinson, which is the primary means by which literary figures of the past have been linked to disability, I am less inclined to emphasize Dickinson's biographical relationship to disability – that is, to assert that she was disabled – than to posit that she was a poet of disability, attuned to how bodily and cognitive impairments altered her poems' content and, more importantly, their material form. This essay considers what editorial practices we might elaborate from understanding the complex role of disability in Dickinson's poetics. I consider, in particular, how disability studies might help editors resist the triumphalism inherent to Dickinson scholarship: to understand instead how bodily (as well as cognitive) limitations are central to Dickinson's compositional practices and how restraint, in turn, should inform our editorial practices with the hopes of keeping her textual idiosyncrasies in place. However, this simultaneous orientation toward both writerly and readerly disabilities presents a significant tension: the editorial practices that Dickinson's body calls for do not always align with the potential needs of readers' bodies, which may be best served by greater editorial interventions like description to render her poems accessible. This essay considers the concerns of each even as it attempts to work through these contradictions. I offer prospects, rather than firm solutions, for practicing editorial restraint (that is, allowing Dickinson's poems to exist as her body made them) and editorial intervention (that is, rendering her poems in multiple formats for a diverse range of readers).

Editorial Theory Meets Disability Studies

Since Thomas Johnson's publication of Dickinson's full collection of poems in 1955, debates about how to properly edit her work abound. Late twentieth-century critics have reacted against the editorial "normalization" of Dickinson's irregular verse – the intrusive methods by which Todd and Thomas Wentworth Higginson regularized Dickinson's punctuation and eliminated her use of dashes (what Johnson called "textual emendations in the direction of conformity").[5] Suggesting that twentieth-century editions of Dickinson's texts are still too limiting, McGann, Alexandra Socarides, Marta Werner, Martha Nell Smith, and others have argued that the unique presentation of Dickinson's poems in manuscript rather than print form – a fairly unusual phenomenon for nineteenth-century poets – challenges conventional editorial theory and practices. Modeling Franklin's edition, recent Dickinson scholars have often strived to maintain the idiosyncrasies of her texts – her unique handwriting and ample spacing between words and individual letters, among other characteristics – without fixing them. In *Open Folios*, a collection of Dickinson's late drafts, Werner attempts, for example, to "undo" prior editorial work and strives to maintain "all vagrant spellings, stray marks, and disturbances – drives, tractions – on the surfaces of the manuscripts" as well as "accidentals – dashes, quotation marks, underlinings, and other flourishes."[6] In her words, she "abnormalize[s] readers" by refusing to alter Dickinson's punctuation or line breaks. Whereas Johnson and Millicent Todd Bingham's early editions were made "for the sake of legibility and conformity," this second wave of editorial theory resists the standardization of Dickinson's writing, refusing to make her poems conform to nineteenth- and twentieth-century conventions of book production.[7] However, these deliberations among Dickinson's editors have not explicitly considered disability. We might, I suggest, practice editorial restraint in order to keep texts "abnormal" not for the poet's *ability* but to prevent the erasure of potential *disability*. Even as editors like Werner and Bervin retain a poem's "disturbances," they often do so through an ableist narrative of liberation and triumph. When read through a disability studies framework, the poems' idiosyncrasies, like Dickinson's dashes or her varied use of space on the page, might not always confirm her poetic creativity or genius but might also be understood as the effects of a bodily and/or mental condition. In addition, although some forms of editorial restraint have focused on making the manuscripts more widely accessible, such editing has not always approached "accessibility" in terms of differently abled readers.

To better consider how disability transforms the conventions of manuscript and print culture, we can turn to the term "print disabilities," coined in the 1960s by George Kershner, a leading developer of talking books, to refer to people who have difficulty writing and reading due to physical or cognitive impairments. Print disabilities include physical disabilities that prevent individuals from being able to turn a book's pages, visual impairments (like eyestrain or blindness, which Dickinson experienced) that make it hard for a writer or reader to see the page, and cognitive processing disorders that may make comprehending a text's content difficult. As historian Mara Mills notes, "Unlike dyslexia, medically defined as an impairment of the brain, the category of print disability focuses attention on the built environment (i.e. media) rather than physiology."[8] That is, rather than disability being located in the mind or body, it materializes via a person's encounter with text. As the interdisciplinary field of disability studies has firmly established, if disability is a "condition" it is one determined, in large part, by the material world. To crip editorial practices is to register how people with print disabilities engage with texts and how texts, in turn, reveal traces of that interaction.

A crip approach to editing takes literally the trope of bodies as texts and texts as bodies. In the context of disability studies, this trope can help us see how the impaired body undermines the latent assumption in textual studies scholarship that writers' and readers' bodies are able. Take, for instance, Dickinson's poem "A Word made Flesh is seldom" (F1715A), which explicitly names a relation between the physically limited as opposed to able body and the physical text. The first stanza of the poem reads:

> A Word made Flesh is seldom
> And tremblingly partook
> Nor then perhaps reported
> But have I not mistook
> Each one of us has tasted
> With ecstasies of stealth
> The very food debated
> To our specific strength –

Although the poem is most often read as a commentary on religious communion, it also recognizes how specific bodies might align, or misalign, with textual experiences. For Dickinson, the "Word" can only be made "Flesh" when we acknowledge the particularity of a body and its limitations: its "specific strength."[9] In this striking phrase, Dickinson implies that texts are not inherently primed for the liberation of bodies (nor bodies primed for the liberation of texts) but that "[e]ach one of us" makes of language what we can, "tast[ing]" or consuming what proves suitable for our individual needs. In Helen Vendler's reading of the poem, she argues, "The poet is the creative spirit who prepares us food precisely 'debated / To our specific strength' – that is, sustenance professionally weighted against our capacity to digest it . . . Dickinson expresses her wonder at the miraculous individual accommodation of word to need."[10] In other words, Dickinson does not cast strength as universal but understands it as calibrated according to the demands of bodies and their particular capacities as they confront language. An orientation to disability helps us reconsider how writing and reading practices are embodied via the physicality of a poem as well as the body and its "specific strength[s]."

Dickinson continues to convey these bodily limitations in her late poems. In the fall of 2013, Werner and Jen Bervin published *Emily Dickinson: The Gorgeous Nothings*, a 255-page volume featuring fifty-two of Dickinson's late poems, which she wrote on envelopes.[11] Praised for their careful assembly of the poet's most fragile materials, Bervin and Werner made these transitory objects widely accessible to readers. Their book resurrects the late poems, which until recently were considered the unfortunate remains of what Werner describes as a "prolonged period of diminished or blocked productivity."[12] And their resurrection is a mighty one: in Holland Cotter's *New York Times* review, he describes the 4-pound "coffee table size" book as "an impressive object" – "indispensable" and "complete."[13] By transcribing what Bingham once deemed "a jumble of words on odds and ends of paper" into more legible reproductions of Dickinson's poems (the book includes both facsimiles and transcriptions), *The Gorgeous Nothings* transforms Dickinson's "faint" and often chaotic strokes into more permanent marks, orienting the late scraps toward a viable future rather than an end.[14] When the brittle fragments are converted into high-quality photographs and bound in a hefty book, the poems are recovered, even rehabilitated, and are no longer subject to the disintegration and eventual erasure they might have met had they been left in Dickinson's desk drawer. Bervin and Werner's volume is not, of course, the only attempt to preserve Dickinson's late poems: in addition to the Emily Dickinson Collection at Amherst College's Library, Werner's own digital archive *Radical Scatters* contains Dickinson's other late poems that were not written on envelopes. However, Bervin and Werner's editorial practice – the collation of these small scraps into one large book aimed at preserving the fragility of the original fragments – offers a particularly triumphant narrative about Dickinson's life and her poems. In the volume's accompanying essay, Werner writes, "Ideally, the reader of these writings will assume the role of 'liberator,' releasing them high up into the ether, following them until they are out of sight, noting their vanishing points."[15] But what exactly does Werner's notion of liberation imply for a book that might paradoxically render Dickinson's transitory scraps permanent? Liberation from what and for whom?

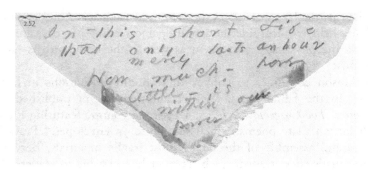

Figure 16.1 "In this short life" (F1292). About 1873. Six lines written in pencil on the inside of an upside-down envelope flap. The seal is partially present. MS252. Courtesy of Amherst College Archives and Special Collections, Amherst, MA.

I turn to one of these envelopes, which appears in Bervin and Werner's volume, as an example of how Dickinson's poems might resist *The Gorgeous Nothing*'s editorial emphasis on recovery, preservation, and liberation.[16] In her 1873 poem (F1292A; see Figure 16.1), which was written just prior to Dickinson's abandonment of formal sheets, she scribbles on the flap of a torn envelope:

> In this short Life
> that only lasts an hour
> merely
> How much – how
> little – is
> within our
> power

The smallness of the scrap, which measures roughly 4 by 2 inches at its widest, illustrates "this short Life." Dickinson's verse fills the entirety of the fragment; the quantity of "much" is written on the larger half of the envelope flap whereas "little" takes up smaller space. The word "power" is squeezed "within" the tip of the envelope's flap, suggesting that our capacities are severely limited when confronted with a finite amount of time and an ever-restricted amount of paper. "[L]ittle," for instance, breaks after "how," abiding by the narrowing space of the envelope seal, thus illustrating – via the size of the paper – "this short Life." In bridging what McGann calls "bibliographic" and "linguistic codes," the envelope flap thus symbolically but also materially forces Dickinson to confront "this short Life," which constrains her body and its capacity to write. In addition to her choice of writing surface, Dickinson's use of pencil as opposed to pen intensifies the scrap's impermanence. As Werner suggests in the introduction to *Open Folios* (1995), "the exchange of ink for lead point may ... mark Dickinson's increasingly acute sense of transience."[17] Her shift from pen to pencil, which becomes most obvious following 1879, was also in response to her worsening vision impairment. Her ophthalmologist, Dr. Henry Willard Williams, claimed that pencil would lessen the severity of her eyestrain because it is softer on the eyes than ink.[18] More broadly, the poem advocates for restraint – that we respect the poem's and poet's right to expire.

In an effort to restore these late poems into circulation, recent editorial practices thus risk dismissing Dickinson's own moves, deliberate or not, to articulate what Alfred Habegger described as "a certain loss of energy."[19] Indeed, as "In this short Life" reveals, both Dickinson's body and the material form and content of her late poems counter efforts at textual rehabilitation. The virtue of ephemera is that they are, as Dickinson wrote in an 1885 letter to the Norcross cousins, "permanent temporarily" (L962). If, as Bervin says, the scraps "remind us of the contingency, transience [and] vulnerability ... embodied in our messages," *The Gorgeous Nothings* (what New Direction publishing calls a "large-scale edition") endures in a way that Dickinson's poems do not.[20] For a volume that aims for editorial restraint, there exists a formal disjunction, in other words, between Dickinson's fragile poem fragments and the representation of those fragments in book form.

Elsewhere, I explore more fully (1) how Dickinson's physical and mental differences impinged on/shaped her writing practice and (2) how she represented disability both through her poems' content and their material forms.[21] I suggest, for example, that her reclusion (or what turn-of-the-century psychiatry termed agoraphobia) inspires her poems' implantation of spatial constraints, which assuaged her possibly chronic fear of open space and her references to material enclosures and broad spacing of words on the page; I also propose that Dickinson's eyestrain in the mid-1860s influenced the presentation of her poems in bound form because the act of stitching her poems together offered a mode of authorship centered on touch rather than sight. An orientation toward new modes of depicting these limitations as they manifest in her poems' textual forms might counter the ableism – that is, the privileging of an individual's bodily and mental capacities – that has long informed textual criticism and editorial practices.

An editorial practice that is specifically "crip" resists narratives of enablement, which typify the majority of Dickinson scholarship since the 1990s. Reproducing facsimiles of her manuscripts was understood as liberating the poet from the presumably constricting conventions of print. For instance, Smith, in illustrating the "corporealization" of Dickinson's work, describes Dickinson's handwriting as a "calligraphic orthography ... freed from the regulation of typography and unique page design."[22] Here, Smith takes note of Dickinson's presentation of her poems, but, like Werner, she again resorts to a rhetoric of liberation. Smith similarly reads Dickinson's iconic dashes as an "intentional appropriation of rhetorical notation learned at the Amherst academy" rather than what Johnson considered an "'equally capricious' accident of emotional 'stress.'"[23] She attributes each element of Dickinson's manuscripts to agency, even ability. I am sympathetic to Smith's impulse to preserve traces of Dickinson's embodiment in her poems by maintaining the inconsistent dashes (rather than, like Johnson, "correcting" them), but I want to challenge her rationale. As "A Word made Flesh" asserts, texts are not just evidence of what a person *can do*; texts might also articulate the difficulties experienced while writing.

Attending only to the ways in which disability is superseded and subsequently effaced is what disability studies terms the "overcoming narrative," which – in the words of Simi Linton – "emphasizes personal triumph over a personal condition" and fails to recognize the social and indeed material circumstances that perpetuate the presence of ableism or what might also be likened, in Werner's terms, to liberation.[24] We fail, then, to realize how impairment plays a central role in Dickinson's poetic project. Attributing Dickinson's dashes to signs of emotional stress is pathologizing, but it also might heed Dickinson's call "In this short Life" to recognize her depletion of "power." In the case of these late scrap poems, an ethical mode of editing might mean having no texts at all (neither in the library nor a book) – which, of course, sacrifices their accessibility, or availability, for reading. In "cripping" the norms of reading and writing, we might consider how to reproduce Dickinson's texts in ways that recognize the poet's bodily limitations alongside her "specific strength[s]."

Crip Editorial Practice: "Dont put up my Thread + Needle"

In the section that follows, I think less about the enabling narratives attributed to editorial intervention or restraint and consider instead what a "crip" editing might look like in practice. To do so, I return to

Dickinson's "Dont put up my Thread + Needle." Likely written just prior to the onset of Dickinson's vision impairment, this poem is relevant because of both its editorial history and its depiction of blindness. It describes a seamstress – the poem's speaker – who temporarily stops working because she is having difficulty seeing. This poem, in particular, offers two levels of representation; disability appears in the text through Dickinson's portrayal of dashes as stitches and its thematization of impairment:

> These were bent – my sight
> got crooked –
> When my mind – is plain
> I'll do seams – a Queen's
> endeavor
> Would not blush to own –

I am primarily concerned with how editors might acknowledge disability in their reproduction of the poem. "Dont put up my Thread + Needle" is instructive in this regard because it focuses on how a bodily impairment materializes via the poem's material form (see Figure 16.2). The "bent" and "zigzag" stitches make visible the seamstress's "crooked" sight. "[C]rooked" is an odd descriptor for the act of seeing; it refers, instead, to the garment itself. The reference to "these" denotes an equivalency between poem and garment, dash and stitch. Disability moves off the body and onto the poem's surface. When poorly executed, the stitch offers evidence not of the effacement of disability but of its rematerialization on the page. The poem also advocates for what we might liken to editorial restraint in order to keep disability present: "Leave my needle in the furrow – / Where I put it down –," the seamstress warns. The speaker thus resists any intervention – or attempt to rectify her impaired condition – until her strength, which she indeed casts as specific, is reactivated: "I can make the zigzag stitches / Straight – when I am strong –" the penultimate stanza concludes.

It is worth thinking through the various publications of "Dont put up my Thread + Needle" to show how editorial practices influence the poem's depiction of disability both thematically and materially. The poem was first published in Martha Dickinson Bianchi and Alfred Leete Hampson's *Further Poems of Emily Dickinson* (1929). Like all early editions of Dickinson's work, this volume regularized Dickinson's capitalization and eliminated most dashes, replacing them with commas or periods. More recent print editions like Johnson's and Franklin's include the dashes but

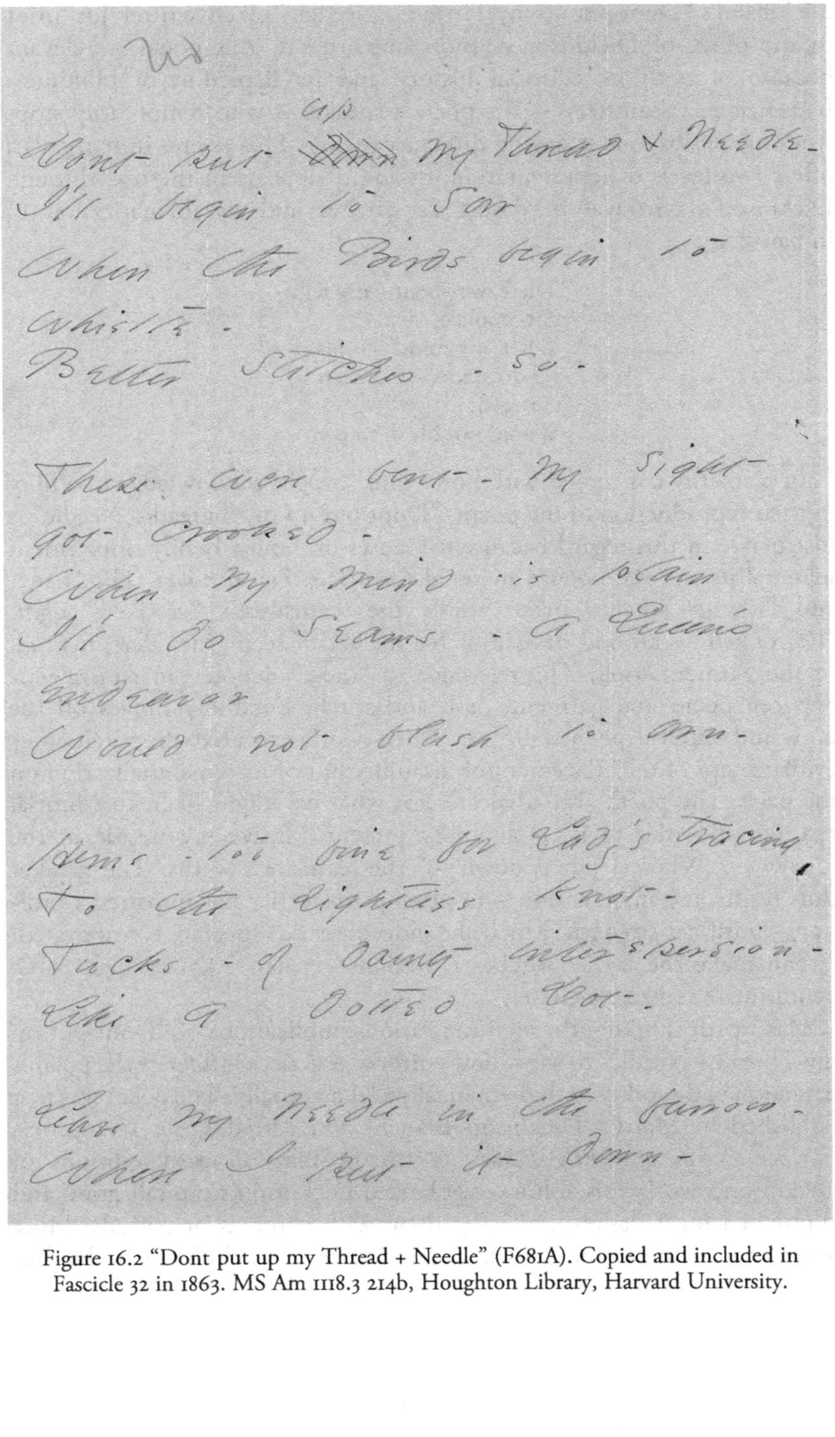

Figure 16.2 "Dont put up my Thread + Needle" (F681A). Copied and included in Fascicle 32 in 1863. MS Am 1118.3 214b, Houghton Library, Harvard University.

translate them into uniform type. The uneven dashes are more than just symbols of the seamstress's messy and all-too-visible stitches but serve, instead, as literal, material inscriptions of Dickinson's visual difficulties. Her blurred vision undoubtedly influenced her investment in the "bent" and "crooked" dash. As I noted earlier, an attention to textual representations of disability means resisting excessive emendations, which attempt to correct a text's anomalies. A crip editorial practice would retain Dickinson's unpredictable dashes in their varied forms – some long, others short; some straight, others crooked.[25] In the specific context of "Dont put up my Thread + Needle," the importance of the seamstress's uneven stitches is made less clear when the dashes are presented in even lines, and, again, Dickinson's visual impairment is eclipsed via these editorial interventions. By contrast, in *Open Folios*, Werner hand-draws Dickinson's dashes (along with commas, quotation marks, and "deletions and mutilations on the surfaces of the manuscripts") to convey the particularity of their presentation. Werner's graphic reproductions of the dashes are not identical to Dickinson's. Instead, her transcriptions take creative liberties; the dashes often appear longer, thicker, and more "crooked" than Dickinson first composed them. But regardless of the dashes' accuracy, Werner importantly addresses how central these often overlooked "abnormalities" of Dickinson's poems are to their overall presentation. In juxtaposing the dashes' irregularities with print, Werner's transcriptions ensure that they are not to be overlooked by readers. She notes, too, that these "'accidentals' . . . are, wherever possible, both graphically figured and narratively described."[26] These hand-drawn dashes have been read as innovative visual art, but they also reveal how Dickinson's difficulty seeing – that is, the poet's "specific strength" – informed her compositional practices. Werner adopts what could be read as both editorial restraint and intervention; she keeps Dickinson's dashes as they were originally drafted but reproduces them with her own hand.

Editing for Readers: Intervention and Restraint

If, thus far, I have explored how best to practice editorial restraint in preserving traces of Dickinson's body (and its limitations) in her poems, we also need to turn our attention to what editorial interventions are necessary for making Dickinson's poems accessible to a broad range of readers with bodily and cognitive impairments. Dickinson's work challenges a crip editorial practice that attends to readers in part because her unique modes of composition (her widely diverse use of paper and her difficult handwriting) make it hard for people with print disabilities to access her poems in their original manuscript forms. (I will also argue, however, that the diversity of Dickinson's authorship – in particular, her emphasis on haptic modes of textual engagement – offers disabled readers a number of access points for understanding her poetry.) Her poems have been primarily described as visual artifacts (what Susan Howe calls "visual productions" and what Smith refers to as having "visual nuances"), and – as I also noted in the essay's opening – they remain largely inaccessible to blind or visually impaired readers as Dickinson herself was.[27] These readers, for instance, would not be able to read Dickinson's poems in the archives, the facsimile reproductions of her fascicle poems in Franklin's edition, or the visual reproductions of her late scrap poems in *The Gorgeous Nothings*. Nearly all editions of texts are aimed toward accommodation for their readers, even if they do not specifically address disability. When deciding on an edition's content and layout, editors must consider what their readers know, what they do not know, and, finally, how to assist them in understanding the edited text, whether through an introduction, transcriptions, images, or explanatory footnotes. No edition, in other words, assumes total literacy, or ability, on behalf of the reader. As for Dickinson, the content of her poems have been made accessible in a number of ways but not always in ways that make crucial manuscript details available to readers with sensory and/or cognitive impairments. These editions show neither adequate editorial restraint nor enough editorial intervention to make the manuscripts and their "specific strengths" accessible to people with print disabilities.

Dickinson's poems have a specific editorial history for disabled readers. Throughout the twentieth century, the poems have been presented in a number of accessible formats for people with print disabilities. According to the National Library Service for the Blind and Physically Handicapped, they first appeared in braille in 1936.[28] Printed in three volumes, this first edition was based on Martha Dickinson Bianchi and Alfred Leete Hampson's *Unpublished Poems of Emily Dickinson*, which appeared that same year. In 1946, 1960, 1978, 1986, and 2001, additional braille editions of Dickinson's poems were published, each modeled after a different standard-print edition. Although braille has existed since the early 1800s in the United States, by the mid-twentieth century, a range of specialized, textual formats to assist blind or visually impaired readers began circulating through homes, schools, and libraries. These accessible versions of texts included large-print books, tactile and talking books, and, more recently, e-books, which can easily be read aloud via text-to-speech software for those who are unable see Dickinson's poems but can hear them. In the latter half of the twentieth century, oral recordings of Dickinson's poems became available. In 1986, a selection of poems were issued by a recording agency at the National Library Service for the first time as a sound recording on a cassette tape, and in 2004 the National Library Service made Johnson's complete edition into a sound recording lasting a total of twenty-five hours and six minutes. Today, with the widely available digitization of Dickinson's poems, recordings are no longer essential because speech synthesis software can translate digitized print into sonic files.

Editions designed specifically for readers with visual impairments are necessary, but it is also useful to consider how such editions can benefit a range of users. This principle is what disability scholars and activists call universal design – the idea that accessible practices benefit not just one person with a specific disability but everyone. In their work on what they term "critical access studies," Aimi Hamraie notes that universal design does not only pertain to built space but also to "Web design, education, and critical humanistic structure," and, I argue, the material form of texts.[29] Good accessibility requires that architects, web designers, and editors manipulate the material world to achieve equality for a range of minds and bodies, and it addresses "how we structure knowledge, interact with material things, and tell stories about why the users of built environments matter for belonging and justice."[30] As Werner and Beth Staley have recently argued, being able to hear Dickinson's poems changes how we make sense of the way they are visualized on the page.[31] The experience of hearing poems spoken aloud is beneficial not just for readers with visual impairments; it might, for example, provide people who do not read an opportunity to listen to the poems and learn them well enough to recite them. In addition, deaf people encountering Dickinson's poems may not benefit from audio versions in the traditional sense, but feeling the vibrations of a poem spoken aloud might offer an orientation to poetic rhythm.

To consider how to make Dickinson's manuscripts and not just their print transcriptions accessible to a broad audience challenges editors to devise new ways of presenting Dickinson's poems that account both for *her* relationship to disability and her readers' relationship to disability. What makes Dickinson's work a special, if not unique, case is the way her own writerly disabilities conflict with those of her readers. If Dickinson's impairments are made most legible in her manuscript (for instance, via her crooked "stitches"), what about a reader who is unable to see Dickinson's poem? We might, then, begin with the following questions:

Can all of the visual features of Dickinson's poems be translated into oral form? For instance, should her poems' differently lengthened dashes determine the length of a recording's pause? (And why might an editor decide to record Dickinson's poems rather than having a reader rely on text-to-speech technology?) How do we verbalize the other non-verbal features of the poems – their size, texture, spacing, and bindings? And can these features be conveyed through sensory forms independent of linguistic registers?

As I noted in the essay's introduction, description offers one way of reconciling the tension between editorial restraint and intervention. These audio descriptions of texts require editorial intervention because, if editors choose to include them, they would position the descriptions alongside facsimiles of Dickinson's poems, thus potentially displacing the centrality of the manuscript. However, the descriptions also embody editorial restraint because they allow the poem and its textual features to be presented in a form largely faithful to the unique attributes of her manuscripts. To include description as central to our editing practices is to attend to the triangulated configuration of the poet's body, the reader's body, and the body of the poem. As descriptive practices reveal, a turn to disability suggests that long-standing debates about whether Dickinson's poems are primarily visual or sonic, and whether they belong in manuscript or print, are misplaced. A disability studies perspective allows us to understand her poems' sensory modes of presentation not as an either/or but rather a both/and; that is, her poems – in privileging a range of abilities and disabilities – are uniquely capable of being translated into multiple mediums. While I argue for an editing practice that attends to writerly disability by retaining the visual anomalies of her manuscripts, attention to readerly disability means that print is essential for the sake of accessibility. Print, for instance, is more easily translated into different mediums (whether they be visual or auditory) than handwriting. A crip editorial practice extends what Magdalena Zapedowska calls the "manuscript turn" in Dickinson studies but advocates for reproducing key features of the manuscripts.[32] Werner's digitization of Dickinson's late scraps in her database *Radical Scatters* is an incredibly useful model of access for the ways it presents Dickinson's poems in multiple formats. It offers both a "Facsimile" version and a "Reading View," which is easy to input into screen-reader technology, which many visually impaired people use. Also crucial in Werner's digital edition are its "Physical Descriptions," which offer information about what type of paper Dickinson wrote on, its dimensions, media, and hand. What is not included, though, is a description of the ways poems are spaced on the page. The Houghton Library's *Emily Dickinson Archive* is another example of editorial practices that begin to make the poems more accessible. Because an image of each manuscript is placed alongside a print transcription, blind readers can hear Dickinson's poems through screen-reader technology. Visually impaired readers can also enlarge text through the database's "zooming-in" function. More broadly, the digitization of texts has also proved useful for people with physical impairments that make it difficult to hold a codex book (especially collections as large and heavy as Franklin's) and turn its pages. The Kindle and other e-readers, as well as the iPad, have been beneficial in this regard because they require little arm movement to navigate from one page or volume to another. The digitization of Dickinson's poems allows for what Smith describes as the "democratization" of the digital: "Democratizing access to primary materials is the most obvious value that multimedia research archives bring to humanities education."[33] Smith's "democratization" refers to the reproduction of archival manuscripts for public viewing (which enable those who are unable to travel to archives to easily access rare materials from a computer), but here, too, we might amplify this democratization by using such digital spaces as a collaborative commons in which users can, for example, add additional audio descriptions of Dickinson's manuscript layouts, along the lines of what I map out above for "Dont put up my Thread + Needle." No single bibliographic or audio description, of course, holds authority. Each has a "specific strength," and having multiple accounts of a poem's visual features (for instance, layering audio descriptions) can only enhance its meaning.

If audio description is one way to address the tension between depicting Dickinson's writerly disability and accommodating readerly ones, an emphasis on the tactile qualities of poems might be another way to bridge these two objectives. Digital formats are not accessible to all readers because they fail to facilitate touch; being able to interact with poems as physical objects would benefit blind, deaf, and autistic individuals alike. The possibilities of foregrounding touch – what many have called a universal sense – as a primary mode of access to Dickinson's poems seems key. For future editions of Dickinson's poems, is it possible to make tactile reproductions of her texts? Or is touch only reserved for the archive? Embossed recreations of Dickinson's handwriting (as opposed to print) would mirror the embossed type of the nineteenth century. As Sari Altschuler and David Weimer have recently shown in their project "Accessible Print," this printing technology might be likened to an early version of universal design, because it was capable of being used by blind and sighted people alike.[34] Embossed reproductions of Dickinson's poems might be one way of helping blind readers to access the often unique spacing of Dickinson's poems independent of their description. Imagine, for instance, an embossed recreation of "In this short Life," one that retains the cramped layout and the unruliness of the lines, attending to the body of the text, while making itself legible to blind readers. Such a solution, though, is not fully sufficient – accessible verbal descriptions of poems are also needed to grasp textual features that cannot be accessed through touch alone. And of course, these editorial interventions and manipulations would undermine the ephemerality of Dickinson's late scrap poems, which I have argued resist efforts at preservation.

Altogether, these various reflections on reading reveal that what constitutes the so-called best version of Dickinson's poems becomes more complicated when we take disability into account. An editorial approach toward Dickinson's work that employs universal design demands that scholars think more seriously about the ways disability is made present in Dickinson's poems while also making those poems accessible to disabled readers. Unlike prior editorial theorists, my goal in this essay is not to liberate Dickinson and her texts from the constraints of prior editorial practices but to consider how disability asks us to imagine what new forms her poems might take. As she makes clear in "Dont put up my Thread + Needle," Dickinson writes alongside disability (both her own and the seamstress's), making impairment central to her poetic practice, and she also encourages us to take the term "access" in open access seriously by casting her poems as multi-modal objects that can be continuously repurposed for new sets of readers. In widening Dickinson's readership and widening access to the manuscripts to include readers and scholars with disabilities, we all stand to learn a great deal.

Notes

1. See R. W. Franklin, ed., *The Manuscript Books of Emily Dickinson*, vol. 2 (Cambridge, MA: The Belknap Press of Harvard University Press, 1981), 760.
2. For more on the importance of description and its relation to accessibility, see Georgina Kleege, "Audio Description Described," *Representations* 135.1 (2016), 89–101.
3. Jerome McGann, *The Textual Condition* (Princeton: Princeton University Press, 1991).

4. The term "crip" is short for "cripple," a term reclaimed by disability rights activists to take ownership of non-normative embodiments.
5. Thomas H. Johnson, ed., *The Poems of Emily Dickinson; Including Variant Readings Critically Compared with All Known Manuscripts*, 3 vols. (Cambridge, MA, and London: The Belknap Press of Harvard University Press, 1955), lxi, xlv.
6. Marta Werner, *Emily Dickinson's Open Folios: Scenes of Reading, Surfaces of Writing* (Ann Arbor: University of Michigan Press, 1995), 50.
7. Lena Christensen, *Editing Emily Dickinson: The Production of an Author* (New York: Routledge, 2007), 79.
8. Mara Mills, "What Should We Call Reading?" *Flow* 17 (December 2012), web.
9. See Helen Vendler, *Dickinson: Selected Poems and Commentaries* (Cambridge, MA: Harvard University Press, 2010), 508.
10. Ibid., 508.
11. Jen Bervin and Marta Werner, *The Gorgeous Nothings: Emily Dickinson's Envelope Poems* (New York: New Directions, 2013).
12. Marta Werner, "'Most Arrows': Autonomy and Intertextuality in Emily Dickinson's Fragments," *Radical Scatters* (The University of Nebraska-Lincoln), last modified June 2010.
13. Holland Cotter, "A Poet Who Pushed (and Recycled) the Envelope," *New York Times*, December 5, 2013.
14. Ibid.
15. Bervin and Werner, *The Gorgeous Nothings*, 219.
16. Ibid., 63.
17. Werner, *Open Folios*, 23.
18. Johnson, lxiv.
19. Qtd in Alexandra Socarides, *Dickinson Unbound: Paper, Process, Poetics* (Oxford: Oxford University Press, 2012), 130.
20. Socarides writes, "While Mabel Loomis Todd may have been invoking the sense of discardability that she saw as intrinsic to these texts when she first called them 'scraps,' critics who have chosen to take up these materials have done everything to avoid reading this assumption back into the work itself" (131).
21. Clare Mullaney, "Not to Discover Weakness is the Artifice of Strength: Emily Dickinson, Constraint, and a Disability Poetics," *J19* 7.1 (forthcoming).
22. Martha Nell Smith, "Corporealizations of Dickinson and Interpretive Machines," in *The Iconic Page in Manuscript, Print, and Digital Culture*, ed. George Bornstein and Theresa Lynn Tinkle (Ann Arbor: University of Michigan Press, 1998), 106.
23. Smith, *Rowing in Eden: Rereading Emily Dickinson* (Austin: University of Texas Press, 1992), 19.
24. Simi Linton, *Claiming Disability: Knowledge and Identity* (New York: New York University Press, 1998), 18.

25. For more on Dickinson's dashes, see Paul Crumbley, *Inflections of the Pen: Dash and Voice in Emily Dickinson* (Lexington: University Press of Kentucky, 1997).
26. Werner, *Open Folios*, 56.
27. Susan Howe, *The Birth-Mark: Unsettling the Wilderness in American Literary History* (Middletown, CT: Wesleyan University Press, 1993), 141 and Martha Nell Smith, *Rowing in Eden: Rereading Emily Dickinson* (Austin, University of Texas Press, 1992), 63.
28. Despite these reproductions, the World Blind Union suggested in 2016 that less than 10 percent of all published texts are made accessible to disabled readers in the world's wealthiest countries. In developing nations, the number is closer to 1 percent. This lack of accessible materials has been termed the "book famine."
29. Aimi Hamraie, *Building Access: Universal Design and the Politics of Disability* (Minneapolis: University of Minnesota Press, 2017), 6.
30. Hamraie, 6.
31. Staley and Werner presented their work on Dickinson's soundscapes at the Emily Dickinson International Society Annual Meeting in Amherst, MA (2017).
32. See Magdalena Zapedowska, "Critical History II: 1955 to the Present," in *Emily Dickinson in Context*, ed. Eliza Richards (New York: Cambridge University Press, 2013), 425.
33. Martha Nell Smith, "Democratizing Knowledge," *Humanities: The Magazine for the National Endowment of the Humanities* (September/October 2005).
34. The details of this project were presented by Altschuler at the American Studies Association Annual Meeting in Chicago, IL (2017), and by Weimer at the Society for Nineteenth-Century Americanists Conference in Albuquerque, NM (2018).

CHAPTER 17

Emily Dickinson in Baghdad

Naseer Hassan

I had not heard of the name "Emily Dickinson" until the day I started reading an Arabic translation of *Poetry and Experience* by Archibald MacLeish.[1] That was in 1996, a time when my passion for reading and writing was at its peak, a period that eventually became a turning point in my relation to poetry.[2] The only American poet who was well known among Iraqi readers, and Arab readers generally, was Walt Whitman. And this is only because a prominent Iraqi poet, Saadi Yousuf, translated *Leaves of Grass* in the 1970s. When I read the chapter on Emily Dickinson's poetry in MacLeish's book and encountered Dickinson's poems in Arabic there, I felt immediately that I was before something different: a sort of strangeness in the words, in their way of combining, in punctuation, and in the style of sentences. I was curious to see the texts in their original English form, to see how they looked on paper, to see that unique, strange creature called an *Emily Dickinson poem*. I had not felt this kind of curiosity before.

At that time it was hard to find any book in English in Iraq, particularly a book of American poetry. The Internet and satellite television were forbidden under Saddam Hussein, and bringing a book from abroad was almost impossible. The mail and banking systems had deteriorated. And to receive a book sent from abroad, or to have a postman knock on your door to deliver a book by or about an American poet, was not wise – especially when you yourself were suspected of opposing the regime because some members of your family did. Two of my uncles were killed under Saddam. One of them, Adanan Hassan, was poisoned with cyanide in prison in May 1980 and then set free only to die three days later in the hospital, where doctors were helpless to save him. When another uncle of mine, Abdul Mun'im Thani, was tortured and executed in 1983, the regime didn't inform us. We learned of it years later from the documents that were found in Intelligence Centers after the collapse of the regime. I, myself, refused to be a Baathist for about twenty-five years. Of course, I paid a lot for this, like other members of my family.

My search for more books by and about Emily Dickinson in bookshops was in vain. Arabic translations of her simply did not exist. "Who is Emily Dickinson?" the bookshops' owners used to answer me; many of them knew Whitman and the novels of Hemingway, and some of them knew something about Ted Hughes, Robert Frost, or William Faulkner's *The Sound and the Fury*. Beyond this, almost nothing. Today I know their unfamiliarity with Dickinson was not strange. There are very few Arabic translations of Dickinson's poetry, and even fewer that would have reached Baghdad by 1996. Interestingly, the very first edition of Dickinson's poems was reportedly translated into Arabic in Syria; according to several American newspaper reports in July 1891, the translation even went through multiple reprints.[3] Copies of this edition remain lost, however. Her poems also made an appearance in Arabic in the 1950s by means of Yusuf al-Khāl, a Lebanese poet of Syrian descent who founded the magazine *Majallat Shi'r* in Beirut, aiming to bring Arabic literature into conversation with American modernism. The first issue in January 1957 included a translation of an essay by MacLeish, as well as translations of Pound's First Canto and a number of Dickinson's poems, along with an introduction to her and her importance to American poetry.[4]

Unable to find Emily Dickinson in shops, another idea came to mind: I could go to the Central Library in Baghdad. There I might find a book on Emily Dickinson among those books that remained undisturbed on the shelves during the sanctions years, when Iraq was disconnected from the world. As I browsed the old, weary drawers in the Central Library, my exultation was sudden when I found some English books about Dickinson (unfortunately I can no longer recall the titles). At last I had the chance to see that "creature" in its original form: a poem by Emily Dickinson. I borrowed two of the books and made photocopies of them in a nearby shop. Because of external sanctions, as well as Iraqi restrictions on freedom of thought, including publishing, exchanging, or bringing in books from outside the country, photocopying was often the only option for sharing or circulating forbidden books or for keeping a copy for oneself. This practice came to be known among Iraqis in the 1990s as "the culture of photocopying."

I'd had the sense since reading MacLeish's book that the translations of Dickinson's poems in that book were inadequate. When I read them, I knew ambiguously on one hand that I was before something important, but at the same time, the poems were not presented with enough coherence and unity to convey this importance. So, when I found the original texts, it was natural to ask myself: What if I tried, in one or two poems, to catch the secret that lies at the heart of her poems? What would be the Arabic result if I tried to translate such a text – a text that seems strange even within its own English language? It would be my first attempt at translating poetry. For someone to make a first attempt at translating poetry with difficult poems like Emily Dickinson's might seem unwise – but it is not so for someone fond of trying to solve enigmas and big challenges. And why not? Inside the huge solitude that envelopes us from all sides, why not live with the biggest enigmas rather than the simplest?

Of course, when I had read the translated poems in MacLeish's book, I sensed an atmosphere of solitude, death, fear, the futility of meaning, and all that characterizes the general climate of many of Dickinson's poems. It was natural that such a poetry made its echoes in myself. We had been living through a painful chapter in the history of Iraq. Successive losses in our lives; deaths of loved ones; time that was flowing with no change under a primitive, abominable dictatorship; youth that was going afar, day after day, with all its dreams and first fresh expectations – all this was a proper environment, for a person like me at least, to find in such poetry strong echoes in his soul. I felt some spiritual kinship, a friendship of two worlds distant in space and time. Indeed, don't we read the most ancient things written in history, poetry, and philosophy, and ask and interact, object and accept, as if we are in a direct, living dialogue with that human who is now not even mere dust but who was once full of life and expectations?

Questions jumped before me when I started the experiment: What makes this poem in front of me a masterpiece? Where does its mysterious secret lie exactly? Seizing this elusive secret would lead to choosing the proper alternatives of words and sentence structures, so that the final result might be a "poem of translation," not a "translation of a poem" – I wanted to create in Arabic a "living twin" to that distant and distinct English creature.[5] The initial result was a translation of three poems and a critical essay reflecting on the translation process.[6] The first poem I translated begins "Because I could not stop for Death – / He kindly stopped for me" (F479). What initially drew my attention to it was the paradox of the first two lines – not a mental or logical paradox but a poetic one rather – a paradox that expresses an important aspect of our relation, all of us, with death. Death is related usually to fear and awe, and in spite of that we all know it is inevitable in this existence that we live. Still, we have the gift of not knowing exactly when the moment of death will be. So, hope and endeavor can remain parts of human life. This fact enriches the moment of death and gives it an atmosphere of mystery and of openness to various possibilities; without it, the nature of human life would be quite different in ways that we can't imagine. However, when we sense that moment approaching – or in instances where death is not sudden – then all of our expectations, questions, fears, and readiness come to the fore. Would we be ready? And if we were to hesitate in that moment – or the last part of that moment – how would it be?

The poet in this poem is seemingly not ready for that moment. She goes on her way as if she doesn't notice Death, like anyone who ignores something that she actually sees. But that terrible visitor who is in fact there doesn't complain about this superficial ignorance because he seems to understand the human and to have already faced countless cases of such moments that made him wise enough to stop the person "kindly" and with "Civility," not with aggression. It is this strange sense of kindness that I wanted to capture in my translation.

But this sense of kindness was also the hardest point in the translation process, for the English words bear different connotations and tones in Arabic. If I were just to put the supposedly accurate alternatives for "kindly" and "Civility" in the translated text, it would harm the poem aesthetically.

Wanting a poetically effective alternative, I chose the Arabic word *lutf* for both "kindly" in the first stanza and "Civility" in the second stanza. Another translation for "kindly" would have been *a'tf*, but this would not be exactly right, since *a'tf* can suggest sympathy, too, which is not quite the case here. Phonetically, *a'tf* is heavier than *lutf*, especially due to the first sound /a'/ (a sound that doesn't exist in English). For "Civility," I might have chosen *kayasa*, but it is not phonetically suitable for the poem, and it lacks the sense of a touch of kindness implicit in the word "civility." I might have instead chosen *tahaddur*, which can also mean "civilized," but, like "civilized," *tahaddur* refers not only to one's manner but also to large cultural groups. If I'd used *tahaddur*, I would have needed to add other words for accuracy – for example, *tassarrufihi al mutahhdir* ("his civilized manner"). But the word *tahaddur* would already be too heavy and clumsy for the poem, and adding additional words would make it even clumsier. *Lutf*, again, is a much softer sound. Thus, despite the differences in meaning between "kindly" and "Civility," I chose *lutf* in both cases.

Still, while this translation maintains the poem's poetic energy, I found it necessary to indicate to Arabic readers the difference in the English original words by using footnotes. I have often adopted this strategy in translation because I think in this way we present to the reader an aesthetically poetic text on one hand (a living twin), and, on the other hand, draw the reader's attention to what she should be aware of in the original text. If the Arabic reader reads the word *lutf* in the two stanzas without referring to the original difference, she might think it is the same word in English, too, and then she would lose the beautiful, significant difference between kindness and civility in this context, since the *lutf* of death in the first stanza is responsive to the awful moment of facing death, while "Civility" relates to his courtesy in the driving process, especially significant because the poet "put away" her "labor and [her] leisure" – her whole life – for that civility. Thus, I put footnotes showing the original English words, with an explanation that *lutf* in the first stanza comes with the meaning of *atf*, while *lutf* in the second comes with the meaning of *kayasa*.

Ultimately, the syntax and punctuation I used in the Arabic translation aim to keep the meditative, relatively slow, distracted atmosphere of the poem, although I opted to leave out her dashes: Dickinson's style is already difficult enough for Arabic readers. Here are the two texts, the original and the translation:

> Because I could not stop for Death –
> He kindly stopped for me –
> The Carriage held but just Ourselves –
> And Immortality.
>
> We slowly drove – He knew no haste
> And I had put away
> My labor and my leisure too,
> For His Civility –
>
> We passed the School, where Children strove
> At Recess – in the Ring –
> We passed the Fields of Gazing Grain –
> We passed the Setting Sun –
>
> We paused before a House that seemed
> A Swelling of the Ground –
> The Roof was scarcely visible –
> The Cornice – in the Ground –
>
> Since then – 'tis Centuries – and yet
> Feels shorter than the Day
> I first surmised the Horses' Heads
> Were toward Eternity –

لأني لم أستطعِ التوقفَ للموت،
فانه بلطفٍ*توقفَ لأجلي؛
العربةُ ما حملتْ أحداً، سوانا
والخلود.

ببطءٍ قُدْنا. هو لا يعرفُ العَجَلة
وأنا هجرتُ عملي
وفراغي أيضاً،
من أجلِ لطفه**.

مررنا بالمدرسة حيث لعبَ الأطفالُ
في عطلةٍ، المصارعةَ في حلبةٍ؛
مررنا بحقولٍ من الحبوب المحدَّقة،
مررنا بالشمسِ الغاربة.

توقفنا أمام بيتٍ بدا
كبروزٍ في الأرض؛
السقفُ بالكاد يُرى،
والإفريزُ محضُ أكَمة.

مذ ذاك وهي قرون؛ ولكن كلّاً منها
يُحسُّ أقصرَ من نهار
أنا أولُ من خمن ان رؤوسَ الجياد
كانت باتجاه الأبدية.

---

* Kindly. بلطف، بعطف :
** Civility. لطف، كياسة :

In the atmosphere of dictatorship, fear, sanctions, and solitude, there were not enough motives for an ambition to continue a complete project on Emily Dickinson, such as a book. This applied to my own poetry, too. I published a single collection of my poems in 1998 using a photocopy machine (publishing small quantities of books this way was necessary in the 1990s, part of the so-called culture of photocopying). But after that I was not able to find enough motivation to keep writing.

It was also safer to stay in the shadows than to present yourself as a cultural or literary figure under a fascist dictatorship that might ask you to create propaganda: to write a poem in praise of the dictator, to glorify a nihilistic war, or to show that "all the people are happy," for example. If you did not comply, it would be highly possible that you would expose yourself to serious dangers. Artists and cultural figures in Iraq at that time were divided into three groups: the propaganda "intellectuals" of the dictatorship; intellectuals who emigrated or were forced into exile; and those who chose to stay as far in the shadows as they could. In this environment, it was especially unwise to translate American writers. Authorities were promoting an anti-American propaganda on a large scale as a part of its policy at that period. Nevertheless, I translated a few more poems of Dickinson's and kept them unpublished.

Things changed radically in 2003 after the collapse of Saddam Hussein's regime. By 2007, in spite of the widespread violence that prevailed, my enthusiasm for literary activity moved again in a much freer air of publishing and Internet access to books and other materials. I had been able to obtain a book of Emily Dickinson's complete poems. The idea came back to me again – to translate more of Dickinson's poems, or even to publish a book of translations of her poetry. I completed a book manuscript of translations of her poems in 2009. I first self-published it in Baghdad: I asked a printing center only to print the cover of the book, while I printed a limited number of copies of the text myself on my home printer. In 2012, I published the book again with a well-known publisher, Arab Publishing House, in Beirut-Lebanon. The book was entitled *Emily Dickinson: Selected Poems and Critical Articles*. As far as I know, it is the first book-length translation of Dickinson's poetry in Arabic (apart from the lost 1891 edition). My book includes fifty poems and five translated critical articles on her poems, in addition to my own critical article, which I wrote in 1996. I found it important to include critical articles on Dickinson's poetry in the book, since I assumed that the reader would face the strangeness of the style and might need some guidance as she encounters the poems.

But what might seem strange is that the style and disposition of Emily Dickinson's poems about death align harmoniously with the general disposition of Iraqi people, who have endured disasters, wars, tragedies. Because of the conditions Iraqis have lived under, from the dictatorship until the present day, questions about death, fear, futility, and time take root continuously in Iraq's soul and mind, and death is an almost permanent obsession in Iraqi life. Iraqis are a people with ancient roots of this feeling of anxiety and instability, since the early myths of creation in Sumerian and Babylonian civilizations (*Gilgamesh* is the earliest known epic in human history) and then through a long history that has been generally unstable and violent. Of course, the ways people deal with the question of death are different. Religion and belief in the afterlife are major ways for many Iraqis to cope with the continuous losses that death brings to them. Dickinson's poems don't often approach death from this point of view but rather in a more personal, psychological way. Still, there are many similarities that cross different cultures and circumstances: the fear of death, images of the tomb, how the world might look like in the eyes of a dying person, how "life" in the grave might look. Moreover, Iraqi intellectuals – however much in the minority they are – generally speaking are inclined to look at death from an existential point of view rather than a religious one.

When Emily Dickinson says things like "After great pain, a formal feeling comes – / The Nerves sit ceremonious, like Tombs," it expresses exactly the feeling of a whole people which she almost didn't hear of (F372). But the contemplative human soul has its own ways of transcending the limits of time and space and reaching out to other worlds it doesn't know about. When a scene of death is repeated continuously in our daily life, in acts of terrorism or the like, our sense of death itself takes another form. It turns from a sharp shock to monotony and ongoing sorrow, akin to what Dickinson says in "There's been a Death, in the Opposite House": "It's easy as a Sign – / The Intuition of the News – / In just a Country Town" (F547). When I see an image of a woman or a man or a child, innocent, dying, I remember that sincerity of the "look of Agony" which cannot be "sham[med]" or "simulate[d]" (F339). And when I think of the pages of history and life where long sadness and transitory happiness succeed each other, or in the big question of why pain is naturally extended and not momentary like a moment of joy (life is a losing deal, as Schopenhauer says, and this seems true at least for those generations who are condemned to live the dark pages of history), I can't help remembering that "For each extatic instant / We must an anguish pay / In keen and quivering ratio / To the extasy" (F109).

But we should not forget, in the end, MacLeish's important note: he argues that dealing with issues like death and fear usually leads to the failing of art because an artistic vision should exceed personal experience. He contends that the tone in which Emily Dickinson handled these issues was what saved her poetry from falling into a negative, broken air and what made her offer great poetry. And this description might apply, too, to a whole people's attitude: to keep a tone of hope inside a disastrous page of history.

Notes

1. Palestinian writer and translator Salmaa Al Khadraa Al Jayyusi translated MacLeish's 1961 *Poetry and Experience* into Arabic in 1963 for the Franklin Institute.
2. Editor's note: in the Introduction to this volume, I enlist Hassan's essay at some length to think about the stakes and realities of a global Dickinson readership.

3. According to Willis J. Buckingham, *Emily Dickinson's Reception in the 1890s: A Documentary History* (Pittsburgh: University of Pittsburgh Press, 1989), 158, the mention of an "Arabic translation made in Syria [that] has passed through several editions" appeared in "Notes," *Nation* 53 (July 16, 1891), 48, (reprinted in *Chicago Post* [July 17, 1891], 4) and in "Notes," *Critic* n.s. 16 (July 18, 1891), 36, (reprinted in *Christian Union* 44 [July 25, 1891], 195; *Philadelphia Press* [July 25, 1891], 11; and *Current Literature* 8 [October 1891], 317). Buckingham notes that "[t]his report of an Arabic edition gained currency in the nineties, owing perhaps to the *Nation*'s affiliation with Higginson, its regular poetry reviewer. Evidence of the translation remains to be discovered" (158).
4. *Majallat Shi'r* 1.1 (1957): 3–4, 82–87. See Huda J. Fakhreddine, *Metapoesis in the Arabic Tradition: From Modernists to Muhdathūn* ([Leiden; Boston: Brill, 2015], Brill Studies in Middle Eastern Literatures, vol. 36), 31–32.
5. See also Nabil Alawi, "Translating Emily Dickinson's 'There came a Day at Summer's full' into Arabic," *EDJ* 6.2 (1997): 84–89. Alawi discusses nineteenth-century points of contact between Dickinson's poetry and Arabic translation and readerships, and he offers his own Arabic translation and a discussion of the obstacles he encountered in translating her poem.
6. At this time, I also translated "Surgeons must be very careful" (F156) and "Exultation is the going" (F143). These three translations, as well as a critical essay which I wrote reflecting on the translation process, were published in a local Iraqi newspaper and another Arabic one, too. I was not able to locate these issues for citations.

Suggested Further Reading

Alawi, Nabil. "Translating Emily Dickinson's 'There came a Day at Summer's full' into Arabic." *EDJ* 6.2 (1997): 84–89.

Barrett, Faith. *To Fight Aloud Is Very Brave: American Poetry and the Civil War.* Amherst: University of Massachusetts Press, 2012.

Behar, Katherine, ed. *Object-Oriented Feminism.* Minneapolis: University of Minnesota Press, 2016.

Boggs, Colleen Glenney. *Animalia Americana: Animal Representations and Biopolitical Subjectivity.* New York: Columbia University Press, 2013.

Burr, Zofia. *Of Women, Poetry, and Power: Strategies of Address in Dickinson, Miles, Brooks, Lorde, and Angelou.* Urbana: University of Illinois Press, 2002.

Chow, Juliana. "'Because I See – New Englandly –': Seeing Species in the Nineteenth-Century and Emily Dickinson's Regional Specificity." *ESQ* 60.3 (2014): 413–449.

Cohen, Michael C. *The Social Lives of Poems in Nineteenth-Century America.* Philadelphia: University of Pennsylvania Press, 2015.

Coole, Diana, and Samantha Frost. "Introducing the New Materialisms." In *New Materialisms: Ontology, Agency, and Politics*, ed. Diana Coole and Samantha Frost, 1–46. Durham: Duke University Press, 2010.

Crumbley, Paul. "Back Talk in New England: Dickinson and Revolution." *EDJ* 24.1 (2015): 1–21.

Crumbley, Paul, and Karen Kilcup. "Dickinson's Environments." Special issue of *ESQ* 63.2 (2017).

Davidson, Michael. "Disability Poetics." In *The Oxford Handbook of Modern and Contemporary American Poetry*, ed. Cary Nelson. Oxford: Oxford University Press, 2012.

Davis, Theo. *Ornamental Aesthetics: The Poetry of Attending in Thoreau, Dickinson, and Whitman.* Oxford: Oxford University Press, 2016.

Deppman, Jed. *Trying to Think with Emily Dickinson.* Amherst: University of Massachusetts Press, 2008.

Deppman, Jed, Marianne Noble, and Gary Lee Stonum, eds. *Emily Dickinson and Philosophy.* Cambridge: Cambridge University Press, 2013.

Dimock, Wai Chee. "Introduction: Genres as Fields of Knowledge." *PMLA* 122.5 (2007): 1377–1388.

Through Other Continents: American Literature Across Deep Time. Princeton: Princeton University Press, 2006.
Eberwein, Jane Donahue, Stephanie Farrar, and Cristanne Miller, eds. *Dickinson in Her Own Time: A Biographical Chronicle of Her Life*. Iowa City: University of Iowa Press, 2016.
Emerson, Lori. *Reading Writing Interfaces: From the Digital to the Bookbound*. Minneapolis: University of Minnesota Press, 2014.
Fletcher, Angus. *A New Theory for American Poetry: Democracy, the Environment, and the Future of Imagination*. Cambridge: Harvard University Press, 2004.
Fretwell, Erica. "Emily Dickinson in Domingo." *J19* 1.1 (2013): 71–96.
Garland-Thomson, Rosemarie. *Extraordinary Bodies: Figuring Physical Disability in American Literature and Culture*. Columbia: Columbia University Press, 1996.
Gerhardt, Christine. *A Place for Humility: Whitman, Dickinson, and the Natural World*. Iowa City: University of Iowa Press, 2014.
"Emily Dickinson Now: Environments, Ecologies, Politics." *ESQ* 63.2 (2017): 329–355.
Giles, Paul. "'The Earth Reversed Her Hemispheres': Dickinson's Global Antipodality." *EDJ* 20.1 (2011): 1–21.
The Global Remapping of American Literature. Princeton: Princeton University Press, 2011.
Gray, Janet. *Race and Time: American Women's Poetics from Antislavery to Racial Modernity*. Iowa City: University of Iowa Press, 2004.
Haraway, Donna. "Encounters with Companion Species: Entangling Dogs, Baboons, Philosophers and Biologists." *Configurations* 14 (2006): 97–114.
Hsu, Hsuan L. *Geography and the Production of Space in Nineteenth-Century American Literature*. Cambridge and New York: Cambridge University Press, 2010.
Hsu, Li-hsin. "Emily Dickinson's Asian Consumption." *EDJ* 22.2 (2013): 1–25.
Jackson, Virginia. *Dickinson's Misery: A Theory of Lyric Reading*. Princeton: Princeton University Press, 2005.
Kelly, Mike, et al., eds. *The Networked Recluse: The Connected World of Emily Dickinson*. Amherst: Amherst College Press, 2017.
Kohler, Michelle. "Ancient Brooch and Loaded Gun: Dickinson's Lively Objects." *ESQ* 63.2 (2017): 79–121.
Miles of Stare: Transcendentalism and the Problem of Literary Vision in Nineteenth-Century America. Tuscaloosa: University of Alabama Press, 2014.
Kuhn, Mary. "Dickinson and the Politics of Plant Sensibility." *ELH* 85.1 (2018): 141–170.
Linton, Simi. *Claiming Disability: Knowledge and Identity*. New York: New York University Press, 1998.
Loeffelholz, Mary. "The Creation of Emily Dickinson and the Study of Nineteenth-Century American Women's Poetry." In *A History of Nineteenth-Century American Women's Poetry*, ed. Jennifer Putzi and Alexandra Socarides, 406–421. Cambridge: Cambridge University Press, 2017.

"Networking Dickinson: Some Thought Experiments in Digital Humanities." *EDJ* 23.1 (2014): 106–119.
The Value of Emily Dickinson. Cambridge: Cambridge University Press, 2016.
Marrs, Cody. "Dickinson in the Anthropocene." *ESQ* 63.2 (2017): 201–225.
Nineteenth-Century American Literature and the Long Civil War. Cambridge: Cambridge University Press, 2015.
McAbee, Leslie. "Through the Tiger's Eye: Constructing Animal Exoticism in Emily Dickinson's 'Big Cat' Poems." *EDJ* 26.1 (2017): 1–26.
Meiners, Benjamin. "Lavender Latin Americanism: Queer Sovereignties in Emily Dickinson's Southern Eden." *EDJ* 27.1 (2018): 24–44.
Miller, Cristanne. *Reading in Time: Emily Dickinson in the Nineteenth Century.* Amherst: University of Massachusetts Press, 2012.
   ed. "Special Section: The Global Translation and Reception of Emily Dickinson." *EDJ* 18.1 (2009): 69–104.
Mitchell, Domhnall, and Maria Stuart, eds. *The International Reception of Emily Dickinson.* London: Continuum, 2009.
Mullaney, Clare. "Not to Discover Weakness is the Artifice of Strength: Emily Dickinson, Constraint, and a Disability Poetics." *J19* 7.1 (forthcoming).
Muresan, Maria Rusanda. "Dickinsonian Moments in African American Poetry: Unsettling the Map of the Lyric." *Women's Studies* 47.3 (2018): 286–301.
Murray, Aífe. *Maid as Muse: How Servants Changed Emily Dickinson's Life and Language.* Durham: University of New Hampshire Press, 2009.
Osborne, Gillian. "Dickinson's Lyric Materialism." *EDJ* 21.1 (2012): 57–78.
Peterson, Katie. "Surround Sound: Dickinson's Self and the Hearable." *EDJ* 14.2 (2005): 76–88.
Pollak, Vivian R. *Our Emily Dickinsons: American Women Poets and the Intimacies of Difference.* Philadelphia: University of Pennsylvania Press, 2017.
Pugh, Christina. "Dickinson's Ambivalence: Lyric Resistance to Rhyme." In *On Rhyme*, ed. David Caplan, 143–160. Liege: Presses Universitaires de Liege, 2016.
   "Ghosts of Meter: Dickinson, After Long Silence." *EDJ* 16.2 (2007): 1–24.
Putzi, Jennifer, and Alexandra Socarides, eds. *A History of Nineteenth-Century American Women's Poetry.* Cambridge: Cambridge University Press, 2017.
Richards, Eliza. *Battle Lines: Poetry, Media, and the U.S. Civil War.* Philadelphia: University of Pennsylvania Press, 2019.
   ed. *Emily Dickinson in Context.* Cambridge: Cambridge University Press, 2013.
Richards, Eliza, and Alexandra Socarides. "Networking Dickinson." Special issue of *EDJ*. 2015.
Scarry, Elaine. *The Body in Pain: The Making and Unmaking of the World.* Oxford: Oxford University Press, 1987.
Socarides, Alexandra. "Consuming Dickinson." *Legacy* 34.2 (2017): 377–386.
   Dickinson Unbound: Paper, Process, Poetics. Oxford: Oxford University Press, 2012.
Uno, Hiroko. "Emily Dickinson and Japanese Flowers: Her Herbarium and Perry's Expedition to Japan." *EDJ* 26.1 (2017): 51–79.

"Emily Dickinson's Encounter with the East: Chinese Museum in Boston." *EDJ* 17.1 (2008): 43–67.

Wheeler, Lesley. *The Poetics of Enclosure: American Women Poets from Dickinson to Dove*. Knoxville: University of Tennessee Press, 2002.

Wolfe, Cary. *What Is Posthumanism?* Minneapolis and London: University of Minnesota Press, 2010.

Index

Dickinson's poems are indexed here by their first lines.

"A Death blow is a Life blow, to Some" (F966B),
    273–274
  Chin's "Nocturnes" and, 273–274
  eternity in, 273–274
"A not admitting of the wound" (F1188), 113
  carpenter of, 113
  crucifixion trope of, 114
  temporality of, 113–114
  visual obstruction in, 113
"A Pang is more conspicuous in Spring" (F1545),
    108–110
  figuration in, 110
  pain in, 108–110
  phenomenological field of, 108
"A Precious – mouldering pleasure – 'tis –"
    (F569), 199–200
  participation in world literature,
    199
  reading in, 38–39, 199
"A Route of Evanescence" (F1489), 198–199
  Africa in, 198
  globalization in, 198–199
  Latin America in, 198
  Shakespeare in, 198–199
"A solemn thing – it was – I said –" (F307),
    95–96
  black/white dichotomy in, 277
  female subjectivity in, 96
  gendered constraints of, 95
  objects in, 95
  race in, 261
  sneering in, 95–96
  transcendence of, 95
  whiteness in, 96, 99, 263
  wifehood in, 95–96
  women's subjectivities in, 95–96
"A Toad, can die of Light –" (F419), 129–130
  death in, 129–130
  egalitarianism of, 130

  Umwelt of, 130
  wine metaphor of, 130
"A word made Flesh is seldom" (F1715A),
    284–285
  physical limitation in, 284
ableism
  in editorial practices, 283
  perpetuation of, 288
  See also disabilities
abolition
  Dickinson and, 216–217, 276
  women's rights and, 217
Acker, Kathy, 259
Africa
  in Dickinson's poetry, 198–199
  in "A Route of Evanescence," 198
African American authors
  trickster figures of, 211
African Americans
  identification with Christian Bible, 264
  nationalism among, 277
  See also poetry, African American; women of
    color
"After great pain, a formal feeling comes –"
    (F372), 35–36
  distance in, 37
  Iraqi readers of, 306
  letting go in, 36
  Longfellow and, 37
  poetic form of, 35–36
"After the Sun comes out" (F1127A), 59–60
  human communication in, 59
  mass media in, 59
  nature/media exchange in, 60
  wagon trope of, 59–60
agency
  Dickinson's, 3, 5, 288
  in Dickinson's handwriting, 288
  disidentification as, 277–278

Index

in lyric dis-reading, 267
of women of color poets, 259
Ahmed, Sara, 96
Alawi, Nabil, 307
Alexander, Meena, 259
"All the letters I can write" (F380B), 75–77
  aural experience of, 76
  figurative relationships of, 75
  hyperbole of, 76–77
  meiosis in, 76
  meter of, 76
  rhyme of, 76
  rose trope of, 75–76
  self-diminishment in, 76
  silence in, 75–77
Alvarez, Julia, 259
American studies
  exceptionalism in, 187
  transnational, 187–188
Amherst (Mass.)
  in Dickinson's geography, 168
  ecology of, 140
  electrical lighting in, 56
  soundscapes of, 80
Amherst Academy
  Dickinson's education at, 41, 169, 189–190, 288
Amherst College
  Dickinson permission policy, 248
  geography at, 171
  scientific inquiry at, 178
  See also online archives, Dickinson's (Amherst College)
Angelou, Maya, 259
animals
  Dickinson's engagement with, 129, 133
  equality among, 129
  fusion with machines, 64
  as poor in the world, 121
  relationship to surroundings, 121
animal studies
  Dickinson and, 7
  posthumanism and, 120
Anthropocene era, 161, 165
anthropocentrism
  ecopoetics on, 138
anthropomorphism
  Dickinson's engagement with, 62, 133
  posthumanism and, 120–121
Arabic
  Dickinson translations in, 300–304, 307
  See also readers, Iraqi
archives, Dickinson's
  access to, 248, 250
  comprehensive, 248
  critical analyses from, 249
  early and late works in, 249
  first generation of, 249
  flexibility in, 249
  gestural interface of, 254
  intimacy with Dickinson through, 254
  role in reception, 254
  selection principles of, 249
  technology enabling, 248
  texture and gesture in, 250–254
  Todd's, 226–227, 247–248
  visual analysis of, 251
  See also manuscripts, Dickinson's; online archives, Dickinson's
Aristarkhova, Irina, 90
Asahina, Midori, 135
Asia
  in Dickinson's poetry, 197–198
  European exploitation of, 197
  in New England print culture, 197
"As Sleigh Bells seem in Summer" (F801), 77–78
  disappearance in death of, 77–78
  lettering of, 77–78
  memory in, 78
Atlantic cable
  laying of, 190
Atlantic Monthly
  physics articles in, 157
atomic theory, 167
  ancient, 160
  in "The Chemical conviction," 160
  nineteenth-century, 160
attention
  in Dickinson's poetics, 137
Attridge, Derek, 67
authorship
  legitimacy of, 18
"Awake ye muses nine, sing me a strain divine" (F1), 118

Baathist regime (Iraq), 11, 299
  collapse of, 305
  literature under, 304–305
  violence under, 299
  See also Hussein, Saddam; Iraq
Babylon
  creation myths of, 305
Baghdad Central Library
  Dickinson editions in, 300
Baldwin, James, 1
Bang, Mary Jo
  on Dickinson's influence, 258
"Banish Air from Air–" (F963), 159–160
  inadequacy of language in, 159

314　Index

"Banish Air from Air–" (F963) (cont.)
　natural science in, 159–160
　suffering in, 163
　transformation in, 159
Barrett, Faith, 8, 24
　To Fight Aloud Is Very Brave, 218
Bate, Jonathan
　The Song of the Earth, 143–144
Baym, Nina, 178–179
"Because I could not stop for death" (F479)
　Arabic syntax of, 303
　Arabic translation of, 9, 301–303
　Arabic word choice in, 302–303
　civility in, 302
　footnotes for, 302–303
　kindness in, 302
　paradox of death in, 301–302
"Before I got my eye put out –" (F336)
　sight and blindness in, 25–26, 34
Behar, Katherine, 91, 93, 97
　on feminist politics, 90–91
　on object-oriented feminism, 90–91
　on objects, 96
　on praxis of care, 92
Bennett, Paula Bernat, 25, 46
　on Dickinson's reading, 33
Berg, Peter, 134
Bervin, Jen, 9, 46, 249–250
　editorial practices of, 283
　on transience, 287
　See also Gorgeous Nothings, The
Bianchi, Martha Dickinson
　Further Poems of Emily Dickinson, 289
　Unpublished Poems of Emily Dickinson, 292
Bingham, Millicent Todd, 285
　normalization of Dickinson's texts, 282, 285
biodescription
　in Dickinson's poetry, 145
biological essentialism, 86
biopoetics, Dickinson's, 119–120, 123–127, 131
　cross-species encounters in, 131
　environmental relations of, 62, 130–131, 144
　of "The Robin's my Criterion for Tune," 124–126
　self and world in, 130
　subject-forming in, 131
　subjectivity via, 124, 132–133
bioregionalism, 134
　in Dickinson's poetry, 140, 143
　of nineteenth-century poetry, 139
　reading in, 140
　Tuckerman's, 140, 144
biosemiotics, 7
　Dickinson and, 132–133
　Uexküll's, 124, 132

birdsong
　in Dickinson's poetry, 134
　in nineteenth-century music, 75–76
　in Tuckerman's poetry, 142
Bishop, Elizabeth, 259
Black Arts Movement, 264, 269, 275
Blackmur, R. P., 114
Blackwood, Sarah, 130
Blanchard, Donald L., 101
Bobadilla, Francisco de, 196
Bobadilla, Isabel de, 196
bobolinks
　decline in numbers of, 143
　in Dickinson's poetry, 137, 143, 145–147
　of "Some keep the Sabbath going to Church," 123
body
　being-in-the-world of, 7
Boggs, Colleen Glenney, 7
bookmaking, women's, 69
Bowles, Samuel, 170
　Dickinson's correspondence with, 190
braille
　Dickinson's poetry in, 292, 296
Brontë, Charlotte, 191
　Dickinson's poem about, 20
Brooks, Gwendolyn, 9, 260
　in Black Arts movement, 269
　black identity of, 268
　black people's experience in, 268
　break with tradition, 268
　creative influences on, 268
　at Dickinson's Homestead, 269, 278
　engagement with Dickinson, 259, 267–269, 278
　influence on Chin, 270
　lyric dis-reading by, 268–269
　rhymes of, 267–268
　at Seton Hall celebration, 267–268, 276
Brown, Charles Brockden, 171
Brown, Nathan, 115
Brown, William Wells, 211, 218
Browning, Elizabeth Barrett, 190–191
　Dickinson's poem about, 20
Bryant, Levi R., 90
Buckingham, Willis J., 307
Burke, Tarana, 99
Burr, Zofia, 275
　on Dickinson's canonization, 258
Burt, Stephanie, 144
"Flowers – Well – if anybody" (F95B)
　mass media transport in, 60
Byerly, Alison, 192–193
Byron, Lord
　"Darkness," 143–144

Index

Calvinism
  Dickinson's, 192
Cameron, Sharon, 7, 25, 166
  on choosing not choosing, 78
  on Dickinsonian pain, 100
  and Dickinson's feminist critics, 97
  on Dickinson's principle of exchange, 81
  on Dickinson's relationship to music, 72
  Lyric Time, 103–104, 106
  on maelstrom metaphor, 105
  on repetition, 104
  on simile, 106–107
  on temporality, 105
Carlo (Dickinson's dog), 119–120, 132
  Dickinson's poetic engagement with, 119, 133
Carr, Jean Ferguson, 41
"Celebration of Emily Dickinson and American Women's Poetry" (Seton Hall University, 1986), 260, 276
  Brooks at, 267
  women of color poets at, 276
Chin, Marilyn, 9, 260
  aesthetic lineage of, 270
  biculturalism of, 270–271
  Brooks's influence on, 270
  Chinese-American quatrains of, 270–271
  and Dickinson's metaphysics, 270
  dis-reading of Dickinson, 273–274
  engagement with Dickinson, 267, 270–274
  "From a Notebook of an Ex-Revolutionary," 271–272
    Dickinson in, 271–272
    irony in, 271–272
    Plath in, 271
    quatrains of, 271
  "Goodbye"
    Dickinson's tropes in, 274
  Hard Love Province, 270
  in Iowa Writers Workshop, 270
  "Nocturnes"
    "A Death blow is a Life blow, to Some" and, 273–274
    Dickinson in, 273
    eternity in, 273
    injustice in, 273
  political poetics of, 270
  race in poetics of, 270–271
  silence in poetry of, 272–273
Chow, Juliana, 136
  on deforestation, 150
Cisneros, Sandra, 259
"Civilization – spurns – the Leopard!" (F276), 197–198
  Asiatic other in, 197
  Oriental commodity in, 197–198
  transversing of categories in, 197–198
Civil War, U.S., 11
  culture of, 24
  Dickinson on, 64, 164
  mass media during, 50
  news of dead in, 26–27
  technologies of, 25
Civil War poetry, 24–27
  Dickinson's, 24–25, 27–28, 116, 164
  readers of, 29
  response to casualty lists, 32
Clausius, Rudolf, 157, 162
Cohen, Michael, 6
  on historical poetics, 138
  on nineteenth-century poetry, 138
collaboration
  among women authors, 18, 30
  aspects of, 19
  communities', 20–21, 27
  destabilization of authorship, 18
  Dickinson's, 18–31
  in Dickinson's fascicles, 21, 31
  effect on readers, 18
  materiality of, 21
  nineteenth-century, 19, 30
  poetic, 19
colonialism
  in Dickinson's poetry, 196–197
"Color – Caste – Denomination –" (F836), 207
  racial difference in, 262
Columbus, Christopher, 196
computer analysis, of Dickinson's poetry, 250–254, 257
  e-texts in, 251
  of handwriting, 252
  macro analyses using, 250–251
  visual, 251
  See also online archives, Dickinson's
Concord (Mass.)
  ecology of, 150
consciousness
  material interactions of, 4
Cotter, Holland, 285
Crane, Hattie, 224
Crawford, Joan, 277–278
creativity
  individualistic forms of, 64
  literary, 6
  nineteenth-century conventions of, 38
"Crisis is a Hair" (F1067), 155
criticism, historical
  knowledge of poetry in, 138
  See also ecocriticism

Crumbley, Paul, 1–2
  on gift culture, 22
cuckoo
  parasitism of, 125–126
culture
  black literary, 278
  sound-based, 66
  visual, 251
culture, African American
  Biblical themes in, 264
  Dickinson's poetry and, 264
culture, nineteenth-century
  of Civil War, 24
  diary-keeping in, 220, 222, 233
  mementos in, 228
  poetic, 40–41
  print, 190, 197
  scribal, 47
  spelling books in, 48
  transatlantic, 190–191
  white supremacist, 266–267

Dalton, John, 160
Darwin, Charles, 148
  natural selection theory, 136
Dasmann, Raymond F., 134
Davis, Theo, 63–64
  on Dickinson's "attention," 137
  on Dickinson's mutuality, 121
  Ornamental Aesthetics, 111
"Death sets a Thing significant" (F640)
  memorial objects in, 228
Degaulle Manor (New Orleans), 12
  evictions from, 1–2
Deleuze, Gilles
  on repetition, 112
Deppman, Jed, 7, 158, 184
Derricotte, Toi, 260
  engagement with Dickinson, 261–262, 267
  on politics and poetry, 277
  reading of "I took my Power in my Hand –," 263–264
  "Sitting with Myself in the Seton Hall Deli . . . ," 260–261, 263, 276
Derrida, Jacques, 118
description
  in Dickinson online archives, 294–295
  of Dickinson's manuscripts, 280, 294
  relationship to accessibility, 296
  of texts, 280–281, 294
  See also biodescription
description, audio
  of Dickinson's manuscripts, 280–281, 295
  in disability studies, 280–281

  of "Dont put up my Thread & Needle," 280–282
  of texts, 294
diaries
  Dickinson's fascicles and, 222–223, 233
  physical format of, 223
diary writing, nineteenth-century, 234
  among Dickinson's friends and family, 222, 224–227, 230–231, 234
  association with memory, 220–224
  Austin's, 225
  communities of, 222–227
  dangers of, 232–233
  Dickinson on, 220–221, 227, 231
  in Dickinson's poetry, 220–234
  Dickinson's skepticism concerning, 222–223, 233–234
  diverse practices of, 227
  female experience and, 221–222, 234
  gendered associations of, 220, 222, 231
  in "I cautious, scanned my little life," 230
  influence on Dickinson, 233
  Lavinia's, 220, 224–225
  literary status of, 221, 234
  marginalization of, 222, 233
  material formats of, 227
  at Mount Holyoke Female Seminary, 222–224, 230–231
  in nineteenth-century culture, 220, 222, 233
  prevalence of, 227
  purposes of, 227
  relationship-building in, 223–224
  representation in, 220
  scholarship on, 221–222
  self-scrutiny in, 223–224
  sharing in, 230–231
  Todd's, 225–227
Dickinson, Austin, 140
  affair with Loomis, 225
  diary of, 225, 235
  Dickinson's correspondence with, 220, 224–225, 231
Dickinson, Emily
  agency of, 3, 5, 288
  as American poet, 270
  anthropocentrism of, 63
  astronomical language of, 184
  authorial self of, 156
  and being poor-in-the-world, 122–123, 127
  biopoetics of, 119–120, 123–127, 132–133
  biosemiotics and, 132–133
  Calvinism of, 192
  canonization of, 258–259
  Civil War poetry and, 24–25, 116, 164
  collaborative poetics of, 18–31

confinement of, 205
connections to science, 155–156
consumption of poetry, 35
correspondence, 20, 119
  account of father, 177
  Austin Dickinson, 220, 224–225, 231
  Bowles, 190
  choices in, 225
  circulation of poems in, 221
  Civil War in, 164
  concerning eye ailment, 101–102
  Gilbert, 48
  Gould, 118
  Higginson, 39–41, 94, 101, 130, 145, 164, 190
  Huntington, 102, 243–244, 248
  Lord, 116
  Lyman, 177–178
  Norcross sisters, 287
  Root, 42
  Sarah Tuckerman, 140
  Todd, 190
  travel in, 190
  volcanos in, 177–178
creative process of, 6
cultural engagement of, 3, 222
cultural myths concerning, 3
decentering of, 2–5, 12
destabilization of, 3, 5–6
deviance of, 3
diary communities of, 222–227
and eco-mimesis, 136
economic privilege of, 99
education, 48
  at Amherst Academy, 41, 169, 189–190, 288
  foreign studies in, 189–190
  international aspects of, 189
  at Mount Holyoke Female Seminary, 170, 174, 189–190, 223
  in science, 158
  through poetry, 41
engagement with world, 4, 43, 85, 118, 122
and environmental literary history, 136
environmental subjectivity of, 123–127, 130–132
epistemological thought of, 184
exceptionality of, 34
in ExhibitBE, 1–2
experience of gender roles, 205, 269
eye problems of, 101–103, 115–116, 287
feminism of, 3, 258
feminist scholarship on, 12, 85–97
gender stereotypes concerning, 259–260
"generic" aspects of, 33–45
George Moses Horton and, 204–216
and global aesthetic heritage, 200

haptic textual engagement of, 292
Higginson's depiction of, 131–132
historical ecopoetics of, 136–148
historical/political study of, 6
humanism of, 3–4
identification with the exploited, 197
influence on women's poetry, 258–260
influences of, 233
intellectual interests of, 6
intellectual sovereignty of, 118
interiority of, 221
isolation of, 3, 17–19
literary culture and, 223
marginality of, 1
material formats of, 4, 18, 21–29, 31, 165, 223
meaning-making by, 34, 124
memory receptacles of, 227–233
metaphors of, 54, 116, 119–120
modes of communication for, 29
mythologies of, 3
naturalism of, 135, 195
networks of, 69
as New England poet, 124, 187–188
and nineteenth-century poetry, 30, 33–35, 41
nineteenth-century women poets and, 30
and nineteenth-century world, 3, 6, 148, 163, 205, 251, 261
and non-canonical women poets, 217
opinions
  abolition, 216–217, 276
  animals, 129, 133
  Civil War, 64, 218
  diary-keeping, 220–222, 227, 231, 233–234
  education, 40
  ephemera, 287
  geography, 175
  heaven, 178–183
  her home, 177–178
  imagination, 50–63
  memory, 227
  metaphor, 54, 119–120
  nineteenth-century women, 99
  reading, 38–40
  thinking, 63
  Transcendentalism, 166
originality of, 33
outer archives of, 233–234
personal papers of, 220
persona of, 222, 234
as poet of negation, 33–34, 72
poetry
  absence in, 143
  accessibility of, 11, 248, 250, 285
  Africa in, 198–199

Dickinson, Emily (cont.)
    African American culture and, 264
    afterlife in, 113
    animal, 119
    anthropomorphism in, 62
    Arabic translations of, 300–304, 307
    Asia in, 197–198
    autobiographical aspects of, 222
    biblical allegory in, 119
    biodescriptive, 145
    bioregional reading of, 140, 143
    birdsong in, 134
    blackness in, 218
    bobolinks in, 143
    bodily limitation in, 284–285
    bodily withdrawal in, 35
    boundary crossing in, 158
    braille editions, 292
    camaraderie in, 97
    circulation in letters, 218, 221
    Civil War in, 24–25, 27–28, 164
    colonialism in, 196–197
    communications technologies in, 50
    compressed space of, 8
    confinement in, 8, 208
    cross-species relationships in, 122
    dashes in, 291, 298
    death in, 272, 305–306
    destabilization of meaning in, 3
    diary-keeping in, 8, 220–234
    digital concordances of, 257
    disability in, 282–283, 287, 293–294, 296
    distance from conflict in, 32
    distance in, 199
    doggerel, 118–120, 124, 131
    early, 118
    editorial intervention for, 291–296
    editorial theory for, 282–283
    electricity in, 62–63
    enslavement in, 196, 205, 216
    environmental/human media in, 60–61
    environment in, 62, 130–131, 134, 136–137, 144, 161, 184
    epistemological experience through, 137
    everyday life and, 156, 191
    external environments of, 62
    flowers accompanying, 144
    force in, 7, 155
    foreign imagery in, 189
    foreign places in, 8
    future critical reception of, 77, 240–241
    geography in, 8, 168–184
    heaven in, 179–183
    on her dog, 119, 133
    hills in, 140
    historical-constructivist critique of, 240
    human/nonhuman boundary in, 162
    impermanence of, 285–287
    individual experience in, 201
    instruction in, 179
    intellectual context of, 156
    interiority of, 189
    interiors in, 168–169
    isolation in, 17–18
    lack of development in, 104
    Latin America in, 194–197
    listening to, 293
    lyric pain of, 7
    lyric reading of, 66–67, 265–266
    mass media and, 50–53, 62
    memory in, 78, 227–233
    meters of, 67
    modes of composition, 291–292
    movement and immobility in, 204–206
    multiple mediums of, 294, 296
    mutuality in, 119–121
    names in, 144–145, 202
    national metaphor in, 119
    nature-culture matrix of, 142
    nature in, 140, 156, 158, 161–163
    "New Englandly" aspects of, 124
    new materialism and, 149, 156
    nonhuman world in, 119–120, 136–137
    non-verbal forms of, 294
    normalization of texts, 282, 289–291
    ocular instability in, 116
    oral forms for, 293–294
    other worlds in, 188–189
    overlapping connections in, 166
    pain in, 100–101, 114
    pairing in, 119
    participatory poetics of, 144–145
    physics in, 155–166
    political scope of, 6
    pronoun ambiguities of, 215
    as proto-ecological, 136
    race in, 204, 207, 216–217, 260–263, 266, 269
    racial/ethnic stereotypes in, 8
    receptions of, 8, 187, 254
    recovery of, 285
    relationality of, 148, 163
    religious aspects of, 113
    renunciation in, 122
    repetition in, 104–105
    scientific inquiry in, 178
    secular/postsecular interpretations of, 165
    self-critical strand of, 79
    sequences in, 163

silences in, 67, 75–77, 273
slavery in, 196, 205, 216, 261–262
social/cultural engagement of, 69
sonic features of, 6–7, 66–79, 294
sonic files of, 293
subject-world relations of, 121–122
substance and form in, 104
suffering in, 100
temporality in, 104, 113, 199
textual idiosyncrasies of, 283
thought projects in, 184
titles of, 145
transference in, 162–164
transformation narratives concerning, 97
transitive aspects of, 137
transnational, 189–201
Tuckerman's poetry and, 140
Umwelt of, 124
universal design standards for, 296
the unknowable in, 178
vision metaphors of, 116
visual aspects of, 54, 66, 292, 294
volcano tropes in, 169, 171–174, 184–185
whiteness in, 216, 262–263
world-making in, 119
posthumanistic study of, 5–8, 120–123, 127–129, 132, 156, 161, 165–166
powers of recognition, 35
productivity of, 142
racial/class politics of, 5–6
reading, 234
  ecohistorical, 139
  international affairs, 190
  of Longfellow, 37
  opinions on, 38–40
  travel writing, 190
reading habits, 183, 190
reclusiveness of, 132, 287
rejection of publication, 207
relationship to music, 67, 72
religious doctrine of, 68
selfhood of, 3, 118
sensory perception of, 139–140
servants
  African American, 278–279
  Irish, 190
social/cultural engagement of, 69
sovereignty of, 85, 87, 89
studies
  animal, 7
  botanical, 144, 150
  foreign, 189–190
  ornithology, 125–126
stylistic influences on, 41–43

Tuckerman and, 139–140
understanding of permeability, 141
as unexceptional Other, 5
unfamiliar contexts of, 2
white privilege of, 205
women of color and, 96, 259–260, 265
women's expression and, 221
workshop practices of, 20
writing practice of, 285–288
See also archives, Dickinson's; fascicles, Dickinson's; manuscripts, Dickinson's; online archives, Dickinson's
Dickinson, Lavinia, 177–178, 224–225
  diary of, 220
Dickinson, Susan Huntington, 179
  Dickinson's collaboration with, 20, 244
  Dickinson's correspondence with, 102, 243–244, 248
Dickinson Electronic Archives (Smith), 243, 247–248
  digital articles of, 248
  exhibitions of, 248
  See also online archives, Dickinson's
digitization
  democratization in, 295
  of Dickinson's handwriting, 252
  See also computer analysis; online archives, Dickinson's
Dimock, Wai Chee, 6
  on aesthetic heritage, 200
  on American international studies, 187–188
  on deep time, 199
  on planetary unity, 11
  on temporal measurement, 201
  Through Other Continents, 10–11
disabilities
  accessibility to Dickinson and, 283
  Dickinson as poet of, 282–283, 287, 293–294, 296
  effacing of, 288
  effect on manuscript culture, 283–284
  readers', 9, 282
  textual condition and, 281
  as textual experience, 288
disabilities, print, 283–284, 291–292
  among Dickinson's readers, 292–296
  braille for, 292
  cognitive, 283–284
  physical, 283
  reading formats for, 292–293
  sonic formats for, 293
disability studies, 7, 103
  audio description in, 280–281
  Dickinson and, 7, 282, 294

disability studies (cont.)
　editorial theory and, 281–288
　overcoming narrative of, 288
　textual idiosyncrasies in, 281
　universal design in, 293, 296
disidentification, 264–265
dis-reading, lyric, 9, 265–266
　agency in, 267
　Brooks's, 268–269
　of Dickinson, 12, 260, 265–267, 272–274
　by women of color, 266–267
　See also poetry, lyric
Donne, John
　"A Valediction Forbidding Mourning," 73
"Dont put up my Thread & Needle" (F681), 86–87
　audio description of, 280–282
　creativity metaphors of, 87
　crip editorial practice of, 288–291
　dashes in, 291
　editorial practices for, 288–291
　female subjectivity in, 87, 91
　"I cannot dance opon my Toes" and, 88, 93
　interpretations of, 87
　layout of, 295
　levels of representation in, 289
　manuscript of, 87, 280
　object-oriented feminism on, 86, 89
　objects of, 87, 89, 91–93
　resistance to subjectification in, 92
　sovereign poet-speaker of, 87, 89
　stitches in, 87, 98, 291, 293
　subjunctive and actual in, 92
　transformative potential of, 91–93
　visual impairment in, 288–289, 291, 296
Doppler Effect, 156
Doty, Mark, 80
　on poetic sensorium, 69
Douglas, Jeremy, 251
Dove, Rita, 259
Du Bois, W. E. B.
　The Souls of Black Folk, 269

Early English Books Online
　page images of, 246
Earth
　deep time of, 199
　temporal expanse of, 200
ecocriticism
　in Dickinson scholarship, 184
　in historical ecopoetics, 138
　human/nonhuman in, 138
　See also ecopoetics, historical
ecomimesis, 149

Dickinson's resistance to, 136
ecopoetics, historical, 7, 149
　bioregion in, 139
　crisis of relevance, 138
　Dickinson's, 136–148
　ecocriticism in, 138
　emphasis on content, 138
　of English romantics, 143–144
　historical poetics and, 137, 139
　poetic agency in, 137–138
　poets' use of, 137
　reception in, 137
　relationality in, 147–148
　tenets of, 138
　of Tuckerman's poetry, 142
　See also ecocriticism
editorial practice, crip, 9, 284, 288, 291–292
　of "Dont put up my Thread & Needle," 288–291
　meaning of "crip" in, 297
　readers' knowledge in, 292
editorial theory
　for Dickinson's poetry, 282–283
　disability studies and, 281–288
education
　Dickinson on, 40
　nineteenth-century, 41
electrical lighting
　in Amherst, 56
　in "The farthest Thunder that I heard," 56
　See also technology
electricity
　aesthetic, 57
　in Dickinson's poems, 62–63
　illumination and, 56
　imagination and, 57
　in lightning, 53
　in "The Lightning playeth – all the while –," 53–54
　metaphors of, 57
　nineteenth-century discoveries in, 156–157
　in telegraph lines, 53
electromagnetic induction, 156
Emerson, Lori
　Reading Writing Interfaces, 255
Emerson, Ralph Waldo, 132
　atomic theory in, 160
　"Books," 38
　on imagination, 49–50
　interest in physics, 158
　"The Poet," 49
　on relationship to nature, 205
　on transparent eyeball, 116
　Tuckerman and, 144

Emily Dickinson Archive (Harvard University)
   See online archives, Dickinson's (Harvard University)
Emily Dickinson Collection
   See online archives, Dickinson's (Amherst College)
Emily Dickinson International Society, 85
Emily Dickinson Journal, 85
Emily Dickinson Lexicon, 257
enslaved people, female
   imagery of, 214
Envelope Poems (Werner and Bervin), 66
environment
   deforestation of, 142–143, 150
   in Dickinson's poetry, 62, 130–131, 134, 136–137, 144, 161, 184
   meaning-making in, 124
   planetary thought on, 138–139
   twenty-first century problems with, 161
environmental relations
   subjectivity of, 126–127
equality
   among living creatures, 129
e-Readers
   for disabled readers, 295
Erkkila, Betsy, 99
eroticism
   Dickinson and, 7
   of pedagogical death, 40
essentialism
   biological, 125
eternity
   phenomenology of, 2
Europe
   as center of civilization, 200
   Dickinson's references to, 191, 193
exceptionalism, American, 187
exclusion
   binary structures of, 4
ExhibitBE (New Orleans, 2014), 1
explorers, Latin American
   in Dickinson's poetry, 196
"Exultation is the going" (F143)
   Arabic translation of, 307

Faraday, Michael, 156
   "On the Conservation of Force," 158
   theory of force, 157, 166
Farr, Judith, 75, 159
Fascicle 3 (Dickinson)
   collaborative logic of, 23–24
   community in, 24
   death in, 23
Fascicle 16 (Dickinson), 25–27

Fascicle 32 (Dickinson)
   construction of, 280
Fascicle 37 (Dickinson), 29
fascicles
   exchange as gifts, 22
fascicles, Dickinson's, 21–29
   access to her poetry through, 31, 231
   collaboration in, 21–23, 29–30
   community in, 24, 27–28
   construction of, 22, 24, 31, 233
   diaries and, 222–223, 233
   discovery of, 21–22
   imagined recipients of, 22
   materials of, 21, 223
Felski, Rita, 142
   on deforestation, 150
Felstiner, John
   Can Poetry Save the Earth?, 138
feminism
   Dickinson as progenitor of, 258
   material, 86
   recovery of nineteenth-century authors, 46
feminism, object-oriented (OOF), 98
   "being things" in, 91
   on "Dont put up my Thread & Needle," 86, 89
   experimentation in, 91, 93, 96
   "I cannot dance upon my Toes" and, 93
   intersectional, 96
   and object-oriented ontology, 89
   sneering in, 96
   in study of Dickinson, 7, 85–97
   on subject and object, 91
   transformative potential of, 92–93
   See also ontology, object-oriented
Feminist Critics Read Emily Dickinson (1983), 85
feminist theory
   Dickinson and, 7
figuration, 115
   of chronic pain, 7
figuration, Dickinson's, 115
   the material and, 131
   of pain, 100, 103–104, 107
   of "'Twas like a Maelstrom, with a notch," 105–107
   of "We send the wave to find the wave," 107–108
Finch, Annie, 70
Finnerty, Páraic, 8, 31
   Emily Dickinson's Shakespeare, 20
   on racial difference, 216
Fletcher, Angus
   on environment poems, 63–64
   A New Theory for American Poetry, 62

flowers
  accompanying Dickinson's poetry, 144
Flynt, Eudocia, 75
folk ballads
  meter of, 68
Folsom, Ed, 217
force
  connecting power of, 155
  in Dickinson's poetry, 7, 155
  in nature, 155, 158
  in nineteenth-century poetry, 158
Ford, Karen Jackson
  Gender and the Poetics of Excess, 275
formalism
  in Dickinson scholarship, 136–137
Foucault, Leon
  pendulum of, 156
"Four trees – opon a solitary Acre –" (F778), 161–162
  unknowable nature in, 162
François, Anne-Lise, 33
Franklin, R. W., 47, 56, 247
  on Dickinson's handwriting, 255
  on early Dickinson, 118
  The Manuscript Books of Emily Dickinson, 243, 280
  normalization of Dickinson's text, 289–291
  The Poems of Emily Dickinson: Variorum Edition, 244–247, 283
Fretwell, Erica, 216–218
Friedlander, Benjamin, 276
"If I could bribe them by a Rose" (F176), 201
Fulton, Alice, 259
"Further in Summer than the Birds" (F895), 109
Fuss, Diana, 115

Gelpi, Albert
  "Emily Dickinson's Long Shadow," 275
gender
  in Dickinson scholarship, 85, 97
geography, Dickinson's, 8, 168–184
  Amherst in, 168
  displacement of self in, 192
  European analogies in, 191
  external world in, 168
  function of, 168
  global references in, 189–190
  heaven in, 168–169, 178–179, 181–183
  implementation of, 176
  at Mount Holyoke Female Seminary, 174
  sources for, 168–171
  specificity of, 177
  subjectivity in, 178
  in "volcano" poems, 171–175
  See also volcano poems, Dickinson's

geography, nineteenth-century
  as academic discipline, 171
  accessibility of, 171
  American literature and, 185
  Dickinson's attitude toward, 175
  discourse of, 169, 175, 184
  and nature of heaven, 178–179
  primers, 169
  representative texts of, 169–171
  travel writing and, 170
Gerhardt, Christine, 136
  on bioregionalism, 134
Gibbons, Reginald, 80
gifts
  culture of, 22, 47
Gilbert, Sandra M., 85, 87
  on renunciation, 122
Gilbert, Susan
  Dickinson's correspondence with, 48
Giles, Paul
  on American international studies, 188
  local and foreign in, 188
Gilgamesh (epic), 305
Gilmore, Paul, 50
  on electrical metaphors, 57
  on telegraph, 50
globalization, Dickinson's, 8, 187–201
  alternating forces in, 188
  exoticism in, 199
  fluidity in, 201
  in her reading, 190
  international independence in, 189
  in "A Route of Evanescence," 198–199
  subjectivity in, 194
  traversing of globe in, 201
  in "We see – Comparatively –," 194
  See also transnationalism, Dickinson's
globalization, nineteenth-century, 187–188
  Dickinson's reading concerning, 190
  normalization of, 189
"Going to Him! Happy Letter!" (F277), 44–45
  address to letter in, 45
  desire for communication in, 45
  emotional sincerity in, 45
  fear of unresponsiveness in, 45
  material form in, 45
  recognition in, 44–45
  versions of, 48
Goodrich, Samuel Griswold, 171
Gorgeous Nothings, The (Werner and Bervin), 66, 77, 249–250, 285
  editorial practice of, 285–287
  late poems in, 285
Gould, George H.
  Dickinson's correspondence with, 118

Index

graffiti artists, 1
Gray, Janet, 217
Gubar, Susan, 85, 87
  on renunciation, 122
Guthrie, James R., 115–116

Habegger, Alfred, 287
Haitian Revolution (1791–1804), 196–197, 216
Hampson, Alfred Leete
  Further Poems of Emily Dickinson, 289
  Unpublished Poems of Emily Dickinson, 292
Hamraie, Aimi, 293
handwriting, Dickinson's
  affective investments in, 241, 245
  agency in, 288
  assumptions concerning, 239
  as calligraphic orthography, 288
  chronology of, 242–243, 255
  digital reproductions of, 252
  embossed recreations of, 295–296
  emotion in, 242–243, 245
  entrenched attitudes toward, 241
  frottage of, 252
  in online archives, 239–240
  value as property, 247
Haraway, Donna
  on companion species, 121
  "A Cyborg Manifesto," 13, 64
  posthumanism of, 133
Harjo, Joy, 259
Hartman, Saidiya, 218
Harvard University
  Dickinson permission policy, 248, 250, 256
  ownership claims of, 248, 256–257
  See also online archive, Dickinson's (Harvard University)
Harvard University Press
  Dickinson permission policy, 248, 250
Hassan, Adanan, 299
Hassan, Naseer, 9–12, 306
  "Because I could not stop for death" translation, 9, 301–303
  Emily Dickinson: Selected Poems and Critical Articles, 305
  "Exultation is the going" translation, 307
  "Surgeons must be very careful" translation, 307
Hawthorne, Nathaniel, 105, 171
Hayles, N. Katherine, 120
H.D.
  Dickinson's influence on, 259
heaven
  nineteenth-century inquiry into, 178
heaven, Dickinson's, 178–183

earthly counterparts of, 179
geography of, 168–169, 178–179, 181–183
  in her poetry, 179–183
home and, 183
primers for, 180
scientific inquiry and, 178
Heidegger, Martin
  on relationship to world, 121–122
Henderson, Desirée, 8
Henderson, Stephen, 278
Henry, Joseph, 157
Higginson, Thomas Wentworth, 17
  abolitionist views of, 276
  affiliation with *Nation*, 307
  on Amherst environs, 140
  Civil War service of, 164
  depiction of Dickinson, 131–132
  Dickinson's correspondence with, 39–41, 94, 101, 130, 145, 164, 190
  on Dickinson's handwriting, 131
  on Dickinson's meter, 68
  naturalist studies of, 135
  normalization of Dickinson's texts, 282
  ornithological studies of, 131
hills
  in Dickinson's poetry, 140
Hirshfield, Alan, 166
"his mistress's rights he doth defend –" (L34), 118–119
history, environmental, 149
  decline in, 138
  earth history and, 138
Hitchcock, Edward, 178
  The Religion of Geology, 160
  teaching of geography, 171
Holmes, Oliver Wendell
  on mass communication, 50
  on reading, 39
Horton, George Moses, 8, 204–216
  circulation of manuscripts, 207
  enslavement of, 205–206
  "Fearful Traveller in the Haunted Castle, The," 208–211
    animality in, 213–214
    comic ending of, 210, 214–216
    gender identities in, 213
    immobility in, 211
    movement and immobility in, 208
    resistance to slavery in, 208–209, 215
    slaves' fear in, 209–210
    "The Soul has Bandaged moments –" and, 211, 213–214
    speaker of, 209
    tonal shifts in, 213
    Turner rebellion in, 209–211, 213

Horton, George Moses (cont.)
    white woman's perspective in, 215
    Hope of Liberty, The, 206
    life of, 218
    paternalistic patronage of, 207
    as poet-for-hire, 206–208, 213, 217
    Poetical Works, 206
        courtly love in, 208
        historical references in, 208
        race in, 216
        resistance to slavery in, 206, 208
        speakers of, 208
    poetic persona of, 206–207
    Poetic Works
        movement and immobility in, 204–206, 208
    student audiences of, 210
    twentieth-century editions of, 217
Howe, Susan, 66
    Dickinson's influence on, 259
    My Emily Dickinson, 243
Hsu, Li-hsin
    on idea of the "Orient," 197
Hubbard, Melanie, 223
Hughes, Langston, 261, 276
Hunter, Jane, 224
Hussein, Saddam, 9, 299
    See also Baathist regime (Iraq)
hymns
    meter of, 68

"I cannot dance upon my Toes" (F381B)
    artist's subjectivity in, 89
    "Dont put up my Thread & Needle" and, 88, 93
    female artist of, 88
    feminist politics of, 94
    fullness in, 94
    helplessness in, 94
    narrative of, 93
    object-oriented feminism and, 93
    objects of, 88–89, 93–94
    transcendence in, 94
"I cant tell you – but you feel it" (F164), 179–180
    Peter Parley series in, 180
    saints in, 179–180
"I cautious, scanned my little life" (F175), 228–231, 235
    autobiographical memory in, 228–229
    barn trope of, 229–231
    diary form in, 230
    gendered space in, 232
    lost memories in, 230
    speaker of, 232
    survival of memory in, 230

"I could bring You Jewels – had I a mind to –" (F726), 195–196
    Bobadilla family in in, 196
    speaker-trader of, 195
    transcontinental movement in, 195
"I dreaded that first Robin, so" (F347)
    slant rhyme of, 267
"I dwell in Possibility" (F466), 141
"If any sink, assure that this, now standing –" (F616), 164–165
    transference in, 165
"I felt a Funeral, in my Brain" (F340), 80
    aural aspects of, 74
    beating in, 74
    repetitiveness in, 74
    rhyme in, 75
    sensorium of, 74
    silence in, 74–75
    subjective being in, 74
"I have a Bird in spring" (F4), 134
"I know where Wells grow – Droughtless Wells" (F695)
    heaven in, 179
"I like to see it lap the Miles" (F383)
    sound in, 73
imagination
    circuitry of, 6
    Emerson on, 49–50
    eye trope for, 49
    Kant on, 49
    mobility of, 49–51
    poetic, 49–50
    romantic electricity of, 50
    Transcendentalists on, 49–50
imagination, Dickinson's, 50–63
    adaptation to media environments, 53
    circuitry of, 62
    communication technologies and, 50, 61
    delocalized, 51
    elemental and cultural in, 62
    environmental, 60–61
    externalization of, 51
    mass media and, 51–53
    media pathways of, 50–51
    mediated, 51
    networks of, 50
    object and subject in, 62
    observation and invention in, 62
    present and future in, 61
    travel in, 190
immigration, nineteenth-century, 190
impairment
    in Dickinson's poetics, 288
    See also disabilities

Indicator, The (Amherst College)
  Dickinson's poetry in, 118
"In Ebon Box, when years have flown" (F180)
  memorial objects in, 228
informatics, 64
International Reception of Emily Dickinson, The (2009), 188
"In this short Life" (F1292A)
  envelope of, 286
  fragmentary nature of, 286–287
  legibility for blind readers, 296
  right to expire in, 287
  use of pencil for, 286–287
"In thy long Paradise of Light" (F1145)
  isolation in, 17
Iraq
  Dickinson's readers in, 9–10, 299, 306
  readers of American poetry in, 299–300
  See also Baathist regime; Hussein, Saddam
"I think the Hemlock likes to stand" (F400), 191–192
  binaries of, 192
  racial ideologies of, 191
  transnational perspective of, 192
"It is an honorable Thought" (F1115)
  Egyptian civilization in, 200–201
"It knew no lapse, nor Diminution –" (F568), 162, 164
  change in, 164
  transference in, 162
"I took my Power in my Hand –" (F660)
  Derricotte's reading of, 263–264
"I went to Heaven –" (F577), 179
"I held a Jewel in my fingers" (F261)
  gem imagery of, 227–228
  memory in, 227–228
"I would not paint – a picture –" (F348), 71–73
  balloon trope of, 73
  metal trope of, 72–73
  meter of, 73
  painting in, 72
  rhyme in, 73
  sound in, 71–72

Jackson, Helen Hunt, 170
  Dickinson's correspondence with, 20
Jackson, Leon, 217
Jackson, Virginia, 6, 10, 35
  on Dickinson's lyricism, 66–67, 75–76
  on Dickinson's manuscripts, 240
  on figuration, 109
  on lyric poetry, 79, 255, 265, 277
Jacobs, Harriet, 211, 218
Al Jayyusi, Salmaa Al Khadraa, 306
Johnson, Thomas H., 87, 288

  on Dickinson's eye problems, 101
  normalization of Dickinson's text, 283, 289–291
  variorum edition of, 242, 247, 282
Jordan, June, 261, 276
Juan Fernandez island
  remoteness of, 177
  volcano of, 177
jue-ju (Chinese quatrain), 270, 279
Juhasz, Suzanne, 85

Kant, Immanuel
  on imagination, 49
Katz, Adam, 98
Keats, John
  on negative capability, 33
  "Ode to Autumn," 143–144
Kern, Robert
  on ecomimesis, 149
Kerns, Michael
  on Dickinson's education, 158
Kershner, George, 283
al-Khāl, Yusuf, 300
King, Martin Luther, Jr., 1
Knickerbocker, Scott, 136
Kohler, Michelle, 118
  on Dickinson's metaphoric vision, 54, 116
  on Dickinson's ocular poetics, 116
  on estrangement from landscape, 116
  on imagination, 49
Kumbier, Alana
  Ephemeral Material, 20–21

labor, industrial
  deadening, 73
Laird, Holly
  Women Coauthors, 18
Latin America
  in Dickinson's poetry, 194–197
  in "A Route of Evanescence," 198
  slavery in, 196–197
Lejeune, Philippe, 221–222
lightning
  electricity in, 53
  in "The Lightning playeth – all the while –" (F595A), 55
Linton, Simi, 288
literary imagination
  new thought on, 6
literature, American
  culture of, 223
  geography and, 185
  international studies on, 187–188
  nationalist, 188
  transamerican, 194
  See also poetry, American

locale
  in production of texts, 7
Loeffelholz, Mary, 251
London, Bette
  Writing Double, 18
Longfellow, Henry Wadsworth, 33, 40
  conventionality of, 36
  Dickinson's reading of, 37
Lord, Judge
  Dickinson's correspondence with, 116
Lorde, Audre
  "Coal," 274
  Dickinson's influence on, 259
Luciano, Dana, 115
Lyman, Joseph
  Dickinson's correspondence with, 177–178

MacLeish, Archibald, 300
  on Dickinson, 306
  Poetry and Experience, 299–301, 306
Majallat Shi'r (literary magazine), 300
man
  "world-forming," 121
Manheim, Daniel, 92
Manovich, Lev, 251
manuscript culture, nineteenth-century
  Dickinson's response to, 223
  scholarship on, 221
  traditions of, 221
  women's, 221
manuscripts
  diplomatic transcription of, 256
  materiality of, 255
manuscripts, Dickinson's, 66–67, 148
  affective experiences of, 241, 245
  at Amherst, 247
  as artistic structures, 243
  audio descriptions of, 280–281, 295
  circulation of, 207, 215, 218
  commodification of, 241, 247, 249–250
  description of, 280, 294
  Dickinson's personhood in, 242
  as drawings, 243
  on envelopes, 66, 77, 252
  facsimiles of, 66, 285, 288
  at Harvard, 247
  images of, 239
  impermanence of, 285–287
  as intellectually generative, 245
  intimacy with Dickinson through, 241–242, 250, 254
  materiality of, 69, 136, 145, 240, 252
  physical interaction with, 295
  possession and control of, 247, 256–257
  posthumous division of, 247–248
  and readers with print disabilities, 292
  recovery of, 285
  resistance to rehabilitation, 287
  scholarship on, 221, 239–240
  smaller collections of, 256
  substitutive claims for, 242
  textual idiosyncrasies of, 283
  textual/gestural dimensions of, 241
  Todd on, 242
  use of pencil in, 286–287
  visual aspects of, 67, 294
  visual field of, 243
  See also archives, Dickinson's; fascicles, Dickinson's; online archives, Dickinson's
Maron, Jean-Luc, 103
Marrs, Cody, 8, 25, 58
  on Dickinson's conception of poetry, 31
  on Dickinson's distance from conflict, 32
  on Dickinson's privacy, 27
Martin, Wendy
  on Dickinson's renunciation, 122
Marvel, Ik, 33
Massachusetts
  deforestation of, 142–143
  ecology of, 139
  reforestation of, 147
materialism, new, 13, 86
  Dickinson and, 98, 149
materiality
  of books, 47
  of collaboration, 21
  of memory, 233
  of zines, 21
materiality, Dickinson's, 18, 165
  of "The Birds reported from the South –," 29
  of Dickinson's manuscripts, 69, 136, 145, 240, 252
  figuration and, 131
  formats of, 4, 21–29, 31, 223
  scholarship on, 96
  of "Some keep the Sabbath," 124
material objects
  worldless, 121
matter
  in feminist discourse, 86
  and sovereign humanist subject, 86
McAbee, Leslie, 197–198
McGann, Jerome
  Rossetti Archive, 246
  on textual condition, 281
McIntosh, James, 68, 78
McSweeney, Kerry, 115
meaning-making
  and being-in-the-world, 7
  Dickinson's, 34, 124

Index

media
  as communication, 53
  as environment, 57
media, elemental, 52–53, 55
  and cultural media, 62
  voicelessness of, 53
media, mass
  during Civil War, 50
  in Dickinson's poetics, 50–53
  effect on creation, 64
  as nervous network, 50–51
  nineteenth-century, 50–51
Melville, Herman, 105
  atomic theory in, 160
memory
  association with diary writing, 220–224
  role of objects in, 228
  spatial qualities of, 222–223
  textual qualities of, 222–223
memory, Dickinson's, 227–233
  in "As Sleigh Bells seem in Summer", 78
  autobiographical, 228–229
  dangers of, 231–233
  of the deceased, 228
  of herself, 228
  in "I held a Jewel in my fingers", 227–228
  materiality of, 232–233
  receptacles of, 227–233
  skepticism concerning, 227
  in textual form, 233
  in "That sacred Closet when you sweep –," 231–233
metaphors
  Dickinson's, 54, 116, 119–120
  vehicle and tenor of, 78
meter
  cultural aspects of, 70
  narrative, 68
  of prayer, 68
meter, Dickinson's, 67
  of "All the letters I can write," 76
  choice of, 69
  destabilizing effect of, 68
  irregularity of, 68
  of "I would not paint – a picture –," 73
  resistance to iambic pentameter, 70
  tetrameter, 67
#MeToo movement, 99
Michaels, Walter Benn, 243, 255
Miles, Josephine, 259
Miles, Susan
  on Dickinson's prosody, 68
Mill, John Stuart

  on lyric poetry, 277
  on solitude, 19
Miller, Cristanne, 47, 257
  on Dickinson's foreign imagery, 189
  on Dickinson's meter, 68, 75
  on nineteenth-century music, 69–70
  on the "Orient," 197
  Reading in Time, 67
Mills, Mara, 284
"Mine – by the Right of the White Election!" (F411), 262
Moore, Marianne, 259
"More Life – went out – when He went" (F415), 193
Morris, Leslie A., 245
Morrison, Toni
  on enslavement, 216
  Playing in the Dark, 204
Morse, Jedidiah
  American Universal Geography, 170
  ministerial career of, 171
Morton, Timothy
  on ecological thought, 149
  on eco-mimesis, 136
Mount Holyoke Female Seminary
  diary writing at, 222–224, 230–231
  Dickinson at, 170, 174, 189–190, 223
  manuscript culture of, 223
  texts assigned at, 185
Mullaney, Clare, 7, 9
Muñoz, José Esteban, 260
  Disidentifications, 264
Murray, Aífe
  Maid as Muse, 96
music, nineteenth-century
  birdsong in, 75–76
  Dickinson's relationship to, 67, 72
  poetry and, 70
  popularity of, 69–70
"My friend must be a Bird –" (F71)
  death in, 24
"Myself can read the Telegrams" (F1049A), 51–52
  failure of imagination in, 51
  individual and mass in, 51
  mobile information in, 52
  natural and cultural media in, 52
  telegrams in, 51–52
  world's motions in, 52

names
  in Dickinson's poetry, 144–145, 202
nationalism, black American, 277
nature
  accuracy in writing of, 144
  comprehension of, 162

nature (cont.)
  and cultural circuitry, 57, 62
  cultural networks imposed on, 50
  Dickinson's interest in, 158
  in Dickinson's poetry, 140, 156, 158, 161–163
  "end of," 161
  force in, 155, 158
  harnassing of, 54
  nineteenth-century theory of, 136
  in Young's *Complaint*, 42–44
  See also physics
Nayar, Pramod K., 4, 10
negation
  in Dickinson's poetry, 33–34, 72
  poets of, 33
Networked Recluse, The (Morgan Library, 2017), 69
networks
  Dickinson's, 69
  women's, 69
New Criticism
  African American critics and, 277
  close reading hermeneutic of, 265
  women of color and, 265–266
New England
  association with Europe, 192
  in Dickinson's poetics, 124, 187–188
New Historicism
  historical poetics and, 138
  human/nonhuman in, 138
newspapers
  telegraph bulletins in, 52
Noble, Marianne, 114
Noble, Mark, 160
"No Bobolink – reverse His Singing" (F766), 143
nonhuman, the
  atomic theory and, 160–161
  in Dickinson's poetry, 119–120, 136–137
  other as, 5
  production of meaning, 7
  subjectivity of, 120
Norcross sisters, 48
  Dickinson's correspondence with, 287
Norton Anthology of Modern and Contemporary Poetry
  Dickinson in, 258
"Not in this World to see his face –" (F435), 43–44
  child's primer trope of, 43–44
  life in the world in, 43
  Young's influence in, 43

objects
  democracy of, 90
  as things in themselves, 90
  women as, 90
  See also feminism, object-oriented; ontology, object-oriented
Odums, Brandan "BMike," 1
"Of nearness to her sundered Things" (F337), 27
O'Neil, Joseph D.
  on *Umwelt*, 123
"One Sister have I in the house" (F5), 120
online archives, Dickinson's, 239–254
  as artifacts of present, 240
  collaborative commons in, 295
  curators of, 246
  Dickinson's handwriting in, 239–240
  features for disabled readers, 294
  images of, 246
  influence on literary interpretation, 241
  lyrical response to, 254
  markup language for, 249, 256
  Martha Nell Smith's, 243
  physical descriptions in, 294–295
  readers' interactions with, 250
  reading habits in, 246
  responses to poems in, 240
  scraps in, 294
  strengths of, 239
  structural analysis of, 241
  technologies of, 240–241
  textual apparatus in, 239
  textual information in, 241
  textural dimensions of, 252–253
  See also archives, Dickinson's; computer analysis; *Dickinson Electronic Archives* (Smith); manuscripts, Dickinson's; *Radical Scatters*
online archives, Dickinson's (Amherst College), 8–9, 239
  automated data collection of, 251
  images in, 246, 251–252
  thumbnails of, 246
online archives, Dickinson's (Harvard University), 239, 254
  as companion to published editions, 246–247
  e-texts in, 251
  features for disabled readers, 295
  gestural interface of, 253–254
  images of, 246, 251–252
  launch of, 256
"On my volcano grows the Grass" (F1743), 175–177
  appearance of volcano in, 176
  geographic discourse of, 175–176
  nature of volcano in, 176
ontology, object-oriented (OOO), 86, 98

human subject and, 89–90
nonhuman world in, 90
objectification in, 90
and object-oriented feminism, 89
praxis of care in, 92
truth claims of, 91
See also feminism, object-oriented
opera
  ballet in, 98
"Opon a Lilac Sea" (F1368), 110–112
  bee of, 111
  claustral space of, 112
  enforced realism of, 112
  figuration of, 111
  pain in, 111
  rhythms of, 112
  syncopations of, 110
  temporality of, 112
Osborne, Gillian, 7–8, 111–112
Other
  nonhuman, 5
"Our lives are Swiss" (F169), 192–193
  alternative selfhood in, 193
  American self-division in, 192

pain
  chronicity of, 7
  duration of, 110
  figuration of, 7, 110
  narrative theory and, 103
  ontologically relational, 110
  phenomenality of, 110
  temporality of, 110
pain, Dickinsonian
  agential vertigo in, 116
  chronicity of, 104, 113
  distance in, 100
  eye problems, 101–103, 115–116, 287
  figuration of, 100, 103–104, 107
  figurative lexicon of, 101
  her poetry and, 102–103
  heterosexualization of, 116
  numbness in, 102–103
  in "A Pang is more conspicuous in Spring," 108–110
  persistence of, 104
  phenomenal field of, 101, 103
  physical, 101
  in physical object-world, 100
  psychical, 100–101
  responsiveness of, 100
  subject-object of, 103
  temporality of, 104
  in "'Twas like a Maelstrom, with a notch," 105

vantage in, 100
in "We send the wave to find the wave," 107–108
Parmar, Nissa, 270
Pass, Gregory, 256
Patterson, Rebecca, 194–195
Pearce, Roy Harvey, 45
pencil
  Dickinson's use of, 286–287
Perlow, Seth, 8–9
permeability
  Dickinson's understanding of, 141
Peter Parley's Geography for Beginners, 169–171, 180
Peter Parley's Universal History on the Basis of Geography, 180
Peters, John Durham, 53, 62
  on electrical environment, 57
  The Marvelous Clouds, 52–53
Peterson, Katie
  on self-scattering, 72
  "Surround Sound," 71
Petrino, Elizabeth, 172
phenomena
  imperceptible, 110
physics, Dickinson's, 155–166
  energy in, 163
  in her correspondence, 164
  human/nonhuman in, 156
  as model for writing, 165
  in nature poems, 158, 162–163
  related motions in, 155
  shaping of poems, 163–164
  in "We pray – to Heaven –," 180
physics, nineteenth-century
  artistic uses of, 157
  discoveries in, 156–158
  Emerson's interest in, 158
  entropy in, 162, 164
  periodical publications, 157
  Thoreau's interest in, 158
  Transcendentalists' interest in, 157–158
  transference in, 157
  See also nature
"Pink – small – and punctual" (F1357)
  biodescription in, 145
planetary intelligence, 138–139, 149
planet earth
  wholeness of, 11
plant-study
  poetical associations of, 150
Plath, Sylvia, 259
Poe, Edgar Allan
  collaborations of, 19

Poems: Second Series (Dickinson, 1891)
   holograph image of, 242
poetics, Dickinson's
   African American poets and,
      204–205
   attention in, 137
   collaborative, 18–30
   Dickinson's control over, 3
   geographic, 168–183
   impairment in, 288
   mediated, 163
   New England in, 124, 187–188
   ocular, 116
   remediation in, 291
   transcendence in, 86, 88–89, 95
poetics, historical, 149
   crisis of reading in, 138
   cultural knowledge in, 138
   emphasis on content, 138
   in interpretation of Dickinson,
      137
   interpretive method of, 137
   New Historicism and, 138
   nineteenth-century, 137
   poetic agency in, 137–138
   time and place in, 147
poetry
   Asian American, 266
   community production of, 27
   Dickinson's conception of, 31
   as embodied activity, 7
   influence of hip-hop on, 79
   negatives in, 46
   nullifications in, 147
   relationships comprised in, 7–8
   relationship to politics, 264
   in *Umwelt*, 124
poetry, African American
   Dickinson and, 204–205
   discursive contexts of, 205
   Whitman and, 261
   See also women of color poets
poetry, American
   antinomianism of, 33
   Dickinson's influence on, 258–259
   Iraqi readers of, 299–300
   people of color and, 266
   protest, 266
poetry, Chinese
   death in, 272
   quatrains, 270, 279
poetry, lyric
   audience of, 277
   Dickinson's as, 184
   John Stuart Mill on, 277

   music in, 67, 79
   pain of, 7
   political purpose of, 277
   reading of, 10
   regenerate, 150
   See also dis-reading, lyric
poetry, nineteenth-century
   bioregional reading of, 139
   collaborative, 30
   conventions of, 33–34
   crisis of reading for, 138
   Dickinson and, 30, 34–35
   Dickinson's consumption of, 35
   environmental, 63–64
   genres of, 158
   innovation in, 68
   loco-descriptive, 145
   molding of social/intellectual life,
      35
   pain in, 36
   relating to world in, 64
   social roles in, 46
   theories of force in, 158
   verse culture of, 40–41
Poet's Seat (Deerfield, Mass.), 140
Pollak, Vivian, 96, 99, 267
Porter, David, 12
Porter, Noah
   Books and Reading, 39
posthumanism, 10, 120
   animal studies and, 120
   decentering of subject, 156
   the human in, 4–5, 122
   materialism of, 4–5
   networks of, 11–12, 156
   origins of, 13
   in study of Dickinson, 5–8, 120–123, 127–129,
      132, 156, 161
   subjectivity and, 120, 130
   technology and, 120
poststructuralism
   Dickinson scholarship and, 118
Pound, Ezra
   Arabic translation of, 300
Pratt, Ruth, 70
Price, Kenneth M., 217
Price, Leah
   How to Do Things with Books in Victorian
      Britain, 47
Primack, Richard B., 150
Prins, Yopie
   on lyric poetry, 265, 277
print disabilities
   readers', 284, 292–296
"Publication – is the Auction" (F788)

print marketplace in, 207
slavery in, 261–262, 276
whiteness in, 207, 218
Pugh, Christina, 6–7
Putzi, Jennifer, 5

queer phenomenology, 7
queers of color
  sense of self, 264
queer theory
  Dickinson and, 7

race
  in Dickinson's work, 204, 207, 216–217, 260–263, 266, 269
  nineteenth-century ideologies of, 216
race theory, critical, 205
racial politics, U.S., 10
racism, Dickinson's, 216
  women of color poets and, 263–264
Radical Scatters (database, Werner), 247, 249, 285, 294–295
  diplomatic transcriptions of, 249
  innovation in, 249
  as open archive, 249
  See also online archives, Dickinson's
readers
  bodies of, 282, 294
  effect of collaboration on, 18
  global civil society of, 11
readers, Dickinson's
  affective experiences of, 241, 245
  American innocence for, 187
  with cognitive impairment, 291
  Dickinson's dialogue with, 29
  editing for, 291–296
  future, 11, 33–34
  global, 11, 306
  idealization of Dickinson, 34
  imagined, 25
  Iraqi, 9–10, 13, 299, 305–306
  with print disabilities, 292–296
  reading habits of, 241
  relationship to disability, 293
  of spoken poems, 293
  stance of removal, 36
  with visual impairment, 292, 296
readers, disabled, 9, 282
  access to books, 298
  with print disability, 284, 292–296
readers, Iraqi, 299
  of Dickinson, 9–10, 299, 305–306
  view of death, 305–306
reading
  bioregional, 140

communicative power of, 44
companionship in, 40
contingencies of, 4
cultural truisms about, 39
Dickinson on, 38–40
Dickinson's, 183, 190
effect of violence on, 9–10
Emerson on, 38–39
environmental, 139, 142, 148
Holmes on, 39
of lyric poetry, 10
nineteenth-century practice of, 34, 38
and physicality of poem, 285
physical pleasure of, 39
postcritical, 142
in "A precious – mouldering pleasure – 'tis –," 38–39, 199
protocols of, 44, 48
self-cancellation in, 39
transgression of boundaries in, 11
See also dis-reading, lyric
realism, speculative, 86
reliefs, Assyrian
  perspective of, 111
rhyme, Dickinson's
  in "All the letters I can write," 76
  feminine, 76
  irregularity of, 68
  in "I would not paint – a picture –," 73
  slant, 67, 79, 267
Rich, Adrienne, 45
  Dickinson's influence on, 259
  "Vesuvius at Home," 85, 172
Richards, Eliza, 6, 19, 27
  on Dickinson's mediated poetics, 163
  on dissemination of news, 25
romantic racialism, Dickinson's, 262, 276
Root, Abiah
  Dickinson's correspondence with, 42
Rosson, Grant, 8
Russell, Malinda
  Domestic Cookbook, 217

"Safe in their Alabaster Chambers" (F124), 244–245
  "deep time" in, 200
  textual history of, 244–245
  Venice in, 200
  versions of, 244
Sagan, Dorion, 124
Sánchez-Eppler, Karen
  on embodiment in Dickinson, 217
  on enslaved women, 219
Santo Domingo
  in Dickinson's poetry, 196–197

Index

Scarry, Elaine
  on bodily pain, 103, 117
scholarship, Dickinson
  critical tendencies in, 217
  ecocriticism in, 184
  feminist, 12, 85–97
  formalism in, 136–137
  gender in, 85, 97
  on her influences, 233
  historical-constructivist, 240
  international, 188
  manuscript studies in, 221, 239–240, 294
  on materiality, 96
  posthumanistic, 5–8, 120–123, 127–129, 132, 156, 161, 165–166
  poststructuralism and, 118
  prejudices in, 114
  racial attitudes in, 260
  reading habits in, 241
  slavery in, 262
  sound-based culture in, 66
  subjectivity in, 96
  web-based, 248–249
  whiteness in, 263
  women of color's influence in, 266
Schopenhauer, Arthur, 306
science, nineteenth-century
  Dickinson's connections to, 155–156, 184
  Dickinson's skepticism concerning, 159
Scott, Sally Ann Brown, 278–279
self-determination, black
  and Dickinson's poetics, 278
sensorium, poetic, 69
Sewall, Richard B., 115
  on Dickinson's education, 48
Shakespeare, William
  in "A Route of Evanescence," 198–199
Shelley, Percy Bysshe
  on music, 78
Sherman, Joan, 217
Sheurer, Erica, 41
Shockley, Evie, 9, 12
Sigourney, Lydia
  collaboration with readers, 30
  elegies of, 19
Sinor, Jennifer, 222
slavery
  in Dickinson's poetry, 196, 205, 216, 261–262
  writers of color on, 205
  See also women, enslaved
Small, Judy Jo, 79
Smith, Lorrie, 278
Smith, Martha Nell, 20
  on Dickinson's handwriting, 288

"Emily Dickinson Writing a Poem," 243, 245, 248
  See also Dickinson Electronic Archives
Snediker, Michael, 7
"So bashful when I spied her!" (F70)
  death in, 24
Socarides, Alexandra, 5–6, 255
  on Dickinson's manuscripts, 69, 223, 240
  on Dickinson's mediated poetics, 163
  on Mabel Todd Loomis, 297
  on poems about death, 11
society, male-oriented
  Dickinson in, 85
"Some – keep the Sabbath – going to church" (F236B), 122–123, 143
  bobolink of, 123
  diminution in, 123
  materiality of, 124
  mutuality in, 123
  relational poetics of, 123
  subjectivities in, 123
  world of God in, 123
"Some things that fly there be –" (F68)
  death in, 24
sound
  domestic dialects, 70
  industrial, 70
  role in poetry, 78
  as synecdoche for senses, 69
sound, Dickinson's, 66–79
  as critique, 79
  Dickinson's relationship with, 71
  ecstatic absorption of, 71
  environmental, 70–71
  everyday, 67, 70–71
  extra-poetic, 67, 69–71
  governing rhyme and meter, 78
  industrial, 70–71
  in "I would not paint – a picture –," 72
  listening to, 67
  networked aspects of, 69
  in portrayal of death, 78
  power of, 72–73
  reception and ontology of, 78
  separation of syllable from, 76
  silencing of, 77
  visual information and, 78
soundscapes
  of Amherst, 80, 298
space
  individual self and, 177
Spahr, Julia, 148
Springfield Republican
  Atlantic cable in, 190
  foreign news in, 190

Index 333

Staley, Beth, 293
  on soundscapes, 298
Stanton, Elizabeth Cady, 215, 219
St. Armand, Barton Levi, 228
Stearn, Franz, 25
Stewart, Susan
  on lyric poetry, 67
Stowe, Harriet Beecher, 171
subjectivity
  autonomous, 4
  of being poor in world, 122
  in Dickinson scholarship, 96
  disidentification in, 264–265
  environmental, 123, 125–127
  extranational, 193
  global, 189
  identification/counteridentification in, 264
  of the nonhuman, 120
  in object-oriented ontology, 89–90
  posthumanism and, 120, 130
  relational, 120
subjectivity, Dickinson's, 121–122, 124
  artist's, 89
  Dickinson's reconfiguration of, 120
  environmental, 123–127, 130–132
  the global in, 194
  in nature poems, 156
  planetary, 200
  posthumanist, 132
  of "The Robin's my Criterion for Tune," 125–126
  in "A solemn thing – it was – I said," 96
  "Soul" in, 132
  via biopoetics, 124
  white womanhood in, 261
Sumeria
  creation myths of, 305
"Surgeons must be very careful" (F156)
  Arabic translation of, 307

Tate, Allen, 113
technology
  of Civil War, 25
  communication, 50, 61
  in nineteenth-century life, 190
  of online archives, 240–241
  posthumanism and, 120
  See also electrical lighting
telegraphs
  circulating messages of, 52
  Dickinson and, 64
  electricity in, 53
  letters and, 52
  in "Myself can read the Telegrams," 51–52
  natural systems and, 52
  published in newspapers, 52
temporality
  in Dickinson's poetry, 104, 113, 199
  Dickinson's refusal of, 2
  of "A not admitting of the wound," 113–114
texts
  audio descriptions of, 294
  descriptions of, 280–281, 294
  discursive circumstances of, 156
  transit routes of, 11
  universal design principles for, 293
textuality
  as material/social condition, 281
  of memory, 222–223, 233
Thani, Abdul Mun'im, 299
"That sacred Closet when you sweep –" (F1385)
  alienated memories of, 232
  dangers of memory in, 233
  gendered space in, 232
  memory in, 231–233
"The Birds reported from the South–" (F780), 28–29
  materiality of, 29
  modes of communication in, 29
  mourning in, 29
  sharing in, 29
"The Bobolink is gone – the Rowdy of the Meadow –" (F1620), 143
"The Chemical conviction" (F1070), 160, 162
  atomic theory in, 160
  conversion in, 160
  Hitchcock and, 160
"The Farthest Thunder that I heard" (F1665B), 55–57
  electricity in, 55
  enlightenment in, 56
  lightning in, 56–57
"The Future never spoke –" (F638B), 61–62
  as environment, 62
  present and future in, 61
  sign language in, 61
  telegraph in, 61
"The Lassitudes of Contemplation" (F1613), 155
"The Lightning playeth – all the while" (F595A), 53–54
  circus metaphor of, 54–55
  electricity in, 53–55
  imagination in, 55
  lightning in, 53–55
  motion in, 53
  utterance in, 53–54
  vision in, 54–55
"The Malay – took the Pearl –" (F451)
  race in, 261

"The Robin's my Criterion for Tune" (F256),
    125–127
  biopoetics of, 125–126
  contingency in, 125
  cross-species encounters in, 120, 126
  cuckoo trope of, 125–126
  environmental issues of, 125–126
  habituation imagery of, 125
  mutuality in, 126
  seasonal change in, 125
  subjectivity of, 125–126
  Umwelt of, 124–126
"The Soul has Bandaged moments –" (F360),
    211–213, 219
  bee imagery of, 212, 214
  embodiment in, 212–213
  enslavement imagery in, 214–215
  "The Fearful Traveller in the Haunted Castle"
    and, 211, 213–214
  female embodiment in, 214
  gender roles in, 215
  male embodiment in, 214
  movement and immobility in, 211–212
    bondage imagery of, 211
  sexual assault in, 211–212, 214–215
  shackle imagery of, 214–215
  soul figure of, 212–214
  tonal shifts in, 213
  whiteness in, 215
"The Soul selects her own Society –" (F409),
    269, 278
"The Truth – is stirless" (F882), 155
"The way Hope builds his House" (F1512)
  materiality of, 252–253
"The Way to know the Bobolink" (F1348), 143,
    145–147
  interiority of, 146–147
  naming in, 146
  relational experience in, 146–147
"The Wind took up the Northern Things"
    (F1152A), 57–59
  as Civil War poem, 58
  elemental/mass media in, 59
  human versus environmental media in, 58–59
  hyperbole in, 58
  observation in, 57
  trope of wind in, 58–59
"There is no Frigate like a Book" (F1286), 190
"There's been a Death, in the Opposite House"
    (F547)
  Iraqi readers of, 306
"They leave us with the Infinite" (F352), 194
  international aspects of, 194
"This is my letter to the World" (F519), 33–34,
    187

Thomas, Shannon, 64
Thompson, William, 157
Thomson, J. J., 160
Thoreau, Henry David
  interest in physics, 158
  phenological records of, 150
  on women's immobility, 206
thought
  Dickinson on, 63
  as interference in world, 63
Todd, Mabel Loomis, 297
  affair with Austin, 225
  diary writing of, 225–227, 235
  Dickinson archive of, 226–227, 247–248
  Dickinson's correspondence with, 190
  on Dickinson's manuscripts, 242
transcendence
  biopoetics of, 125–127
  in Dickinson's poetics, 86, 88–89
Transcendentalists, American
  Dickinson and, 166
  on imagination, 49–50
  interest in physics, 157–158
transference
  in Dickinson's poetry, 162–164
  force in, 165
  in "If any sink, assure that this, now
    standing –," 165
  in physics, 157
transnationalism, Dickinson's, 189–201
  Africa in, 198–199
  alternatives to nationalism in, 190–191
  Asia in, 197–198
  European references in, 191, 193
  the everyday in, 191
  hemispheric patriotism in, 194–195
  of "I think the Hemlock likes to stand," 192
  Latin America in, 194–197
  multicontinental imagery of, 193
  natural world in, 195
  North-South binary in, 192–193
  power relations of, 195
  See also globalization, Dickinson's
travel
  in Dickinson's correspondence, 190
  travel writing, nineteenth-century, 170, 190
  personal fragmentation in, 192
trickster figures, African American, 211
Tuckerman, Edward, 140
Tuckerman, Frederick (son of Frederick
    Goddard), 140
Tuckerman, Frederick Goddard, 139–140
  bioregional reading of, 140, 144
  "Cricket, The" 139
  Dickinson's poetry and, 140

Emerson and, 144
hills in poetry of, 140–141
naming in poetry of, 151
"Once on a day, alone but not elate," 141–142
   birdsong in, 142
   ecopoetics of, 142
   reading in, 141–142
   sensory perception of, 139–140
   understanding of permeability, 141
Tuckerman, Sarah
   correspondence with Dickinson, 140
Turner, J. M. W., 111
Turner, Nat
   rebellion of, 209–211, 213
"'Twas like a Maelstrom, with a notch" (F425)
   chronicization of, 105–106
   figuration of, 105–107
   limitlessness of, 105
   maelstrom metaphor of, 105
   pain in, 105
   repetition in, 105–106
   self of, 106–107
   simile of, 106–107
Tyndall, John, 157

Uexküll, Jacob von
   on animal subjects, 129
   biosemiotics of, 124, 132
   environmental subjectivity of, 126–127
   influence on Heidegger, 123
   Umwelt of, 123–124
Umwelt
   in Dickinson's poetry, 124
   poetry in, 124
   Uexküll's, 123–124
unity, global, 11

Vendler, Helen, 80, 163, 284
"Volcanoes be in Sicily" (F1691), 172–174, 193
   geographic discourse of, 172, 175
   space in, 173
   speaker of, 172
   speaker's agency in, 173
   speaker's interiority in, 174
   volcano's exterior in, 173
   volcano's interior in, 173–174
Vetter, Lara
   "Emily Dickinson Writing a Poem," 243
Victorian Literary Studies
   Hyper-Concordance of, 257
volcano poems, Dickinson's, 169, 171–176, 184, 193
   Dickinson's character and, 171–172
   lyric reading of, 172
   rage in, 193

repressed potentiality in, 193
sources for, 185
space in, 172
transcriptions of, 176
See also geography, Dickinson's
volcanos
   birth of, 175
   in Dickinson's correspondence, 177–178
   of Juan Fernandez island, 177
   mutable physicality of, 174–175
   in *Universal Geography*, 174–175

Wallinger-Schorn, Brigitte, 279
Wang, Dorothy, 266
   on Chin, 271
Ward, Theodora
   on Dickinson's handwriting, 242–243
Wardrop, Daneen, 70
"We dream – it is good we are dreaming –" (F584)
   Egyptian civilization in, 200–201
   immortality in, 201
   metaphysical possibilities of, 201
Welch, Elizabeth, 224
Wells, Harriet, 224
"Went up a year this evening!" (F72)
   death in, 24
"We pray – to Heaven –" (F476), 180–183
   geography in, 181–183
   heaven's geography in, 180–183
   physics in, 180
   prattling in, 180
   primer imagery of, 181–182
   three-term structure of, 181–182
   time and space in, 181
Werner, Marta, 9, 77
   editorial practices of, 283
   on diplomatic transcription, 249, 256
   on envelope manuscripts, 66
   on listening to Dickinson, 293
   Open Folios, 283, 291
   on recovery of poems, 285
   on soundscapes, 80, 298
   See also Gorgeous Nothings, The; Radical Scatters
"We see – Comparatively –" (F580), 193–194
   global relationships in, 194
   presence and absence in, 193
"We send the wave to find the wave" (F1643), 107–108
   figuration of, 107–108
   pain in, 107–108
"What would I give to see his face?" (F266), 195
Wheare, Degory
   Of the Reason and Method of Reading Histories, 142

Wheatley, Phillis
  Biblical themes of, 264
whiteness
  in Dickinson's poetry, 216, 262–263
  in "Publication – is the Auction," 207, 218
  in "The Soul has Bandaged moments –," 215
white supremacism, 266–267
  in Horton's poetry, 213–214
Whitman, Walt
  African American poets and, 261, 276
  archive of, 245–246
  canonization of, 258
  Iraqi readers of, 299
  Jack Engle, 246
  in *Norton Anthology of Modern and Contemporary Poetry*, 258
  on slavery, 261
  supervision of publication, 246
Willard, Emma Hart
  educational reform work, 171
  Universal Geography, 170
  on volcanoes, 174–175
Williams, Henry Willard, 287
"Within my reach!" (F69), 24
Wolfe, Cary
  on cross-species relationships, 120–121
Wolosky, Shira, 46
women, nineteenth-century
  Dickinson's attitude toward, 99
  dress codes of, 206, 218
  forms of expression, 221
  immobility of, 205
  manuscript practices of, 221
  sexual vulnerability of, 213, 215
  struggle for rights, 215, 217
  votes for, 219
  white, 215–216, 219
women authors
  as amateurs, 18
  collaborative works of, 18
  feminist recovery of, 46
  use of enslaved women's experience, 205
  in world of men, 28
women, enslaved, 205
  imagery of, 214
  rape of, 218
  See also slavery
women of color
  dis-reading of Dickinson, 266–267
  in #MeToo movement, 99
  New Criticism and, 265–266
  participant spectatorship, 277–278
  self-authorizing of lyric, 266
women of color poets
  agency of, 259
  choices of, 259
  Dickinsonian inheritance of, 259–275
  Dickinson's mythology and, 274–275
  and Dickinson's racism, 263–264
  disidentification with Dickinson, 265
  engagement with Dickinson, 9, 259–260
  marginalization of, 260
  racializing of Dickinson, 260
  at Seton Hall celebration, 276
women poets
  Dickinson's influence on, 258–260
  lyric poetry of, 259
  marginalization of, 5
  sisters, 19
  subjectivity of, 19
Wood, Alphonso, 155
Woodbridge, William Channing
  educational reform work, 171
  Universal Geography, 170
  on volcanoes, 174–175
Wordsworth, William, 136
World Blind Union
  on accessibility of books, 298

X, Malcolm, 1
XML (markup language), 249, 256

"You'll know Her – by Her Foot" (F604), 151
  biodescription in, 145
Young, Edward: *The Complaint, or Night-Thoughts*, 42–43
  book of nature in, 42–44
  influence on Dickinson, 43
  practices of reading in, 42
  Protestant piety in, 42
"Your Riches – taught me – Poverty" (F418), 195
Yousuf, Saadi, 299

Zapedowska, Magdalena, 294
zines
  collaborative, 21–22
  materiality of, 21